MUSIC AND PHIL

Is music just matter of hearing and producing notes? And is it of interest just to musicians? By exploring different authors and philosophical trends of the Roman Empire, from Philo of Alexandria to Alexander of Aphrodisias, from the rebirth of Platonism with Plutarch to the last Neoplatonists, this book sheds light on different ways in which music and musical notions were made a crucial part of philosophical discourse. Far from being mere metaphors, notions such as harmony, concord and attunement became key philosophical tools in order to better grasp and conceptualise fundamental notions in philosophical debates from cosmology to ethics and from epistemology to theology. The volume is written by a distinguished international team of contributors.

FRANCESCO PELOSI is Lecturer of History of Ancient Philosophy at the University of Pisa. His main field of study concerns the interaction between music and philosophy in ancient Greece, with a special focus on the mind-body relationship and theories of perception. He is the author of *Plato on Music, Soul and Body* (Cambridge, 2010).

FEDERICO M. PETRUCCI is Professor of History of Ancient Philosophy at the University of Turin. His main research areas are Plato and the Platonist Tradition and his publications include the first English translation of the texts of the Platonist Taurus of Beirut (2018).

MUSIC AND PHILOSOPHY IN THE ROMAN EMPIRE

EDITED BY

FRANCESCO PELOSI

University of Pisa

FEDERICO M. PETRUCCI

University of Turin

CAMBRIDGE
UNIVERSITY PRESS

CAMBRIDGE
UNIVERSITY PRESS

University Printing House, Cambridge CB2 8BS, United Kingdom

One Liberty Plaza, 20th Floor, New York, NY 10006, USA

477 Williamstown Road, Port Melbourne, VIC 3207, Australia

314-321, 3rd Floor, Plot 3, Splendor Forum, Jasola District Centre, New Delhi - 110025, India

103 Penang Road, #05-06/07, Visioncrest Commercial, Singapore 238467

Cambridge University Press is part of the University of Cambridge.

It furthers the University's mission by disseminating knowledge in the pursuit of education, learning and research at the highest international levels of excellence.

www.cambridge.org
Information on this title: www.cambridge.org/9781108940955
DOI: 10.1017/9781108935753

First published 2021
First paperback edition 2022

A catalogue record for this publication is available from the British Library

Library of Congress Cataloging in Publication data
NAMES: Pelosi, Francesco, editor. | Petrucci, Federico M., 1985– editor.
TITLE: Music and philosophy in the Roman Empire / edited by Francesco Pelosi, Federico M. Petrucci.
DESCRIPTION: New York : Cambridge University Press, 2020. | Includes bibliographical references and index.
IDENTIFIERS: LCCN 2020039512 (print) | LCCN 2020039513 (ebook) | ISBN 9781108832274 (hardback) | ISBN 9781108935753 (ebook)
SUBJECTS: LCSH: Music – To 500 – Philosophy and aesthetics. | Music and philosophy – History – To 500. | Philosophy, Ancient.
CLASSIFICATION: LCC ML169 .M9 2020 (print) | LCC ML169 (ebook) | DDC 781.1/70937–dc23
LC record available at https://lccn.loc.gov/2020039512
LC ebook record available at https://lccn.loc.gov/2020039513

ISBN 978-1-108-83227-4 Hardback
ISBN 978-1-108-94095-5 Paperback

Contents

Notes on Contributors

ANDREW BARKER is Emeritus Professor of Classics at the University of Birmingham. He is the author of eight books on ancient Greek music and musical theory, including *Greek Musical Writings* (2 volumes, Cambridge 1984–1989), *Ancient Greek Writers on their Musical Past* (Pisa and Rome 2014), and most recently *Porphyry's Commentary on Ptolemy's* Harmonics*: a Greek Text and Annotated Translation* (Cambridge 2017). He has also published over a hundred articles on topics in these and related areas.

LAURA M. CASTELLI is research and teaching Fellow at the Munich School of Ancient Philosophy (MUSAPh), LMU, Munich. She is the author of several publications on ancient metaphysics and logic, among which are *Aristotle,* Metaphysics *Iota. Introduction, Translation and Notes* (Clarendon, Oxford 2018); *Alexander of Aphrodisias, On Aristotle. Topics II* (Bloomsbury 2020); *Alexander of Aphrodisias, On Aristotle. Topics III* (Bloomsbury, forthcoming).

BRAM DEMULDER is currently substitute lecturer at KU Leuven and postdoctoral researcher at the University of Liège / F.R.S.-FNRS (Fonds de la Recherche Scientifique). His main research interest is the interplay between cosmology and ethics in the Platonist tradition. In his PhD thesis (KU Leuven 2018) he explored this theme in the work of Plutarch of Chaeronea.

STEPHEN GERSH, Emeritus Professor of Medieval Philosophy, University of Notre Dame. Author of numerous books on the ancient, medieval, and early modern Platonic traditions, among which are *Middle Platonism and Neoplatonism. The Latin Tradition* (Notre Dame 1986) and *Concord in Discourse. Harmonics and Semiotics in Late Medieval and Early Modern Platonism* (Berlin and New York 1998).

GIOVANNA R. GIARDINA is Professor of Ancient Philosophy at the University of Catania. Her studies focus in particular on the Aristotelian philosophy and on Neoplatonism. Among her recent studies are *Fisica del movimento e teoria dell'infinito. Analisi critica di Aristotele,* Phys. *III* (Sankt Augustin 2012); 'Providence in John Philoponus' *Commentary on Aristotle's Physics*', *CHORA* 13 (2015), 149–72; 'Jean Philopon Commentateur d'Aristote, *Physique* II 8', *Revue de Philosophie Ancienne* 32 (2014), 177–221; 'Aristotle vs. Empedocles in *Physics* II.8', in *Proceedings of the World Congress Aristotle 2400 years,* ed. D. Sfendoni-Mentzou (Thessaloniki 2019), 78–82; 'Platone, *Eutidemo* 294e2–3', *Museum Helveticum* 75/2 (2018), 129–37; *To Metron. Sur la notion de Mesure dans la Philosophie d'Aristote*, ed. by G. R. Giardina (Paris-Brussels 2020).

CHRISTINA HOENIG is Associate Professor in Classics at the University of Pittsburgh. Her main areas of research are the Greek and Roman Platonic traditions. She mostly works on topics in natural philosophy and theology, and a central theme of interest is the translation of Greek philosophical vocabulary into Latin. Representative publications include 'Calcidius and the Creation of the Universe', *Rhizomata* 2/1 (2014); further, 'Calcidius', in Tarrant, H., Baltzly, D. *et al.* (eds.), *A Companion to the Reception of Plato in Antiquity* (2018). Her monograph *Plato's* Timaeus *and the Latin Tradition* was published in *The Cambridge Classical Series* with Cambridge University Press (2018).

CARLOS LÉVY is Emeritus Professor of Roman Philosophy and Literature at the Université de Paris-Sorbonne (Paris IV). His main research interests are Philo of Alexandria, Hellenistic philosophy, and Cicero. Among his publications are *Cicero Academicus. Recherches sur les* Académiques *et sur la philosophie cicéronienne* (Rome 1992); *Philon d'Alexandrie et le langage de la philosophie* (Turnhout 1998); and the article *Philo of Alexandria* in the *Stanford Encyclopedia of Philosophy*.

ALEXANDRA MICHALEWSKI is Research Fellow at the CNRS (Centre Léon Robin, Paris-Sorbonne). Her work focuses on Plotinus and the ancient Platonic tradition. One of her main research interests is the interplay between Aristotelianism and Platonism from the beginnings of the Imperial era to Late Antiquity. She is the author of a monograph on intelligible Forms as causes from Antiochus to Plotinus: *La puissance de l'intelligible. La théorie plotinienne des Formes au miroir de l'héritage médioplatonicien* (Leuven 2014). Recently she has published, as co-editor with M.-A. Gavray, *Les principes cosmologiques du platonisme. Origines, Influences et systématisation* (Turnhout 2017).

DOMINIC J. O'MEARA is Emeritus Professor of Philosophy at the University of Fribourg (Switzerland). He has published widely on Plato and the history of Platonism in Antiquity and Byzantium. His books include *Pythagoras Revived. Mathematics and Philosophy in Late Antiquity* (Oxford 1989); *Plotinus* (Oxford 1993); *Platonopolis. Platonic Political Philosophy in Late Antiquity* (Oxford 2003); *Cosmology and Politics in Plato's Later Writings* (Cambridge 2017).

FRANCESCO PELOSI is Lecturer of Ancient Philosophy at the University of Pisa. His main field of study concerns the interaction between music and philosophy in ancient Greece, with a special focus on the mind–body relationship and theories of perception. In recent years he has been the principal investigator of a project devoted to the collection, translation, and analysis of the ancient Greek sources on the interplay between music and philosophy, from the Presocratics to late Antiquity (*Megiste mousike*, 2 vols., forthcoming De Gruyter). He is the author of *Plato on Music, Soul and Body* (Cambridge University Press 2010).

FEDERICO M. PETRUCCI is Professor of History of Ancient Philosophy at the University of Turin. He studied and obtained his PhD in Pisa. He was fellow of the Humboldt Foundation in Würzburg, of the Scuola Normale Superiore, and of the Durham University. He is particularly interested in Plato and the Platonist tradition. His publications include a translation and commentary of Theon's *Expositio* (Sankt Augustin 2012) and the monograph *Taurus of Beirut. The Other Side of Middle Platonism* (London and New York 2018).

HAROLD TARRANT studied at Cambridge and Durham UK, and taught Classics for thirty-eight years in Australian universities. After retiring to live in the UK from 2012 he remains Professor Emeritus at the University of Newcastle Australia. Recent publications include *Proclus: Commentary on Plato's Timaeus*, vol. 6 (Cambridge 2017); François Renaud and Harold Tarrant, *The Platonic* Alcibiades *I: The Dialogue and Its Ancient Reception* (Cambridge 2015); and (edited with D. A. Layne, D. Baltzly, and F. Renaud) *Brill's Companion to the Reception of Plato in Antiquity* (Leiden 2018).

MÁTÉ VERES is a Postdoctoral Fellow at the Collaborative Program in Ancient and Medieval Philosophy at the University of Toronto. He was a Postdoctoral Researcher at the University of Hamburg, at the University of Geneva, and at Eötvös Loránd University, Budapest. He works mainly on Hellenistic philosophy, with a focus on epistemology and ethics. He received his PhD from the Central European University in November 2016, and was a postdoctoral researcher at the University of Hamburg and at the University of Geneva. His recent publications include 'Sextus Empiricus on Religious Dogmatism', *Oxford Studies in Ancient Philosophy* 58 (2020); 'Keep Calm and Carry On: Sextus Empiricus on the Origins of Pyrrhonism', *History of Philosophy and Logical Analysis* 23 (2020); 'Theology, Innatism, and the Epicurean Self', *Ancient Philosophy* 37 (2017).

Acknowledgements

This volume has its roots in the International Conference 'The Harmony of Reason. Music and Philosophy from the Early Imperial Age to Late Antiquity', held at the Scuola Normale Superiore (Pisa) in September 2016, in the framework of the three-year Research Project 'I filosofi e la musica' ('Futuro in Ricerca 2013' programme), supported by the Italian Ministry of Education, Universities and Research. We would like to thank all the participants in the Conference and the Scuola Normale Superiore for its generous support to the event. Some of the papers given at that conference were selected as the core of the present volume, while others were added upon invitation. As editors, we wanted different areas of international scholarship to be represented, and we especially sought to combine papers by younger researchers with ones by more experienced scholars. For his qualified proofreading of the chapters of non-native English authors, we would like to warmly thank Sergio Knipe.

Abbreviations

LCL: Loeb Classical Library
SVF: von Arnim, H. *Stoicorum Veterum Fragmenta*. Indexes by M. Adler, 4 vols. Stuttgart, Teubner, 1903–1924

***

As a rule, references to ancient authors and works follow the *Oxford Classical Dictionary*.

***

As a rule, we transliterate Greek words and short phrases (not sentences) in the main text; all Greek words and sentences in the main text – either transliterated or not – are accompanied by a translation.

Introduction

Francesco Pelosi and Federico M. Petrucci

In the last forty years, two fields of research have progressively emerged with an initially pioneering and then central role in the scholarly debate on Antiquity: ancient music on the one hand, and post-Hellenistic and late antique philosophy on the other. This volume is the first attempt to discover the huge links between these two fundamental areas in the study of the ancient world by drawing a thorough and complex picture of the various ways in which musical notions entered the philosophical debate during the first centuries of the Christian era and contributed to shaping its content.

After decades of non-systematic enquiries, in the Eighties two groundbreaking volumes on ancient Greek music brought to classicists' attention an extraordinary collection of literary and philosophical texts concerning music, from Homer to Late Antiquity (Barker 1984, 1989). Andrew Barker's seminal works made many technical, and somewhat obscure, issues related to ancient musical culture completely accessible to non-specialists and initiated a process that in a couple of decades was to lead to the stable inclusion of ancient music among the branches of classical studies. Following Barker's inspiration, many scholars have embarked on in-depth enquiries into music in Antiquity, by unveiling the religious, political, and social values embedded in musical experience, the theoretical background of harmonic theories, and the historical development of musical culture.[1] As a result, topics such as contexts and practices associated with musical performances, the educational and social role of music, and its scientific study have become common in Classical scholarship nowadays.

[1] Two fundamental technical and historical surveys are West 1992 and Hagel 2009. On harmonics, the reference work is Barker 2007. The essays collected in Murray and Wilson 2004 provide a wide-ranging enquiry into the social, political, and religious role of music in Classical Athens. On the interesting yet undeveloped branch of ancient Greek musical historiography, see Barker 2014.

Recent decades have also witnessed the flourishing of studies on Imperial and late antique philosophy as a momentous phase in the history of the ancient thought. Also in this case, crucial aspects of post-Hellenistic and late antique thought have emerged in an intriguing development of the field of enquiry, from the critical engagement with the major philosophical traditions of the Classical and Hellenistic periods to some cultural exchanges of paramount importance (above all the encounter of ancient Greek philosophy with Judaism and Christianity), and from exegetical strategies to the focus on specifically philosophical issues. As a consequence, the actual intellectual import of these centuries for the history of philosophy has come to the forefront.[2]

Despite these impressive advances in our knowledge both of ancient music and of post-Hellenistic and late antique philosophy, the intersection between these two fields still remains unexplored to a large extent. Before delving into the reasons why it deserves special consideration, let us add a few remarks on how the study of the interplay between music and philosophy can generally contribute to our knowledge of Antiquity. The main contributions can be illustrated by considering three points – the first two are preliminary and related to our appreciation of the sources, the third is more strictly related to the goal of this book. First, our knowledge of ancient Greek music relies heavily on philosophical texts: ancient philosophers discuss at length many issues concerning both the theory and practice of music, and this rich amount of evidence is one of the principal sources for the reconstruction of musical culture throughout Antiquity. A rather clear picture of this phenomenon emerges as soon as one skims through fundamental books in the field, for instance Andrew Barker's above-mentioned collection (especially vol. 2, 1989) or David Creese's *The Monochord in Ancient Greek Harmonic Science* (2011). Both authors extensively draw upon philosophical texts, whose contribution to our understanding of ancient Greek music and its scientific study is crucial not only quantitatively, but also qualitatively: philosophical accounts such as those by Archytas, Philolaus, Plato, Aristotle, and Porphyry provide

[2] After the classic monographs by Baltes 1976, Dillon 1977, and Donini 1982, interest in post-Hellenistic philosophy has been considerably increasing, especially with respect to the Peripatetic and the Platonist traditions. As to the former, the study of Alexander has advanced considerably, and we have at our disposal a fundamental sourcebook on Peripatetic philosophy (Sharples 2010). Research on post-Hellenistic and late antique Platonism is even better developed: along with reference books such as Gerson 2010, Tarrant et al. 2018, and Boys-Stones 2018, and the ongoing project *Der Platonismus in der Antike*, several works have shed light on the philosophy and exegetical methods of post-Hellenistic and late antique Platonism (see Bonazzi 2003 and 2015, Ferrari 1995 and 2001, Gersh 1986, Hoenig 2018, Michalewski 2014, Opsomer 1998, O'Meara 2003, Petrucci 2018a).

a clear image of the development of the reflection on music and harmonics from both a technical and a methodological point of view. This picture indicates how pressing a properly philosophical analysis of these musical passages is: even if one focuses only on the philosophers' contributions to musical theory, it is of paramount importance to have adequate knowledge of their philosophical use of music – and this is a crucial contribution of this book. Second, and very interestingly, it is not simply the case that philosophers develop discussions on music and harmonics: what has also emerged is that music theorists fully exploit philosophical notions and adopt specific philosophical approaches which lie at the basis of their technical works on music. This is the case with Aristoxenus, Ptolemy, and Aristides Quintilianus, just to mention three prominent figures, whose intellectual enterprises in musical fields presuppose specific philosophical theories. Indeed, the philosophical background of these music theorists strongly influences the way in which they contribute to shaping the technical domain of music and harmonics and to interpreting its study: this clearly emerges, for instance, when one focuses on Aristoxenus' conception of harmonics as an 'Aristotelian' science, or once Ptolemy's methodological revolution is investigated by considering not only its final technical outcome but also, and above all, its philosophical assumptions and aims.[3] This leads us to the third point (the most important one for our purposes): in Antiquity music is not a topic occasionally dealt with by philosophers but rather a *philosophical* topic, inasmuch as it plays a role in argumentative and exegetical strategies. As a matter of fact, although it would be difficult to argue that *all* ancient philosophers regard music as a fundamental topic, it is quite fair to say that there has not been a moment in the history of ancient philosophy when leading figures have not reflected on a number of aspects of harmonics and music, and have not exploited musical notions for philosophical purposes. This is blatantly true for the Pythagoreans, Plato, Aristotle and the Early Peripatetics, the Stoics and the Epicureans (especially, but not only, Philodemus), and – as recent scholarship has shown – for a Platonist such as Porphyry, if we wish to leap directly from the late Hellenistic age to the third century AD. Taking into account how and why ancient philosophers deal with music has suggested innovative ways of approaching much-debated questions concerning some major philosophical figures and movements (e.g. Pythagoreanism and Plato's philosophy, especially his ethics and psychology) and has led to the project of a comprehensive survey of the interplay between music and

[3] On Aristoxenus, see Bélis 1986 and Barker 2007, 136–259; on Ptolemy, see especially Barker 2000a.

philosophy in Antiquity.[4] However, even though a systematic interest in musical topics has become increasingly common among scholars of ancient philosophy, there is still much work to be done. This is particularly true in relation to the post-Hellenistic and late antique philosophical use of, and debate on, music and harmonics, which has received little attention compared to the consideration given to the interplay between music and philosophy in the Classical and Hellenistic periods.[5]

The point is even more astonishing if one considers that from the Imperial Age to Late Antiquity, especially in the context of the Platonist tradition, music and harmonic theory are mostly exploited from a philosophical point of view. During these centuries music becomes a privileged instrument to conceptualise philosophical doctrines and discuss them. Notions borrowed from the musical culture are employed in the investigation of fundamental philosophical fields, such as ethics, cosmology, and metaphysics, and strongly contribute to shaping them. More specifically, in works from this period, an interest in music lies at the core of fundamental philosophical activities, from exegetical practices to the development of ethical, epistemological, and cosmological doctrines. This makes an enquiry into the philosophical use of music and harmonics in this period not only promising but also crucial for getting to the core of the links between music and philosophy in Antiquity and for exploring a new and effective path towards a fresh understanding of post-Hellenistic and late antique philosophy.

The present volume is designed to fill this gap in the scholarship by drawing a picture of the relationship between music and philosophy across a long time span, from the work of Philo of Alexandria at the beginning of the Imperial age to that of John Philoponus at the end of Antiquity. All the philosophers and philosophical movements dealt with in the volume make interesting use of musical notions to address crucial philosophical issues and provide some clear examples of how sophisticated the dialogue between music, as a highly technical field, and philosophy was during the last centuries of ancient thought. In particular, the reader will be struck by the presence of some central topics common to different philosophical approaches: the use of musical notions for exegetical purposes, the presence of philosophical accounts in technical works on music, the use of musical

[4] This is the aim of our project for a collection, with a translation and commentary, of texts testifying to a philosophical use of music from the Presocratics to Middle Platonism: Pelosi forthcoming; Pelosi and Petrucci forthcoming.

[5] Some remarkable, yet isolated, attempts to survey the links between music and philosophy in Late Antiquity can be found in O'Meara 2005 and 2007, and Sheppard 2005.

images and notions in argumentative accounts with the aim of demonstrating the superiority of a particular philosophical view or way of life, and the use of concepts borrowed from the musical field as paradigms in the description and interpretation of ethical, ontological, cosmological, and metaphysical elements. This is an entirely new narrative, whose development really sheds light on the philosophical debates and theoretical constructions of a fundamental period of ancient thought.

The structure of the book aims to bring together both a diachronic perspective, focused on the different philosophical approaches to music across time, and a thematic point of view, centred on the main topics and notions characterising the interplay between music and philosophy in the Imperial age and Late Antiquity. By broadly following a chronological order, the book aims to show how the exchange between music and philosophy unfolds throughout key moments in the history of ancient thought in this period, and what philosophical trends emerged – or remained constant – throughout the centuries. At the same time, the thematic structure of the volume allows the reader to fully appreciate the main concepts at stake when music is intertwined with philosophy: for instance, in the first part of the book, a section including chapters on Alexander of Aphrodisias, Sextus Empiricus, and Ptolemy provides analyses of the role played by musical notions in the conceptualisation of ontological matters, as well as reflections on the very status of music and its scientific study in the post-Hellenistic age. This section is designed to draw attention to some ontological and epistemological issues which prove to be essential tenets underpinning the interplay between music and philosophy in the works of this period (see below, pp. 10–12, for a more detailed introduction to this point).

Before illustrating the main contents of the volume in detail, an overview of earlier philosophical approaches to music may be useful, so as to put our enquiry in the right historiographical perspective. By the dawn of the Imperial age, the philosophical use of music has already undergone crucial developments in different philosophical traditions rooted in the Archaic, Classical, and Hellenistic periods. As is widely known, music plays a pivotal role in the investigations of some Pythagoreans such as Hippasus, Philolaus, and Archytas, who extensively discuss musical notions and lay the foundations for their philosophical use from a range of points of view. Although mainstream views on the Pythagorean approach to music, from Aristoxenus onwards, tend to emphasise its mathematical aspects – that is, roughly speaking, the tendency to analyse musical phenomena in terms of numerical ratios – the Pythagorean investigations, at the crossroads between music and philosophy, are far more diverse than this feature might suggest. Indeed, they provide insights into central areas of ancient philosophical thought, such as the philosophy of science, and in particular acoustics, epistemology, and cosmology.[6] Therefore, at the beginning of the Classical age the encounter between music and philosophy already shows its thought-provoking potential and produces some important outcomes.

With Plato's reflection, which stands out as the first articulate and sustained analysis of the philosophical import of music, the link between the two fields is further explored and definitively established as the fundamental interaction between two central areas of ancient Greek culture. As is well known, music plays a crucial role in Plato's accounts of ethics and politics, both in the *Republic* (books 2–3) and in the *Laws* (books 2 and 7). Behind these treatments there lies a refined analysis of the psychophysical impact of music, hinging on Plato's view about body and soul and their relationship. By investigating how music stimulates sense-perception, emotions, and cognitive processes, Plato fully exploits the pedagogical and psychagogical qualities of music, not least by making it a valuable resource within a higher educational programme – the one conceived for rulers in *Resp.* 7 – in which harmonics plays an important part. Midway between the sensible and the intelligible, music is a hot philosophical topic in Plato, providing a number of insights into the core of his philosophy (i.e. the distinction between two ontological and epistemological domains). The philosophical relevance of music, and its twofold nature as something both sensible and intelligible, is further explored in the *Timaeus*, where some perceptive analyses of sound and hearing are combined with the notion of an entirely intelligible music, namely the harmonic ratios out of which the world soul is fashioned (*Ti.* 35a-36e). The account of the world soul, which will have an extraordinary influence on philosophers in the Imperial age and in Late Antiquity, as well as on Renaissance conceptions of the links between man and the cosmos, clearly shows how pervasive musical notions are in Plato's philosophy, as they touch upon all areas of his thought – ontology, epistemology, psychology, ethics, politics, and

[6] To summarise the contribution of the three above-mentioned Pythagoreans in a handful of lines (which hardly do justice to them): Hippasus is credited with one of the first experiments in acoustics (18B12 DK), while Philolaus' theories imply complex relationships between music theory and cosmology, based on the notion of *harmonia*, a key concept both in music and in the cosmological theory (44B6 DK); as for Archytas, his works on acoustics and harmonics are landmark ones (47B1 DK, 47B2 DK), and his authority in the musical field is acknowledged throughout Antiquity. On the Pythagorean view and use of music, see especially Burkert 1972, 350–400, Barker 2007, 263–307, Zhmud 2012a, 285–313, and Horky 2013, 222–58.

cosmology. Plato's account provides a key to grasping the close link between the place of music in human life and its role in the intelligible world.[7]

Plato's analyses of musical phenomena – and particularly his interpretation of the ethical and political role of music – have a great impact on Aristotle, who acknowledges that music can significantly shape a person's character and dwells at length on the social and political impact of music in the eighth book of the *Politics*. More originally, perhaps, he also makes room for the non-educational purposes that music can be used for, such as amusement and catharsis. Besides the extensive account of *Politics* 8, some important references to musical notions and theories appear in the treatises *On the soul*, *On sense and the sensible*, and *On the generation of animals*, where Aristotle deals with the physics of sound – that is, its production and propagation – and with the process by which sound, with its specific qualities, is perceived. This side of Aristotle's interest in music exerts a strong influence within the Peripatetic milieu, where his research on sound and hearing is further developed – as is especially evident from *Problems* 11 and 19, from the treatise *De audibilibus*, and from Theophrastus fr. 716 FHS&G.[8] Most importantly, Aristotle's thought (his conception of science and knowledge more than his 'philosophy of music', so to speak) deeply influences the most renowned music theorist of Antiquity: Aristoxenus of Tarentum, whose work on harmonics is thoroughly imbued with Aristotle's ideas on scientific knowledge and its principles. Aristoxenus' enterprise of theorisation in the field lies at the basis of the substantial technical development of music and harmonics in the Hellenistic age. On the one hand, Aristoxenus' establishment of harmonics as an Aristotelian science determines the progressive canonisation of an empirical model of music. On the other, especially through the *Sectio canonis* and the first technical exegeses of the *Timaeus* (e.g. Crantor's),[9] a different approach to harmonics is developed, one based on pure calculus and heavily depending on Platonic assumptions. The divergence between these approaches underlies the (often implicit) debate between a rationalistic and an empirical approach to harmonics characterising the following centuries.[10]

7 On Plato's appeal to, and discussion of, music see Barker 1984, 124–69, 1989, 53–65, 2007, 308–27, and Pelosi 2010.

8 See Barker 1984, 190–204, 1989, 85–118, 2007, 411–36, Pelosi 2009, and Petrucci 2011 (especially on the relevant sections of the *Problems*); on Theophrastus see now Raffa 2018.

9 On the *Sectio canonis* see Barker 1989, 190–209, 2007, 364–410, Barbera 1991, and Busch 1998. On Academic and Platonist exegeses of Plato's *divisio animae*, see Petrucci 2019a.

10 On Aristoxenus, see the references provided in footnote 3 above.

Interest in music undergoes obvious transformations in the Hellenistic age, reflecting the peculiar philosophical traits of this period. Of course, the main issue becomes the epistemological and ethical value of music (i.e. whether music has a real impact on the soul and, if so, of what kind). The scarceness of extant testimonies strongly limits our possibility of investigating this issue, but at least one valuable witness has been transmitted, testifying to the fact that there was an intense debate on these questions: it is, of course, Philodemus' *De musica*, which illustrates the intriguing interlacement of ethics and epistemology which distinguishes the quarrel about music between the Stoics and the Epicureans.[11]

In the period that is the focus of our narrative, then, music on the one hand lies at the centre of an advanced technical debate, while on the other it is already a fundamental philosophical topic of discussion and a means of philosophical elaboration, although its impact on the various parts of philosophy varies from case to case. Interestingly enough, in Philo of Alexandria – the point of departure for our story – one encounters a rich use of musical notions as philosophical paradigms, where both the influence of previous approaches and the presence of a new and pervasive use of music in philosophical argumentations are remarkable. Philo's interest in music is as known as it is overlooked in its philosophical implications. As **Carlos Lévy**'s contribution shows, the importance of the musical paradigm in Philo's thought clearly emerges by means of a comparison with the other complementary model adopted by the philosopher: the pattern of the *scala naturae*, inherited from Stoicism. Lévy's analysis reveals that the musical paradigm turns out to be the most powerful expression of the notion of transcendence, from both a philosophical and theological point of view, as it describes – in a way that the model of the *scala naturae* cannot do – the harmony of the world and its distance from God. More specifically, Philo's appeal to the notion of harmony introduces the idea of an orderly discontinuity in nature, implying both the transcendence of God and the limited condition of men: the world is indeed governed by harmony, but only in the very qualified sense that it implies harmonically defined relationships between very distant entities. This 'vertical' harmony, however, is combined with a 'horizontal' one, for God also exerts his providence according to harmony, while, in turn, music is the intellectual means allowing human beings to contemplate the heavens and to draw closer to God. Interestingly,

[11] See Martinelli 2009 for a collection of essays on music in the Hellenistic age, including some studies on philosophical texts. On Philodemus' *De musica* see especially Delattre's monumental edition (2007). Recently scholars have proposed that music also played some role in Stoic physics: see Scade 2017 and Salles 2017.

these are *not* mere metaphors: rather, music represents now a proper philosophical model, and moreover it is applied to aspects which will prove fundamental in the post-Hellenistic age.

Indeed, a wide-ranging use of musical notions and a tendency to build up a philosophical system by appealing to them are among the major features emerging from the Middle Platonists' treatment of music. This is especially the case with the writings of one of the most prolific authors of the early Imperial age, namely Plutarch. Through an in-depth enquiry into the *Moralia*, **Bram Demulder** emphasises that Plutarch's notion of cosmic and divine music represents a paradigm for all kinds of sensible music. Indeed, in Plutarch's view the existence of a cosmic and divine music implies that there is a paradigm–image relationship between this dimension and all sensible instances of music. Two conclusions follow from this. On the one hand, it is somewhat misleading to draw too strict a comparison between sensible and cosmic music inasmuch as cosmic music is intrinsically pure and perfect; on the other hand – and most interestingly – even if sensible music as such is impure and potentially damaging, it can be used as a therapy for the human soul precisely because it complies with the embodied condition of the latter. In other words, music plays a fundamental role in all dimensions of reality, although in each case its status and effectiveness have distinctive features and mechanisms. This paves the way for focused enquiries into the philosophical use of music with respect to specific – and crucial – philosophical issues. Now, it would be hard to find an issue which is more important for a Platonist than the status of God and his relationship with the world, and, interestingly, such a relationship concerns music, for a Platonist could hardly fail to regard the world as being harmonically arranged. Theology is, in effect, one of the fields in which the appeal to musical notions proves most effective and powerful, as the paper by **Federico M. Petrucci** shows. Middle Platonists developed different theological models in order to build up philosophically consistent cosmologies, and one of the main tools applied to achieve these models is the use of two specific notions of cosmic harmony and divine harmonisation. On the one hand, a dynamic notion of harmony is crucial for those authors who regard God as a divine craftsman and uphold a temporal cosmogony, for it ensures God's direct engagement in the *production* of harmony between opposite cosmological powers. On the other hand, a static notion of harmony paves the way for a sempiternalistic cosmology and a non-artisanal theology, as it ensures the intrinsic order of the world. Harmony is, in both cases, a philosophical model, and by understanding its role in each Middle Platonist doctrine one is in a position also to enter an intriguing debate on the sense in which God is to be regarded, according to the Middle Platonists, as the harmoniser of the world. At the same time, music is seen as a philosophical key to interpret reality not only by the Middle Platonists, but also by the Peripatetics, as **Laura M. Castelli** shows. By focussing on Alexander of Aphrodisias' use of two essential musical notions – *harmonia* and *symphōnia* – as paradigms in non-musical fields, she demonstrates that Alexander resorts to harmonics in order to shape a specific philosophical model, namely an ontological one. Alexander rejects the idea that harmony can play a role in the constitution of being, and thus engages in a polemic against a view which, in its strongest formulation, has clear Pythagorean and Platonist echoes. But Alexander goes much further than this, for he rethinks the role of harmonic patterns in the constitution of beings by transforming it into an ontological model according to which it is possible to state that harmonic relations – that is, proportional ones – can grasp specific quantitative aspects of reality. Through a close reading of some relevant passages from Alexander's *De anima* and his commentaries on Aristotle's *Metaphysics* and *De sensu*, Castelli demonstrates that Alexander's enquiry – with its adoption of some Pythagorean elements and rejection of others – interestingly bears traces of a debate on formal causes within the Peripatetic tradition.

From a more general perspective, however, these Platonist and Peripatetic treatments of musical notions are framed within a broader intellectual context. As a matter of fact, the wide-ranging treatment of and appeal to music also highlight the need for a new and deeper understanding of the very status of music: *if* thinkers of the post-Hellenistic age appeal to music and harmonics in order to develop a proper philosophical reflection, what is the status of music itself in their view? It is particularly crucial to answer this question because it is far from clear whether music – and, more generally, the so-called 'liberal arts' – have any epistemic value, any therapeutic function, and – even more radically – any grasp on reality at all. This is what comes to the fore in Sextus' discussion of music, as emerges from **Máté Veres**' detailed analysis, which extensively discusses Sextus' well-known criticism of 'musicologists'. Veres first detects and explains Sextus' argumentative strategy, consisting in a complex synergy of arguments aiming to radically undermine the idea that music can have any ethical function, while at the same time suggesting that fundamental notions of music theory do not correspond to anything in reality, and thus that music itself is no science at all. On the one hand, this discussion is of particular interest as regards Sextus and his Pyrrhonian project, for Veres sheds light on the relationship between these arguments and the overall sceptical agenda articulated in the *Outlines*, and interestingly indicates that Sextus' arguments are entirely consistent with the suspensive stance. On the other hand, this has a huge impact on our narrative, for Sextus' criticism could have undermined any kind of strong philosophical appeal to music. The reasons why this never really happened are of course complex, and after all one should not assume that non-Sceptics really heeded Sextus' criticism. However, there is at least one very good argument which could have been formulated in support of a philosophical use of music, and it is related to the epistemological rethinking which the discipline underwent during the late-Hellenistic and early post-Hellenistic age, and which reached its culmination with Ptolemy's *Harmonics*. The Sextan (or Sextus-like) criticism just outlined might not have been accepted by all post-Hellenistic thinkers, but the questions it raised about the status of music and its relationship with reality were still waiting to be answered. Regardless of whether Ptolemy was aware of such criticism, the mission of providing harmonics with a stronger epistemological foundation is key to Ptolemy's agenda, as **Andrew Barker**'s chapter shows. Through a fine-grained reading of some key passages of the *Harmonics*, Barker reconstructs the stages by which Ptolemy's investigation shifts from acoustics to harmonics, that is, from the science of sounds in general to the science of those sounds that are musically relevant. As Barker shows, this transition keeps pace with the passage from a descriptive to an evaluative enquiry, in which qualities such as 'pleasing', 'homogeneous', and 'beautiful' play a crucial role as pivotal aspects defining the principles governing the musical field. This raises a crucial question, which lies at the very heart of Ptolemy's epistemological approach to music: whether and how these evaluative judgements are integrated into his scientific approach to music, based on rigorous logical procedures and empirical confirmations. In addressing this question, Barker focuses on a topic that is central both to the *Harmonics* and, more generally, to the philosophical debate on music from the Hellenistic age to Late Antiquity: the relationship between reason (*logos*) and sense-perception (*aisthēsis*) in the study of musical phenomena. As is well known, Ptolemy's harmonics is firmly grounded in the use of both these criteria, as it is deeply imbued with the idea that the conclusions derived from rational assumptions must always be submitted to the test of sense-perception. Within this methodological framework, the role of evaluative assessments in harmonics is highlighted by focusing on the relationship between the mental and acoustic processes involved in musical experiences: in Ptolemy's view, the beauty of musical structures is but the perceptual expression of the fact that relations between sounds can be given specific mathematical representations, and this close link between the two domains is what ultimately justifies the shift of perspective from acoustic to harmonics. Barker's analysis throws new light on Ptolemy's impressive project, which is designed to provide the scientific study of music with a new and solid epistemological foundation: besides emphasising some far from obvious implications of Ptolemy's approach to knowledge in the musical field, the analysis demonstrates the fundamental role of this reflection in highlighting the philosophical import of harmonics, in the encounter between the ontological domain of musical phenomena and the perceptual and cognitive resources of human knowledge. As Barker shows, therefore, with Ptolemy harmonics become established on more solid and effective epistemological foundations, and their status as a science is not only defended against a sceptical approach but greatly strengthened.

Buttressed by both technical and epistemological conceptualisations, music enters the last centuries of ancient thought as a crucial philosophical instrument. It is not surprising, then, that in the same centuries such use of music deeply penetrated also another intellectual context whose relationship with Greek philosophy lies at the centre of scholarly debate, that is Christian thought. This is the intriguing and understudied field which **Francesco Pelosi** turns to by focusing on some musical notions and images in the works of Clement of Alexandria and Origen. Through an analysis of metaphors in which Christian elements and pagan musical notions merge (e.g. Christ-Orpheus, Christ the Word as the New Song, man as God's instrument, and *symphōnia* as an expression of the deep consistency between all parts of Scripture) Pelosi shows that the use of music stands out as a momentous feature in the apologetic and exegetical activities of these Christian writers, raising some crucial issues: the Christian attitude to pagan culture, the relationship between Christianity and philosophy, the allegorical interpretation of Scripture, and the demonstration of the superiority of Christianity.

All this sets the foundations for an extensive exploitation of music in Neoplatonism. As the following chapters in the volume show, this happened in a surprisingly rich and systematic way. Music turns out to have strongly affected all fields of Neoplatonist philosophy, from cosmology to theology, from ethics to epistemology. This already emerges in the description of cosmological and causal process provided by Plotinus' references to music, as **Alexandra Michalewski**'s chapter reveals. By analysing Plotinus' use of musical images, Michalewski proves that Plotinus heavily relies on a rich repertory of musical notions in order to illustrate the cosmic order and different causal relationships. At the same time, however, within such a common scenario one can clearly detect philosophical aspects which properly belong to Plotinus' philosophy and which reshape the Platonist appeal to music from within. Indeed, although music still plays a fundamental role in human education, it now becomes a purely individual stepping stone in the elevation towards the intelligibles; and it achieves this goal not as one of the mathematical disciplines, but as a direct training of the irrational part of the soul. But this is possible only because there is a kind of correspondence between the human soul, the constitution of the world, and the intrinsic order of the world's causes, that is, the forms. In this sense, Plotinus also strongly refashions similar Middle Platonist accounts. First, the world's order (i.e. the one established by the world soul) is indeed harmonic, but only in a non-mathematical sense; second, not only is the internal structure of the intelligible realm harmonic, but music – especially in terms of harmony and rhythm – represents a model for the very causality of forms with respect to sensibles. Through a specific focus on dance and rhythm, and an interesting analysis of the hapax *arrhythmiston*, Michalewski argues that the concept of *rhythmos*, far from being confined to the artistic field, is used to express the dynamic productivity of the intelligible realities. Post-Hellenistic Platonists and, in a very specific way, Plotinus thus provide a multi-focal and complex interpretation of music. Setting out from these premises, later Platonists exploited and developed them from different perspectives.

One would now expect the well-known Porphyrean discussion of Ptolemy's *Harmonics* to be a follow-up to Plotinus' perspective, and indeed scholars usually take Porphyry's *Commentary on Ptolemy's Harmonics*, which stands out as the only writing by a Platonist philosopher programmatically devoted to music, to be a 'Neoplatonist' work.[12] However, **Harold Tarrant** proposes a very fresh reading of both Porphyry's overall intellectual perspectives and the contents and aims of the *Commentary*: the chapter aims to define the tradition in the light of which Porphyry undertakes his exegetical task and the main traits of the intellectual figure of Porphyry at the time of the composition of the *Commentary*, whose

[12] In fact, while the importance of this work for the reconstruction of otherwise unknown musical theories has been all too evident to scholars, its philosophical relevance in relation both to Porphyry's activity and to the links between music and philosophy in Neoplatonism has only lately (and partly) been acknowledged, especially thanks to the recent publication of two annotated translations of Porphyry's *Commentary* (Barker 2015, Raffa 2016a), which has paved the way for further research on the interesting interconnections between the philosophical and musical topics to be found in the text.

content is argued to be fairly independent from Plotinus' thought. By considering the various sources on which Porphyry draws to explain Ptolemy's text and by dwelling in particular on Porphyry's consideration of *logos* and sensation, Tarrant discusses whether and in what sense Porphyry's *Commentary on Ptolemy's Harmonics* can be considered a Pythagorean exercise, and what its relationship with Platonism is.

With Porphyry we properly enter Late Antiquity, that is, the age in which Platonism becomes the dominant philosophical movement. Interestingly enough, this philosophical supremacy is accompanied by an increased focus on music, as the last contributions of the volume show. **Dominic O'Meara**'s chapter leads us into the ethical field by analysing the paradigmatic role played by harmonics in relation to practical philosophy, and in particular ethics, in the works of some prominent Platonists of Late Antiquity – namely, Iamblichus, Proclus, and Damascius. Taking as a frame of reference the twofold hierarchy – of types of music and types of virtues – that these philosophers introduced under the inspiration of Plato's *Republic*, Nicomachus of Gerasa, and Ptolemy, O'Meara demonstrates how harmonics relates both to the ethical virtues and to the theoretical ones. Indeed, while on the one hand there are four dimensions to music, from the sensible one to that embodied by the life of the gods, on the other these kinds of music can be associated with levels of virtue and hence represent fundamental steps in men's progression towards the divine. Interestingly, this is not a mere exercise in matching notions; rather, the progression towards higher levels of music and that towards higher virtues share the same structural model, namely the tendency towards unification and simplicity. This way of conceiving the ethical import of music, therefore, recovers certain elements of Plotinus' peculiar way of conceiving human being's ascent to the intelligible; at the same time, however, it is worth emphasising that, as O'Meara shows, late Neoplatonists also strongly resorted to a 'Platonist' mathematical definition of music, namely Nicomachus' one, by re-framing it according to their new philosophical outlook. Indeed, one of the most intriguing effects of such re-framing is a peculiar treatment of the very mathematical core of the notion of harmony: the appeal to the mathematical nature of harmony does not imply that Neoplatonists really regarded those items as having a 'harmonic' structure, or nature, or that they were mathematically structured. As we have seen, this intriguing puzzle is particularly important for Plotinus and in turn plays a fundamental role in Proclus. Indeed, as **Stephen Gersh** shows, in Proclus' *Commentary on the Timaeus* – and, accordingly, in his theology in general – it is possible to discover a notion of harmonic theology designed to reveal the essence, intelligible relations, and causality of the soul by taking its harmonic structure as a starting point. The fact that the soul is made of specific means and proportions is key, for it paves the way to the claim that the soul's essence consists in a *logos*. Interestingly enough, this does not represent just an exegetical remark related to Plato's *divisio animae*, or the mere use of an image: Proclus regards Plato's account of the soul's harmonic structure as a specific key to access theology. From Gersh's survey of the harmonic component within Proclus' iconic theology, a clear analysis of both the 'theological' implications of Proclus' study of the harmonic structure of the Platonic world soul and of the metaphysical-theological function of the ambivalent notion of *logos* emerges. However, the wide-ranging philosophical impact of harmonics is also evident in the case of direct exegeses of Plato's text, as **Christina Hoenig** shows in her chapter on Calcidius' *Commentary on Plato's Timaeus*. Indeed, while the exegesis of Plato's *divisio animae* is a fundamental passage for the introduction of music as a crucial aspect of reality, it must be regarded only as a starting point, for the idea that reality mirrors a harmonic structure and entails harmonic mechanisms can be detected not only in relation to the world soul but also with respect to the overall arrangement of the world – that is, of the various ontological levels into which reality is articulated – and of the human soul itself. Through the influence of the harmonic structure of the soul on the heavenly motions, Calcidius introduces a specific correlation between the cosmic order and the human soul, aspiring to reproduce the perfect condition of the world soul. Such a radical affinity proves important, first of all, from an exegetical point of view. On the one hand, this is how Calcidius seeks to make the cosmological representation of the myth of Er and the *Timaeus*' cosmology and psychological theory interact. On the other, we are well beyond mere textual exegesis here: the chapter reveals that the presence of a harmonic structure ensures the consistency and overall unity of reality from the superior God to the human soul. And we are far beyond mere exegesis also with Philoponus' discussion of music, as **Giovanna R. Giardina** shows in the last chapter of this book. Of course, the idea that the universe, its soul, and human souls have a numerical structure stems directly from the *Timaeus*, but this idea is only a starting point – albeit a crucial one – for Philoponus' discussion. Focusing on the remarks on harmonics to be found in Philoponus' *Commentary on Nicomachus' Introduction to Arithmetic*, Giardina conducts a detailed investigation of the different meanings of Philoponus' references to harmonics, with the aim of demonstrating that all these connotations contribute to shaping a conception of the world in which harmonics as a mathematical science can lead men to grasp both divine and absolutely immaterial entities and the revolutions regulating the heavens.

What we have illustrated thus far emerges from the diachronic perspective that the book invites readers to adopt by leading them on a six-century journey to discover a complex process of exchange between music and philosophy. However, as already mentioned, this is not the sole approach to the matter: a web of synoptic readings is also possible and strongly suggested by the content of this book, for its chapters encourage us to detect a sort of implicit debate on several crucial issues characterising the history of the interplay between music and philosophy in the period under consideration. Taking the Classical and Hellenistic background as a starting point, one can notice how refined and complex the philosophical use of music became in the post-Hellenistic and Imperial Age. In what follows, we shall briefly outline four aspects which the volume synchronically emphasises, leaving the stimulating task of completing this picture to the reader, by exploring the various concepts and fields touched upon by this enquiry.

First, it immediately emerges that musical notions (especially those pertaining to the semantic field of harmony) played a crucial role in cosmological debates. In principle this is not astonishing at all: already with Heraclitus (22B8, 10, 51 DK) and Philolaus (44B6 DK) the orderly constitution of the world is depicted in terms of 'harmony'.[13] In spite of the difficulty of assessing whether and to what extent these philosophical uses of musical notions imply a reflection on the relationship between the two fields, it is beyond doubt that these authors fully acknowledge and exploit the semantic power of 'harmony' (even in its strictly musical sense) in their philosophical accounts of the cosmic order. The foundations of the exchange between music and philosophy are firmly laid out, and Plato's abundant use of musical notions in areas that are central to his philosophical enquiry constitutes a clear demonstration of how much further this exchange could have been developed. Particularly in relation to the notion of cosmic harmony, musical notions play an important role in the cosmological and astronomical account included in the well-known myth of Er at the end of the *Republic* (616c-617d), where in allusive terms the world and the heavens are said to move harmonically. However, the reference work here is the *Timaeus*, whose mathematical account of the world soul brings technical aspects of harmonics into the philosophical discourse and literally leads to a representation of the world as a harmonically structured object.[14] This paved the way for a series of

[13] For bibliographical references, see above, footnote 6, and, more generally, Barker 2007, 263–307.

[14] See works quoted in footnote 7 above, and more specifically Barker 2007, 318–26. It is worth mentioning that the centrality of the *Timaeus* in the development of philosophical thought has been widely emphasised in the last few decades: see Reydams-Schils 1999 and 2002.

technical interpretations of the *divisio animae*: we know, for instance, that Crantor (see Plut. *De an. procr.* 16.1020C3–D9) produced a well-known reading of the *divisio*, and interest in this exercise was probably taken up also in the Peripatos;[15] moreover, in the wake of Plato's *Timaeus*, a flourishing of references to harmony and music in cosmological accounts came to characterise philosophy in the post-Hellenistic age and Late Antiquity. Focusing on the philosophical traditions explored in this book, we can see that, at the dawn of our era, the use of notions and conceptual models borrowed from the musical fields appears in Philo, who insists on the notion of harmony in order to appropriate and supplement Stoic cosmology in Platonist terms, as **Lévy** shows. However, it is within the Platonist tradition that one can discover a number of ways in which Plato's original idea of cosmic harmony is exploited. As **Demulder**, **Petrucci**, and **Michalewski** show, for Platonists discussing the order of the world meant reasoning on – and exploiting – the notion of cosmic harmony. In other words, it meant evaluating what the relationship between pure harmony and its sensible images, or how the idea that the world is harmonically arranged is related to more general issues, especially the causal role of God (or, more broadly, of the intelligible realm) with respect to the world. All this coexists with a further development of technical exegesis: as emerges from **Hoenig** and **Giardina**'s chapters, a mathematising conception of the world's order can be used as the basis for a more general harmonic conception of the dynamics regulating the world itself. The relationship between the cosmic order and music also emerges in Christian literature, especially in a passage of Clement's *Exhortation to the Greeks* where the cosmological role of Christ's Word, significantly defined as the New Song, is illustrated through an impressive use of musical terms such as *emmelōs*, *diaphōnia*, *symphōnia*, and *harmonia*. As **Pelosi** argues, in resorting to technical musical notions to illustrate how the Word-song has accomplished universal harmonisation, Clement adopts and reinterprets a method of explanation combining music and cosmology which finds its earliest application in Presocratic thought. To put it briefly, by following a long tradition that fully explored the link between music and cosmology, and in particular by expanding the *Timaeus'* account of cosmic harmony, thinkers of the post-Hellenistic age and of Late Antiquity developed an intriguing narrative addressing major cosmological issues through the exploitation of musical notions as a philosophical tool.

[15] For an overview of the interpretations of Plato's *divisio animae*, see Petrucci 2019a.

A second important field of debate explored in this volume is epistemology. Also in this case, music, and particularly harmonics, was involved in epistemological discussion already in the Classic and Hellenistic times. Just to mention some fundamental pieces of this history, in the seventh book of the *Republic* (530d-531c) Plato describes two approaches to the harmonic science: the rationalistic approach, championed by the Pythagoreans and characterised by mathematical methods of analysis, and the empirical one, whose distinctive feature is the tendency to rely on hearing as the essential criterion for harmonic investigation. The distinction sketched out in this account – a fundamental piece of evidence on musical epistemology, since it is the first source to explicitly account for the existence of two competing approaches to harmonics – provides the basic coordinates for later discussions on musical epistemology, from Aristotle (*An. post.* 78b-79a) to Late Antiquity (Barker 2007, 311–18). In the Hellenistic period, when the criterion of truth becomes a major topic in philosophy, the epistemological debate on harmonics is given a wider theoretical context within which the role of sense-perception and reason in the assessment of musical events could be analysed (Barker 2009). Hence, at the dawn of the post-Hellenistic age the epistemological status of music and harmonics lay at the centre of a powerful debate. To this, one must add the last stage of the debate, which potentially is in a position to undermine all positive use of music and harmonics, that is, the sceptical attack carried out by Sextus Empiricus in a Pyrrhonian perspective – a topic which **Veres** explores in this volume. All in all, then, authors of the post-Hellenistic age are called to answer questions concerning the very possibility that music and harmonics have an epistemological status – or, at least, questions concerning the specific role of these disciplines. A first crucial reply to both questions is provided by Ptolemy, as **Barker** shows. Not only does Ptolemy justify the idea that harmonics has a specific epistemological status but, in order to do so, he establishes a new relationship between perception and *logos* allowing human beings to properly evaluate harmony. This is, however, just one of the ways in which one could claim a role for harmonics in epistemological discourse. First, a Platonist development of this conception is to be found in Porphyry. Scholars have widely explored the epistemological core of Porphyry's *Commentary on Harmonics*, but **Tarrant**'s fresh interpretation of the treatise and of its philosophical orientation leads to a new appraisal both of the overall theory offered in the text (which he regards not as post-Plotinian but rather as Pythagorean) and of the specific definition of the crucial notion of *logos*. As **Castelli** demonstrates, a different option is provided by Alexander. With Alexander harmonics is granted a special epistemological role, for it allows us to grasp quantitative aspects of reality: far from being confined to aesthetic experience, musical notions are exploited to develop a new ontological conception of the constitution of things; consequently, we can gain special access to things by grasping them in harmonic terms. To put it briefly, Ptolemy, Alexander, and Porphyry represent music as a specific means to access reality. Interestingly, a similar pattern can be discovered in Proclus: as **Gersh** indicates, in Proclus too music represents a model by which we can access a specific dimension of reality – in this specific case, it is a key instrument in theological discourse.

Finally, the book will show that music played an important role in the development of ethics. Also in this case, Plato had a lot to say on the issue. The contribution of music to virtuous behaviour is a crucial point in both his major political works, the *Republic* and the *Laws*, where the idea that music has an impact on character – a traditional belief in ancient Greek culture – is interpreted in the light of the psychological and ethical doctrines championed in these dialogues.[16] Analogously, the ethical impact of music is acknowledged and investigated by Aristotle in *Politics* 8, whereas it becomes a matter of controversy in Hellenistic schools, as testified by the extant parts of Philodemus of Gadara's *On Music*, where the Epicurean author presents and criticises the doctrines of the Stoic Diogenes of Babylon.[17] Consistently with what happens in the fields of cosmology and epistemology, from Philo onwards we witness a strong exploitation of music and harmonics also with respect to ethics. Indeed, depending on the different philosophical systems one considers, music can be seen as a means to lead human beings to become conscious of their limited condition in the world – in Philo, as **Lévy** shows – or as a therapy for the soul – in Plutarch, as **Demulder** suggests. Greek theories and myths on the ethical power of music flow through Christian literature, as illustrated by **Pelosi**, with particular reference to Clement of Alexandria, who reinterprets the link between music and ethics as part of the strategy that characterises his general approach to Greek culture. These ethical appeals to music, however, clearly reach their culmination in Neoplatonism, as **O'Meara** argues: music is used as a model for a system of virtues and the progressive ascent towards ethical perfection.

As both the diachronic perspective and the synchronic approach reveal, the intertwining of music and philosophy from the early Imperial age to Late Antiquity produced a great variety of views and theories, which can only partially be confined within the boundaries of interpretative

16 On Plato, see Pelosi 2010. 17 See especially Delattre 2007.

categories, be they historical or thematic. Nonetheless, both the chronological and the thematic perspective point to the common background that lies behind this rich and multifaceted representation: in all the cases considered in this volume, music provides a fundamental tool to produce effective philosophical accounts in fields such as cosmology, ontology, epistemology, and ethics. As we have seen, moreover, this is true not only for specific problems but, more generally, for the attempt to establish connections between different issues and aspects of reality. Even more interestingly, music is not referred to just as a repertory of metaphors: from harmony to numeric concords, from attunement to *logoi*, music provides philosophy with a powerful conceptualisation, which was exploited in philosophical discourse. This also means that, by following such a narrative, one is in a position to reconstruct the progressive reworking and rethinking of these notions, which were redefined on a case-by-case basis, acquiring new functions and roles in an ever-expanding debate. From the beginning of the Imperial age to the end of Antiquity, therefore, music never ceased to be key to philosophical discourse, in a continuous production of harmonies of reason.

CHAPTER 1

The Scala Naturae *and Music*
Two Models in Philo's Thought

Carlos Lévy

In the history of ancient philosophy there is a kind of fascinating black hole between Cicero's last philosophical treatises and the first works of Seneca and Philo. From this period very little has survived via direct transmission. The causes of this silence are multiple and complex. One of them is certainly the Roman civil war, the *commune nefas*, as the poet Lucan put it.[1] Not only was it a major political trauma, but it had momentous consequences for Roman philosophy. The period before the war was that of Lucretius, Cicero, Cato and many other Romans with profound philosophical interests. After this war, most gifted young men preferred poetry or rhetoric to philosophy, as though the age of desire and the imagination had succeeded that of reflection. John Glucker also stressed the fact that this century of silence of our sources on Platonism is a huge obstacle for our general knowledge of the Academy.[2] It must be added that when new philosophical (or paraphilosophical) texts appeared, the situation changed. The last great witness of the philosophy of the Hellenistic period was a Roman magistrate, Cicero. The first great witness of what is commonly called "Middle Platonism" was a leading citizen of the Jewish community of Alexandria, soaked in both traditional Greek *paideia* and the themes and categories of Hellenistic Judaism.[3] It is precisely this articulation between Hellenistic philosophy and Middle Platonism that I will tackle here through the presence in Philo's work of two different models (i.e., that

[1] Lucan, *Bell. civ.* 1.6.

[2] Glucker 1978, 121: "It is a well-known fact (or, at least, it deserves to be well-known), that between Theomnestus' lectures attended by Brutus in 44 BC (Plut. *Brut.* 24.1) and Ammonius the teacher of Plutarch, some hundred years later, we meet with no philosopher living in Athens and described in our sources as an 'Academic' or a 'Platonist.'"

[3] The Middle Platonic identity of Philo is a tantalizing problem. It could not be otherwise, since the concept of Middle Platonism is a product of modern erudition. The bibliography on this topic has increased considerably. The problem, however, has been well formulated by Runia 1993, 112–40 and Sterling 1993, 96–111.

of the *scala naturae* and that of music).[4] In *De congressu* 76, Philo, who very rarely speaks about himself, evokes the role of music in his education:[5]

> Again my ardour moved me to keep company with a third; rich in rhythm, harmony and melody was she, and her name was Music, and from her I begat diatonics, chromatics and enharmonics conjunct and disjunct melodies, conforming with the consonance of the fourth, fifth or octave intervals. And again of none of these did I make a secret hoard, wishing to see the lawful wife a lady of wealth with a host of servants ministering to her.

Everything seems to be simple and clear in this text. Music, the daughter of geometry, is a path to philosophy, and philosophy herself leads to wisdom. But we will see that this apparent simplicity is somewhat fallacious. Music is omnipresent in the Philonian corpus and pervades much of his vocabulary. Here I shall not stress the problem of his musical competence. One of the few papers devoted to the problem of the presence of music in Philo is that published by Siegmund Levarie in the *Journal of Musicology* in 1991.[6] Through a fine analysis of some passages from *De agricultura* 137 and *De somniis* 1.27–9, he reached the conclusion that, without having all the skills of a professional musician, Philo had a strong musical culture. In my opinion there is, however, a gap in Levarie's article: he seems to consider the musical model as the only one at work in Philo. In any case, this model is the only one that he evokes. Now, it seems to me that the presence of another model, that of the *scala naturae*, and the articulation between the two models constitute an interesting aspect of Philonian thought. Eclecticism and syncretism are words often used to characterize Philo's way of thinking and writing. In my opinion, however, the main hallmark of Philo's thought is its fluid and dynamic quality. What would seem contradictory in the case of a "professional" philosopher finds a kind of superior coherence in Philo, owing to the omnipresence in his thought of the revealed word of an absolutely transcendent God. The philosophical context itself was an ever-evolving one. Stoic dogmatism was somewhat shaken by the criticism from the New Academy. The Neo-Academic scepticism of Arcesilaus and Carneades had itself evolved, with Philo of Larissa, into a kind of mild dogmatism. Aristotelianism had made a comeback after a long period of decline. In Rome, a new form of Pythagoreanism had appeared with Nigidius Figulus and, some years after, the Sextii tried to promote a strange synthesis of Stoicism, Pythagoreanism, and the Roman tradition.[7] Pythagoreanism was probably a rather strong

[4] On the meaning of the *scala naturae* in Stoicism, see Bénatouïl 2003, 297–331.
[5] Unless specified, the translations are those of the LCL. [6] See Levarie 1991, 124–30.
[7] See Hadot 2007, 179–210.

presence in the Alexandrian and Roman intellectual milieus, but it was by and large a reformulated doctrine, as we can see from the last book of Ovid's *Metamorphoses*.[8] There were more than four centuries between Philolaus and Philo, who in his commentaries on the *Law* did not present the various doctrines in isolation. His aim was rather to subordinate them all to his own particular research. The time of the big Hellenistic systems was over, and Philo had even more reasons than did other thinkers to consider himself free from this kind of rigid rationality.

1.1 The Philonian Use of the *Scala Naturae*

To describe the world, Philo could draw upon a model – with Aristotelian antecedents especially in the *Historia animalium* – which he had inherited from Stoicism.[9] It presented the universe in terms of the continuity of a nonmusical scale, organized around the four categories of *hexis*, *physis*, *psychē*, and *logos*, embodied in minerals, plants, nonrational animals, and rational animals.[10] These are terms that he often uses in his work. However, contrary to what happens in Stoicism, in his case the *scala naturae* was not a closed, self-sufficient model. I shall try to demonstrate this through three examples.

The first one is a passage from the *De opificio mundi*.[11] Philo wants to explain the most famous verse of *Genesis*, where God says: "Let us make the soul in our image." In his commentary, he refers to the *scala naturae* but in a way that only partially corresponds to what we find in the Stoic description of this structure. First of all – and this is more than just a nuance – the *scala* is no longer presented as a dogma, but only as a plausible hypothesis, since Philo states: "The absolutely true cause, it is necessary that it is only God who knows it. But the cause which seems persuasive and probable for a conjecture of some appearance must not be hidden." A Stoic would never have professed such incapacity to achieve true knowledge. For the Stoics, it might happen that even the sage must suspend his assent, but this suspension is only occasional and temporary. For Philo, by contrast, ignorance of the ultimate cause is ontological, since only God knows such a cause. The second difference is that animals, as a general category, are not mentioned. On one side of the scale there are the plants and brute beasts; the former are devoid of the faculty of representation, while the latter have

[8] See Hardie 1995, 204–14.

[9] On this point see Granger 1985, 181–200 and Besnier 2003, 51–64.

[10] Sext. Emp. *Math*. 9.78.

[11] *Opif.* 73.

neither intellect nor reason. At the other end are the stars, presented as living beings endowed with intellect. They are the visible aspect of the universal *logos*, the emanation of an ineffable and unknowable God. At the center are human beings, who embody a mixed nature and the combination of opposites. For their creation God employed other craftsmen, "so that the Father was not responsible for evil toward his children."[12] Here the compatibility between human freedom and the rational order of the world, a crucial point of the Stoic system, is reformulated through the biblical problem of sin. The Stoic idea of a fundamentally good world, characterized by a perfect continuity between individual and universal reason, without any transcendental perspective, was fundamentally foreign to the Jewish Alexandrian thinker: even though he often adopted Stoic terms and themes, he always did so outside their perfectly systematic context. The Stoic dogma that evil is only an error of perspective due to human inability to see the perfection of the world could not be accepted by someone imbued with the idea that evil was due to the sin of Adam and Eve and to their expulsion from paradise.

In *Leg.* 2.22, there is a rather complex passage, where Philo describes the powers of the mind, when it is naked and isolated from the body. He evokes the four categories of *dynameis*: *ektikē*, *physikē*, *psychikē*, and *logikē*, stressing the difference between rational and irrational animals and the similarity between human and divine rationality.[13] All this sounds thoroughly Stoic. There are, however, at least two differences between Philo's thought and this doctrine. First, the idea of isolating the mind from the body is much more Platonic than Stoic. Even in a somewhat Platonizing Stoic like Panaetius we do not find anything of the sort.[14] Second, when he speaks of reason as being common to humans and gods, he adds "probably" (*tacha*), which is an elegant way of distancing himself from the Stoics, for whom this was simply a dogma.[15] In a letter to Lucilius, Seneca does not hesitate to say that in a certain sense a human being can be superior to the gods, since by his own efforts he can gain a perfection that is instead

[12] *Opif.* 74: διὰ τοῦτ᾽ ἐπὶ μόνης τῆς ἀνθρώπου γενέσεώς φησιν ὅτι εἶπεν ὁ θεὸς "ποιήσωμεν," ὅπερ ἐμφαίνει συμπαράληψιν ἑτέρων ὡς ἂν συνεργῶν, ἵνα ταῖς μὲν ἀνεπιλήπτοις βουλαῖς τε καὶ πράξεσιν ἀνθρώπου κατορθοῦντος ἐπιγράφηται θεὸς ὁ πάντων ἡγεμών, ταῖς δ᾽ ἐναντίαις ἕτεροι τῶν ὑπηκόων· ἔδει γὰρ ἀναίτιον εἶναι κακοῦ τὸν πατέρα τοῖς ἐκγόνοις.

[13] See the useful commentary in F. H. Colson and G. H. Whitaker's translation of Philo (1929, 480). They quote *Quod deus* 35, the most complete explanation of the Stoic theory of the *scala naturae*.

[14] It is probable that Philo's approach must be interpreted within the context of the Platonic revision of Stoicism, of which Eudorus was at least one of the promoters: see Bonazzi 2007, 109–32.

[15] *Leg.* 2.22: πάλιν ἡ διανοητικὴ δύναμις ἰδία τοῦ νοῦ ἐστι, καὶ ἡ λογικὴ κοινὴ μὲν τάχα καὶ τῶν θειοτέρων φύσεων, ἰδία δὲ ὡς ἐν θνητοῖς ἀνθρώπου.

inherent to the divine nature.[16] This affirmation certainly would have seemed monstrous to Philo.

My third example is found in *Quod deus* 48. Philo expresses an idea that is common to both Judaism and Stoicism, namely the absolute superiority of the human being over other living beings. At the same time, he deviates from Stoic orthodoxy in that he does not use the opposition "rational animal(s)" (*zōion logikon / zōia logika*) to characterize this human superiority. From his point of view, it is freedom of choice that allows man to dominate nature. Of course, in Stoicism freedom is associated with assent, which exists only in the human soul and is one of the powers of the *logos*, but it is not this angle that Philo chooses to adopt. For him:

> the soul of man alone has received from God the faculty of voluntary movement, and in this way especially is made like to Him, and thus being liberated, as far as might be, from that hard and ruthless mistress, necessity, may justly be charged with guilt, in that it does not honour its Liberator.

It is in the choice between good and evil that freedom manifests itself, and this choice ultimately leads to the God of transcendence.

It is easy to appreciate the difference between Philo and the Stoics by comparing these passages with the exposition of the *scala naturae* in Sextus.[17] According to the sceptic thinker, who in this rather long passage expounds the Stoic doctrine before refuting it, everything in the right perception of the universe shows that God exists and that he is nowhere else than in the rational perfection of the world, "intelligent, virtuous, and immortal."[18] For Philo, the *logos* is the ultimate limit of human finitude, but God is beyond this limit. The divinity cannot be identified with reason, which is only what the human mind can perceive of His powers.[19] The model of the *scala naturae* developed by the Stoics, therefore, presented two contrasting aspects for Philo:

- a positive one: to preserve human specificity and to emphasize the eminent place of human beings in the universe. No doctrine before the Stoics had so strongly emphasized the fact that, though at his/her

[16] *Ep.* 53.11: *Est aliquid quo sapiens antecedat deum: ille naturae beneficio non timet, suo sapiens. Ecce res magna, habere inbecillitatem hominis, securitatem dei.*

[17] Sext. Emp. *Math.* 9.74–91, where he deals with the argument of the perfection of the world, after having refuted that of the *consensus omnium*, the general and unanimous opinion about the existence of God.

[18] *Ibid.* 85: ἀλλ' εἰ ἀρίστη ἐστὶ φύσις ἡ τὸν κόσμον διοικοῦσα, νοερά τε ἔσται καὶ σπουδαία καὶ ἀθάνατος. Τοιαύτη δὲ τυγχάνουσα θεός ἐστιν. εἰσὶν ἄρα θεοί.

[19] On the complexity of the concept of *dynamis* in Philo of Alexandria, see the many articles recently dedicated to that question in Calabi, Munnich, Reydams-Schils, and Vimercati 2015.

birth a human being is no different from any other animal, since he/she is subject to the law governing the whole of nature (i.e., spontaneous adaptation to his/her own nature),[20] he/she then becomes a rational being, although in most humans this rationality is a feeble and defective one;
- a negative one: the erroneous identification of human nature with that of God and the idea that reason is the key to absolute truth.

So, Philo could adopt some aspects of the Stoic *scala naturae*, but it was impossible for him to adhere to a doctrine that he regarded as only a partial representation of the reality of the world.

1.2 The Musical Model

In what sense, then, was the musical model a means for Philo to escape the limitation inherent to the Stoic *scala naturae* and to take into account the transcendent nature of God? Before sketching out an answer to this question, I would like to make two preliminary remarks.

1.2.1 The Double Theological Approach

Things would be clearer, perhaps, if Philo had explicitly rejected the Stoic *scala naturae*, but this was not the case. In fact, he had no fundamental contempt for the immanentist attitude, just the ambition to proceed further in the direction of truth.[21] In *Praem.* 41–43, he defines two different perceptions of the world and of the idea of God: that of the rationalists – probably the Stoics even though they are not explicitly mentioned – and that of Israel. Contrary to what could be expected, he does not condemn the former perception, which asserted the existence of God based on a description of the world and a reflection on its nature. He even presents those who chose this approach as incomparable men, who deduced the Demiurge from His works through what is at least a probable reasoning:

> Entering the world as into a well-ordered city they have beheld the earth standing fast, highland and lowland full of sown crops and trees and fruits and all kinds of living creatures to boot. Also spread over its surface seas and lakes and rivers, both spring fed and winter torrents. They have seen too the air and breezes so happily tempered, the yearly seasons changing in

[20] For a general presentation of the concept of *oikeiōsis*, see Radice 2000.

[21] Runia 2001, 394 rightly writes: "In Philo's view Judaism is in its fundamental aspects a reasonable religion." On the relation between God and humans, see Calabi 2007.

> harmonious order, and over all the sun and moon, planets and fixed stars, the whole heaven and heaven's host, line upon line, a true universe in itself revolving within the universe. Struck with admiration and astonishment, they arrived at a conception according with what they beheld, that surely all these beauties and this transcendent order have not come into being automatically but by the handiwork of a demiurge and world maker (οὐκ ἀπαυτοματισθέντα γέγονεν, ἀλλ' ὑπό τινος δημιουργοῦ κοσμοποιοῦ); also that there must be a providence, for it is a law of nature that a maker should take care of what has been made. These no doubt are truly admirable persons (οἱ θεσπέσιοι) and superior to the other classes. They have as I said advanced from down to up by a sort of heavenly ladder and by reason and reflection happily inferred the Creator from his works. But those, if such there be, who have had the power to apprehend Him through Himself without the cooperation of any reasoning process to lead them to the sight, must be recorded as holy and genuine worshippers and friends of God in very truth (ἐν ὁσίοις καὶ γνησίοις θεραπευταῖς καὶ θεοφιλέσιν ὡς ἀληθῶς ἀναγραφέσθωσαν).

While Philo is generally quite harsh toward the Chaldeans, whom he criticizes for affirming that the universe is the only thing in existence,[22] he is much friendlier toward the "admirable persons," precisely because they do not deny the existence of a Creator. The second attitude is that of Israel, the people who were allowed to see God when God revealed Himself to them on Mount Sinai. In Philo's perception of the Jewish faith, there is no indifference toward the beauty and the perfection of the world, but he does not consider this to be the ultimate revelation of the divine nature. For him Israel is fundamentally the nation who sees not the Creation but the Creator.[23] That is his interpretation of the very name of his people, for example in *Ebr.* 83, where he says that Israel means perfection, since it means the vision of God.

It is striking, however, that the existence of this double approach finds musical expression in *Somn.* 2.27–28:

> For both the work and his Fashioner need to be celebrated by two quite perfect melodies, not the same in each case. For since the theme of the praise was different, it was necessary for the corresponding musical harmonies to be distinct also, the conjunct assigned to the conjunct universe, compacted as it is of different parts, the disjunct reserved for Him who is in virtue of his existence disjunct from the whole of creation (τὴν δὲ διεζευγμένην τῷ πάσης γενέσεως διεζευγμένῳ κατὰ τὴν οὐσίαν θεῷ).

[22] See Frick 1999, 120–33. [23] Delling 1984, 29–30.

While the model of the *scala naturae* stressed the perfect continuity of the universe and was unable to express a more authentic perception of reality, music could express not so much the perfection of the world but the distance separating the Creator from his Creation. Though music, being both conjunctive and disjunctive, was not identified with disjunctive harmony, this aspect was privileged by Philo as the most powerful expression of the gap between God and His creation. Philo accuses the Chaldeans of having used music exclusively as a way of affirming the unity and perfect intelligibility of the universe:[24]

> They have set up a harmony between things on earth and things on high, between heavenly things and earthly. Following as it were the laws of musical proportions, they have exhibited the most perfect symphony of the universe, produced by a concord and sympathetic affinity between its parts, separated indeed in space, but housemates in kinship.

The Chaldeans, a recurrent target for Philo's attacks, were unable of drawing a distinction between the *scala naturae* model and the paradigm of music. They considered both ways of expressing the evident rationality of a universe they perceived to be as bright as the stars they were always contemplating.

1.2.2 Philo and Pythagoreanism: Some Remarks

My second remark concerns the relation of Philo to Pythagoreanism, a vast subject that I shall refrain from investigating in detail here, since I have devoted an article to many aspects of it.[25] While Philo rarely cites his sources, in *Opif.* 100 he explicitly mentions the Pythagoreans in relation to the number seven. He says that they are the only ones to identify it with the Rector of the universe. What is more, a few lines later, he quotes Philolaus, the famous Pythagorean of the fifth century BC: "For there is a Rector and Head of all things, God, who is for everlasting, unchanging eternity, like unto himself, different from all other beings." I will refer to Runia's commentary on *De opificio* and to C. A. Huffman's edition of the fragments of Philolaus for a comparison between this passage and a fragment of Lydus.[26]

[24] *Migr.* 179, transl. Frick 1999, 120.

[25] See Petit 1998, 471–82 and Lévy 2007, 11–28. On the various aspects of Pythagoreanism in Antiquity, see now Huffman 2014a.

[26] Lydus, *Mens* 2.12.33.8–34.3. See Runia 2001, 273–5, Huffman 1993, 335–6, Petrucci 2012a, 417–27, and related tables.

There is, however, a contradiction between the two treatises. In *Leg.* 1.15, the number seven is no longer identified with God. Philo says that "the Pythagoreans, indulging in myth, liken seven to the motherless and ever-virgin Maiden because neither she was born of the womb nor shall she ever bear." Perhaps this was a turnabout on Philo's part, who would have blamed himself for having too closely connected the God of the Bible with a pagan author in the *De opificio*. Other references are also significant. In *Probus* 2–3 it is said that "the most holy company of the Pythagoreans teaches this too among other excellent doctrines: 'walk not on the high-ways.'" About this principle he says that "all genuine votaries of philosophy have obeyed the injunction, divining in it a law, or rather super-law, equivalent to an oracle" (νόμον αὐτὸ μᾶλλον δὲ θεσμὸν ἰσούμενον χρησμῷ ὑπετόπησαν).[27] Finally, in the *Quaestiones in Genesim* Pythagorean friendship is defined as the firmest concord among habits (*symphōnia bebaiōtatē ethōn*),[28] which is – to the best of my knowledge – the only reference in Philo that explicitly associates a musical concept with Pythagoreanism. It is therefore undeniable that all this testifies to a strong Pythagorean influence. But it would be an error to think that all of Philo's musical culture was of Pythagorean origin. The wide diffusion of this rather varied philosophy and the presence of some of its themes in other philosophical systems always leave the possibility of one or more intermediate sources open. Here I will give just one example. Philo frequently draws upon the theme of the efficacy of melody on the soul, which allows her to acquire good dispositions, in a process comparable to that of gymnastics. But this theme is present in Philodemus' *De musica*, where it is attributed to the Stoics and more precisely to Diogenes of Babylon.[29] This analogy between music and gymnastics is a very good example to show how multifaceted Philo's thought on music, and many other themes, truly is. Diogenes, who had previously accepted the ideas of Heraclides in a much broader way, had said that it was clear from these statements that music was useful in many areas of life. In his opinion, its assiduous practice could give the human mind dispositions appropriate to a fairly large number of virtues and even all of them. It is therefore necessary to remain prudent and to take this circulation of doctrines into account, especially in relation to a thinker like Philo, who does not identify with any of them.

[27] See *Opif.* 143. On this Pythagorean theme, see Diog. Laert. 8.17.

[28] *QG* 1 17b: Φιλία γὰρ οὐκ ἐν τῷ χρειώδει μᾶλλον ἢ κράσει καὶ συμφωνίᾳ βεβαιοτάτῃ ἠθῶν, ὡς ἕκαστον τῶν συνελθόντων εἰς φιλικὴν κοινωνίαν τὸ Πυθαγόρειον ῥῆμα ἐπιφθέγξασθαι ὅτι "ἆρά ἐστι φίλος ἕτερός τις ἐγώ."

[29] *De musica* D, col. 49.

1.2.3 Music, Providence, and Transcendence

Music and Providence

Let us now try to understand how the musical model could be a way for Philo to emerge from the conceptual confinement that the *scala naturae* represented for him. First, it must again be emphasized that in his thought the musical model does not abolish Stoic providentialism but rather extends it, allowing us to abolish its finitude. I will take the *De posteritate* as my point of departure. Here Philo affirms that it is nature that has given the human being the paradigm of music by installing in him a perfect phonatory system and by giving him the most beautiful of all musical instruments, the voice:[30]

> Most appropriately does he give to sounding speech the title of father of music and of all musical instruments (πατέρα μουσικῆς καὶ τῶν κατὰ μουσικὴν πάντων ὀργάνων τὸν γεγωνὸν λόγον προσφυέστατα καλεῖ). For nature, when she had wrought the organ or instrument of sound of living creatures as the chief and most perfect of all instruments, went on at once to bestow upon it the concords and various kinds of melodies to the end that it might be a pattern made ready beforehand for the instruments that were to be fashioned artificially. So too with the ear. Nature turned it with her lathe and made it spherical, drawing circles within circles, lesser within larger in order that the sound that approached it might not escape and be dispersed outside of it, but that the thing heard might be collected and enclosed within by the circles and being as it were poured through them, be conveyed into the receptacles of mind.

It is worth noting the resemblances between this eulogy of the way in which nature constructs the senses, and thus hearing, and what we find in Cicero's *De natura deorum*, in the speech of the Stoic Balbus.[31] Significantly, Cicero too emphasizes how musical instruments reflect the natural perfection of the ear: "at the entrance the ears are hard as horn and represent many folds, which in bodies of this nature, amplify the sound they reverberate, which is why, in lyres too sound is returned by shell or horn, and why noise is amplified in closed and tortuous places." There is in Philo, as well as in Cicero, the idea that music has been developed through the imitation of natural paradigms. In what way does the Alexandrian's thought differ from the Roman's? It seems to me that part of the answer can be found in *Quod deterius* 75:[32]

[30] *Post.* 103. [31] *Nat. D.* 2.144.

[32] *Det.* 75: ὥσπερ γὰρ μουσικοῦ τινος ἢ γραμματικοῦ τελευτήσαντος ἡ μὲν ἐν τοῖς ἀνδράσι μουσικὴ καὶ γραμματικὴ συνέφθαρται, αἱ δὲ τούτων ἰδέαι μένουσι καὶ τρόπον τινὰ βιοῦσιν ἰσοχρόνιοι τῷ κόσμῳ, καθ' ἃς οἵ τε ὄντες καὶ οἱ μέλλοντες διαδοχαῖς ταῖς εἰσαεὶ μουσικοί τε καὶ γραμματικοὶ

> When a musician or a scholar has died, the music or scholarship, that has its abode in individual masters, had indeed perished with him, but the original patterns of these remain, and in some way (*tropon tina*) live as long as the world lasts; and by conforming to these the men of this generation in perpetual succession will attain to be musicians or scholars. In exactly the same way, if what is sensible or modest or brave, or just or, to say it in one word, wise be destroyed, none the less does there stand, inscribed on the undying tablets of the universe, good sense with a life that dies not, and all virtue exempt from decay.

The interpretation of this text is less easy than it seems. In particular, one may wonder about the meaning of *tropon tina* and the significance of the difference between the ideas of music, which are said to last as long as the world, and the virtues, which are all simply referred to as being immortal. Actually, Philo's thought appears clearer in the *De mutatione*:[33]

> For it may happen that there are many musical, grammatical and geometrical items as well as acts of justice, prudence, courage and temperance. But what is in itself the musical or the geometric, as well as the just, the temperate, the prudent or the courageous, is something unique; it has the highest place, and does not differ in any way from the Archetype-Idea, from which most replicas have been formed, and they are innumerable.

Here we see that the nature of music is not essentially different from that of wisdom, represented in this passage through the enumeration of the four cardinal virtues. It is a perfect replica, but only a replica, of a transcendental reality.

Another example of Philo's transformation of traditional philosophical patterns is *Cher*. 109 ff. In this passage there are clear elements of the *scala naturae*, for example at the beginning of §111: thus love draws "lifeless to living, unreasoning to reasoning" (ταύτῃ καὶ ἄψυχα ἐμψύχων καὶ ἄλογα λογικῶν). However, it soon becomes evident that Philo does not aim to describe an easily knowable world, organized according to a strict hierarchy. The deconstruction of the traditional *scala* is led by the Empedoclean principle of love (*philia*), probably through a Platonic intermediary source: "Thus love draws lifeless to living, unreasoning to reasoning, trees to men, men to plants, cultivated to wild, savage to tame, each sex to the other." The musical model crops us again here, through the mention of a lyre, as a way to reconcile coherence and difference (§110): "Thus through reciprocity and

γενήσονται, οὕτως καὶ τὸ ἔν τινι φρόνιμον ἢ σῶφρον ἢ ἀνδρεῖον ἢ δίκαιον ἢ συνόλως σοφὸν ἂν ἀναιρεθῇ, οὐδὲν ἧττον ἐν τῇ τοῦ παντὸς ἀθανάτῳ φύσει φρόνησις ἀθάνατος καὶ ἀρετὴ σύμπασα ἄφθαρτος ἐστηλίτευται, καθ' ἣν καὶ νῦν εἰσιν ἀστεῖοί τινες καὶ αὖθις γενήσονται.

33 *Mut*. 146, my translation.

combination, even as a lyre is formed of *unlike* notes, God meant that they should come to fellowship and concord and form a single harmony, and that an universal give and take should govern them, and lead up to the consummation of the whole world." But this musical model is not self-sufficient. It is the best expression of what can be understood about divine Providence. It is God who decided that the differences could be integrated into a coherent whole, but the presence of unlike notes is not insignificant. It means that, unlike in the system attributed to the Chaldeans by Philo, essential differences cannot be dismissed by invoking an allegedly complete perception of reality. When music is discordant, for Philo it is as useful from an ontological point of view as when it is harmonious, since it reminds us of the fact that God is the ultimate cause and that the human mind can attain only what the Divinity places within his/her reach.

Music as a Liberation

Music is therefore a path to transcendence, a threshold between the variety of sensation and the perfection of the archetype that it reproduces. Thus man creates musical instruments by imitation of nature, but the music he creates is itself the imitation of an archetypal music. This relationship between music and the archetype is particularly interesting because it constitutes a radically new element with respect to the *scala naturae*. The human being is no longer defined as a merely rational being, as in the Stoic doctrine, but rather as a musical being. Here I am referring more precisely to *Mut.* 184:[34] "We are born in a form of mixtures where the divine and the mortal are mingled together and harmonized according to the perfect musical relations." In Stoicism that of *krasis* was quite an important concept: it meant a complete mixture and was one of the most controversial aspects of the doctrine. As Diogenes Laertius states,[35] "a small amount of wine thrown into the sea will extend alongside of it and then be destroyed along with it." Plutarch says that Arcesilaus joked about this dogma, saying that if the leg of a wounded soldier extended across the whole sea, Xerxes' fleet and the Athenian one would be included in a leg.[36] Actually, Philo does not use *krasis* here but *krama*, a word expressing not the action but the result of the action and explicitly requiring the presence of someone who produces the mixture. In Stoicism, since the

[34] *Mut.* 184: ἐπειδὴ καὶ ἡμεῖς γεγόναμεν κράματα, θείου καὶ θνητοῦ συγκερασθέντων καὶ κατὰ τοὺς τῆς τελείας μουσικῆς λόγους ἁρμοσθέντων.

[35] Diog. Laert. 7.151 = *SVF* 2.479, see Lewis 1988, 89, who – *contra* the traditional interpretation – affirms that the constituents are not preserved but destroyed. See also Stobaeus, *Ecl.* 1.17.4, 153.24–155.14.

[36] *Com. not.* 1078C.

universe is one and perfectly rational, the complete mixture does not encounter any ontological obstacle; hence, the mixture may be said to be self-produced. Philo is faced with the obstacle that confronts all dualistic ways of thinking: how to explain the union of two different substances? For him the musical paradigm had the advantage of lending the whole a unity that did not presuppose a perfect continuity from the first Cause down to individuals. For the Stoics, the human soul and the body cannot be separated from one another. Both are corporeal and belong to the universal rational whole. Their union could be imagined as a *krasis*. But in Philo's thought, "perfect musical relations" meant a system integrating differences without abolishing them.

In *De opificio* 69–70 Philo illustrates this intermediate situation more precisely.[37] It is said that by means of the arts and sciences the intellect opens great paths in all directions. It then rises on the side of the ether and the celestial revolutions: "it then evolves with the chorus of the planets and the fixed ones according to the laws of perfect music, carried away by the love of wisdom which leads his race, and dominates from above all sensible substance, and, at this point, covets the intelligible." Actually music is not explicitly mentioned here among the *technai* that allow the intuition of the intelligible, but it is the only one in relation to which the supraterrestrial referent is evoked. The reference to the guide of the universe becomes explicit when Philo says that God preordained the universe in such a way that it was ready to receive the human being, since He organized

> the most wonderful motions and rhythmic dances performed in harmonic sequences by means of numerical proportions and concordant revolutions. You would not be mistaken if you said that in all these movements the original and true and paradigmatic science of music was embodied. The human beings who came later inscribed the images of this music on their souls, and so handed down to human life a most indispensable and useful art (ἀναγκαιοτάτην καὶ ὠφελιμωτάτην τέχνην τῷ βίῳ).[38]

In *De somniis* 1.37, heaven is called "this archetype of musical instruments", and it is said that it was precisely adjusted only to provide musical accompaniment for the hymns sung to the glory of the Father and the Universe. The archetype of music is not foreign to matter but, at the same time, music is directed toward the one who is (i.e., toward the absolute cause). Celestial music is a perfect harmony, while human music includes dissonances. For Philo, music allows the perception of an ontological ladder extending from humans to God, but it

[37] See Plato, *Phaedrus* 249c.

[38] It is worth recalling that in *Opif.* 126, music and grammar are called "the best of the sciences". On the mystical function of arithmology, see Staehle 1931.

also has the advantage of making it easier to intuit the transcendence that the *scala naturae* seeks to exclude.

From Music to Prophecy

In what way, according to Philo, does the musical paradigm free the human being from the aporias of the *scala naturae*? It does so inasmuch as the Stoic model sees only the perfection and *sympatheia* of the world and refuses to define the human being, however imperfect he may be, other than through his rationality. The musical model, on the other hand, allows more complex approaches. We will see this through some additional remarks. The first concerns the numerical nature of music, which – as we have seen – is capable of pointing to that which is beyond the world, unlike the *scala naturae*. The richness of the arithmological approach appears most explicitly in *De opificio*.[39] Philo begins by emphasizing the perfection of the tetrad, which is at least implicitly perceived as the most appropriate number to describe the harmonious order of the celestial world. But the tetrad is also presented in the same passage according to the variety of its musical aspects: "And then the tetrad contains the relations of the musical chords, the fourth, the fifth, the octave and also the double octave, which realize the most perfect system." Nevertheless, the perfection of the tetrad is a relative perfection, for it contains only virtually absolute perfection, that of the decade, which is called the totally perfect, the *panteleia*. It is in *De decalogo* that we find the perfection of the decade illustrated through several approaches. The decade, we are told, corresponds to the ten categories that "those who care for nature" claim to be consubstantial with it.[40] Incidentally, the specificity of the Aristotelian categories according to Philo lies in the fact that time and space are presented as categories without which the other categories could not exist.[41] The musical meaning is not immediately mentioned, in any case not in the same way as it is for the tetrad. But this does not mean that it is absent. Some paragraphs later, we find this meditation about the way in which God spoke to Moses on Mount Sinai:[42]

> I should suppose that God wrought on this occasion a miracle of a truly holy kind by bidding an invisible sound to be created in the air (κελεύσας ἦχον ἀόρατον ἐν ἀέρι δημιουργηθῆναι) more marvellous than all instruments and fitted with perfect harmonies, not soulless, nor yet composed of body and soul like a living creature, but a rational soul, full of clearness and

[39] *Opif.* 47. [40] *Decal.* 30. [41] On Philo and Aristotelianism, see Lévy 2011, 17–33.
[42] *Decal.* 33–4.

> distinctness, which giving shape and tension to the air and changing it to flaming fire, sounded forth like the breath through a trumpet an articulate voice equally audible to the farthest as well as the nearest.

Thus music serves as a guide – from the imperfect sound of human instruments to the unprecedented voice of God expressed through its logical power. To this one must add what is said about Moses' own hymn in *Virt.* 72–74:

> He convoked a divine assemblage of the elements of all existence and the chiefest parts of the universe, the earth and heaven, one the home of mortals, the other the house of the immortals. With these around him he sang his canticles with every kind of harmony and sweet music in the ears of both mankind and ministering angels: of men that as disciples they should learn from him the lesson of like thankfulness of heart; of angels as watchers, observing, as themselves masters of melody, whether the song had any discordant note, and scarce able to credit that any man imprisoned in a corruptible body could like the sun and moon and the most sacred choir of the other stars attune his soul to harmony with God's instrument, the heaven and the whole universe.

It is through the music of his hymns that Moses succeeds in taking his place in the celestial choir. We shall note here two differences with respect to the *Somnium Scipionis*, with which the text also presents certain resemblances. In Cicero, access to the celestial spheres is conditioned, if one may say so, by the double filter of the dream of the Second Africanus and the death of the First. In Philo, on the contrary, it is a living Moses who participates in the choir of the universe. Moreover, Scipio participates in the music of the spheres only as a dazzled and mute listener, while Moses becomes an active part of this choir. It must be noted, however, that there is a point at which Cicero approaches Philo: in §18 he evokes the educated men who on the strings of the lyre and in their songs produced relations between sounds similar to the music of the heavenly spheres, saying that they thus opened a path to return to heaven. Music and right political action are two different ways for a human being to reach the highest kind of life.[43]

Music and Stoicism: Two Contrary Positions

I would now like to return to the problem of sin, which we have seen to lie at the very heart of Philo's critical approach to the *scala naturae*. Here I will

[43] Cic. *Rep.* 6.18: *quod docti homines nervis imitati atque cantibus aperuerunt sibi reditum in hunc locum, sicut alii, qui praestantibus ingeniis in vita humana divina studia coluerunt.*

recall what Jacques Brunschwig wrote about the conjunctive model in one of his most enlightening articles:[44]

> Just such a moral hypersensitivity seems to be what is expressed in the Stoics' conviction that a partial imperfection is enough to spoil the whole, that anything that is not totally successful is no better than something that is completely unsuccessful and that one fumbled note is enough to warrant going back to replace the piece of music right from the beginning. The Stoics, more than anyone else in Antiquity, had a sense of the contagious nature of defilement, impurity that spreads like an oil-stain. Using psychological terminology, one might say that there is something obsessional about their perfectionism.

Now, I will say that if there is any obsession in Philo, it is one of exactly the opposite sort: an obsession not to be perfect, but to always have a most lucid awareness of human imperfection, and even of human nothingness (*oudeneia*), one of the central concepts in his thought. Music, however, is far from being a nihilistic tool for him. It is primarily an instrument by which the soul rises to the contemplation of the heavenly order. It is compared to gymnastics, which gives the body its strength, and is associated with grammar, mathematics, and philosophy.[45] The mind, which – as Philo is keen to specify – exists in a mortal body, is thus confronted with "creatures who enjoy happiness and bliss, arousing in it a passionate aspiration." Music cares, tutors, and repairs the soul, but it also teaches her the impassable limit that separates the created from the Creator. Israel sees God, because God has revealed Himself to Him.

> For he who claims to be in the second rank, he will see only the good of the second order, the sensible heaven, the harmonious order of his stars, and their dance which is really all Music. The race or kind that strives for second place sees the second best, that is the heaven of our senses, and therein the well-ordered host of the stars, the choir that moves to the fullest and truest music.[46]

To conclude, I will spend some words on the metamorphosis of the concept of harmony in the transition between the Stoics and Philo. In Stoicism, the concept of harmony plays a modest role, with the exception

[44] See Brunschwig 1994a, 90.

[45] *Spec.* 2.230: τὸ μὲν οὖν σῶμα διὰ τῆς γυμναστικῆς καὶ ἀλειπτικῆς ὠφέλησαν εἰς εὐτονίαν τε καὶ εὐεξίαν σχέσεις τε καὶ κινήσεις εὐμαρεῖς, οὐκ ἄνευ ῥυθμοῦ καὶ τοῦ πρέποντος, τὴν δὲ ψυχὴν διά τε γραμμάτων καὶ ἀριθμῶν γεωμετρίας τε καὶ μουσικῆς καὶ τῆς συμπάσης φιλοσοφίας . . .

[46] *Congr.* 51: τῷ μὲν οὖν ἀρίστῳ γένει τὸ ἄριστον ὁρᾶν, τὸ ὄντως ὄν, συμβέβηκεν – Ἰσραὴλ γὰρ ὁρῶν θεὸν ἑρμηνεύεται –, τῷ δὲ δευτερείων ἐφιεμένῳ τὸ δεύτερον, τὸν αἰσθητὸν οὐρανὸν καὶ τὴν ἐν αὐτῷ τῶν ἀστέρων ἐναρμόνιον τάξιν καὶ πάμμουσον ὡς ἀληθῶς χορείαν.

of Diogenes of Babylon, in whose thought harmony is certainly present, albeit essentially within an ethical context. We find very little in the first Stoics, not a single occurrence in Epictetus or Musonius Rufus, and two references in Marcus Aurelius, one of which is particularly interesting:[47] "In the end, there is a harmony and, like the world, this great body, is completed by all bodies, so fate, this great cause, is completed by all causes." The concept of harmony is thus framed within the Stoic perception of the world as a universal system of causes, outside which nothing can exist. Though the musical conjunctive model is at least implicitly present in the Stoic doctrine of the unity of the world, the Stoics seem to have avoided the term "harmony", perhaps because of its Platonic and Pythagorean echoes.[48] Philo, who is also deeply Platonic, uses the concept of harmony throughout his works. It is probably in *De fuga* that its function is most clearly described.[49] Harmony is the manifestation of the *logos desmos*, which represents the universal bond of the world and is thus found equally well in the balance of the four elements as in the human body and soul and at all levels of the universe. Insofar as it is the most immediate expression of this universal harmony, music allows the human being to have a precise idea of his abilities and of his finitude. All this is also expressed in a passage about the sacrifices of Abel and Cain:[50]

> Service pleasing to God and to virtue is like an intense and severe harmony, and in no soul is there an instrument capable of sustaining it, without such frequent relaxation and unstringing of the chords that it descends from the higher forms of art to the lower. Yet even these lower forms demand much toil.

The Stoic *scala naturae* was based on an understanding of the universe, from the lowest beings to the universal *logos*. The Philonian musical paradigm is much more flexible, as it integrates fallibility and regards both ascent and descent as being inherent to human nature.

47 Marcus Aurelius 5.8.
48 On the notion of harmony and the conjunctive model in Stoicism, see Long 1996, 202ff, Scade 2017.
49 *Fug.* 112. 50 *Sacr.* 37.

CHAPTER 2

Music and Plutarch's Platonic Cosmos

Bram Demulder

At a symposium in Chaeronea, Plutarch's home town, the guests once had a discussion about the appropriateness of 'things heard' (*akroamata*) at dinner. Or, at least, that is what Plutarch reports in *Quaestiones convivales* (7.8), the nine-book work devoted to sympotic questions in which he often stages himself as a character.[1] Near the end of this particular discussion, the character 'Plutarch' defends the presence of lyre and aulos at the banquet on the grounds of tradition: the lyre has been around since Homer and the *aulos* is part and parcel of traditional libations. There are, however, certain restrictions. The lyre should avoid dirges and laments and stick to soothing, innocuous songs (*euphēma*). Similarly, the *aulos* is welcome as long as it 'keeps due measure, and avoids emotional display, so as not to rouse into ecstasy (*parexistas*)' (713A).[2] Instead of instilling anything, *aulos* and lyre should be used to calm down the part of the soul which 'has no notion of reason and no response to it' (*axyneton logou kai anēkoon*: 713B).[3] This already fairly limited endorsement of music is restricted even further when 'Plutarch' comes to his second point. In a consciously controversial statement, he bans instrumental music from the dinner table:[4]

[1] Throughout this chapter, I will use 'Plutarch' to refer to the character as distinguished from the author. On several aspects of *Quaest. conv.*, including the tensions between history and fiction and between Plutarch (the author) and 'Plutarch' (the character), see Klotz and Oikonomopoulou 2011. On music and musical terminology in *Quaest. conv.*, see Smits 1970, 82–8, García López 1999 and 2002. On *Quaest. conv.* 7.8 and how it relates to contemporary culture, see Pernigotti 2009.

[2] Greek texts and translations for Plutarch's works are taken from the LCL editions. I have tacitly substituted '*aulos*' for 'flute'; other modifications are indicated.

[3] A similar calming effect of music is described in *De superstitione* 167B-C (with Van der Stockt 2009, 402–7); cf. also *De virtute morali* 441E on Pythagoras. In *Quaest. conv.* 7.5, on the other hand, a discussion about the dangers of arousing music ensues after an *aulos* performance has gotten out of hand; see Smits 1970, 54–7, Barker 2016 and 2018.

[4] With the untranslated particle (οὐ) μήν, with which this passage begins, 'the character-narrator anticipates (and contradicts) the possible conclusions that his addressee(s) may draw from the facts presented earlier' (Wakker 1997, 223; cf. Denniston 1954, 28–30). Aristotle, for one, seems to allow for purely instrumental music (*Pol.* 1339b20-21). Plato's stance is more complicated. In *Leg.* 669d-670a

> If I may express my own opinion, I should never commit a party to the music of *aulos* or lyre by itself without words to be sung (χωρὶς λόγου καὶ ᾠδῆς), as if it were committed to the whim of a stream on which it floats. We must form the habit, whether working or playing, of enjoying the words (*logou*) and including words (*logōi*) in our pastimes. We should regard melody and rhythm as a sauce so to speak, added to the words (*tōi logōi*), rather than use or prize them for their own sake. (713B-C; transl. modified)

A moment ago, 'Plutarch' was still recommending music for its effect on the non-rational part of the soul. Now, all of a sudden, *logos* is all he can talk about and music is radically subordinated to it. In the end, it does not even seem to matter very much whether or not words are sung: in whatever form, they should be omnipresent in our lives. These words, not the music itself, appeal to 'our rational part' (*ton en hēmin logon*: 713C). Music receives another blow in the final part of the speech. If a symposium is already entertaining through the presence of philosophical discourse – as it should be[5] – it would be plain wrong to introduce musical entertainment.[6] The right time for music is when the party runs the risk of being disrupted by quarrels. Overall, 'Plutarch's' philosophical appreciation of music might be rather disconcerting to the reader looking for a vigorous defence of music. There is no doubt that music is playing second fiddle: talking about music is preferable to listening to it.[7]

the Athenian warns against instrumental music not because it lacks the potential of beneficial expression, but because this kind of expression is much harder to understand for humans; see Pelosi 2010, 59–62 and 197. 'Plutarch' seems to have slightly different reasons: he treats instrumental music not as something which is (too) hard to understand, but as something which cannot be an object of understanding.

5 See esp. *Quaest. conv.* 1.1 on 'Whether philosophy is a fitting topic for conversation at a drinking-party'. Cf. Kechagia 2011.

6 Cf. *Coniugalia praecepta* 143D, as well as the previous question of *Quaest. conv.* (7.7), where the issue of the *aulos* player, sent away in Plato's *Symposium* (176e) and belittled in *Protagoras* (347c-e), is brought up. The character 'Plutarch' does not take part in this question, which is a discussion between two Stoics.

7 Cf. *De tuenda sanitate praecepta* 133F: '[I]t is less onerous to exchange opinions about an *aulos* and a lyre than to listen to the sound of the *aulos* and the *aulos* itself.' In the anti-Epicurean dialogue *Non posse suaviter vivi secundum Epicurum* 1095C-1096C, the character Theon, an intellectual ally of Plutarch, criticises Epicurus for banning music from the symposium. On closer inspection, however, what Theon recommends are *discussions* about music instead of music itself (1095C: *προβλήμασι* [. . .] μυσικοῖς; *ibid.*: μουσικῶν καὶ ποιητικῶν *προβλημάτων*; 1095E: περὶ συμφωνιῶν *διαλεγομένου*; 1096A: κριτικῶν καὶ μουσικῶν *λαλιάν*; 1095A: οἱ περὶ χορῶν *λόγοι* καὶ διδασκαλιῶν καὶ τὰ διαύλων *προβλήματα* καὶ ῥυθμῶν καὶ ἁρμονιῶν; 1095A-C: several examples of such musical topics for discussion); cf. Van der Stockt 2009: 410–13. (On Plutarch's criticism of the Epicurean disdain for matters of music, see also *Non posse* 1094F-1095A with Jufresa 2001.) Similarly, in *Quaest. conv.* 9.15 (on the elements of dance), Plutarch prefers a speech about dancing to a dance performance, as Schlapbach 2011 (see now also Schlapbach 2018, 25–74) points out. On dance in *Quaest. conv.*, see also Martins de Jésus 2009.

In what follows, I want to show that, indeed, an unconditional defence of music cannot be found in Plutarch. This is largely the result of his reading of Plato's *Timaeus*, the text at the very heart of his philosophy.[8] This claim may sound surprising, given the ethical and even cosmological value Plato attaches to music in this dialogue.[9] For instance, Timaeus mentions that music has a beneficial effect on the wise, since its sounds are an 'expression (*mimēsin*) of divine harmony in mortal movement' (*Ti.* 80b). Plutarch, to be sure, acknowledges the potential implied by this statement: music can reflect divine harmony. As we will see, however, he also acknowledges its limitedness: we should keep in mind that music is only a (necessarily imperfect) *mimēsis* of divine harmony. Putting the two on a par would be as foolish as confusing a sensible object with an intelligible form.[10]

The sympotic discussion on *akroamata* shows us a fairly non-technical expression of this general view: 'Plutarch' subsequently rejects the ecstatic force of music, postulates the pre-eminence of *logos* over music itself, and emphasises the strictly remedial role of music. This may read like a slightly more pessimistic version of *Timaeus* 47c-d, where Timaeus complains that nowadays most people use music for 'irrational pleasure' (*eph' hēdonēn alogon*), points out that as regards the benefits of sounds *logos* plays a bigger part than music itself (*logos* contributes 'the greatest part', τὴν μεγίστην μοῖραν), and describes the harmony expressed by music as 'an ally in the fight to bring order to any orbit in our souls that has become unharmonized'.[11] However, some peculiar aspects of Plutarch's take on the view expressed in *Timaeus* will emerge in due course.

In order to outline the role of music in Plutarch's philosophy, and particularly in his Platonic cosmology, I will take up these three themes, albeit in a different order. First I will look at how Plutarch, interpreting Plato's *Timaeus*, combines the subordinate status of music to *logos* with its cosmic importance. For this purpose, I will continue along the lines of Federico Petrucci's chapter in this volume and show in what sense the demiurge is compared to a musician in Plutarch's *De animae procreatione*

[8] On the paramount importance of *Timaeus* for Plutarch's Platonism, see Hershbell 1987, 235 (with further references in n. 3); Ferrari 2004. For an introduction to Plutarch's Platonic philosophy, see Froidefond 1987, Dillon 1996, 184–230, Ferrari 2000, and Opsomer 2005a.

[9] See Barker 2000b, Pelosi 2010, and Lyon 2016.

[10] On this combination of potential and limitedness see Hirsch-Luipold 2002, esp. 159–62.

[11] Translations of Plato are from Cooper 1997; for the Greek, the Oxford Classical Texts edition is used. Plutarch paraphrases part of this passage from *Timaeus* in *De superstitione* 167B. The interpretation of *Ti.* 47c-e is, of course, much more complex than I make it seem here; see esp. Pelosi 2010, 68–113.

in Timaeo.[12] This will lead, in the second section, to the theme of music as a remedy, which I will approach through Plutarch's interpretation of the music of the spheres. As we will see, the idea that music is first and foremost a remedy will prompt Plutarch to question the notion of heavenly music and to confine music to the earthly realm. In the third section, I will dwell briefly on the connection between ecstasy and music in order to show that Plutarch, once again cautious about giving music too elevated a status, tries to distance music from the notion of divine inspiration or enthusiasm (*enthousiasmos*). As this line of argument will reveal, music plays an important yet strictly limited role in Plutarch's philosophy: music is a road to divine harmony, but due to its sensible character it can only ever be an indirect road.[13]

2.1 The Demiurge and the Musician

While the first part of *De animae procreatione* discusses how the demiurge created the mixture of the cosmic soul by blending together intermediate being, sameness, and difference (*Ti.* 35a-b), the second part turns to the *divisio animae*, the final composition of the cosmic soul through the mathematical distribution of that mixture (*Ti.* 35b-36b).[14] After having discussed the numbers used by the demiurge to distribute the mixture, as well as the way in which these numbers should be arranged, Plutarch turns to the question of the function (*dynamis*) of these numbers. Let us jump right to the very last sentence of the treatise:

> Just as one is ridiculous, then, who looks for the ratios (*logous*) of 4:3, 3:2, and 2:1 in the yoke and the shell and the pegs of the lyre (for, while of course these too must have been made proportionate to one another in length and thickness, yet it is in the sounds [*phthoggōn*] that that concord [*harmonian*]

[12] On this work, see Cherniss 1976, 133–57, Hershbell 1987, Ferrari and Baldi 2002, 7–91, and Opsomer 2004.

[13] Smits 1970, written in Dutch, is the only monograph about music in Plutarch. It provides an admirably extensive overview of musical theory and practice in Plutarch's works. Written as a study in the history of musicology, however, it does not engage thoroughly with the philosophical issues I am tackling here. Other, more limited overviews of the subject are García López 2000, Durán Mañas 2005, Araújo da Rocha Júnior 2008, and Görgemanns and Hirsch-Luipold 2010. As a collection of Plutarchan passages on music, Weil and Reinach 1900, liii–lxix, is still valuable. It should be noted that Weil and Reinach firmly believed that the treatise *De musica* was written by Plutarch, whereas today most scholars consider it to be spurious; see Fera 2011, although D'Ippolito 2011 holds a different view. Cf. also Tassi 2009, an index of Plutarchan passages involving sound.

[14] See Moutsopoulos 1959, 352–75, Lippman 1964, 20–9, Barker 1989, 58–61, and Pelosi 2010, 189–95 on how this passage from *Timaeus* relates to Plato's views on music. On its connection with Plutarch's views on musical theory, see Smits 1970, 10–25.

> is to be observed), so is it reasonable (*eikos*) to believe that, while the bodies of the stars and the intervals of the circles and the velocities of the revolutions are like instruments commensurate in fixed <ratios> with one another and with the whole though the quantity of the measurement has eluded us, nevertheless the product of those ratios and numbers used by the artificer is the soul's own harmony and concord (*emmeleian kai harmonian*) with herself, whereby she has filled the heaven, into which she has come, with countless goods and has arrayed the terrestrial regions with seasons and measured changes in the best and fairest way for the generation and preservation of things that come to be. (*De an. procr.* 1030B-C; transl. modified)

Most of the section on the *dynamis* of the numbers used by the demiurge is devoted to interpretations of the *divisio animae* which are centred on astronomical observations (1028A-1029D). As it appears from the comparison just quoted, Plutarch's criticism of these interpretations is nuanced. On the one hand, they are not completely wrong: the heavenly bodies are harmonious in the same way as well-tuned musical instruments are. On the other hand, it would be misguided to assume that the heavenly bodies are the reason for which (cf. 1028B: *heneka toutōn*) the demiurge forged the cosmic soul. That would be like saying that music exists for the sake of musical instruments.[15]

The comparison of divine *harmonia* and musical *harmonia* (I will call this 'comparison 0') comprises three aspects: (1) the heavenly bodies are compared to the musical instrument, (2) the cosmic soul is compared to music (*phthoggoi*), (3) the demiurge is (implicitly but unmistakably) compared to the musician. In the course of *De animae procreatione*, Plutarch makes three further comparisons which can be paired with the three aspects which I have just enumerated. These further comparisons can help clarify what Plutarch is doing here.

(1) The heavenly bodies can be compared to a musical instrument. The idea that the harmonious cosmic soul is prior to the heavenly bodies and is the cause of the goods present in them and the harmony exhibited by them is

[15] The point that it is ridiculous (γελοῖος) to look for the essence of music in the instruments can be compared to the position which Plutarch defends in *Quaestiones Platonicae* 9 (on which see Opsomer 2012, 328–30). There, he interprets a passage in *Republic* (443d), 'where Plato likened excellently well the consonance of the rational and mettlesome and appetitive to a concord of intermediate and topmost and nethermost strings (ἁρμονίᾳ μέσης καὶ ὑπάτης καὶ νήτης)' (1007E). In the course of his interpretation, Plutarch suggests that it is 'ridiculous (γελοῖον) to allot to local positions the status of first and intermediate and last, seeing that the topmost itself, while on the lyre it occupies the position further above and first, on the pipes occupies the one underneath and last and that intermediate, moreover, wherever it is located on the lyre, if tuned in the same way, sounds higher than the topmost string and lower than the nethermost'. For the strings of a lyre used in a moral context see also *De virtute morali* 444E-F, *De genio Socratis* 589D-E.

fully in line with Plato's *Timaeus* (34b-c). It should be noted, however, that Plutarch understands this priority of the cosmic soul over the cosmic body as a chronological and not merely ontological priority: the demiurge forged the soul before he started working on the cosmic body (*De an. procr.* 1013D-F).[16] If we follow the logic of the comparison, then, the harmony which can be found in sounds (*phthoggoi*) precedes and causes – odd as it may seem – the musical instrument which plays these sounds (*phthoggoi*).[17]

Earlier in *De animae procreatione*, Plutarch tells an anecdote about Zeno of Citium which is interesting in this regard. Zeno made his pupils attend a performance by *aulos* players 'to observe what a sound is produced (*phōnēn aphiēsi*) by bits of horn and wood and reed and bone when they partake of ratio and consonance (*logou metechonta kai symphōnias*)' (*De an. procr.* 1029F). This is brought up as a comparison for the demiurge's work on the pre-cosmic soul (the irrational soul-stuff which the demiurge used to forge the cosmic soul) and, through this, on soulless matter. The suggestion is that a musical instrument, in a way, only comes into being when a skilled musician starts playing it. It is the musician who applies the *logoi* of which his tool partakes and by which the *phōnē* is caused. All the instrument really does is *apheinai* ('produce', or more literally 'put forth').

Plutarch dishes up the same story in *De virtute morali* (443A), only now Zeno is sending his pupils to a performance by a *kithara* singer (*kitharōidos*) instead of an *aulos* concert. In that treatise, which shows interesting parallels with *De animae procreatione*, Zeno's field trip is not brought up in the context of the demiurge's work on the pre-cosmic soul, but as an illustration of how the body and the irrational parts of the soul can be made to work together with reason.[18] In this version of the story, it becomes clear

16 Cf. *Quaest. Plat.* 4.1002E-1003B, *De an. procr.* 1016A and D, 1023A-C.

17 Plutarch, then, would seem to disagree with Simmias in Plato's *Phaedo* (85e-86d), who states that the harmony is obviously destroyed along with the musical instrument and infers from this that the soul, which he thinks is a kind of harmony, dies with the body. Although, as Plutarch knows well (see n. 49 below), the thesis that the soul is a harmony is eventually rejected, this does not explain why Simmias and Plutarch would have a different take on how harmony relates to the instrument. Rather, they are thinking of different kinds of harmony. While Simmias means the attunement of the material instrument, Plutarch is referring to music in a more abstract sense (i.e. not tied to a particular instrument). See Rowe 1993, 203 for these two meanings of harmony; cf. also Gottschalk 1971. On the different ways in which Plutarch uses the word *harmonia*, see Smits 1970, 34–41.

18 On the connections between *De animae procreatione* and *De virtute morali* see Opsomer 1994 and 2012, 313–15. On how this anecdote about Zeno (= *SVF* 1.299) relates to Stoic views on music see Scade 2017, 200–1. However, one should be aware that, both in *De animae procreatione* and in *De virtute morali*, the anecdote is used in an anti-Stoic context in which Plutarch argues for the existence and importance of an irrational part of the (cosmic and human) soul. That being said, Plutarch is careful not to distort the anecdote by ascribing such a view to Zeno: in both works, he inserts the anecdote in such a way that it can be taken to pertain, strictly speaking, only to the non-rational and

how the source of harmony can be the musician rather than the instrument: musical instruments themselves are 'void of soul' (*apsycha*); what they actually do is 'reproduc[e] the judgements, the experiences, and the morals of those who use them (τὰς κρίσεις ἀναφέροντα καὶ τὰ πάθη καὶ τὰ ἤθη τῶν χρωμένων)'. Once again, it is the musician who by using *logoi* – and in this version of the story Plutarch hesitantly allows the non-rational parts of the soul to play a role as well – causes music to appear in soulless matter, thus turning that matter into a musical instrument.[19]

(2) Plutarch also offers a more complex version of the comparison between music and the cosmic soul:

> As some sound is not speech and not significant but speech is an utterance in sound that signifies thought, and as concord is what consists of tones and intervals and a tone is one and the same thing, an interval the diversity and difference of tones, and the mixture of these results in song and melody, so the affective part of the soul was indeterminate and unstable and then was bounded when there came to be limit and form in the divisible and omnifarious character of the motion.[20]

Here, the ingredients of the cosmic soul are linked to the elements constituting music. Interestingly, Plutarch insists on including the human voice as an essential constituent in the comparison. According to Plutarch's interpretation of *Timaeus* 35a-b, the demiurge created the cosmic soul in two steps. First, he blended divisible and indivisible being. Only after establishing this preliminary mixture as a basis was he able to add the two more extreme ingredients, sameness and difference. Plutarch compares the first phase of the soul's creation to the composition of the lyrics to the song. These lyrics (*logos*) are a combination of sound (*phōnē*) and thought (*dianoia*). The second phase is compared to setting the lyrics to music by applying tones (*phthoggoi*) and intervals (*diastēmata*).

soulless rather than irrational soul. It is the context added by Plutarch which makes it clear that the anecdote serves to illustrate the harmonising of the irrational soul.

19 On Plutarch's hesitance see Babut 1969, 145, who also points out that, in this passage, Plutarch is manifestly more tolerant than Plato in his selection of accepted instruments.

20 *De an. procr.* 1026A, transl. modified: ὡς δὲ φωνή τίς ἐστιν ἄλογος καὶ ἀσήμαντος λόγος δὲ λέξις ἐν φωνῇ σημαντικῇ διανοίας, ἁρμονία δὲ τὸ ἐκ φθόγγων καὶ διαστημάτων καὶ φθόγγος μὲν ἓν καὶ ταὐτὸν διάστημα δὲ φθόγγων ἑτερότης καὶ διαφορά, μιχθέντων δὲ τούτων ᾠδὴ γίγνεται καὶ μέλος· οὕτως τὸ παθητικὸν τῆς ψυχῆς ἀόριστον ἦν καὶ ἀστάθμητον, εἶθ' ὡρίσθη πέρατος ἐγγενομένου καὶ εἴδους τῷ μεριστῷ καὶ παντοδαπῷ τῆς κινήσεως. On this passage, see also Opsomer 1994, 40–1, Demulder 2017b, 206–9 (with a discussion of the parallel passage *De tranquillitate animi* 473F-474B).

(3) For the comparison of the musician and the demiurge as well we can turn to a passage earlier in the treatise. As has been noted, Plutarch's interpretation of *Timaeus* is temporal. According to his reading of Plato's dialogue, which is opposed to that of most ancient Platonists, there really must have been a beginning of the cosmos.[21] The demiurge did not, however, create the cosmic soul and the cosmic body *ex nihilo*. Rather, he took over and ordered both the pre-cosmic soul and the pre-cosmic body. In this respect, Plutarch points out, he acted like a musician, who 'is expected not to create sound or movement either but to make sound tuneful and movement rhythmical' (*De an. procr.* 1014C).[22]

By now, two things will have become clear which seem to contradict each other. On the one hand, the comparison between music and the cosmos is not made casually: it occurs several times throughout the treatise and, as such, it seems to be important for Plutarch's understanding of Platonic cosmology. On the other hand, the picture which appears when we piece the several iterations of the comparison together is rather blurry. Several inconsistencies regarding the most crucial aspects of the exegesis of *Timaeus* can be pointed out. In the comparison with which we started the discussion (comparison 0), the ontological and temporal priority of soul over body (and that of music over the musical instrument) was the whole point. This is hard to square with comparison 3: there, the generation of the cosmic soul and the cosmic body is compared to the generation of tuneful sound and rhythmical movement (Plutarch does not spell out which corresponds to which). It would be hard to conceive of either rhythm or sound as coming first in a musical performance. Moreover, the same comparison insists on including both body and soul in the analogy, whereas comparison 2 compares only the soul to music, and the original comparison even distances the body from soul / music by comparing the former to the instrument. This comparison of the body to the instrument, in turn, does not quite fit with comparison 1, where the instrument is compared to the pre-cosmic soul, which is harmonised by the demiurge. However, the anecdote about Zeno itself (in comparison 1), if detached from the context, could again suggest that the instrument is soulless. To make matters worse, the instrument from comparison 1 is the *aulos* in a performance of *aulētai* (*De an. procr.* 1029F): the human voice does not play a role here, nor does it really in comparisons 0 and 3, while it is essential to comparison 2.

[21] On the two main strands of interpretation of Timaean cosmology see esp. Baltes 1976. Cf. also Boys-Stones 2018, 184–211.

[22] Cf. *De Iside et Osiride* 373C-D, where Osiris plays the role of the demiurge. See Petrucci's chapter in this volume.

Where does this leave us? Is Plutarch being sloppy and inconsistent?[23] I would rather suggest that the blurry picture is an indication that, while music and the cosmic soul can be compared, their different ontological statuses severely limit the comparison. Plutarch is very much aware that the demiurge *is not* a musician. This is why, after reporting the ancient practice of 'put[ting] musical instruments into the hands of the statues of the gods', he adds that this does not mean that the gods play 'the lyre and the *aulos* but that no work is so like that of gods as concord and consonance' (*De an. procr.* 1030B; transl. modified). Similarly, in *De primo frigido*, he wishes to avoid confusion after reporting that some call the demiurge 'harmonizer and musician':

> He does not receive these names for bringing sounds of high and low pitch, or black and white colours, into harmonious fellowship, but because he has authority over the association and disunion of heat and cold in the universe [. . .]. (946F; transl. modified)[24]

By creating harmony on a human level, the musician is certainly doing a good job, which can to some extent be compared to the demiurge's creation of harmony on a divine level. This does not mean, however, that the musician's job is even close to being on the same level as that of the demiurge. This sounds fairly obvious, but a perfect comparison between the musician and the demiurge could easily obscure this. Rather, the apparent inconsistencies point to different aspects of the general, necessarily imperfect comparison. In Plutarch's philosophy, for instance, it makes perfect sense to compare the musical instrument both to the heavenly bodies (comparison 0) and to the pre-cosmic soul (comparison 1): the demiurge makes both partake in harmony (cf. *De an. procr.* 1014C), which is the point of comparison 3, where, however, the reference to an instrument is omitted.

The fact that Plutarch chose to couch his reflections on music in comparisons is significant in itself. As Rainer Hirsch-Luipold has shown, Plutarch's use of imagery is closely connected with the notion taken from Plato's *Timaeus* that the sensible cosmos is a likeness (*eikōn*) of an intelligible model (*Ti.* 29b).[25] If this is taken into account, the original

[23] On contradiction and consistency in Plutarch see Nikolaidis 1991 and the contributions in Opsomer, Roskam, and Titchener 2016.

[24] The Loeb translator ironically adds to the confusion by translating 'he does not receive these names *merely* for bringing [. . .]' (my emphasis), which is not warranted by the Greek.

[25] Hirsch-Luipold 2002, 159–224. Cf. esp. Plutarch, *Adversus Colotem* 1115B-1116B, *De Iside et Osiride* 372F.

comparison reveals two *eikōn* relations. The first is expressed through the content of the comparison: as Plutarch explicitly states earlier, the ratios which we can observe in the visible parts of the cosmos are likenesses (*eikones*) of the *logoi* of the cosmic soul (*De an. procr.* 1029D-E). The second is suggested by the form of the comparison: music is an image of the cosmic soul.

These two parallel *eikones* – the sensible cosmos and music – can be taken to mirror the parallel treatment of sight and hearing as ways of using the sensible realm to learn about the cosmic soul in *Timaeus* 47a-e. A good discourse involving an *eikōn* – an *eikōs logos*, as Timaeus would describe it – is indeed valuable as a hermeneutical effort, since it allows us to explore things in our investigation which we could not otherwise explore. At the same time, however, such a discourse is also limited: at best it can aspire to be likely.[26] Plutarch, therefore, makes sure to introduce his statement about the harmony of the heavenly bodies with the words 'it is likely' (*eikos esti*) and adds that 'the quantity of the measurement has eluded us'. The same limitations apply when music is considered as an *eikōn* of the cosmic soul. We cannot possibly expect the results to be perfect or even fully consistent.[27]

Plutarch's position on the cosmic significance of music is subtle. There is, to be sure, a connection between the harmony of the cosmos and the harmony expressed by music, but this should not lead us to confuse the work of the demiurge and the work of a musician (i.e. someone concerned with music, a sensible phenomenon).[28] The relation between the two is one between paradigm and image. Insight into the nature of this relation is of paramount importance and cannot be furnished by music itself. This might explain, then, why a *logos* about music is more important than music itself.

[26] On this much-discussed issue, Burnyeat 2005 is a seminal paper which has evoked many responses such as Betegh 2010, which has the particular merit of showing how εἰκώς is at the same time a positive standard and a limitation.

[27] Cf. *Ti.* 29c: 'Don't be surprised then, Socrates, if it turns out repeatedly that we won't be able to produce accounts on a great many subjects – on gods or the coming to be of the universe – that are completely and perfectly consistent and accurate.'

[28] One could turn this around and argue that the demiurge is the only true musician, in the same fashion as Socrates is Athens' only true politician by abstaining from politics (*Gorgias* 521d). This is not, I think, what Plutarch is suggesting. As we have seen, in the only two passages where the demiurge is presented as a musician (*De prim. frig.* 946F and *De an. procr.* 1030A-B), this is a characterisation which Plutarch does not make in his own name but which he ascribes to tradition. Moreover, both times he feels the need to nuance this traditional characterisation by going on to distance the god from music as he understands it (i.e. as a sensible phenomenon).

2.2 The Song of the Muses

The same subtle position feeds into Plutarch's reception of a notion which establishes a very strong link between music and cosmology and which, as we shall see, also plays a role in *De animae procreatione*: the so-called music of the spheres.[29] This Pythagorean notion could not be ignored by a Platonist like Plutarch, given its importance for Plato's myth of Er (*Republic* 614b-621b). From Plato we learn about Sirens standing on the rims of the eight whorls which are parts of the spindle of the universe. Each Siren emits a single tone and the eight tones together form a harmony, which serves as the background to the song of the Fates, who sing about the past, the present, and the future (617b-c).

In his own eschatological myths, Plutarch enjoys playing with this motif. The myth which concludes *De sera numinis vindicta* tells a *post mortem* story very similar to Plato's myth of Er. In Plutarch's myth, the character who is guided through the cosmos suddenly hears a woman's voice. It turns out to be the Sibyl, who is singing (*aidein*) about the future while being stationed on the moon (566D-E). Similarly, in *De genio Socratis*, a myth is told about a certain Timarchus, who descended into a cave and experienced something which he could only describe as the temporary release of his soul. During this release, the heavenly bodies appeared to him like islands

> [. . .] and he fancied that their circular movement made a musical whirring in the aether, for the gentleness of the sound resulting from the harmony of all the separate sounds corresponded to the evenness of their motion. (590C)

Again, in the myth at the end of *De facie in orbe lunae*, we learn that during a lunar eclipse the moon accelerates because the good souls inhabiting the moon at that time complain that they cannot hear the 'harmony of the heaven' (*hē peri ton ouranon harmonia*) as the moon is traversing the earth's shadow (944A).

The consistent presence of the music of the spheres in Plutarch's three great myths suggests that it has a certain place in his thought.[30] However, this should also give us pause: a Platonist indulging in myths should never be taken at face value. Indeed, all three myths are preceded by a disclaimer distinguishing them from *logos* (*De sera* 561B; *De gen.* 589F; *De fac.* 940F).

The music of the spheres from Plato's myth of Er receives a seemingly less veiled treatment at one of the symposia evoked by Plutarch. The ninth

[29] For a recent introduction to this notion see Viltanioti 2015, 1–10 and Pelosi 2018.
[30] Cf. Vernière 1977, 175–6.

book of *Quaestiones convivales* is aptly dedicated to the nine Muses. In this last book of sympotic questions we find ourselves in the company of a young 'Plutarch'. The host of the symposium which takes up the entire book is Plutarch's teacher Ammonius. We learn that the symposium was held during some festival of the Muses and the subjects are appropriately 'musical' in the broad sense of the word, including poetry, language, cosmology, and music proper. Unfortunately, three of the talks about music are lost. Only titles remain for the discussions about the division of melodies into diatonic, chromatic, and enharmonic (9.7), about the difference between 'consonant intervals' (*emmelē diastēmata*) and 'melodic intervals' (*symphōna diastēmata*) (9.8), and about the causes of 'consonance' (*symphōnēsis*), including the question why the melody, as the Greeks perceived it, goes with the lowest pitch when two notes sound together (9.9). The last question of *Quaestiones convivales*, a light-hearted finale, offers a discussion on dance (9.15).[31] When the music of the spheres is mentioned, however, it is in a discussion about music *sensu lato* rather than *sensu stricto*.

After singing Hesiod's verses about the birth of the Muses, Ammonius and his guests begin to ponder how many Muses there actually are (9.14).[32] In the course of this long discussion, the connection between music and cosmology (specifically the cosmology of the myth of Er) comes up repeatedly and in various forms.[33] It is worthwhile to follow the course of the three speeches which touch upon this.

(1) In his first contribution to the discussion, 'Plutarch' starts from the ancient belief that there were three Muses instead of the conventional nine. This is an element he takes over from what his brother Lamprias said earlier (744C-F).[34] Lamprias, moreover, criticised traditional accounts which associated the Muses exclusively with music, thus incorrectly limiting their domain of influence. For this mistaken view, he cited some people (*enioi*) who believe that the reason for the number of Muses lies in the three types of melody (diatonic, chromatic, and enharmonic). The Delphians,

[31] Cf. n. 7 above.

[32] As Teodorsson 1996, 345 points out, this unusually long *quaestio* is the culmination point of the whole work. On *Quaest. conv.* 9.14 see also Smits 1970, 78–9, Van der Stockt 2009, 407–10, Klotz 2011, 171–7, and Dillon 2014a.

[33] Earlier in book nine (9.5), we find Ammonius and his guests discussing another aspect of the myth of Er: the fate of the soul of Ajax (*Resp.* 620b).

[34] There are, indeed, several attestations of three Muses instead of nine. However, Hesiod, who sparked this sympotic discussion, already mentions nine Muses (*Theog.* 75–79). See Teodorsson 1996, 353 for further references.

moreover, went wrong in a similar way by naming the Muses after the notes which limit the main intervals of a scale (*nētē*, *mesē*, and *hypatē*).

'Plutarch' does not approve of his brother's attack on Delphic religion. Although Lamprias was right in pointing out that the Delphians call the Muses *Nētē* (or *Neatē*), *Mesē*, and *Hypatē*, he mistakenly concluded that this entails an exclusive association with the science of music. Rather, the Muses *Neatē*, *Mesē*, and *Hypatē* are named in accordance with the region of the cosmos over which they preside: the fixed stars, the planets, and the sublunary region respectively.[35] Although these three regions are 'all knit and ordered together in harmonious formulae' (745B), the Muses are not the cause of the music of the spheres. This much 'Plutarch' makes clear by referring to the myth of Er:

> Plato, too, put this in a disguised form, calling them [i.e. the Muses] by the names of the Fates, Atropos, Clotho, and Lachesis; observe that it was Sirens, not Muses, that he set to preside over the revolutions of the eight spheres, one for each. (745B-C)

(2) Ammonius does not fully agree with his pupil's interpretation of the myth of Er. According to his own interpretation of the myth and contrary to that of the young 'Plutarch', Plato did intend to identify the eight Sirens with the Muses, adding one additional Muse assigned to the earth.[36] After connecting the Sirens as they appear in Homer with the fate of souls in the afterlife, Ammonius describes their influence on our earthly life:[37]

> Here on earth a kind of faint echo of that music reaches us, and appealing to our souls through the medium of words (*dia logōn*), reminds them of what they experienced in an earlier existence. The ears of most souls, however, are plastered over and blocked up, not with wax, but with carnal obstructions and affections. But any soul that through innate gifts is aware (*aisthanetai*) of this echo, and remembers that other world, suffers what falls in no way

[35] There seems to be a subtle yet significant difference between the two brothers' takes on the process of name-giving. According to Lamprias' account (744C; cf. 745A-B, where 'Plutarch' reiterates it), the Muses were named *after* the notes, which could suggest that sensible music precedes its divine overseer and that the latter is an imitation of the former instead of the other way around. In his own interpretation, 'Plutarch' seems to be careful to avoid the suggestion that the Muses were named *after* the cosmic regions (745B).

[36] In *Vita Pythagorae* 31, Porphyry too places the Muses in charge of the cosmic spheres when describing Pythagoras' experience of cosmic music. His distribution of the Muses is, however, understandably more Pythagorean. Ammonius appears to count – with *Timaeus* 36d-38e in mind – the fixed stars and the seven wanderers (Saturn, Jupiter, Mars, Venus, Mercury, sun, moon), adding a ninth Muse for the earth. Porphyry, on the other hand, reports that Pythagoras assigned the ninth Muse to the counter-earth. See Boyancé 1946 for the occurrence of this theme in other sources.

[37] Cf. Viltanioti 2015, 64–6.

> short of the very maddest passions of love (*tōn emmanestatōn erōtōn*), longing and yearning to break the tie with the body, but unable to do so. (745E-F)[38]

Here, the music of the spheres is couched in the language of Plato's *Phaedrus*.[39] In *Phaedrus* (249d-252b), Plato describes how a small minority – the philosophers – succeed in using earthly beauty as a reminder of true beauty. Whereas Plato emphasises the vision of beauty, Plutarch's Ammonius transmits the experience to the hearing of music by postulating an earthly echo of the Muses' heavenly music. The paradoxical consequence of this adaptation is that the human reception of the Muses' heavenly music does not happen under the aegis of the Muses, who instil their own kind of madness in humans if we follow *Phaedrus* (245a; 265b). Rather, the receiver of the song of the Muses experiences the madness called love, which in *Phaedrus* is reserved for the philosopher. Accordingly, the echo is transmitted to us not as music but 'through the medium of words' (*dia logōn*). Ammonius does not elaborate on this. Does he mean words as part of music or even words about music? Or should we maybe even understand *logoi* in the sense of (mathematical) ratios?

In any case, it is clear that Ammonius is not thinking about the music of the spheres as a superior kind of sensible music caused by the mechanics of the heavenly bodies. Unlike others, he does not ask why we do not hear the sounds of the heavenly music.[40] That very question would be hard to reconcile with his conception of transmission *dia logōn*: there is no sign that there is anything to be heard. By the time he describes the reception of heavenly harmony with the word *aisthanetai*, the reader is already aware that this verb should be understood metaphorically, since the reception is done by the 'ears of the soul'.[41] The apparent departure from Plato's take on kinds of madness, then, turns out to be an endorsement of Plato's true

[38] Right after this, Ammonius remarks that he does not agree with all these statements (οὐ μὴν ἔγωγε παντάπασι συμφέρομαι τούτοις, 745F). This should not be taken to refer to the part just quoted, but rather to the statements presented by the young 'Plutarch': Ammonius' distancing remark marks the transition from his defence of 'Plutarch's' interpretation (the Sirens are not inhumane, contrary to what one of the interlocutors objected in 745C-D) to the points where he disagrees (the Sirens are the Muses).

[39] Teodorsson 1996, 364.

[40] Porphyry (*VPyth.* 30) gives human inferiority as an explanation, adding that Pythagoras himself could hear the music; cf. also Maximus of Tyre, *Or.* 37.5; Aristides Quintilianus, *De musica* 3.20. Aristotle, who himself does not believe in the music of the spheres, reports the explanation that we are not aware of the music due to our life-long familiarity with it (*de Caelo* 2.9.290b); cf. also Cicero, *De re publica* 6.23 Powell.

[41] This seems to be inspired by Plato's notion of an 'eye of the soul' (*Resp.* 533d), which is better than ten thousand regular eyes (527e). Cf. Van der Stockt 2009.

intention: claiming the Muses for philosophy and establishing philosophy as the only true 'music'.[42]

(3) Ammonius ends his contribution by emphasising its tentative character and invites the others to respond. This sparks the young 'Plutarch's' second speech (746B-747A), in which he comes up with a third way of locating the Muses in the cosmos. After having expressed his own first impression that the Muses are the three Fates from Plato's myth and having learnt Ammonius' view that they are the Sirens from the same myth, 'Plutarch' now concludes that the majority of the Muses should be assigned to earth, since the earthly realm is most in need of guidance. Therefore, only one Muse, Urania, is placed in the heavens. The eight others are given functions on earth. As in 'Plutarch's' first speech, the work of the Muses is musical in a broad sense: this time, he points out that they correct the earthly mistakes and disharmony (*plēmmeleia* and *anarmostia*). Music in the strict sense is the domain of only one Muse, Melpomene.[43] Conversely, while only Urania is occupied with the cosmos in the strict sense, the others are described as bringing 'cosmos' in a more abstract sense: they 'bring order' (*kosmousin*) to human activities on earth. Melpomene, for instance, takes over the 'pleasure' (*hēdonē*) of the ears and turns it into 'enjoyment' (*euphrosynē*). Thus, the discussion closes with a wink to Plato's *Timaeus* (80b), where music is said to bring mere pleasure to fools and enjoyment to the wise.

The sympotic discussion has followed a remarkable trajectory. In all three answers, the connection between music and the cosmos is confirmed, albeit only to a certain extent. What the answers have in common is that they all warn against excessive appreciation of music (a sensible phenomenon). In his first speech, the character 'Plutarch' introduces cosmology to drive a wedge between music and the divine: the names of the Muses do not refer to notes but to regions of the cosmos. Although the young Platonist faithfully invokes the myth of Er, he omits any reference to the tones emitted by the Sirens or the song sung by the Fates. Ammonius, then, comes close to embracing the music of the spheres, but he insists that the transference from heavenly harmony to earth does not happen by way of earthly music, but *dia logōn*. His engagement with Plato's *Phaedrus*

[42] Cf. Plato, *Phaedo* 60d-61a with Murray 2002.

[43] This may seem an odd choice, since Melpomene became known primarily as the Muse of tragedy, but 'Plutarch' is probably thinking about the connection between Melpomene and the verb μέλπω ('to sing'). Cf. Cornutus, *Theol. Graec.* 16.6–7: Μελπομένη δὲ ἀπὸ τῆς μολπῆς γλυκείας τινὸς φωνῆς μετὰ μέλους οὔσης.

suggests that this process points to the practice of philosophy and not to the practice of music. In his second speech, finally, 'Plutarch', as if pointing out the ultimate consequences of his teacher's view, locates music firmly in the earthly realm.

The reader of Plutarch's sympotic questions – and the same goes for his other writings involving *quaestiones* – understandably feels inclined to pick one of the answers. This, however, is not how these zetetic writings work. Although, usually, the last answer seems to carry the most weight, all answers contribute something valuable to the discussion.[44] In this case, the choice of the young 'Plutarch' as a character makes it particularly difficult to gauge the speeches. *De E apud Delphos* is another work where the young 'Plutarch' and his teacher express different opinions.[45] In that case, the writer Plutarch appears to side with the teacher rather than with his younger self. The sympotic discussion could be a similar case. On the other hand, the young 'Plutarch' does get the last word in the debate about the Muses, whereas in *De E* the teacher explicitly corrects him. Moreover, in the last book of *Quaestiones convivales*, Plutarch makes every effort to present his younger self as a star pupil.[46] In this regard, we cannot simply subordinate the pupil's answer to the teacher's, all the more since the teacher explicitly asked for his contribution to be challenged.

A comparison with *De animae procreatione* (1029C-D) can shed some light on this issue.[47] There, Plutarch gives an interpretation of the Sirens from Plato's *Republic* which is akin to Ammonius' take on the matter: both accounts connect Plato's eight Sirens with the nine Muses, assigning one Muse to earth. Before deciding that this is Plutarch's preferred interpretation, we should take the context into account. One of the astronomical interpretations of the *divisio animae* assigns 'to earth the position of the *proslambanomenos*' (1028F), one tone below the *hypatē*, which corresponds to the moon. Plutarch dismisses this interpretation by pointing out that the *proslambanomenos* as an addition to the scale below the *hypatē* is a modern invention. The ancients, including Plato, added the *proslambanomenos* to

44 See Opsomer 1996 for a discussion of Plutarch's zetetic method applied to *Quaestiones Platonicae*. The pervasiveness of the zetetic approach in Plutarch's work can be gleaned from Opsomer 2010, Roskam 2011, 2013, 2014, 2017, Petrucci 2016a, and Meeusen 2016, 84–92.

45 Jones 1967, 206 estimates the dramatic date of *Quaest. conv.* 9 to be near to that of *De E*.

46 König 2007, 52. Klotz 2011, 171–7 offers a discussion of *Quaest. conv.* 9.14 which focuses on his self-presentation as a model student, at the same time respectfully building upon and correcting his teacher's answer. König 2011 discusses self-presentation as a tension between self-promotion and self-effacement in *Quaestiones convivales*.

47 This is a work of a completely different nature: in the introduction, Plutarch indicates that it should be read as his definitive statement on the subject at hand (*De an. procr.* 1012B).

the higher end of the scale. As Plutarch sees it, the story of the Sirens proves this.

The reason is that, in addition to the Sirens assigned to the seven wanderers, Plato adds a Siren for the sphere of the fixed stars and not for earth.[48] If the moon corresponds to the *hypatē*, Plato's *proslambanomenos* would indeed be to the higher end of the scale. However, instead of using his interpretation of Plato to correct the cosmological scale, Plutarch advises against the endeavour as a whole: instead of trying to map the structures of sensible music onto the structure of the physical cosmos, it is better to focus on the imperceptible harmony of the cosmic soul (1029D-E). One can see how, given his temporal interpretation of *Timaeus*, Plutarch would disagree with the chronology implied by the story of the Sirens. In that story, harmony arises out of the tones chanted by the Sirens, who are carried around by the heavenly spheres (1029C). What Plutarch emphasises, instead, is that 'concordant ratios' (*tois kath' harmonian logois*) precede and cause the 'harmonic motions' (*emmeleiais kai kinēsesin*) of the cosmic soul, rendering her 'concordant and docile' (*symphōnon* [. . .] *kai peithēnion*) (1029D-E).[49] The idea that harmony precedes the movements of heaven, then, amounts to a refutation of the interpretation of the story of the Sirens which is presented in *De animae procreatione*.[50] According to this interpretation the story is an attempt to map musical notions (i.e. the names of the notes) onto the structure of the cosmic soul. Plutarch's criticism of such attempts once again points to the fundamental difference between heavenly harmony and earthly music and favours an interpretation like the one advocated by the young 'Plutarch' in the sympotic discussion.

Both in *Quaestiones convivales* and in *De animae procreatione*, the 'Ammonius-style' interpretation of the story of the Sirens is followed by a critical account which warns against exaggerating the importance of music. Both accounts, moreover, emphasise the need of correction on earth. The young 'Plutarch', as we saw, assigns the majority of the Muses to earth as guides for human endeavours. The rest of the cosmos can make do with only one Muse, since the heavenly bodies 'do not need much or varied guidance' (*Quaest. conv.* 746B). Similarly, in *De animae procreatione*,

[48] Cf. Helmer 1937, 62.

[49] The idea that the soul *partakes* of harmony (e.g. *Quaest. Plat.* 1001C and 1003A, *De an. procr.* 1014E and 1016B quoting *Ti.* 36e-37a) without *being* harmony (*De an. procr.* 1013B referring to *Phd.* 92a-95a, cf. 1024E) similarly suggests harmony's priority within the framework of Plutarch's exegesis of *Timaeus*.

[50] For a different interpretation of how the story of the Sirens in *Quaestiones convivales* relates to the version in *De animae procreatione* see Opsomer 2009, 139.

Plutarch points out that, while the cosmic soul is not entirely error-free, since it contains an element of evil in the form of divisible being (1026E-1027A), it is less prone to aberrations than the human soul (1025C-D).

The young 'Plutarch''s suggestion that music and the other works of the Muses are of a corrective, therapeutic nature fits in with Plutarch's general thought on the role of music. As I have argued in the first section of this paper, music is cosmic only in the context of imagery. Music comes to the rescue, for instance, at a symposium where the conversations are 'disorderly' (*ataktoi*, *Quaest. conv.* 9.1.736E) – a word denoting chaos in *Timaeus* (30a; 43b; 46e).[51] Fortunately, someone starts singing to the lyre and the party becomes a cosmos again. Immediately, the music fades to the background and the calmed guests start a *logos* prompted by the appropriateness of the words which have just been sung (736E-737B). As soon as music has done its work, it has to yield to philosophy, as the sympotic discussion at the beginning of this paper has already made clear.

2.3 The Limits of Divine Inspiration

At that introductory symposium, 'Plutarch' warned against the ecstatic potential of music. In the previous section, moreover, we have seen how Plutarch's teacher Ammonius described his understanding of the harmony of the spheres in terms of the philosopher's erotic madness instead of appealing to musical madness proper. In this last section, I will briefly consider if any trace remains of this traditional notion of divinely inspired music and how this notion is evaluated by Plutarch.

In *Amatorius*, Plutarch draws on Plato's *Phaedrus* to construct his own classification of kinds of enthusiasm. Faithfully following Plato, Plutarch distinguishes prophetic enthusiasm (attributed to Apollo), mystic enthusiasm (Dionysus), and musical / poetic enthusiasm (the Muses), attributing the best kind of enthusiasm to Aphrodite and Eros (*Amat.* 758E-759A).[52] After giving a brief overview of this classification, Plutarch works his way back through the list, giving more details about each kind (759A-B). However, the madness which was said to be responsible for 'poetic and

[51] Of course, the word ἄτακτος does not necessarily imply a reference to cosmological vocabulary, let alone to *Timaeus*. However, as I have argued elsewhere, Plutarch sees the symposium as an image of the Platonic cosmos and, accordingly, often uses cosmological vocabulary to describe it, while consciously making it difficult to distinguish between the cosmological and everyday use of certain words; see Demulder 2017a, esp. 37–8.

[52] Interestingly, although it does not pertain to our current purpose, Plutarch adds war-related enthusiasm (attributed to Ares) between musical and erotic madness.

musical creation' is suspiciously absent from this otherwise tidy elaboration. Once again, we might be tempted to think that Plutarch was being sloppy. Once again, I would like to suggest a different explanation: Plutarch had his doubts about musical creation being a divinely inspired activity.[53]

To make sense of this, we can turn to Plutarch's *De Pythiae oraculis*. In this dialogue, the discussion about the apparently disappointing literary quality of contemporary oracles contains a more general theory on the nature of artistic inspiration. The difference between the past, when oracles were mostly delivered 'as poetry and music' (*en metrois kai melesi*: *De Pyth. or.* 402D; cf. 405D), and the present cannot be explained by referring to Apollo. In other words: the musical aspect of the oracle (or the lack thereof) is not part of the divine inspiration. Whether or not the oracles are accompanied by music depends on the nature and the education of the Pythia.

It seems obvious that at least some degree of natural talent and musical education are necessary in order to be able to compose and play music. Still, by pointing this out, Plutarch is going against Plato's description of musical madness, which seizes 'a tender virgin soul' (*hapalēn kai abaton psychēn*, *Phdr.* 245a; also quoted by Plutarch, *Amat.* 758F). It is precisely because she has a 'virgin soul' (*parthenos hōs alēthōs tēn psychēn*) that the Pythia cannot be expected to express the oracles 'in verse of a grandiloquent and formal style with verbal metaphors and with an *aulos* to accompany its delivery' (*De Pyth. or.* 405D). For Plutarch, musical composition is a *technē* (cf. 404F; 405A), not a passive or unconscious experience.[54]

What happens when Apollo inspires an oracle is the following: the god uses the soul of the Pythia as an instrument (*organon*). The Pythia, in turn, uses her voice and her body to express the oracle in a manner suited to her

[53] I would attribute the absence of any justification of these doubts to the fact that this would be out of place in a more or less doxographic enumeration. Moreover, this particular absence has no bearing on the general theme of the work: Plutarch just wants to get to erotic madness.

[54] After quoting Euripides' verses 'Love doth the poet teach, / Even though he know naught of the Muse before' (ποιητὴν δ' ἄρα / Ἔρως διδάσκει, κἂν ἄμουσος ᾖ τὸ πρίν), Plutarch explains that 'Love does not implant in one the poetical or musical faculty (ποιτικὴν καὶ μουσικήν), but when it is already existent in one, Love stirs it to activity [...]' (*De Pyth. or.* 405F). *Quaest. conv.* 1.5 is concerned with the interpretation of the same lines; see Smits 1970, 52–4 and Roskam 2013. On τέχνη in Plutarch, see Van der Stockt 1992. An amusing anecdote which suggests that not only composing music but also listening to music is a question of expertise rather than inspiration or feeling appears in *De recta ratione audiendi* 46B. Plutarch tells how a member of a chorus once received a firm talking-to from Euripides. The man had burst into laughter during the rehearsal of a song in the solemn mixolydian mode, at which Euripides scolded him for being 'stupid and ignorant' (ἀναίσθητος [...] καὶ ἀμαθής). Cf. *De sera* 549E, *Quaest. conv.* 7.8.711C.

own nature and capabilities, in the form of music or otherwise (*De Pyth. or.* 404B-405D).[55] As Jens Holzhausen has shown, this *organon* theory of inspiration is thoroughly influenced by Plato's cosmology: the soul of the Pythia serves as the matter which receives the ideas from god.[56] Now, 'the virtue of an instrument is to conform as exactly as possible (*malista mimeisthai*) to the purpose of the agent' (404C). This process of *mimēsis* brings with it an unavoidable contamination by the nature of the medium (i.e. matter in the case of the demiurge's cosmogonic work; the Pythia in the case of the god's oracular work). Any musical aspect of the Pythia's oracles is situated in this contaminating layer of the process.

With this, our story about music in Plutarch's philosophy has come full circle and we are back at the comparison between the demiurge and the musician. Like the demiurge, the god who inspires the Pythia's oracles is compared to someone who plays a musical instrument.[57] In both cases, however, Plutarch makes it abundantly clear that this comparison should not be taken at face value. A musician is at best an *eikōn* of the god: his music is always a contaminated reflection of the divine. Music, then, is not the direct result of enthusiasm. Conversely, it would be foolish to believe that ecstasy evoked by music could forge a direct connection with the divine. It should, therefore, be avoided. For Plutarch, music is a sensible phenomenon. It is, for better or worse, an 'expression (*mimēsis*) of divine harmony in mortal movement' (*Ti.* 80b).

2.4 Concluding Remarks

'[W]hat truly organizes music in the West is the tension between the inescapable body and the West's deep-seated need to control or transcend that body through intellectual idealism.'[58] Plutarch's thoughts on music are an interesting example of how this tension can be embraced rather than ignored by focusing exclusively on one of the two poles. Plutarch does not deny the connection between music and what transcends the body. This connection, however, is in the form of an *eikōn*. Music, therefore, is placed squarely in the sensible realm – divine harmony and music should not be confused – and overemphasising its importance is as

[55] The idea that the soul is the instrument of the gods, and the body the instrument of the soul, occurs several times in Plutarch; see Holzhausen 1993, 83 with n. 38.

[56] Holzhausen 1993, 83–91. On the connections between cosmology and divination in Plutarch, see also Simonetti 2017. On the role of φθόγγος in Plutarch's thoughts on divination, see Crippa 2009.

[57] Cf. also *De defectu oraculorum* 436E-F. [58] McClary 1995, 83.

dangerous as neglecting it.[59] The benefit of this is that Plutarch's Platonic philosophy, although it is certainly idealistic in some sense, leaves room for music as it is experienced in tradition and culture.[60] Plutarch's particular brand of Platonism, then, allows him to avoid the 'sacrifice of the sensible component',[61] which is the ultimate consequence of Plato's view on music as voiced in *Republic* 7.

At the beginning of this chapter, I connected Plutarch's views to *Timaeus* 47c-d. By way of conclusion it may be useful briefly to return to this passage and to offer a more detailed yet on some points inevitably tentative explanation of how Plutarch understood the elements mentioned there. In *Timaeus*, music – 'an ally in the fight to bring order to any orbit in our souls that has become unharmonized' – is a remedy which is received by the *rational* soul, a compound of being, sameness, and difference.[62] This rational soul is what the demiurge forged with the ingredients which remained after his work on the cosmic soul. Having forged the rational soul, he handed it over to the younger gods who added the irrational soul and mortal body (*Ti.* 41d-42e). Plutarch, however, in his search for consistency across Platonic dialogues, ends up with a far stricter parallel between cosmic and human soul: in both cases the element of difference is associated with irrationality (*De virt. mor.* 441E-442A).[63] This has a consequence for how music, which as a sensible phenomenon is grasped by difference (*Ti.* 37a-c), enters the soul: on Plutarch's account it is possible for music to be received primarily by the irrational, although there is always some degree of combination of rational and irrational (cf. *De an. procr.* 1024F-1025A).[64] This may explain why, in the sympotic discussion about the Muses, the young 'Plutarch' refuses to decide whether the pleasure of music 'belongs mainly to reason or to emotion or is their common property' (*Quaest. conv.* 9.14.746F).

[59] In *Pericles* 1.4–5, Plutarch quotes Antisthenes, who, upon hearing someone being described as an excellent *aulos* player, responded: 'But he's a worthless man, otherwise he wouldn't be so good a piper'. This is followed by an anecdote about Alexander the Great being criticised by his father for playing beautifully: he should not devote himself to such trifles; the Muses should be more than pleased already if he deigns to listen to music. See Bowie 2004, 120. On music in Plutarch's *Vitae* see also García López 2003 and 2005.

[60] Smits 1970 provides many examples of this. Through a very different route from the one taken in this chapter, Petrucci 2019b reaches a similar conclusion.

[61] Pelosi 2010, 112; cf. 114–51. [62] Pelosi 2010, 91–111.

[63] See Opsomer 2012, 314 for a charitable interpretation of Plutarch's endeavour.

[64] As Cherniss 1976, 237 n. f notes, Plutarch seems to disregard Plato's distinction between difference as an ingredient of soul and the circle of difference. On the combination of bi- and tripartition of the soul, see Opsomer 2012, 319–25.

For Plutarch, then, it makes perfect sense to associate the therapeutic effect of music with the irrational part of the soul (*Quaest. conv.* 7.8.713B). That this is how he understood *Timaeus* 47c-d is clear from his paraphrase of the passage in *De superstitione* 167B-C, where music is targeted at the 'disturbing and errant' (*to tarachōdes kai peplanēmenon*) part of the embodied soul. Elsewhere, for instance in the retellings of the myth of Er which I discussed, it is the irrational part of the soul which is described in these terms.[65] By understanding musical therapy in this sense, Plutarch goes beyond *Timaeus*. His interpretation, however, may well be able to recover some Platonic elements which are otherwise hard to reconcile with *Timaeus*, such as the musical education described in *Republic* 2–3 and *Laws* 2 and 7, which engages to a much greater extent with the non-rational parts of the soul.[66]

Plutarch's particular take on the perception of the sensible can also explain why he seems to fear bad music more than is strictly warranted by *Timaeus* 47c-d. As Timaeus has it, the effect of the majority's using music for 'irrational pleasure' is probably just that music falls on deaf ears because it is not understood. For Plutarch (*Quaest. conv.* 7.8.713A), however, 'emotional display' (*pathainomenos*) opens the gates to arousal and ecstasy (*anasobōn kai parexistas*).[67] This relates to Plutarch's doubts about music as divine inspiration: in the case of music, ecstasy should not be trusted. Finally, although Timaeus states that speech plays a larger part in the benefits of hearing than music itself, he conceives of these respective benefits as independent from each other. Plutarch, however, sees words as an essential part of music and has little faith in purely instrumental music. Music may be an image of divine harmony, but words are how we learn about that harmony.[68] Once philosophy enters the stage, the orchestra should fall silent.

[65] *Quaest. conv.* 9.14.746A, *De an. procr.* 1029D, *De virt. mor.* 444A. Cf. *De an. procr.* 1014C and 1026C. Both *Quaest. conv.* 9.14.746B and *De sup.* 167C quote Pindar, *Pythian Odes* 1.13–14.

[66] See Lippman 1964, 45–86 and Pelosi 2010, 14–67.

[67] Cf. also *De cohibenda ira* 456B-C and *Quaest. conv.* 3.8.657A. However, as *De vitioso pudore* 534E-F shows (cf. also *An virtus doceri* 439C, both quoting *Clitophon* 407c-d, which Plutarch regarded as a genuine Platonic work; see Slings 1999, 11 n. 8), the danger of music should not be overestimated: it is not musical discord which causes conflict but discord (πλημμέλεια) in law and justice. On musical imagery in Plutarch's political thought, see Mosconi 2009.

[68] In this respect, as in many other respects, Plutarch is fundamentally opposed to the Stoics, who give a much more elevated role to music – in some ways more in line, perhaps, with an isolated reading of *Timaeus* – as a rational phenomenon which 'can represent the structure of the divine in terms of its underlying ratios, rather than just *describing* that structure in words' (Scade 2017, 209 [his emphasis] on Cleanthes).

CHAPTER 3

The Harmoniser God
Harmony as a Cosmological Model in Middle Platonist Theology

Federico M. Petrucci

3.1 Premiss

It is a commonplace that the notion of cosmic harmony is key in the Platonist tradition, and indeed Middle Platonists frequently appeal to the world's harmony in order to describe the perfect condition of the ensouled world and to state that God is the cause of this harmony.[1] This can be regarded as a testimony to the importance of exegesis in Middle Platonist philosophy, for several Platonic passages – from the myth of Er to the *divisio animae* in the *Timaeus* – would prove good bases for claiming that the world as a whole entails harmony. Relegating the Middle Platonist doctrine of cosmic harmony to the field of mere exegesis, however, risks leading us towards an oversimplification: for this idea, if unqualified, would ultimately amount to a broad metaphor referring to the world's order, a metaphor of no particular philosophical import in itself and simply based *on the fact* that sometimes Plato describes the world as harmonic. On the other hand, this does not imply that speaking of cosmic harmony without referring to Plato's dialogues necessarily entails any intriguing philosophical doctrine: for instance, the notion of a 'cosmic harmony' also occurs in technical writings or Pythagorean-flavoured Hellenistic poems,[2] such as those by

[1] This commonplace is probably the reason why the topic has not been made the object of many focussed enquiries – apart, maybe, from Brague 1999. A more widely discussed topic is the so-called harmony of the spheres (see e.g. Boyancé 1946, Pelosi 2018, and for the Pythagorean and Platonic background see Viltanioti 2015), which however, as this paper aims to emphasise, represents only one – and less interesting – aspect of the whole issue. On this topic in relation to Plutarch's thought see also Demulder's chapter in the present volume.

[2] Interestingly, it emerges both in astronomical texts (e.g. Achilles Tatius' *Isagoge*, at 43.10–13) and musical ones (e.g. Ptol. *Harm.* 3 ch. 8–16), which suggests that the notion of cosmic harmony has no strict disciplinary characterisation.

Alexander of Ephesus.[3] In this chapter I aim to show not only that Middle Platonist views of cosmic harmony went beyond mere exegesis and were part of a complex philosophical reasoning, but also that the notion of cosmic harmony played different roles in Middle Platonism and was invoked in support of rival theological and cosmological models. More specifically, I will suggest that it is possible to detect two Middle Platonist models of cosmic harmony and divine harmonisation. On the one hand, Platonists such as Plutarch and Numenius supported a strictly artisanal notion of divine harmonisation, according to which God harmonises the world by acting directly on its components. On the other, Platonists such as Taurus, Apuleius, and Alcinous made God free from any direct intervention, by positing a world intrinsically provided with a static harmony which God has never directly established through any demiurgic action. Each model of cosmic harmony plays a key role within the theology in which it is framed: by understanding the Middle Platonist doctrines of cosmic harmony one is in a position also to enter an intriguing debate on the sense in which God is to be regarded, according to the Middle Platonists, as the harmoniser of the world.

3.2 Two Preliminary Clarifications

Before entering the narrative, it is important to clarify two notions which I shall be employing in this paper, namely those of 'craftmanship' and 'harmonisation'.[4]

In this paper I will *never* deny that, in the Middle Platonists' view, there is a demiurge God at all, or that this God is associated with Plato's demiurge; rather, what I want to emphasise is that there are different ways in which this figure was regarded and his action defined. In general, all Middle Platonists identified God as the ultimate efficient cause responsible for the generation of the world as it is. In this very sense, for all of them God is a demiurge and an efficient cause.[5] There are, however, different ways in which this claim can be understood. On a maximalist reading, one can regard this cause to be strictly artisanal, and God to be a proper craftsmanlike cause: he directly acts on the world, without any intermediaries; he has the will to accomplish this action, which is directed towards the world; thus, he properly accomplishes

[3] Quoted by Theon of Smyrna at *Exp.* 138.9–142.6: see Petrucci 2012a, *ad loc.*

[4] I am particularly grateful to the Cambridge University Press readers for suggesting the need for these clarifications.

[5] For an overview see now Boys-Stones 2018, chapter 6.

a generative action.[6] On a minimalist reading, one can consider an efficient cause to simply 'determine certain effects' on the world: this is, for instance, the sense in which one could even take the Unmoved Mover to be an efficient cause,[7] and it does not imply any kind of direct, voluntary, and properly craftsmanlike intervention in the world. There are, then, several intermediate nuances between these readings: for instance, Plotinus' God is indeed a generative cause, but he does not act as the craftsmanlike cause of the maximalist reading.[8] In this scenario, I shall argue that some Platonists (namely, Plutarch and Numenius) regarded the harmonising action of God as being closer to a maximalist reading, while others (for instance, Taurus) strongly downplayed the craftsmanlike nature of God's harmonising action according to a model which is closer to a minimalist reading.

The second premiss concerns the overall meaning of musical terms – especially, harmony and harmonisation – as used in this chapter. The idea that the world and the world soul are harmonically arranged could simply be regarded as a metaphor. In this case, one could argue that, after all, any reference to cosmic harmony – and, hence, to divine harmonisation on the part of God – is nothing more than an image, used at most in order to exemplify the world's order. Interestingly, this cannot be the case with any form of Platonism, and especially of Middle Platonism. To the best of my knowledge, the Middle Platonists agreed with the *Timaeus* that the world soul is a harmonic substance, or else has a harmonic structure.[9] It is not by chance that the Middle Platonists showed considerable interest in technical exegesis, namely to the musical pattern implied by the *Timaeus' divisio animae*.[10] If this applies to the soul, which is the principle of motion of the world, then the world too must be regarded as at least involving harmonic patterns, according to which its time and natural rhythms are regulated. The same applies – as I shall show – to a more general and philosophically interesting level: when Platonists appealed to the notion of cosmic harmony, they referred to specific features and mechanisms involved in their cosmologies. This means that, in general terms, what I will discover is not just a shared use of a metaphor, but specific conceptions of the world order

6 These are the features of craftsmanlike causation invoked (e.g. by Chiaradonna 2015).
7 To put it with Opsomer 2005b, 62. In general, this is the way in which Aristotle himself presents this type of cause: *Ph.* 2.3.194b29–32.
8 See esp. Michalewski 2014, Chiaradonna 2015, and Opsomer 2005c.
9 For the former view, see Procl. *in Ti.* 2.153.17–154.1 = Attic. fr. 35 = Num. fr. 39 = Sever. 12T; the latter can be found – as is widely known – in Plutarch's *De animae procreatione*. On both points see now Boys-Stones 2018, 212–18.
10 See Petrucci 2019a.

which according to the Platonists could properly be described in terms of harmony. In this sense, reducing the Platonists' appeal to harmony to a mere metaphor would somewhat mirror a limited contemporary conception of the notion, that is, a merely 'technical' one.

3.3 The (Platonist) Commonplace

Of course, it would be unwarranted to deny that, to some extent, a *broad* idea that the world is organised according to harmony, which ultimately derives from God, occurs in Platonist works as well: on the contrary, such a weak conception of cosmic harmony is key to really appreciate those cases in which the notion turns out to be philosophically crucial.

A quite effective example of a weak appeal to the notion can be detected in *De animae procreatione in Timaeo*. In the second part of this treatise Plutarch outlines three models in which planets and notes had been associated in the tradition (1029A1-C4): in general, each version represents the heavens as being arranged according to a specific scalar system, which is meant to determine the harmony produced by the motions of the heavenly bodies.[11] Although Plutarch apparently dwells on these theories, it is quite clear that this is not the conception of cosmic harmony he subscribes to: Plutarch is explicitly reluctant to endorse any of them, and in general does not express any sympathy for the underlying operation. Elsewhere, however, Plutarch would seem to be more sympathetic to it: for instance when, in *De defectu oraculorum* (430A1-10), Lamprias proposes the idea of a correspondence between the arrangement of the heavenly bodies and that of musical notions such as intervals and tetrachords, both reproducing a pattern based on the number five (transl. Babbit, modified):

> Five, too, are the orbits of the planets, if the Sun and Venus and Mercury follow the same course. The orderly composition of the world too is based on harmony, just as a tune is seen by us to depend on the five collocations of the tetrachords, namely of the lowest notes, of the middle notes, of the conjunct notes, of the disjunct notes, and of the highest notes. And the musical intervals are five: *diesis*, semitone, tone, triple semitone and double tone. Thus it appears that nature takes a greater delight in making all things in fives than in making them round, as Aristotle said.

[11] See Ferrari and Baldi 2002, 366–70 nn. 316–20, on this passage.

Although in this text Lamprias' views are generally close to those which Plutarch agrees with, this specific passage is puzzling and it is likely that the case is made only for the sake of the argument. Indeed, while Lamprias' overall claim in this passage is regarded with favour by Plutarch (as an author),[12] the technical content of these lines is very poor – for there is no connection at all between the number of the tetrachords and that of the intervals, which are speciously selected – and the argument is mainly based on arithmology. A very similar account also occurs in the *De E* (389D1-F2), where the character Plutarch points out that the number 5 is fundamental in the field of harmonics – for there are five concords, five tetrachords, and five intervals – and on this basis builds up an argument in favour of the role of this number in the cosmic arrangement. It has been effectively shown,[13] however, that the character's speech does not mirror Plutarch's own views, and rather encompasses unsatisfying accounts – as Plutarch seems to explicitly declare through the character Ammonius (387F).[14]

Thus, although such accounts of cosmic harmony occur more than once in Plutarch's writings, one must conclude that he did not regard them as philosophically noteworthy. At the same time, their very occurrence can easily be explained by considering the fact that the broad idea of the arrangement of the heavenly bodies according to musical intervals, or systems, was a commonplace in more or less technical writings (as pointed out at the beginning of the chapter). In other words, Plutarch must have taken such an approach simply for what it was, that is, a widespread, but philosophically poor, commonplace. All in all, then, the case of Plutarch shows that a Middle Platonist was in a position to detect a weak and poor sense in which one can say that the world is harmonic, which is also a good starting point in order to be able to move beyond it: this negative assessment represents a suitable beginning for an enquiry into more refined Middle Platonist conceptions of cosmic harmony.

[12] At least, a number of claims proposed by Lamprias coincide with ones we can ascribe to Plutarch himself, as in the case of his insistence on the notion of providence and on the disorderly status of matter (423A-426E) or his account of the causes of the world (435E). This is, however, a specific feature of the work: on the complex status of Lamprias as a character in Plutarch's dialogues see esp. Ferrari 1995, 29–35 and Donini 2011, 36–45 (providing a very effective analysis of Lamprias' commitments in the *De facie*).

[13] See Ferrari 1995, 38–68.

[14] Similar arguments occur, for example, in fr. 110 and *Quaest. conv.* 9.14 (esp. 744C-745D), having in both cases arithmological grounds and showing no particular link with the core of Plutarch's cosmology.

3.4 God as Harmonising Craftsman: Plutarch and Numenius

At the beginning of the *Vita Phocionis* (2.4–5) the planetary motions are compared to the right way of administrating the state (transl. Perrin, modified):

> Now, the Sun, as mathematicians tell us, has neither the same motion as the heavens, nor one that is directly opposite and contrary, but takes a slanting course with a slight inclination, and describes a winding spiral of soft and gentle curves, thus preserving all things and giving them the best blending. And so in the administration of a city, the course which is too straight, and opposed in all things to the popular desires, is harsh and cruel, just as, on the other hand, it is highly dangerous to tolerate or yield perforce to the mistakes of the populace. But that wise guidance and government of men which yields to them in return for their obedience and grants them what will please them, and then demands from them in payment what will advantage the state – and men will give docile and profitable service in many ways, provided they are not treated despotically and harshly all the time conduces to safety, although it is laborious and difficult and must have that mixture of austerity and reasonableness which is so hard to attain. But if the mixture be attained, that is the most concordant and musical blending of all rhythms and all harmonies; and this is the way, we are told, in which God regulates the universe, not using compulsion, but conditioning the necessity by means of persuasion and reason.

Just as the planets' – and especially the Sun's – motions entail some anomalies, while being regular overall, a constitution cannot just abolish people's desires and inclinations, but must negotiate with them in order to lead them towards an orderly community life. At first sight this might appear to be simply a metaphor for Plutarch's political theory, and apparently there is no need to insist on the cosmological description provided here. In this sense, the final reference to the harmony of the heavenly bodies would amount to nothing more than an evocative image related to the fact that the arrangement of the heavens relies on the mathematical structure of the world soul: after all, although in Plutarch's view the soul's essence does not coincide with its mathematical form (*De an. procr.* 1013B-D), the soul has a harmonic structure, which conditions the heavenly motions, as witnessed by the second part of the *De animae procreatione.* Interestingly enough, however, this way of reading the passage would make very little sense in context. First, Plutarch himself clearly hints at the second part of the cosmogonic account of the *Timaeus* as a textual background for his theory by describing harmony as the result of God's persuasion in relation to necessity: this is God's task with respect to 'necessity' as described in

Timaeus, which is not immediately related to the soul's mathematical structure.[15] Second, given that in Plutarch's view God's cosmogonic action consists in the ordering of the irrational pre-cosmic soul, which in turn is embedded in the unqualified matter,[16] Plutarch cannot be merely referring here to the static structure of the world soul, which is indeed mathematical and hence harmonic, but to *the very constitution* of the world and its soul. Moreover, it is noteworthy that this process is related by Plutarch to the above-mentioned section of the *Timaeus*.[17] In other words, here cosmic harmony does not coincide with the shape and structure of the world via that of its soul, but with the action by which God produces the world and its soul by actively mixing up constituents which are, *in themselves*, disharmonic to each other. Such a reading makes much better sense with respect to the political point, for just as a good statesman is meant to produce a suitable mix of rational law and people's desires by establishing a well-ordered state, God's productive action consists in actively arranging the best mix of rationality and irrationality. This cosmological mixture lies at the basis of heavenly harmony, which at the beginning of the passage is significantly said to express 'the best blending' (*tēn aristēn krasin*). Thus, through the reference to cosmic harmony we are led back to a most renowned Plutarchean cosmological doctrine, that of the constitution and preservation of the world on the part of God, who mixes up a part of himself – providing the world with rationality – with the irrational soul and matter, while the mathematical structure of the world soul plays only a secondary role.[18]

This passage of the *Vita Phocionis* is not isolated in Plutarch's *corpus*, for Plutarch resorts to the same notion of cosmic harmony in some key passages, which in turn help better understand what theological point Plutarch wishes to make by referring to the notion of cosmic harmony. Indeed, a similar representation of the heavens lies at the basis of the setting

[15] See esp. *Ti.* 47e3-48a5: Τὰ μὲν οὖν παρεληλυθότα τῶν εἰρημένων πλὴν βραχέων ἐπιδέδεικται τὰ διὰ νοῦ δεδημιουργημένα· δεῖ δὲ καὶ τὰ δι' ἀνάγκης γιγνόμενα τῷ λόγῳ παραθέσθαι. μεμειγμένη γὰρ οὖν ἡ τοῦδε τοῦ κόσμου γένεσις ἐξ ἀνάγκης τε καὶ νοῦ συστάσεως ἐγεννήθη· νοῦ δὲ ἀνάγκης ἄρχοντος τῷ πείθειν αὐτὴν τῶν γιγνομένων τὰ πλεῖστα ἐπὶ τὸ βέλτιστον ἄγειν, ταύτῃ κατὰ ταῦτά τε δι' ἀνάγκης ἡττωμένης ὑπὸ πειθοῦς ἔμφρονος οὕτω κατ' ἀρχὰς συνίστατο τόδε τὸ πᾶν.

[16] See Ferrari 2014 for a survey, and footnote 18 below for the key passages in Plutarch's *corpus*.

[17] See esp. *De an. procr.* 1014E: see Ferrari and Baldi 2002, *ad loc.*

[18] See esp. *De an. procr.* 1014A-1015C and 1016A-C, *Quaest. Plat.* 1001A-B, 1003A-C, 1006F-1007E (on pre-cosmic time), but also – from different points of view – *De E* 393A-394A, *Def. or.* 423C-E and 435E-436D, *Quaest. conv.* 616A and 718A, *De fac.* 926F, 927A-D, *De sera* 559D, *Quaest. Plat.* 1001A-C and 1006F-1007E, *De Is. et Os.* 371A-B and 373A-B (with Petrucci 2016b). This is one of the fundamental aspects of Plutarch's Platonism: see esp. Ferrari 1995, 1996, 2014, Opsomer 2004, Boys-Stones 2018, 187–90.

of the myth of the *De genio Socratis* (590C4-E2, transl. De Lacy and Einarson, modified):[19]

> When he lifted his eyes the Earth was nowhere to be seen; but he saw islands illuminated by one another with soft fire, taking on now one colour, now another, like a dye, as the light kept varying with their mutations. They appeared countless in number and huge in size, and though not all equal, yet all alike round; and he fancied that their circular movement made a musical whirring in the aether, for the gentleness of the sound resulting from the harmony of all the separate sounds corresponded to the evenness of their motion. In their midst lay spread a sea or lake, through whose blue transparency the colours passed in their migrations; and of the islands a few sailed out in a channel and crossed the current, while many others were carried along . . . the sea (?) drifting around in a circle. In places it was very deep, mainly towards the south, but elsewhere there were faint shoals and shallows; and in many parts it overflowed and again receded, never extending very far. Some of it was the pure hue of the high seas, while elsewhere the colour was not unmixed, but turbid and like that of a pool.

As is widely known, the myth of the *De genio* is set within a complex scenario, which clearly represents the structure of the world from the heavens to the Earth.[20] Although Plutarch's commitment to the psychological doctrines expressed in the myth is far from clear,[21] the aspect which is relevant for the present enquiry is clearly stated and consistent with the narrative which has been emerging: rather than emphasising the homogeneity and perfection of the world, Plutarch indulges in a description of different degrees of purity of the sea (i.e. the heavens) and of the diverse sizes and motions of the islands (i.e. the heavenly bodies) moving within it. Interestingly, the world's harmony consists precisely in this variety of motions and dimensions, and more specifically both in the reciprocal relations between the moving bodies and in the overall cosmic arrangement. As a consequence, the harmony at issue is not merely a perfect order, but a combination of *different* degrees of purity. This picture could be regarded as a sort of stable and autonomous condition of the world, and in this case God would play no role in its establishment.

[19] The passage presents some textual difficulties, on which see Nesselrath 2010, 95 n. 206. I accept Arnim's reconstruction of the text only in part: while a minor conjecture is quite reasonable, I prefer to keep a lacuna between συνεφέλκεσθαι τῇ and σχεδὸν ὑποφερομένης, where Arnim proposes an extensive (and quite arbitrary) integration.

[20] On this dialogue see the notes *ad loc.* by Nesselrath 2010 and Donini 2017.

[21] See now Donini 2017, 40–6.

However, this is not the case, as a well-known passage of the *De Iside et Osiride* shows, namely the one referring to the generation of Horus, which is to say the world (373B-C, transl. Boys-Stones, modified):[22]

> While the gods Isis and Osiris were still in the belly of Rhea, Apollo is said to have been born to them – which signifies the fact that, before this cosmos was brought to light and matter was completed by reason (τὸ πρὶν ἐκφανῆ γενέσθαι τόνδε τὸν κόσμον καὶ συντελεσθῆναι τῷ λόγῳ τὴν ὕλην), † it was shown to be wanting in itself † when it brought forth a defective first birth (ἀτελῆ τὴν πρώτην γένεσιν ἐξενεγκεῖν). That is why they also say that the god whom they call the 'Elder Horus' was born in darkness, a cripple – because he was not order, but a kind of image and representation of the order to come. But this Horus is himself well-defined and whole. He has not annihilated Typhon completely, but removed his efficacy and strength.

I have argued elsewhere that the *De Iside* deals, in general, with the post-creational condition of the world and the cosmological powers acting within it. The quoted passage, however, clearly entails a reference to the generation of the world.[23] Although the text is affected by heavy perturbation, the following aspects can be identified with some certainty: the generation of Horos, the world, was preceded by the pre-creational and imperfect generation of an Elder Horos; only the second generation can be regarded as complete, and it derives from the action of reason on matter (i.e. matter *plus* the irrational soul: 'before this cosmos was brought to light and matter was completed by reason'). Now, this account of Horus' generation clearly mirrors the Plutarchean idea that the world is the product of the rational God's action on an irrational component, constituted by matter and the irrational soul which is intrinsically embedded in it: what is at issue, then, is the interaction of opposite powers as established by the intervention of a rational God. However, the interesting point here is that this account is directly related to the myth according to which Hermes produces the strings of a musical instrument from Typhon's sinews, allowing Plutarch's overall conclusion (transl. Babbitt, modified):

> Hence they say that at Kopto the statue of Horus holds in one hand the privy members of Typhon, and they relate a legend that Hermes cut out

[22] This text too is probably corrupted. Since on the one hand all attempts to emend the text are somewhat arbitrary, and on the other the meaning of the section is intelligible even without any intervention, I prefer to keep the corrupted passage with the *cruces desperationis*. For a detailed analysis of the problem see Petrucci 2016b, 351 n. 50.

[23] See Petrucci 2016b, to which I will also refer for *status quaestionis* on the various interpretations of this text which have been put forward. The importance of the treatise in the Plutarchean *corpus* has been mainly emphasised by Ferrari 1995, 74–87, who, however, detects a full discussion of cosmogony within it.

> Typhon's sinews, and used them as strings for his lyre, thereby instructing that reason harmonises the universe and produces concord out of discordant components (τὸ πᾶν ὁ λόγος διαρμοσάμενος σύμφωνον ἐξ ἀσυμφώνων μερῶν ἐποίησε), and that it does not destroy, but only cripples the destructive power.

The constitution of the world *does* involve a destructive power, which is mixed up with a rational one by God (who encompasses it)[24] and in this way it is weakened and put at the service of rationality, although it is not completely removed and still plays a role in the world: it is this *specific* mix that constitutes the world's harmony. While no reference to the notion of harmony as a mathematical pattern is at issue, the fundamental point is that the world's harmony is based on the interaction between rational and irrational powers, whose influence is mirrored by the world's dynamics, and that this interaction is made possible by the intervention of a power establishing *this* harmony between disharmonic constituents.

This scenario finds support in all three passages I have taken into account, albeit in different ways. While all of them emphasise the persistence of some disorder within the harmonic world, the *De Iside* leads us to better understand a hint which was already present in the *Vita Phocionis*, namely the idea that such a complex harmonic mixture *cannot* be achieved without the intervention of a rational power: it is rather the product of the *logos*, that is, God, who in turn is in charge of harmonically regulating the mix of the opposite powers constituting the final harmony. All in all, *if* there is a multiplicity of components, which in themselves are not harmonic to each other and need to be harmonised, then it is also necessary for there to be a harmonising God, that is, a craftsmanlike cause establishing the harmonic mix. Interestingly enough, such activity does not coincide with the mathematical arrangement of the world soul, but represents the necessary condition allowing the achievement of this further step. Indeed, the second part of the *De animae procreatione* opens with the following passage (1027A, transl. Cherniss, modified):

> Thus many considerations make it plain to us that the soul is not God's work entirely, but that with the portion of evil inherent in it, it has been orderly arranged by God, who with the One bounded its infinitude, so that by participation in limit it might become substance and through the agency of sameness and of difference commingled order and change and

[24] This is one of the most intriguing aspects of Plutarch's cosmology: God is at the same time transcendent and involved in a craftsmanlike shaping of the world, for, in order to limit the irrationality of the precosmic soul, he introduces a part of himself into the psychic mixture: see esp. *De E* 393F, *De sera* 559D, and above all *Quaest. Plat.* 1001A-C.

> differentiation and similarity and in all of these produced – so far as it was feasible – amity and union with one another by means of numbers and harmony (κοινωνίαν πρὸς ἄλληλα καὶ φιλίαν ἐργασαμένου δι' ἀριθμῶν καὶ ἁρμονίας).

The production of amity (*koinōnia*) and union (*philia*) is achieved through the application of numbers and harmonic ratios, but it does not properly establish the soul's harmony: rather, it just strengthens a bond which had already been produced by God between opposite powers which are disharmonic to each other. This amounts to confirmation of the fact that, in Plutarch's perspective, the core notion of cosmic harmony, far from being related to the mathematical and static arrangement of the world and the soul, specifically concerns the ontological mix of the world's components and those of the world soul.

All this is crucial inasmuch as it paves the way to a proper understanding of the theological import of Plutarch's notion of cosmic harmony. Of course, Plutarch's conception has some good exegetical grounds, such as the myth of Er, clearly echoed in the *De genio*, and to some extent also relies on technical bases – for instance, it is likely that Plutarch is thinking of the simultaneous production of notes, which is attested in musical practice.[25] However, it would be unwarranted to regard Plutarch's point as resting either on exegesis or on technical grounds alone: on the one hand, the clearest Platonic reference to cosmic harmony is indeed to be found in Plato's *divisio animae*, which, as we have seen, plays a minor role in the account; on the other, the most obvious ground for a technical notion of harmony would be a well-tuned system of notes, but this hardly constitutes an adequately explanatory image for the complex Plutarchean view. In other words, Plutarch must have deep philosophical reasons for his account, transcending both mere exegesis and technicalities.[26] First, as we have seen, the notion of harmony which has been emerging provides a very suitable 'theoretical model' allowing Plutarch to exploit the idea of the presence, and persistence, of an irrational element in the harmonised world. Second, and most importantly, representing cosmic harmony *just* in mathematical terms would have a serious counter-effect, for in principle

[25] See Pelosi 2009, in which it is shown that the commonplace according to which notes were played only in sequence is to be abolished.

[26] This does not mean, of course, that there is no exegetical ground at all. On the contrary, it is likely that Plutarch would have regarded his view as emerging, for example, from the *Philebus*: in the *De animae procreatione* (1014E), for instance, he refers to *Phlb.* 24c ff. as a key passage for the cosmological point he is making, and in turn this passage finds its foundation in some previous pages, in which the idea of a rational mix of limit and limitless is also proposed by appealing to music and notes (18b-c).

a mathematical structure does not require any superior power ensuring its orderly persistence: a mathematical structure is *essentially* and *definitionally* well-ordered (this will prove crucial in the next section). If, on the contrary, the world is harmonic in the sense that it is the result of a rational mix of dishomogeneous components, each preserving its power to some extent, *then* there is the need for an external cause ensuring both that the harmonic mix is suitably achieved and that it will keep existing in its order. This is the reason why both the passage from the *Lives* and that from the *De Iside* revolve around the following implication: if the world is a harmonic composition, then there *must* also be a harmonising craftsmanlike cause, or better, a harmoniser God.[27] First, since the objects of harmonisation are essentially dishomogeneous in themselves, it will never be the case that harmony is achieved without an external intervention achieving a suitable balance for their mixing and allowing each component to contribute to the composition to a suitable extent. Second, nothing can ensure the persistency of the harmonic composition except the continuous 'care' of the harmoniser God. I do not wish to represent this care in too literal a way. However, given that the harmonisation implies a reasoning which must be directed towards the components of the harmony, and that the product of the harmonisation is something different, and more, than the mere sum of the components, then this reasoning *must* at least consist in a form of planning which is directed towards the world's components, so as to produce and preserve their mix. In other words, Plutarch's conception of cosmic harmony is part of a philosophical mechanism allowing him to represent the harmoniser God as an artisanal, providential, and planning cause for the harmonic world, that is, according to the maximalist view mentioned in Section 3.2.

Plutarch's texts, therefore, highlight the fact that there is a strict philosophical link between a non-mathematical and dynamic idea of cosmic harmony and a very specific theological account, one based on craftsmanship and framed within a dualistic cosmology. If this is the case, one should also be in a position to observe the same pattern in some models which present a different cosmological structure, yet share Plutarch's commitment to craftsmanship. This is the case with Numenius, whose account of cosmic harmony confirms my conclusions. The key text in this sense is fragment 18, where we find the renowned image of the demiurge (i.e. Numenius' second God) as a 'pilot' (*kybernētēs*) who saves the material

[27] To this evidence one should also add *De prim. frig.* 946F, which is analysed by Bram Demulder in this volume (see p. 46 above).

world from disorder by turning to the forms and the superior God (transl. Boys-Stones):

> A pilot borne along in the middle of the sea sits high up, above the rudders, and steers the ship by their handles, but his eyes and mind are intent on the sky as he looks towards the heavens, so that as far as he is concerned his route follows a path through the heaven above, although he is sailing over the sea below. Just so the creator, having bound matter together in a harmony (*harmoniāi syndēsamenos*) that it cannot evade or slip away from, is himself seated above matter, as above a ship on the sea. And he directs the harmony (*tēn harmonian d'ithynei*), steering by the forms; and instead of the heavens, he looks to the god above who draws his eyes to him; and he acquires the faculty of judgement from his contemplation, and the faculty of impulse from his yearning.

Numenius' account clearly implies the ordering of a disorderly factor, coinciding here with matter (along with the irrational soul) and its potentially destructive action, and at the same time it points out that its limitation is due to the power of the forms: the forms' ordering of matter gives substance to a harmonic arrangement.[28] This arrangement, however, is neither automatic nor self-produced, for each component is credited with its proper nature, which in itself is completely dishomogenous with respect to the others.[29] This is the reason why the harmonic composition is due to an external cause, namely the harmoniser God – the creator, or demiurge. Of course, Numenius sets God's action within a different cosmological and theological framework compared to Plutarch, as the explicit reference to the superior God shows. Nonetheless, Numenius' second God is a harmoniser God in the very same artisanal sense in which Plutarch's God is, *because* the world can be harmonically fashioned out of opposite factors only provided that there is a craftsmanlike harmoniser God. Finally, it is noteworthy that also in Numenius' case the mathematical structure of the world soul, while playing some role in the orderly structure of the soul itself and of the world, must be regarded as secondary at least with respect to the production of the world's essence:[30] the core of the notion of cosmic

[28] On Numenius' cosmology and theology see Dillon 1977, 361–78, Bonazzi 2004, Opsomer 2005b, 66–73, and Boys-Stones 2018, 106–7, 156–8, 224–6 (on this fragment, in particular, 226).

[29] This clearly emerges from the negative characterisation of matter (or, better, of an irrational soul embedded in matter) provided by several fragments: see esp. fr. 4a, 11, 18, 33, 41, 52.

[30] Proclus, *in Ti.* 2.153.17–25 (= Num. fr. 39), lists Numenius among those who considered the soul to be a mathematical object, thereby suggesting that Numenius too regarded the soul as having a mathematical structure. The fact that Proclus refers here to the soul's essence instead of its structure cannot disprove my argument, for on the one hand it is widely known that Proclus is often unreliable about the details of Numenius' (and other Middle Platonists') cosmology (see

harmony in Numenius' Platonism is related to the artisanal intervention of the second God within the world. All this strengthens my case, for the demiurgic activity and the artisanal one are presented as coinciding: independently of the overall theological account, where craftsmanship is at issue there is also room for appealing to a theological model according to which cosmic harmony is the product of a direct harmonising intervention on the part of the craftsmanlike God.

It is noteworthy that a direct antecedent of this Platonist conception of cosmic harmony can be found in Stoicism. Several sources, ranging from Cleanthes to Cotta's speech in the *De natura deorum* not only testify to the fact that the world is ruled by harmony,[31] which is best mirrored by the heavenly revolutions, but also state that *this* harmony is the product of God's artisanal production of the world. Of course, between the Platonist model and the Stoic one there is a fundamental difference: while Stoic cosmic harmony is somewhat intrinsic to God, who finds no resistance in the passive principle with respect to the establishment of cosmic harmony, the Platonists regard cosmic harmony as having been established by the craftsmanlike God over and against an irrational principle. This divergence, however, does not concern the association of the craftsmanlike God's intervention with the establishment of cosmic harmony. On the contrary, it is determined by the fact that the Platonists, and especially Plutarch, acknowledge that, in order to make craftsmanship consistent, it is necessary to also introduce an irrational principle into the world. Indeed, the Platonists' version of this notion of cosmic harmony aims to be much more consistent in as far as God *has to be* a harmoniser craftsman not only because he directly intervenes within the world, but also – and above all – because the world entails an irrational principle, which stands in need of harmonisation on the part of a rational one.[32]

All this leads us to some preliminary conclusions. The notion of cosmic harmony, far from being a merely rhetorical device, or metaphor, is conceived by Plutarch and Numenius as a philosophical model for the production of the world in a specific philosophical sense: it ensures, and gives substance to, the possibility of the production of the world according

Tarrant 2004 and Petrucci 2014), and on the other, given the interaction between a rational and an irrational principle (see the fragments quoted in the preceding footnote), the soul's constitution must in any case have some priority with respect to its mathematical arrangement.

[31] In general, see for example *SVF* 1.502–503 and Cic. *Nat. D.* 2.153–155. On this aspect of Stoic cosmology see esp. Scade 2017.

[32] On this relationship between Middle Platonist and Stoic craftsmanship, see Petrucci 2018a, 112–15. A fundamental enquiry into the legacy of Stoicism in Middle Platonism is Reydams-Schils 1999.

to the need for a craftsmanlike account of God's action. In this sense, the very appeal to the notion of cosmic harmony works not only as a representation, but as an argument in favour of a specific theological model, that is a precise representation of God as cause. We have seen in Section 3.2 of this chapter that one could define God's causation in either maximalist or minimalist terms. In the light of my analysis, Plutarch and Numenius may be seen to support a maximalist account, for in their view God is a properly craftsmanlike cause, who directly and intentionally acts upon entities which are, in themselves, disharmonic to each other – that is, God acts within a dualistic cosmological framework. On the one hand, either one denies that the world is harmonic and that the cause of the world's order is God, or one accepts that the harmoniser God is also a craftsmanlike cause; but both Platonists and Stoics would find it hard to deny the former claim, from which the acceptance of the latter claim follows. On the other hand, only a dualistic cosmology can really justify God's harmonising task, and this is the reason why the Stoic notion of cosmic harmony is weak: God can be a craftsmanlike harmoniser only provided that he acts over and against an irrational principle, for according to this view harmony implies dragging opposite powers into a synergy. Finally, the mathematical arrangement of the world plays a minor role in this account: it is only a secondary step in the world's arrangement, for it must be preceded by the essential harmonisation of the world's components. Both Plutarch and Numenius agree that the soul has – either directly or indirectly – a mathematical structure, but by considering it a secondary aspect they are able to make a case for its dependence on the harmonisation of more original constituents and for the necessity of a craftsmanlike God harmonising them. This, in turn, makes it impossible to regard the world's mathematical structure as self-preserving and intrinsically stable, for its establishment and persistence will in any case rely on the original artisanal action of the harmoniser God.

3.5 Harmony without Opposition: Taurus, Apuleius, and Alcinous

Although the collected evidence highlights an influential trend in Middle Platonism, it would be unwarranted to regard it as being fully representative of the Middle Platonist views on the issue: as I will show in this section, the contrary is the case, for one can discover other Middle Platonists engaged in showing that a philosophically consistent notion of cosmic harmony can even lead to a minimalist reading of divine causation, namely one avoiding God's direct crafting of the world.

A first piece of evidence in this sense can be drawn from quite a puzzling and obscure reference to the reciprocal relationship between the notes provided by Taurus' T26,[33] that is, the well-known text presenting four non-temporal meanings in which the world can be said to be *genēton*. In Taurus the second non-temporal meaning is presented as follows (T26.7):

> Also what is notionally composed is said to be generated, even if it has not been composed. In this sense the *mesē* too is composed of the *nētē* and the *hypatē*: for even if the *mesē* has not been composed, the intrinsic function of the one with respect to the other can be observed in it. The same applies to flowers and animals. Thus, composition and mixture are observed also in the world, and in the very same way we can reduce it to its first substrate by setting aside and separating its qualities.

It is impossible to discuss here all the implications of the passage and of the overall text.[34] However, at least the key aspect of Taurus' account is clear: the world is generated in the sense that, while being sempiternal, it is composed of a set of items, just as a note is generated in the sense that its intrinsic function (*dynamis*)[35] is determined by the presence of two other notes. In this sense, the world is a harmony because its constituents (whatever they may be in this case) have a specific reciprocal position, ensuring the overall harmonic order. Taurus' use of *krasis* (transl. 'mixture') could suggest that he is referring to the mix of the components involved. This cannot be the case, however, for the reference to the notes' order militates against this reading. In general terms, when the notion of *krasis* is applied to the notes, it does not imply that each of them is annulled by being absorbed into a single mixture; rather, the word is used to describe the interaction between notes having different pitches, which indeed produces a composite sound but does not imply that each note loses its

[33] I am quoting Taurus' texts from my own collection (Petrucci 2018a); T26 Petrucci corresponds to 23F Gioè (2002).

[34] λέγεται γενητὸν καὶ τὸ ἐπινοίᾳ σύνθετον, καὶ εἰ μὴ συντεθῇ. οὕτως σύνθετος ἡ μέση ἐκ νήτης καὶ ὑπάτης· καὶ γὰρ εἰ μὴ συντεθῇ, ἐνορᾶται αὐτῇ δύναμις ἡ τῆς ἑτέρας πρὸς τὴν ἑτέραν. τὸ δ' ὅμοιον ἐπὶ ἀνθῶν καὶ ζῴων. καὶ τῷ κόσμῳ τοίνυν ἐνορᾶται σύνθεσις καὶ κρᾶσις, καθὸ καὶ δυνάμεθα ἀφελόντες αὐτοῦ καὶ χωρίσαντες τὰς ποιότητας ἀναλῦσαι αὐτὸν εἰς τὸ πρῶτον ὑποκείμενον. I have extensively discussed this text in context in Petrucci 2018a. See also the traditional analyses by Baltes 1976, 105–121, Dillon 1977, 237–247, Dörrie and Baltes 1998, 428–435 and 454–460, Gioè 2002, *comm. ad loc.*, Ferrari 2015.

[35] While a standard Aristoxenian notion of a note's δύναμις (the property, or characteristic, which a listener should be able to grasp: see e.g. Aristox. *Harm.* 13.9; 42.13; 43.11) would not fit the present context, another meaning is attested (see e.g. Cleon. *Eis.* 207.10), according to which a note's δύναμις is 'the position of a note within a system' (τάξις φθόγγου ἐν συστήματι).

own specific pitch.[36] But since the specific pitch of a note corresponds to its position within a scalar system,[37] then the notion of composition and *krasis* as applied to the notes, and above all with respect to their reciprocal relationships, just refers to their position within the static structure of a harmonic system. Interestingly enough, this is perfectly consistent with Taurus' example, which implies that the *mesē* is composed on account of the *nētē* and the *hypatē*. While such a claim would be meaningless from a purely acoustic point of view, it makes very good sense if viewed in relation to the position of the three notes in a basic octave, in which the *nētē* (*diezeugmenōn* or *synēmmenōn*) and the *hypatē* (*mesōn*) play the role of boundaries, while the *mesē* in any case occupies an internal, which is to say central, position. This is, of course, quite a simplistic representation of a basic octave, which, however, is paralleled in philosophical (and especially Platonist) texts[38] and has the advantage of depicting the system as being composed by its fundamental notes, which of course are situated within it according to specific numerical ratios corresponding to specific intervals. If this is the case, the underlying idea is that the *mesē* is composed thanks to the *nētē* and the *hypatē* because its position within the system (i.e. its pitch) depends on that of its boundaries, which is to say on the possibility of determining mathematical intervals regulating the distance between the notes of the system. All in all, then, the 'generation' of the notes in a scalar system coincides with the static structure of the system, not resulting from the harmonisation of disharmonic components, but encompassing a series of intrinsic mathematical relations between notes.

The application of this account to the case of the world is not obvious, and it goes beyond the immediate goal of this chapter:[39] it is enough to state that the second meaning represents a structural model according to

[36] See for example the Platonist Aelianus' definition of συμφωνία (Porph. *In Harm.* 35.26–7: συμφωνία δ' ἐστὶ δυεῖν φθόγγων ὀξύτητι καὶ βαρύτητι διαφερόντων κατὰ τὸ αὐτὸ πτῶσις καὶ κρᾶσις). Such use has its bases in technical writings, in which κρᾶσις sometimes describes the production of a concord by two sounds. Also in these cases, however, while the mixture is something 'more' and 'different' with respect to the two notes, its production is still determined by the individual position of each component (see e.g.?Eucl. *Sect. can.* 149.17–24 – I owe this reference to Francesco Pelosi), exploiting this idea in arithmetic terms.

[37] Already according to Aristoxenus' definition (*Harm.* 20.15–17), a note is φωνῆς πτῶσις ἐμμελὴς ἐπὶ μίαν τάσιν; this definition is echoed in the musicological tradition (see e.g. Bacch. *Isag.* 292.15–16 and 306.19–20, Gaud. *Intr. harm.* 329.7–8, Cleon. *Isag. harm.* 179.9–10; with Gibson 2005, 148–52, Rocconi 2009, 191–204).

[38] See for example Plut. *Quaest. Plat.* 1007E-1009B (interpreting *Resp.* 443d5-7), *Quaest. conv.* 744C, Max. Tyr. *Or.* 9.2.

[39] It is not by chance that this meaning of 'generated' is often taken not to be applicable to the specific case of the world (see e.g. Baltes 1976, 109–12, Dillon 1977, 242–6, Karamanolis 2006, 180–4, Ferrari 2012, 106–10). See, however, Petrucci 2018a, 26–75.

which the world can be said to be non-temporally generated, that is a model through which one can describe the internal structure of the world. At the same time, however, it is important to note that the musical structure referred to here is much more than a mere example: Taurus is not just referring to harmony in vague and generic terms, but is drawing from it quite a precise structural model for the interaction of different components. Indeed, through this reference to harmonic structures and the use of the related language (e.g. terms like *krasis*), Taurus is basically claiming that the internal structure of the world is comparable to that of a harmonic system in which each note has its own specific position, with the various components playing different roles, determined by numerical ratios. Therefore, the world has the specifically harmonic arrangement of a static composition of parts, whose order is ensured by reciprocal structural relationships. There is also more to this, however, for the reciprocal bond between these components must be mathematically established. Indeed, what ensures that the harmonic structure of a system is such is the complex web of mathematical relationships between the notes, which is expressed through specific ratios. This point granted, it is clear that there is no need for any external intervention on the notes in order to produce the system, for all notes will be related to each other through the numerical values they represent, and the ratios which this allows them to establish. To put it differently: if one considers numbers which *are* in a double ratio – such as 2, 4, 8, 16 – producing a series of specific mutual relationships is an intrinsic feature of such numbers, which does not require any external intervention. This implies that, according to Taurus' formulation, the world's harmonic structure is intrinsically determined, *and* as such does not need any external cause acting as a craftsman.

These conclusions are even more interesting if read against the background of two key assumptions of Taurus' cosmology. First, as is widely known, Taurus is strongly committed to sempiternalism: in his view, there has been no moment in which the world has been generated, which in turn implies that it has always had the structure it intrinsically possesses. Second, in Taurus' account of God's causation with respect to the world as a whole there is no hint at any intervention on his part; rather, Taurus says (T26.10):

> The world can well be said to be generated also because it gets its being from outside, namely according to God (*para tou theou*), on account of whom it is intrinsically ordered (*pros hon kekosmētai*). In this sense, also for those in whose view the world is definitely everlasting, the Moon receives its light

> insofar as this is generated by the Sun: for there has never been a time in which it has not been provided with light by it.

The world does have its own orderly arrangement and structure, and these do depend, to some extent, on God as a cause. However, this does not imply that God determined them at a certain moment by actively intervening in the world: rather, the most one can say is that the world's order is achieved *on account of* God. Strange as all this might seem, these two key aspects of Taurus' cosmology and theology fit very well with the notion of cosmic harmony which has emerged from my analysis of Taurus' second meaning of 'generated' (*genēton*). All in all, these passages produce quite a consistent picture: there has never been a moment in which God arranged the world harmonically; the world intrinsically has a harmonic structure, and its components are arranged – and continue to be arranged – as they are thanks to their internal constitution, and not thanks to any external intervention. From these points a further overall conclusion derives: there is no need for Taurus to envisage God as a craftsman who directly intervenes in the world in order to produce its harmony. To put it the other way round: the only way in which one can claim both the world to be harmonically structured and God not to intervene in it is to conceive cosmic harmony not as a temporal process though which a superior cause mixes up opposing cosmological powers, but as a sempiternal condition of order intrinsically belonging to the world's structure which, being based on stable relations, is self-preserving and intrinsically orderly.

The picture I am drawing is certainly unconventional, but it rests on two argumentative aspects which cannot be disregarded. On the one hand, no extant testimony by Taurus tells us that God directly intervenes in the world as a craftsmanlike cause. He is indeed responsible for the order of the world to some extent ('The world can well be said to be generated … according to God, on account of whom it is intrinsically ordered'), and in this sense he is an efficient cause and the demiurge, but nothing allows us to project onto him any maximalist reading of this causation. On the other hand, Taurus' model of cosmic harmony makes such a maximalist reading entirely superfluous from a philosophical point of view: if the world's constituents have the intrinsic feature of being mutually arranged in an orderly fashion, then no external cause is required to act in order to produce the cosmic harmony. So, any application of a maximalist reading of God's causation to Taurus' model would be both unsubstantiated and – above all – philosophically uncharitable. Ultimately, it would depend only on the projection of a Plutarch- or Numenius-like model onto Taurus.

All this does not mean that my reading does not give rise to any philosophical problems (which I shall get back to soon), and, as noted above, Taurus' view might seem to be somewhat heterodox and isolated. However, a new reading of the Middle Platonist 'handbooks' by Apuleius and Alcinous shows that this is not the case. The notion of cosmic harmony is given relatively little room in these writings, but in both texts it appears in relation to the world soul's structure. In Apuleius' account (*De dog. Plat.* 1.199) the soul actually consists in a harmonic structure:

> So, the substance of this intelligence (*substantiam mentis huius*) is arranged by means of numbers and musical patterns (*numeris et modis*), doubled and multiplied according to operations of increase and augmentation applied both in themselves and to one another; and for this very reason it is the case that the world moves according to music and melody.

The soul's *substance* is thus made up of harmonically arranged numbers and is therefore a mathematical entity, which *because of this* moves the heavens harmonically and can be thought of as the cause of the world's harmony. In the same passage Apuleius also stresses the sempiternal nature of the soul and its cosmological function: the soul is meant to serve the producer God (*subseruire fabricatori deo et praesto esse ad omnia inuenta eius*), and in this sense *it* organises the whole world on behalf of God, the implication being that the world as a whole is harmonic thanks to the ruling power of the soul. Indeed, although Apuleius apparently depicts God as a craftsman, he does so only in some passages in which he quotes Plato's characterisation of him (e.g. at *De dog. Plat.* 1.190–191),[40] while there is no clear reference to the fact that God directly organises the world and makes it harmonic. On the contrary, Apuleius insists on the fact that the providence exerted by God is the primary and superior one, but has no direct application to the material world, which on the contrary is ruled by a secondary and a tertiary providence, exerted by the heavenly bodies and the daemons (*De dog. Plat.* 1.205–206). This is perfectly consistent with the fact that Apuleius translated the pseudo-Aristotelian treatise *De mundo*,

[40] *Sed haec de Deo sentit, quod sit incorporeus. Is unus, ait, ἀπερίμετρος, genitor rerumque omnium exstructor, beatus et beatificus, optimus, nihil indigens, ipse conferens cuncta.* Apuleius' theology is quite controversial, but in general terms I would agree with the interpretation of it recently provided by Finamore 2006 (see also Boys-Stones 2018, 164–5), according to which Apuleius posits only one transcendent God, who is described as both *primus deus* and *mens*, yet acts within the world via intermediaries, namely the soul, the heavenly bodies, and the *daemons*. In the past, alternative (and in my view overcomplicated) interpretations of Apuleius' theology were provided by Dillon 1977, 312–17, and Gersh 1986, 227–325; see also, more recently, Donini 2002 and Moreschini 2015, 226–9. A new interpretation of Apuleius' exegesis of the *Timaeus* has been provided by Hoenig 2018, chapter 3.

which does not entail any reference to God's craftsmanship, and regards him as a *militiae princeps* or as the administrator of a city (*De mund.* 345), who delegates the task of directly determining the world's dynamics to other entities, such as the heavenly bodies (*De mund.* 351–352). This view also emerges at the beginning of the *De genio* (esp. 121–124), in which Apuleius depicts God by stressing the fact that he is completely free from any concern, compulsion, or commitment to anything apart from his own perfect and blessed existence. Such a representation implies that God, while being the cause of the world to some extent, does not commit himself to a direct intervention in it. All in all, the sole references to God's direct intervention in the world are detectable in quotations from – or paraphrases of – Plato, which as such stand in need of interpretation. When Apuleius proposes his own reading of Plato's theology, he does so without ascribing any direct intervention in the world to God. This makes quite good sense in the light of God's characterisation in the *Apologia* (64), where he is portrayed as a craftsman without crafting (*sine opera opifex*). This is particularly interesting, for one can discover here the peculiar tension characterising (Taurus' and) Apuleius' account: God is indeed the cause why the sempiternal world is as it is, and in this sense he is a demiurge (something on which all Platonists would agree); however, in this reading he is *sine opera*, hence deprived of any commitment to the direct shaping of the world.

I cannot further expand on this point in the present paper,[41] but it is clear that, if God is in principle preserved from any action upon, or plan for, the world, then another entity will be in charge of this, namely the world soul. And indeed, as we have seen, Apuleius explicitly states that the world soul – and the heavenly bodies, whose motions are dictated by the world soul – allows the world to be harmonic, being itself harmonic. One could argue that all this has a limited impact, for the soul – as said above – exercises some of the functions which in other models are ascribed to God. Even if this were the case, the result would be significant: God would be in any case deprived of his direct craftsmanlike causation, and his overall representation would strongly change – that is, one would go from a maximalist to a minimalist causal account of God's action as such. However, what we have is no mere transfer of functions, for the soul's harmony does not consist in any mixture, or conciliation between opposite powers: as we have seen, Apuleius regards the soul as having a mathematical, which is to say harmonic, essence, as it is made up of musical numbers and patterns (*numeris et modis*). As a matter of

[41] For a more extensive discussion see Petrucci 2018a, 76–145.

fact, if the *soul* is harmonic in nature, then providing the *world* with harmony has nothing to do with any planned and intentional action. The passage quoted above clearly indicates that the soul exerts his organising role thanks to its harmonic structure (*et hinc fieri ut musice mundus et canore moueatur*). In other worlds, the fact of being a harmonic entity is a necessary and sufficient condition for the soul to organise the world. If this is the case, however, the soul is not intentionally crafting the world: on the contrary, it orders the world by being what it is, that is, a harmonic entity. The point, therefore, is not just that a feature which is usually ascribed to God – that is, providence – is now transferred to the soul. Rather, the point is that, in Apuleius' account, the soul is essentially a mathematical and harmonic entity, and this perfectly tallies with the fact that Apuleius does not ascribe any kind of external intervention upon the world to God, or any role of *crafting* the world to the soul.[42] Thus, Apuleius' notion of cosmic harmony plays a crucial role in determining the kind of causality which can be ascribed to God and the soul. Indeed, on the one hand Apuleius can regard God as a craftsman without crafting, deprived of any craftsmanship, because the soul as a lower divine entity is in charge of directly determining the world's harmony; on the other, the soul can achieve this task just by being what it is, that is a mathematical, which is to say harmonic, entity whose harmony is automatically transmitted to the world.

Those of Taurus and Apuleius are not the sole cases in which such a perspective emerges: as further confirmation I shall briefly mention Alcinous' account of cosmic harmony.[43] In the fourteenth chapter of the *Didaskalikos*,[44] devoted to the world soul, Alcinous explains the soul's cosmological function by referring to the astronomical order which it

42 The claim that the soul exerts providence does not imply craftsmanship, just as in principle providence does not imply craftsmanship: as is widely known, it is a common Peripatetic view that the heavenly realm is ruled by providence, even though God is never credited with craftsmanship. For a discussion and an overview of relevant sources, see Petrucci 2018a, 104–10 and 123–6. Rather interestingly – as stated above – the threefold model of providence upheld by Apuleius is ascribed to Aristotle by Atticus (fr. 8.9–17; see Mansfeld 1992, 136–8) and apparently lies in the background of Alexander's theory of providence (see Sharples 2003).

43 For a more extensive analysis of Alcinous' model of divine causation, see Petrucci 2018a, 99–104. A more controversial case is presented by Maximus of Tyre, who refers to God as a harmoniser in *Oration* 41.2. Reydams-Schils 2017 has argued that here Maximus regards this harmonising task as ensuring divine craftsmanship, but I do not think this is the case (see Petrucci 2018a, 96–9). At the same time, I will happily take the opportunity to correct footnote 76 on p. 133 of my book: contrary to what my phrasing may suggest, Reydams-Schils 2017 does refer to *Or.* 8 and 11 (on the interpretation of which we diverge, though), although the central text for her purpose is explicitly said to be *Or.* 41 (p. 126).

44 On Alcinous' theological and cosmological model see esp. Loenen 1956, 314–19, Mansfeld 1971, 61–7, Donini 1988, Opsomer 2005b, 79–83, Boys-Stones 2018, 151–2 and 164.

shapes, and then emphasises that this order depends on its mathematical and numerical structure, revealing a harmonic arrangement (169.42–170.14, transl. Dillon):

> It is clear, then, that the world would be a living thing and possessed of intellect; for in wishing to make it best, it follows that God endowed it with both a soul and an intellect, for the ensouled product is in general superior to the soulless, and the intelligent to that which lacks intelligence (the intelligence, we must presume, being unable to exist without soul). Now, since the soul is extended from the centre to the outer limits, the result is that it binds together and encloses all around the body of the world, so that it is co-extended with the whole world, and in this way it binds and holds it together, though its exterior parts have dominance over its interior ones. For the outer (circuit) remained undivided, while the inner was split six ways, into seven circles, according to double and triple intervals (*kata diplasia kai triplasia diastēmata*). That part which is enclosed by the sphere which remained undivided is akin to sameness, while that which is divided is akin to otherness.

Here the hint at cosmic harmony is even slighter, but nonetheless it is clearly implied by Alcinous' reference to double and triple intervals determining the heavens' constitution. So, the notion of cosmic harmony is once again related to the mathematical structure which the soul is provided with, and which in turn regulates the world's dynamics. Now, scholars have authoritatively demonstrated that Alcinous' first God does not exert any craftsmanship (see esp. 10.164.18–27):[45] indeed, Alcinous regards the first God as activating the lower God by remaining unmoved (*akinētos*), just as the Sun is the reason why one's sight can act, and accomplishes this task by making the second God and his soul refer to him (*pros* himself). This means that the direct achievement of the world's order is to be ascribed to another entity, which is of course the world soul and its intellect, that is, the intracosmic God (see esp. 10.164.22–27 and 41, 10.165.3 and 14.169.38). But in this way we are back to the idea that no craftsmanship is needed on the part of the world soul in order to ensure this harmony, for the soul is intrinsically a mathematical and harmonic entity, and because of this very feature the soul determines the world's harmony.

While each stage of the narrative I have been developing would merit a more in-depth examination, already the present analysis suffices to reveal, if not what God's causality is for Taurus, Apuleius and Alcinous, what features *can* be ascribed to God based on the notion of cosmic harmony

[45] See above all Donini 1988 and Opsomer 2005b, 81.

just outlined. Independently of the specific arrangement of Taurus', Apuleius' or Alcinous' theological hierarchies, a strictly mathematical notion of cosmic harmony allows all of these authors to avoid a fundamental aspect of Plutarch's and Numenius' theology, namely God's direct intervention in the world and its crafting – or, in the terms I mentioned in Section 3.2, a maximalist reading of God's causation. For if the world, either in itself or thanks to its soul, is conceived as a sempiternal orderly structure intrinsically entailing harmony, then there is no longer any need to represent God as a harmoniser craftsman resorting to a strictly artisanal form of causation, or planning, in order to produce or preserve its harmonic structure. On the contrary, once one conceives the notion of cosmic harmony in terms of a stable mathematical structure and inserts it within a sempiternalist cosmogony, in order to ensure the world's order *as a fact* there is no need for God's intervention at all, for the harmonic structure will be intrinsically able to persist and regulate the world. To be clear, the point is not that it is inconceivable for God to craft a world which is sempiternal and stable. The point is, rather, twofold: on the one hand, the mathematical – that is, harmonic – description of the world's (and the world soul's) intrinsic constitution and structure, devoid of any internal opposition between disharmonic components, makes any direct crafting by God entirely superfluous; on the other hand, within a sempiternalist model, there is no need for this stable structure to have a starting point, for it has always been in existence. This, then, is the crux of the matter: a mathematical conception of cosmic harmony, far from being a mere exegetical tool, is here crucial in order to justify the world's order without committing oneself to a maximalist conception of God's causation.[46]

3.6 Middle Platonist Models of Cosmic Harmony and Their Theological Import

At this point we have moved beyond a broad idea of cosmic harmony and have discovered two ways in which Middle Platonists philosophically conceived it. On the one hand, harmony is a model ensuring that

[46] Interestingly, the idea of a sempiternal cosmic harmony separated from divine craftsmanship seems to emerge also outside the Platonist tradition, namely in the Hellenistic Peripatos. Philo of Alexandria extensively quotes Critolaus in his *De aeternitate mundi*, and at some point (75; on this passage and its identification as stemming from Critolaus see Sharples 2010, 177–9), when referring to the eternity of the world, Critolaus apparently refers to the world's harmony. This, of course, must be conceived within the framework of a Peripatetic cosmology, which excludes any craftsmanship.

a dualistic cosmology can really bring about a harmonic world and that this process of harmonisation be realised by a harmoniser God. This is a *dynamic conception of cosmic harmony*, which involves the direct harmonisation of dishomogeneous components and marginalises mathematical aspects of the final product (at least, at first). This conception of harmony is exploited by Plutarch and Numenius in the framework of a maximalist conception of God's causation, that is, one which ascribes to God a direct crafting of the constituents at issue. On the other hand, a mathematical conception can be recovered and exploited when framed within a sempiternalist perspective, for in this case it proves effective in order to avoid such a maximalist reading in favour of a minimalist one: God is indeed responsible for the world's constitution and harmony, but he can play this role without directly crafting the world, for instance as the reason for the goodness of the world's intrinsic arrangement and its dynamics.[47] Thus, these different notions of harmony also single out different notions of craftsmanship. While a minimalist notion, simply implying that God has some causal role with respect to the world, can be detected in Middle Platonists such as Taurus, Apuleius, and Alcinous, the maximalist and stronger notion which is implied by Plutarch and Numenius' idea of cosmic harmony *is distinctive* of their models: in order to ensure that kind of cosmic harmony, God must directly intervene on the opposite components of the world and exert a form of planning that regulates their mix. In this scenario, cosmic harmony is neither an image nor a metaphor. Rather, in both cases it represents a structural model for the arrangement of the world (respectively, indicating the need for the dynamic production of a harmonic mix, or pointing out the stable mathematical arrangement of a harmonic system). In this sense, it is key to ensure the internal consistency of the cosmologies at issue.

[47] For an extensive treatment of this conception I must refer to Petrucci 2018a, chapter 3.

CHAPTER 4

Alexander of Aphrodisias and Musical Models for Ontological Enquiries

Laura M. Castelli

4.1 Introduction

At different places in his writings, Alexander develops some (often far from perspicuous) hints by Aristotle about whether and to what extent a certain approach to *harmonia* and *symphōnia* can be used as a model for the ontological analysis of other beings. Most Aristotelian texts in which such hints can be found occur in contexts where Aristotle discusses the doctrines of other philosophers, who make numbers the principles of things that are. Within the discussion of such doctrines, *harmonia* or *symphōnia* are singled out as paradigmatic cases in which such an approach to the principles of being seems to deliver plausible results: *harmonia* and *symphōnia* indeed seem to be objects whose nature and properties are determined by the numbers that define them. For the sake of brevity, I shall refer to this approach as the *harmonia*-model.

Aristotle discusses at least two different approaches making of numbers the principles of things that are: the approach of the Pythagoreans and that of the Academic supporters of ideal numbers. In order to appreciate Alexander's stance, it may be helpful to briefly recall the main features of both approaches and of Aristotle's criticism. Somewhat simplifying, according to Aristotle the Pythagoreans spell out the claim that numbers (and their principles) are principles of things that are by making numbers (and, a fortiori, their constitutive elements) the constitutive principles of physical objects. This approach, focusing on the constituents of physical objects, suggests to Aristotle that the Pythagoreans tend to regard numbers and their principles as the material cause of physical objects.[1] Among the problems of such a view, Aristotle stresses that the Pythagorean principles are not suitable as the matter of physical objects in

[1] Arist. *Metaph.* A5.985b23-986b8, M6.1080b16-21, M8.1083b8-19.

that they are too abstract and cannot explain the fact that physical objects have the properties they have.[2] The Pythagoreans, however, are right insofar as they have realised that, if numbers are to play any role as the causes and principles of objects in this world, they must be immanent in them.[3] The supporters of ideal numbers, on the other hand, think of ideal numbers not so much as the matter of objects in this world, but (in Aristotle's philosophical framework) as their formal causes. Among the problems which make the doctrine of ideal numbers implausible, Aristotle stresses that forms cannot be separate from the objects whose forms they are supposed to be.[4] However, Aristotle suggests at various places that there might be something to be said in favour of the idea that, if numbers play any role at all in the ontology of things in this world, they do so by contributing, in some sense to be specified, to their formal determination. This is particularly true if one spells out the claim that numbers are principles of things that are by saying that the ratios of numbers (e.g. 2:1, 3:2), rather than simple numbers (e.g. 4, 7, 10), are principles.[5]

This description is not fully accurate, in that Aristotle seems to think that both the Pythagoreans and the Platonists endorse more complex (if possibly incoherent) positions. In particular, the Pythagoreans also happen to have been the first to touch upon formal causes, if only in too abstract a fashion,[6] while at least some Academic accounts of numbers conflate the notion of number as the plurality of units constituting the matter of numbers and the notion of number as a unitary form.[7] These

[2] Arist. *Metaph.* A8.989b29-990a29, N3.1090a30-35.

[3] Arist. *Metaph.* M8.1083b8-11, N3.1090a20-31.

[4] See, for example, *Metaph.* N3.1090a29-b5. Aristotle criticizes extensively various versions of the Academic doctrines of numbers and mathematical entities in *Metaph.* M-N. That forms cannot be separate from the objects whose forms they are is a recurrent argument directed against the philosophy of Plato and, more generally, of the Academy.

[5] The two options are clearly distinguished in *Metaph.* N5.1092b8-25, where the idea that the ratio of material components spells out what a blend is fares significantly better than the idea that simple numbers tell what things are. For the idea that quantitative proportions in terms of excess and defect may at least contribute to convey what things are, cf. *Metaph.* H2.1042b24-25 and b34–35.

[6] *Metaph.* A5.987a20-28 and M4.1078b21-23; cf. Z11.1036b7-20; see also the somewhat ambiguous remark in A5.986a16-17 that the Pythagoreans take numbers to be principles 'both as matter . . . and as affections and dispositions' (καὶ ὡς ὕλην . . . καὶ ὡς πάθη τε καὶ ἕξεις); 986b4-8, on the other hand, stresses the difficulty of assigning a precise causal role to Pythagorean principles, but the fact that the Pythagoreans think of their principles as constitutive of substances suggests that they envisage them in terms of matter. Note that Alexander (*in Metaph.* 41.21–42.17) takes the claim in A5.986a16-17 in the sense that the affections of numbers turn out to be the causes of the coming about of the affections of other beings as a sort of efficient cause of them (41.23: ὡς ποιητικὸν αἴτιον). In this way Alexander deflates the 'formal' aspects of the Pythagorean approach which Aristotle emphasizes and turns the Pythagorean approach into a basically materialistic one.

[7] This can be seen in the ambiguity haunting at least some Academic doctrines of the one (e.g. *Metaph.* M8.1084b18-32). For those who enquire into the nature of the one from the perspective of mathematics, the one is identified with the unit, which is a repeatable entity that constitutes numbers. For

complications, however, remain out of the picture as far as Alexander is concerned (although, as we shall see in Section 4.4, they might play some role in the broader narrative on the reception of Pythagorean elements within the Peripatetic and the Platonic tradition). In fact, the two above-mentioned accounts of the sense in which numbers can be said to be principles of things that are – either by being their matter and constitutive elements or by being their separate form – are the two poles between which Alexander moves.

There would be an obvious intermediate position between these two extremes for the Aristotelian philosopher who really wanted to endorse the claim that numbers are principles of beings: one could say that they are immanent formal determinations.[8] However, if one is Aristotelian enough to endorse the principle that no non-substance can be a principle of substances and to accept the ontology of the *Categories*, in which numbers and other quantities are not substances, it may turn out that numbers and quantitative determinations simply cannot figure among the principles of being in the first place, because they cannot be principles of substance. In fact, as I shall argue in the next sections, the general issue of whether and in what way numbers and quantitative determinations can play a role in the explanation of the structure of being turns out to be the pivotal issue in the discussion about whether and in what way the *harmonia*-model is a valuable one. And it is precisely by tracking the different takes on this fundamental metaphysical issue that one can outline the basic divides between philosophical schools (i.e. the Pythagorean, Platonist and Peripatetic) and within the Peripatetic tradition itself with regard to the applicability of the *harmonia*-model in ontological investigations.

4.2 *Harmonia*, *Symphōnia* and the Quantitative Determination of a Certain Substrate

The image of Pythagorean philosophy that emerges from Alexander's writings is an odd mixture of poetry and investigation of natural phenomena. The elements of poetry are spelled out in Alexander's commentary on Aristotle's *Metaph.*[9] A5.985b23-986a21 (Alex. *in Metaph.* 37.6–42.17). To

those who enquire ἐκ τῶν λόγων the one turns out to be a general predicate which is said of all things that are. But one cannot ascribe both properties to the same item. For a discussion of this problem see Castelli 2018, esp. notes on chapters 1 and 2.

[8] At the present stage I am introducing this merely as a theoretical option. I shall later return to the question of whether anybody in the Peripatetic tradition actually endorsed this view.

[9] See Alex. *in Metaph.* 42.15–17. Note that, more generally, the use of *symphōnia* to account for temperance as a disposition of the soul becomes, in Aristotle's and Alexander's hands, the typical example of a mistake (i.e. the mistake of using language metaphorically in accounting for or

start with, Alexander unfolds the train of thought that leads the Pythagoreans to see in numbers and their principles the principles of all things that are. We can distinguish three phases. Firstly, the Pythagoreans believe that it is possible to detect (Alex. *in Metaph.* 37.22–23: *edokoun … horan*) and select (39.18: *eklegontes*) some similarities (e.g. 37.22: *homoiōmata*; 39.18: *homoiotētas*) between the properties of numbers and those of other things: for example (38.10–16), being mutual and equal is a feature of justice but also one of numbers that are obtained by multiplying a number 'an equal number of times' (i.e. by multiplying a number by itself – for example, 2 × 2 or 3 × 3). Secondly, the Pythagoreans assume that 'in each case the primary thing among those that have the same account is that which is said to be [*scil.* what those other things, too, are said to be] in the highest degree' (38.12–14). For example, if we take the property of being 'the same number an equal number of times', four is the first number to satisfy this property.[10] For this reason it is also said to be what is mutual and equal in the highest degree. Thirdly, the number which is identified as the primary object to which a certain account applies is then taken to be the basic constituent of the objects that fall under the same account: other things that have the same properties as a given number have those properties because that number inhabits them and constitutes them. In this sense, numbers turn out to be the matter of other beings and what is causally responsible for their properties (41.19–26; 42.11–15).[11]

Alexander gives a long list of the alleged similarities between the properties of things and the properties of numbers selected by the Pythagoreans. Just to mention a couple of examples, five is the number of marriage since marriage is the union of male and female, the male is identified with the odd, the female with the even, the first odd number is three, the first even number is two, and the union of three and two gives five (39.8–13). Seven is the number of Athena because seven is not generated by nor generates any other number in the decad, just as

explaining something in a scientific or philosophical context); see, for example, Alex. *in Top.* 324.9–15 *ad* Arist. *Top.* 4.3.123a33-37 (cf. Alex. *in Top.* 425.25–426.5 *ad* Arist. *Top.* 6.2.139b32-33) and Alex. *in Top.* 511.12–13 *ad* Arist. *Top.* 7.4.154a20-21. About Aristotle's condemnation of the use of metaphors in philosophical or scientific discourse, see *Metaph.* A9.991a20-22, M5.1079b25-26, *Meteor.* 2.3.357a24-28.

10 Or nine, for those who prefer to choose the square of the first odd number.

11 Steps two and three are mentioned by Aristotle in a different context in *Metaph.* A5.987a20-28, where he praises the Pythagoreans for their rudimentary efforts to grasp the formal cause of things (cf. n.6 above). For Aristotle the steps consist in identifying the primary object that responds to a certain account and in claiming that that object turns out to be the substance of the other things to which the account applies.

Athena is *amētōr* (being born out of Zeus' head, she does not have a mother) and *parthenos* (the virgin goddess who does not beget any children) (39.3–8). Alexander condemns these pieces of Pythagorean philosophy as mere fiction.[12]

Next to these rather far-fetched similarities, however, Alexander emphasizes that there are some cases in which the identification of things with numbers is based on more solid ground, in that some components or aspects of the things at issue can be measured. This is, in particular, the case with *harmoniai*, whose accounts (*logoi*) and affections (*pathē*) are 'in numbers' (38.1–2; 39.19–22; cf. 41.25–26). This is singled out as a paradigmatic case, in which the nature and properties of an object which is not an abstract number can be explained in terms of numbers and of the numerical proportions between its constituents. For example, the octave is identified with the ratio 2:1, the fifth with 3:2 and the fourth with 4:3.

As to the constituents that are measured and allow the 'reduction' or the 'leading back' of *harmoniai* to numbers, we find some more details in Alexander's commentary on *Top.* 1.15.107a13-17 (Alex. *in Top.* 106.20–107.11). In *Top.* 1.15.107a3 ff. Aristotle is spelling out a move one can make in order to check whether a linguistic expression is used equivocally: one should check whether the genera of the predicates, which are used to explain what a certain expression indicates when used with reference to different things, differ. If so, the expression is said in several ways. Aristotle illustrates this point by means of various examples, one of which is the use of *oxy* ('sharp', 'keen', 'piercing', 'acute') when used with reference to vocal sound (*phōnē*) by 'the students of harmonics concerning numbers' (*hoi peri tous arithmous harmonikoi*)[13] and when used with reference to an angle (*gōnia*). In the first case, Aristotle says, *oxy* means that the vocal sound is 'fast' (*tacheia*), in the second case that the angle is smaller than a right angle. Alexander expands significantly on the approach of *hoi peri tous arithmous harmonikoi.*

> [T1] In a similar way one would show that *oxy* is homonymous: for not all things of which it is predicated fall under the same genus. For the *oxy* which is in vocal sound falls under <the category of> acting (*poiein*), if in truth a sharp vocal sound is the one that is fast: for such an impact and such a vocal

[12] See n. 9 above.

[13] Brunschwig opts for the alternative and more intelligible locution οἱ κατὰ τοὺς ἀριθμοὺς ἁρμονικοί, 'the students of harmonics based on numbers' or 'according to numbers'. Alexander spells out (106.24–27) that these are the Pythagoreans who are most trained in mathematical sciences and reduce everything to numbers.

> sound cuts through and divides the air fast – for its motion is fast. In fact, the students of harmonics based on numbers – and these are those among the Pythagoreans who train in mathematics the most; and the students of harmonics based on numbers are those who produce harmonies according to a composition of numbers: for, in leading all things back to numbers, they lead back harmonies as well (οὗτοι δέ εἰσι τῶν Πυθαγορείων οἱ μάλιστα περὶ τὰ μαθήματα γεγυμνασμένοι· περὶ τοὺς ἀριθμοὺς δὲ ἁρμονικοὶ οἱ τὰς ἁρμονίας κατὰ σύνθεσιν ἀριθμῶν ποιοῦντες· πάντα γὰρ ἀνάγοντες εἰς τοὺς ἀριθμοὺς καὶ τὰς ἁρμονίας ἀνῆγον) – these, then, say that sounds (*psophoi*), to which vocal sounds (*phōnai*) belong, come about when there occurs an impact against the air and a motion of the air is caused by it. And when the motion that occurs is fast and stands in a certain numerical proportion (*en arithmōn analogiāi toiāide*), the sound is sharp (*oxy*); and such a [107] motion comes about because of the vehemence of the impact. If, on the other hand, the motion is slow, the sound is deep, just as if the motion of the air is sudden and of a great quantity, the sound is also great and vehement, whereas if it [*scil.* the motion] is gentle and of small quantity, the sound, too, is quiet and small. If, then, moving the air fast is <a sort of> acting, and the sharp (*oxy*) vocal sound is such in that it moves the air fast, it will be such in that it is <a sort of> acting. The *oxy* with reference to an angle, instead, indicates a relative: for what is less belongs in <the category of> what is relative; for it is less than something; and it is the angle that is less than a right angle that is called 'acute angle'.[14]

In comparison with Alexander's commentary on *Metaph.* A5, two points are worth emphasizing in [T1]. First, here, too, the account of *harmoniai* in terms of numbers is presented as part of a more complex project of 'leading things back' to numbers. With respect to this project, the *harmoniai* provide the paradigm for a general model of explanation. Second, the account of *harmoniai* based on numbers relies on the quantitative analysis of some components of sound – in particular, on the measurement of the speed of the motion of air caused by an impact.[15] On this account, not only pitch but also volume are the perceptible outcomes of measurable parameters in the physical constitution of sound. Note that according to this view the use of numbers in the account of various features of sounds does not rely on more or less loose similarities between the properties of sounds and those of numbers, but rather rests on the possibility of measuring some of the physical components of sound. The basic idea is that quantitative features

[14] Translations are mine unless otherwise indicated.

[15] Note that this is not the only way in which one can make sense of the numbers associated with the various intervals: one could, for example, bring in the length of the vibrating body (e.g. the string) that produces the different pitches.

are taken to be ontologically more basic and explanatory of all other features. Note, en passant, that sounds for Aristotle (and for Alexander) are not substances: in principle the problems mentioned at the end of Section 4.1 do not touch the application of the *harmonia*-model to its paradigmatic case.

Between the 'reduction' to numbers based on more or less loose similarities and the reduction to numbers based on the application of the measurement of physical components, Alexander lingers on a third type of case exemplified by the account of the structure of the universe (39.22 ff.). The way in which Alexander spells out this example is quite interesting and revealing of a general strategy. According to the Pythagoreans the universe is a number – Alexander glosses – in the sense that it is composed 'according to *harmonia*' (*kata harmonian*: 39.22–24): the distances of the celestial bodies from the centre around which they revolve stand to one another in determinate proportions, as do the respective speeds at which they move. By moving, each of them produces a sound whose pitch corresponds to the speed at which it moves. The result is the music of the spheres (40.1: *enharmonion ... ēchon*). Alexander's reaction to this account is revealing: Alexander may well agree that the structure of celestial spheres is 'according to proportion' (*kata logon*), but he follows his master in rejecting the idea that the result of this composition is, among other things, a *harmonia*, an attunement strictly speaking, and that the spheres produce some sound according to it. What is obtained cannot be said to be a *harmonia*, but, at most, something that is composed 'according to number and *harmonia*' (*kat'arithmon kai harmonian*: 39.24).

The arguments Aristotle advances in *de Cael.* B9 in order to deny the existence of the music of the spheres are not very impressive. They can be reduced to the point that, if the spheres produced such a sound in their movements, we would notice it (either because we would hear it or because it would be so loud that stones would break). This is likely to be what Alexander had in mind – among other things – when writing his commentary on *Metaph.* A5. However, he may also have some more sophisticated views of his own about the possibility and the limited application of the *harmonia*-model. In his *De anima*, while refuting the thesis that the soul is a harmony, Alexander specifies what criteria must be met in order to properly speak of a *harmonia*:

> [T2] Someone might deny that a proportion is a harmony whenever things are mixed in a certain proportion, since the proportion of 2:1 is not a harmony when it occurs in wine and honey. For there is harmony in a specific kind of composition of melodies and rhythms, not in just any random thing or in any random proportion. But the mixture of hot, cold,

> dry, and moist things – that is, the mixture of elements that the soul is a form of – is not constituted by a determinate proportion. For the same soul persists even when the powers in a mixture are tightened or slackened to a certain extent. For if someone were to say that in general the mixture of just any thing in some proportion is a harmony, this would commit one to saying that everything composed is in harmony, since some proportion is to be found in every composed thing. In contrast, the soul would be a harmony, or a harmonious composition of certain bodies, rather for those who make the soul out of a specific kind of mixture and composition of things.[16]

In this text Alexander voices some reservations about the unrestricted use of the terminology of *harmonia* whenever one is describing a composite object made of determinate amounts of different components. A *harmonia* comes to be once sounds stand in determinate ratios to one another; both the numerical ratios required for a *harmonia* and the substrates carrying the numerical determinations that enter the ratios are subject to restrictions and must be qualified appropriately. The general idea is that, in order to apply the *harmonia*-model, one has to consider both the numerical values figuring in the ratios and the subjects of which those numerical values are quantitative determinations.

While the passage clearly states that one cannot apply the *harmonia*-model in such a way that everything turns out to be a *harmonia*, it does not tell us much about whether and how the *harmonia*-model can be generalized in such a way that things can be analyzed as being more or less complex compounds of certain amounts of material components. The idea that this procedure could be generalized, however, is picked up in another text, namely Alexander's commentary on Aristotle's *Metaph.* A9.991b13-21. In this passage, Aristotle considers the view that ideal numbers are causes of things not in the sense that simple numbers (e.g. two, three, five) are

[16] Alex. *De Anima* 25.19–26.15 (transl. Caston, modified): λέγοι δ' ἄν τις μηδὲ πάντων τῶν κατὰ λόγον τινὰ μιγνυμένων ἁρμονίαν εἶναι τὸν λόγον. οὐ γὰρ ἁρμονία (5) ὁ διπλάσιος λόγος, ὅταν ἐν οἴνῳ καὶ μέλιτι ᾖ. ἐν γὰρ ποιᾷ συνθέσει μελῶν τε καὶ ῥυθμῶν ἡ ἁρμονία, ἀλλ' οὐ τῶν τυχόντων οὐδὲ κατὰ τὸν τυχόντα γινομένη λόγον. πᾶσα μὲν γὰρ ἁρμονία ἐν ὡρισμένῳ λόγῳ. οὐκ ἐν ὡρισμένῳ δὲ λόγῳ ἡ τῶν θερμῶν τε καὶ ψυχρῶν καὶ ξηρῶν καὶ ὑγρῶν μῖξις, τουτέστιν ἡ τῶν στοιχείων, ἧς μίξεως εἶδος ἡ ψυχή. ἡ γὰρ αὐτὴ (10) ψυχὴ μένει καὶ ἐπιτεινομένων καὶ ἀνιεμένων ἕως τινὸς τῶν ἐν τῇ μίξει δυνάμεων. ὅλως γὰρ εἰ λέγοι τις ἁρμονίαν τὴν τῶν τυχόντων μῖξιν κατὰ λόγον τινά, συμβήσεται τούτῳ πάντα τὰ συγκείμενα ἡρμόσθαι λέγειν. εὑρεθήσεται γάρ τις λόγος ἐν πᾶσιν τοῖς συγκειμένοις. μᾶλλον δὲ κατὰ τοὺς τὴν ψυχὴν γεννῶντας ἐκ ποιᾶς μίξεώς τε καὶ συνθέσεώς τινων εἴη ἂν ἡ ψυχὴ ἤτοι ἁρμονία ἢ σύνθεσις καθ' ἁρμονίαν τινῶν σωμάτων. I have modified Caston's translation at l. 26.10, ἐπιτεινομένων καὶ ἀνιεμένων: I keep the musical connotation and translate 'tightened or slackened', whereas Caston translates 'strengthened or weakened'. I would like to thank Dominic O'Meara for drawing my attention to the musical terminology in this passage.

causes, but in the sense that the ratios of numbers are.[17] Alexander's commentary on this point is worth reading in full because Alexander does not confine himself to illustrating Aristotle's criticism but also sketches out a sort of counterfactual scenario in which he makes it clear how one should apply the paradigm of the analysis of *symphōnia* if one wanted to apply it correctly (and not as the Platonists do).

> [T3] Now he takes up the point that the Platonists do not say that the things in this world are numbers, but that they consist in some ratio of numbers, and that this is what they wish to assert; and he shows that not even in this way the Ideas and those eternal numbers can be causes for the things in this world that exist in a ratio of numbers. Wishing to show what it means to say that the things in this world are ratios of numbers, he adds the example of the concord; for a concord is not a number but some ratio of numbers, i.e. certain things having a numerical ratio to one another. For to be in a proportion of 2:1 is to be in a ratio of numbers, precisely that which the concord of the octave has because its being consists in this ratio; and again, the being of another concord consists in turn in the proportion 4:3, and again, that of another concord in turn in the proportion 3:2, and these are ratios of numbers. Not even if one were to say that all the things that are are ratios of numbers – the Ideas and the <ideal> numbers will not be causes for these things, not even in this way; for in that case, numbers will no longer be over those things. For if the things in this world are certain ratios of numbers, there are obviously certain things in them possessing this ratio in which each of them has its being, just as a concord, being a ratio of numbers, has a certain substrate and some underlying nature of which the concord is the definition and formula; and this substrate is sound. If then the things said to have their being by reference to the Forms are in a ratio of numbers, there is some substrate in them which, by receiving the ratio of numbers, becomes at one time man, at another time something else, becoming different things at different times in accordance with the different ratios, as <there are different> concords because of the difference of ratios in their sounds. But this thing <that receives the different ratios> will be found to be nothing other than the substrate and the matter, in the particular number and ratio of which each of the things that are will be, e.g. in the ratio of fire or air or water or earth or of whatever the particular thing might be; for it is in the ratio of these things to one another that the things <composed> out of them have their being and receive a form.[18]

[17] Arist. *Metaph.* A9.991b13-16: εἰ δ' ὅτι λόγοι ἀριθμῶν τἀνταῦθα, οἷον ἡ συμφωνία, δῆλον ὅτι ἐστὶν ἕν γέ τι ὧν εἰσὶ λόγοι. εἰ δή τι τοῦτο, ἡ ὕλη, φανερὸν ὅτι καὶ αὐτοὶ οἱ ἀριθμοὶ λόγοι τινὲς (15) ἔσονται ἑτέρου πρὸς ἕτερον. 'And if <numbers are causes> because things in this world are ratios of numbers, as, e.g., the concord, it is clear that the things of which the ratios are are one certain thing. So if this, i.e. the matter, is a certain thing, it is evident that numbers themselves, too, will be certain ratios of something to something else'.

[18] Alex. *in Metaph.* 108.7–109.10 (transl. Dooley, slightly modified): νῦν δὲ πάλιν λαμβάνει τὰ ἐνταῦθα μὴ ἀριθμοὺς εἶναι λέγεσθαι ὑπ' αὐτῶν, ἀλλ' ἐν λόγῳ τινὶ ἀριθμῶν συνεστάναι, ὃ καὶ βούλονται

The gist of the argument is clear: even if one were ready to admit that things that are turn out to be, in some sense, ratios of numbers, saying that these things are ratios of numbers would not genuinely and fully express what they are. For the ratios will obtain between quantities of something (i.e. quantities of some substrate or of some matter). Accordingly, ratios turn out to be ratios between quantitatively determined portions of matter of a determinate nature and not ratios between separate numbers.

This account of what things are in terms of the ratios of material components seems to be, according to Alexander, the way to go if one really wishes to stick to the idea that things are, in some sense, ratios of numbers. It emphasizes that, if numbers have any role to play in determining what things are, they can only do so by being a certain determination of a substrate (already characterized by its own nature) and not by being separate objects to which things in this world mysteriously relate. Alexander's revised account indirectly shows the merits of the Pythagorean position, making numbers something immanent in things. However, it also indirectly shows its limits: for in the refined account – in opposition to the Pythagorean account – numbers are not themselves the principles and *stoicheia* of things;[19] rather, they are numbers *of* material components.[20]

Even if the revised account is not a genuine option as a general account of what determines what things are,[21] some remarks in Alexander's *De Anima* may suggest that he was willing to make room for a limited application of the revised account of the *harmonia*-model.

λέγειν· καὶ δείκνυσιν ὅτι οὐδὲ οὕτως αἱ ἰδέαι καὶ ἐκεῖνοι (10) οἱ ἀριθμοὶ αἴτιοι δύνανται εἶναι τοῖς ἐνθάδε οὖσιν ἐν ἀριθμῶν λόγῳ. βουλόμενος δὲ δεῖξαι τί ἐστι τὸ λέγειν λόγους ἀριθμῶν τὰ ἐνταῦθα εἶναι, παρέθετο τὴν συμφωνίαν· καὶ γὰρ ἡ συμφωνία οὐκ ἀριθμός ἐστιν ἀλλὰ λόγος τις ἀριθμῶν, τουτέστιν πράγματά τινα λόγον ἀριθμῶν πρὸς ἄλληλα ἔχοντα. τὸ γὰρ ἐν διπλασίῳ εἶναι ἐν λόγῳ ἀριθμῶν ἐστιν εἶναι, ὅπερ (15) ἔχει ἡ διὰ πασῶν συμφωνία· ἐν τούτῳ γὰρ αὐτῇ τὸ εἶναι· καὶ αὖ πάλιν ἄλλῃ ἐν ἐπιτρίτῳ, καὶ αὖ πάλιν ἄλλῃ ἐν ἡμιολίῳ, ἃ πάντα ἀριθμῶν εἰσι λόγοι. εἰ δὴ καὶ τὰ ὄντα πάντα λέγοι τις λόγους ἀριθμῶν εἶναι, οὐδὲ οὕτως αἴτιαι αἱ ἰδέαι καὶ οἱ ἀριθμοὶ ἐκεῖνοι τούτοις ἔσονται. εἰ γὰρ τοῦτο, οὐδὲ ἐπ᾽ ἐκείνοις οἱ ἀριθμοὶ ἔτι ἔσονται. εἰ γάρ ἐστι τὰ ἐνταῦθα λόγοι τινὲς ἀριθμῶν, δηλονότι τινά ἐστιν ἐν αὐτοῖς ἃ τὸν λόγον ἔχει τοῦτον ἐν (20) ᾧ ἑκάστῳ αὐτῶν τὸ εἶναι, ὥσπερ ἡ συμφωνία λόγος ἀριθμῶν οὖσα ἔχει [109] τι ἓν ὑποκείμενον καὶ φύσιν τινὰ ὑποκειμένην, ἧς ὁ ὁρισμός ἐστι καὶ λόγος ἡ συμφωνία, καὶ ἔστι τοῦτο οἱ φθόγγοι. εἰ δὴ τὰ πράγματα τὰ πρὸς τὰς ἰδέας λεγόμενα τὸ εἶναι ἔχειν ἐν λόγῳ ἀριθμῶν ἐστιν, ἔστι τι ἐν αὐτοῖς ὑποκείμενον ὃ τὸν τῶν ἀριθμῶν λόγον ἀναδεχόμενον ποτὲ μὲν ἄνθρωπος γίνεται (5) ποτὲ δὲ ἄλλο τι, κατὰ τοὺς διαφέροντας λόγους ἄλλοτε ἄλλο γινόμενον, ὡς ἡ συμφωνία τῇ τῶν ἐν τοῖς φθόγγοις λόγων ἑτερότητι. τοῦτο δὲ οὐκ ἄλλο τι εὑρεθήσεται ὂν ἢ τὸ ὑποκείμενον καὶ ἡ ὕλη, ἧς ἐν ἀριθμῷ καὶ ἐν λόγῳ τινὶ ἕκαστον ἔσται τῶν ὄντων, οἷον πυρὸς ἀέρος ὕδατος γῆς, ἢ ὅ τί ποτε ἂν καὶ ᾖ τοῦτο· ἐν γὰρ τῷ τούτων λόγῳ πρὸς ἄλληλα τὸ εἶναι τοῖς ἐξ αὐτῶν καὶ εἰδοποιεῖσθαι.

[19] See Alex. *in Metaph.* 38.5–8.

[20] See (Ps.-)Alex. *in Metaph.* 813.34–814.10 (*ad* Arist. *Metaph.* N2.1090a2-5).

[21] I shall return to the reasons why this is so below.

> [T4] One should not assume that people who claim that the soul is a form that supervenes on a particular sort of mixture and blend of the bodies underlying it <also> claim that the soul is harmony. For suppose that the soul cannot be separate from this sort of blend and mixture; it does not thereby follow that it is the same as the soul. For the soul is not a particular kind of blend of bodies – which is what a harmony is – but a power that emerges above a particular kind of blend, analogous to the powers of medicinal drugs, which are assembled from a blend of many [ingredients]. For in their case too, the mixture, composition, and proportion of drugs – such that one of them, it might turn out, is 2:1, another 1:2, and another 3:2 – bear some analogy to a harmony.[22]

The wording at the end of the passage is clearly cautious. However, the passage makes room for the idea that to a certain extent the revised *harmonia*-model can be used to talk about substances: one can perhaps use the *harmonia*-model to describe the material substrate on which a power or – as Alexander would put it – a form can supervene. I shall return to the issues that this account raises in Section 4.4.

4.3 *Harmonia*, *Symphōnia* and the Account of the Perceptible Properties of Material Objects

The cases considered in Section 4.2 provide some elements to spell out the claim that numbers are the principles of things with reference to substance-like objects.[23] However, when Aristotle presents other philosophers' views that numbers are the principles of things that are, he occasionally splits up this claim into two complementary claims: numbers are the principles of the nature or substance of things as well as of their properties (*pathē*).[24] In fact, *Metaph.* N5.1092b15-16 even suggests that there might be a specific difficulty as to how one could claim that affections (*pathē*) are numbers – presumably, even if one were ready to

[22] Alex. *de An.* 24.18–27 (transl. Caston): Οὐ δεῖ δὲ ὑπολαμβάνειν τὴν ψυχὴν ἁρμονίαν λέγειν τοὺς λέγοντας αὐτὴν εἶδος εἶναι γινόμενον ἐπὶ τῇ τοιᾷδε μίξει τε καὶ κράσει τῶν ὑπο- (20) κειμένων αὐτῇ σωμάτων. οὐ γὰρ εἰ χωρὶς τῆς τοιαύτης κράσεώς τε καὶ μίξεως ἀδύνατον αὐτὴν εἶναι, ἤδη ταὐτὸν αὐτῇ γίνεται. οὐ γὰρ ἡ τοιάδε τῶν σωμάτων κρᾶσις ἡ ψυχή, ὅπερ ἦν ἡ ἁρμονία, ἀλλ' ἡ ἐπὶ τῇ τοιᾷδε κράσει δύναμις γεννωμένη, ἀνάλογον ἔχουσα ταῖς δυνάμεσιν τῶν ἰατρικῶν φαρμάκων ταῖς ἀθροιζομέναις ἐκ μίξεως πλειόνων. καὶ γὰρ ἐν ἐκείνοις ἡ (25) μὲν τῶν φαρμάκων μῖξίς τε καὶ σύνθεσις καὶ ὁ λόγος, καθ' ὃν τὸ μὲν αὐτῶν διπλάσιόν ἐστι, τὸ δ' ἥμισυ, τὸ δ' ἡμιόλιον, ἂν οὕτω τύχῃ, ἀναλογίαν τινὰ πρὸς ἁρμονίαν ἔχει.

[23] About the status of mixtures and homogeneous compounds as substances, see pp. 102–3.

[24] For example, Arist. *Metaph.* A5.985b32.

concede that substances or substance-like objects are, in some sense or other, numbers. In this section I shall briefly address some of the things Alexander has to say about whether and how the *harmonia*-model can be applied to properties.

The most obvious place to look for such evidence is Alexander's commentary on Aristotle's *De sensu*. In *De sensu* Aristotle proposes an account of ranges of perceptible qualities (colours, flavours, odours, etc.) such that each range is finite and limited by a pair of basic contrary qualities (e.g. black and white) and intermediate qualities in each range are the result of the mixture, in different proportions, of the corresponding contraries. The details of this account are problematic in several respects.[25] One difficulty is that Aristotle's *De sensu* does not include an account of sounds and it is therefore hard to tell to what extent Aristotle's analysis of colours and flavours can be applied to the case of sounds too.[26] Alexander applies the same account to all types of perceptible ranges;[27] in particular, he specifies by what contraries each range of perceptibles is determined and he explicitly sets out a pair (86.10: *oxy kai ambly*) for sounds.[28]

One more basic difficulty is that Aristotle analyzes the constitution of intermediates through the mixture of contraries, but properties are not the kind of things that can mix.[29] More particularly, in *De sensu* 3.439b18 ff., Aristotle distinguishes three different ways to explain how intermediate colours come about: (1) through the juxtaposition of white and black parts; (2) through the overlapping of white and black; (3) through the mixture of white and black. Alexander is even more explicit than Aristotle in claiming that (3) (unlike [1] and [2]) provides a realist account of intermediate colours, giving them a genuine *hypostasis* and *hyparxis* (i.e. objective extramental existence), while (1) and (2) account for a plurality of colours in *phantasia* ('appearance') only.[30] Furthermore, Alexander explicitly recalls Aristotle's account of mixture in *Gen. corr.* 1.10.327b31 ff.[31] and makes it clear that the mixture of colours takes place insofar as the bodies whose

[25] For a detailed reconstruction of the metaphysical claim that all intermediates are made out of the contraries between which they range see my commentary on *Metaph.* I7 in Castelli 2018.

[26] Ross follows Freudenthal in deleting *De Sensu* 4.440b27-28, which contains a reference to Aristotle's treatment of sound and voice in *De Anima*; Alexander (*in de sensu*, 66.9–17) comments on those lines and provides a brief summary of *DA* II.8 without mentioning Aristotle's remarks about *oxy* and *bary* as differences of sounding things in *de An.* 2.8.420a26-b4 and without giving any hint about differences in pitches.

[27] Alex. *in de sensu*, 65.22–66.5 (*ad* Arist. *De Sensu* 3.440b23-25).

[28] Alex. *in de sensu*, 86.7–12.

[29] Arist. *Gen. corr.* 1.10.327b11-22.

[30] Alex. *in de sensu*, 55.6–7, 12–15; 65.4–19.

[31] Alex. *in de sensu* 63.16–65.3.

colours they are mix.[32] This move suggests that the *harmonia*-model can apply to qualities only derivatively, in that it applies to the bodies in which the qualities inhere.

Furthermore, Aristotle (followed by Alexander) tries to explain not only the way in which perceptible properties come about, but also the way in which some properties of those properties (such as being pleasant or unpleasant) come about by resorting to the analysis of concords (*symphōniai*). Alexander significantly expands on Aristotle's claim in *De sensu* 3.439b30 ff. that 'these things are in the same way as in the case of *symphōniai*':

> [T5] And some of the <colours> present will be in a certain ratio and commensurable with each other whilst others will be in a predominance without qualification. Of these those that are in a ratio in their predominance, being commensurable, will be pleasant and soothing, but those that are incommensurable will not be, in a manner analogous to <sounds> in musical concords. For in their case also the differentiation is in accordance with the ratios of the predominance in numbers. One, being as two to one, is called and is *diapasōn*. Another, that of three to four, *diatessarōn*. When the sounds possess no ratio to each other, that which is heard is disharmonious and discordant but is heard nevertheless. The same is true of the colours produced by the juxtaposition of whites and blacks invisible because of smallness. For example, three are juxtaposed and mixed with two, or four with two or three with four, and some are in a proportion whilst others are not. The <colours> put together in a proportion are pleasant, like purple and red and such-like. Those that are startling and unpleasant are not in a proportion. He says that the pleasant <colours> are few for the same cause as there are few sounds which go together harmoniously [. . .].[33]

In none of these passages does Alexander depart from Aristotle, but he clearly shows awareness of the problems involved in the account of *De sensu* and develops a coherent picture of the application of the *harmonia*-model within this framework. An account of qualities in terms of mixture and, therefore, in terms of amounts of components, can only be spelled out with reference to the sole objects that can, strictly speaking, mix and be quantified: bodies.

[32] See in particular Alex. *in de sensu* 65.1–3: [. . .] οὕτω δὴ μιγνυμένων τῶν σωμάτων ἀνάγκη καὶ τὰ χρώματα τὰ ἐν τοῖς σώμασι τοῖς μιγνυμένοις μίγνυσθαι ἀλλήλοις ὅλα δι' ὅλων. 'And so when the bodies are mixed in this way, it is necessary that the colours in the bodies being mixed are mixed with each other by being fully interpenetrated' (Transl. Towey).

[33] Alex. *in de sensu* 54.7–22 (transl. Towey, slightly modified). See more generally Arist. *De sensu* 3.439b25-440a6, 440a12-15, 440b18-23, and Alex. *in de sensu* 54.1–55.8, 55.25–56.5, 65.12–21.

4.4 Alexander, the Pythagoreans, the Platonists and Other Peripatetics

The issue of the applicability of the *harmonia*-model can be read as the specific version of a more general problem: to what extent can an account of the quantitative determinations of beings disclose the structure of reality? In setting up the general problem in these terms, some important features of Alexander's discussion of the use of the *harmonia*-model come to the fore. In particular, it becomes evident that the genuine issues involved in the applicability of this model do not really concern the use of musical language in more or less loose similarities or metaphors. The metaphorical use of language is, for Alexander as well as for Aristotle, at best a form of poetry which should not find any place in philosophical and scientific discourse. I take it that the dismissal of this aspect of the use of the *harmonia*-model would not impress a Platonist who is mainly interested in developing a 'Pythagorean' metaphysics by ascribing a precise causal role to numbers and their principles. In fact, the genuine philosophical issues concerning the application of the *harmonia*-model emerge once philosophers start to spell out the possible ways in which it might be *literally* true that numbers and, more generally, quantitative determinations play a causal role in the structure of reality. In this final section I would like to set Alexander's remarks on the specific issues considered in Sections 4.2 and 4.3 within this broader framework.

In the formulation of the general problem that I have just given at least three distinct issues come together. The first issue concerns the ontological status of numbers: what are numbers and, more generally, mathematical entities? The second issue concerns the categorial status of the forms of substances. The third issue concerns the extent to which categories other than substance resemble substance as a ground to justify the order in which individual categories are discussed in the *Categories* (substance, quantity, relatives, quality, etc.). The first issue is addressed by Aristotle himself, whereas the other two become objects of debate in the post-Aristotelian tradition. In what follows I shall suggest a way in which these three issues may be intertwined in the discussion of the *harmonia*-model and I shall sketch out a somewhat speculative but, in my view, not implausible backdrop against which the texts discussed in Sections 4.2 and 4.3 can be read.

As already mentioned, Aristotle himself discusses the status of mathematical entities at length in the *Metaphysics*. Despite certain difficulties and puzzling aspects, Aristotle's stance on this matter is fairly clear (at least on some basic points). To put it simply: first of all, mathematical entities are not substances. What exists are substances with quantitative determinations. Mathematical objects are thought of as if they were self-subsistent objects resulting from a mental process of separation or 'subtraction' of all other properties.[34] This account of the ontology of quantities, as Alexander emphasizes, does not distinguish Aristotle's position only from the more extreme Platonist positions, assigning to mathematical entities one or more separate ontological domains. It also distinguishes Aristotle's views from any position which, without separating them from physical objects, makes mathematical entities immanent substances.[35] Furthermore, Alexander is committed to the principle that the parts of substances are substances in their turn.[36] This implies that, if mathematical entities are supposed to be quantities, they cannot be parts of substances (i.e. they cannot be the matter, as the Pythagoreans maintain) nor the form (i.e. the immanent forms) of substances. Note that, in this respect, the account in terms of numerical ratios may not fare significantly better than the account in terms of simple numbers. Ratios are relations between numbers, and, if quantitative determinations cannot be the form of substances, it is not that obvious that relations between numbers can. Nothing seems to stand in the way, however, of the application of the revised *harmonia*-model to some non-substances.

Whether Aristotle himself would allow ratios to be forms or to express the substance of (at least some) substances is a complex question. There are texts in which he seems to make room for this possibility. For example, in *Metaph.* N5.1092b16-23 we read the following remark:

> [T6] It is clear that numbers are not substance nor causes of the form: for it is the ratio that is the substance, and the number is matter. For example, number is the substance of flesh or bone in this way: three parts of fire and two of earth. And a number, whatever it is, is always a number of some things, either of fire or of earth or of units; but the substance <of things> consists in there being this much in proportion to this much in the mixture.

34 *Metaph.* M3.1077b17-1078a31. For the language of separation in thought and 'subtraction' (ἀφαίρεσις), see, for example, M2.1077a36-b11.

35 See, for example, Alex. *in Metaph.* 200.35–201.11, where Alexander spells out how Aristotle's position about mathematical entities differs from that of those who make them immanent and yet ascribe them a distinct nature 'over and above perceptible objects'. I suppose Alexander is here referring to the Pythagorean view according to which numbers are constituents of perceptible objects while retaining their own distinct nature. Cf. Alex. *in Metaph.* 198.16–26, where Alexander emphasizes the absurdities following from positing mathematical harmonics as being about some intermediate mathematical entities that are distinct from the quantitative determinations of a certain substrate (something that can produce sound).

36 An extensive discussion of the evidence can be found in Rashed 2007, 35–81.

> And this is no longer a number, but a ratio of a mixture of bodily numbers or of whatever other kind of numbers.[37]

In this passage Aristotle clearly distinguishes between the claim that numbers are the substance and the cause of the forms of things and the claim that a certain numerical ratio between the amounts of material components of a mixture is the substance of the mixture by being its formal determination. The latter claim is not presented as intrinsically problematic.

As is well known, the only authentic section of the commentary on the *Metaphysics* ascribed to Alexander is the commentary on *Metaph.* A–Δ. The later books are probably the work of the Byzantine scholar Michael of Ephesus. Michael, however, tends to compile his commentaries by borrowing material from earlier Greek commentators.[38] In the light of this, it does not seem impossible that Alexander (or, in any case, someone more cautious than Aristotle himself) was Michael's source.

> [T7] Enquiring into number in this way, then, since each of the things that are is said to be and is precisely what it is according to its proper form and not according to the matter, he shows that the substance of each thing and its form is not number – and this is the same as saying that numbers are not definitions of substances. He says, then, that it is clear that numbers are neither substances nor causes of the form and nature of each thing. For if the substance and being of each thing is its formula and form, but number, if it contributes anything at all to things, is the quantity of the matter of each thing (for the number four is the very quantity and the measure of fire, earth, water and air, i.e. of the bodily elements) – if, then, each thing is said and is according to its proper form and if number is not the form of things nor, in truth, matter, but rather the quantity and measure of matter, it is false that numbers are causes of the form of each thing or that they are the forms of things. To say that numbers are the quantity and measure of the matter of things, without being their forms, Empedocles' words about the composition of bones are enough: '[. . .] received two parts of bright Nestis out of the eight, and four of Hephaestus, and white bones came into being [. . .]'.[39] For he hints at this by saying that 'number is matter', i.e. number is the substance of flesh or of bone in this way: three parts of fire, two of

[37] ὅτι δὲ οὐχ οἱ ἀριθμοὶ οὐσία οὐδὲ τῆς μορφῆς αἴτιοι, δῆλον· ὁ γὰρ λόγος ἡ οὐσία, ὁ δ' ἀριθμὸς ὕλη. οἷον σαρκὸς ἢ ὀστοῦ ἀριθμὸς ἡ οὐσία οὕτω, τρία πυρὸς γῆς δὲ δύο· καὶ ἀεὶ ὁ ἀριθμὸς ὃς ἂν ᾖ τινῶν ἐστιν, ἢ πύρινος ἢ γήϊνος ἢ μοναδικός, ἀλλ' ἡ οὐσία (20) τὸ τοσόνδ' εἶναι πρὸς τοσόνδε κατὰ τὴν μῖξιν· τοῦτο δ' οὐκέτι ἀριθμὸς ἀλλὰ λόγος μίξεως ἀριθμῶν σωματικῶν ἢ ὁποιωνοῦν.

[38] For a comprehensive analysis of the relations between the three extant Greek commentaries on Aristotle's *Metaphysics*, see Luna 2001.

[39] B96 DK: 'Pleasant earth in her well-made channels received two parts of bright Nestis out of the eight, and four of Hephaestus, and white bones came into being, fitted together divinely by the glues of harmony'.

earth. [. . .] What he says is this. And the number and quantity of the material substance of bone was conceived in this way by Empedocles: three parts of fire, two parts of earth; and he has explained in the books *On the soul* [*De anima* 1.5.410a1-6] how Empedocles conceived these things. And since three parts are of fire and two of earth, he adds also that it is always the case that every number is either of fire or of earth, i.e. either of parts of fire or of parts of earth, or of units and incorporeals. But neither the number made of units, i.e. the mathematical number, nor the number of parts of fire or earth is the substance of things; rather fire and earth are the matter and not the form of things, while their number and measure is neither of these. However, the substance of each thing turns out to be according to the mixture of this much in proportion to this much. (οὔτε δὲ ὁ μοναδικός ἐστιν ἤτοι ὁ μαθηματικὸς οὐσία τῶν πραγμάτων, οὔτε ὁ τῶν πυρῶν καὶ γαιῶν, ἀλλὰ τὸ πῦρ καὶ ἡ γῆ ὕλη μὲν καὶ οὐκ εἶδος τῶν πραγμάτων, ὁ δ' ἀριθμὸς αὐτῶν καὶ τὸ μέτρον οὐδέτερον τούτων ἐστίν, ἀλλὰ γίνεται ἡ ἑκάστου οὐσία κατὰ τὴν τοσοῦδε πρὸς τοσόνδε μῖξιν.) For one thing comes to be when there are six parts of fire, five of air, four of water and two of earth, and something else when there are six parts of earth, three of fire, two of air and five of water, and, more generally, different things come to be according to the mixture of different components. And this is not a number, i.e. these incorporeal and mathematical units, but rather a certain ratio of corporeal numbers, i.e. a certain proportion of numbers of bodies. And you must understand that if the simple bodies are not forms of things, but <this is> rather what is accomplished from the ratio of such a blend, the number and measure of simple bodies will hardly be the forms of things (καὶ ἐπίστησον ὡς εἰ τὰ ἁπλᾶ σώματα μὴ ἔστι τὰ τῶν πραγμάτων εἴδη, ἀλλὰ τὸ ἐκ τοῦ λόγου τῆς τοιᾶσδε κράσεως ἀποτελούμενον, σχολῇ ἂν εἴη τὸν ἀριθμὸν καὶ τὸ μέτρον τῶν ἁπλῶν σωμάτων εἶναι τὰ τῶν πραγμάτων εἴδη).[40]

Of course, we cannot be sure that the position voiced in this piece of commentary goes back to Alexander. But the attempts at strengthening Aristotle's position into saying that the substance and form of things is what comes to be 'according to (*kata*) the mixture of this much in proportion to this much' or what is 'accomplished from (*ek*) the ratio of such a blend' suggest that the author has an interest in distinguishing the form from the ratio of the mixture itself. Be that as it may, the question whether Alexander made room for an even limited application of the *harmonia*-model as an account of what some types of substance (e.g. homogeneous stuff, mixtures) are is a legitimate one. That the model cannot work in more complex cases is clear, among other things, for the reasons explained, for example, in [T2]: if a compound can survive the

[40] (Ps.-)Alex. *in Metaph.* 827.34–828.29.

alteration of the quantitative proportions between its material components without losing its nature, it is clear that its nature does not consist in nor is it fully determined by those proportions between material components.

But can the model be applied to the simpler cases of mixtures and homogeneous stuff? If not, then why not? In addition to the idea that quantities and relations between quantities cannot be forms of substances because they just belong to the wrong category, one reason for a negative answer could be that the mere specification of quantities does not spell out the mode of composition of the compound and, therefore, fails to capture the way in which the object at stake is a non-accidental unity. A similar idea can be found, for example, in Aristotle, *Top.* 6.13.150b22-26. If, on the other hand, the model can be applied, how can Alexander remain faithful to the principle that the parts of substances (including matter and form) are substances? One possible way would be to depart from the categorial approach and to lay emphasis on the causal approach: in order to assess whether a certain ontological component of a substance is a substance or not, one should not ask under what category it falls, but rather what causal role it plays in the substance of which it is a component. Furthermore, we cannot exclude that Alexander intentionally played down the role that accounts based on the *harmony*-model might have within the overall picture. Alexander is not explicit on this point, but his choice of examples in his *De anima*, far from being incidental, may suggest that this sort of account is suitable at most for describing the composition of mixtures and homeomerous parts. Even if we do not have Alexander's commentary on *Metaph.* Z16, it seems possible that Aristotle's claims in Z16.1040b5-10 that parts of animals are only substances in potentiality played some role in shaping Alexander's restrictions of the applications of the *harmonia*-model. The idea would be that, if the revised *harmonia*-model can be used with reference to substances at all, it can at best be used to account for the ontological structure of compounds which only serve as the matter of more complex substances and which, considered in themselves, are mere 'heaps' (i.e. amounts of matter). Note, however, that this is not to say that Alexander dismisses compounds of this kind as uninteresting or irrelevant: quite on the contrary, both the *scala naturae* depicted in the first pages of Alexander's *De anima* and the *De mixtione* testify to an interest on Alexander's part in the analysis of the different levels of aggregation of matter. More generally, the idea that the material parts of objects have something to do with quantity emerges at least in one passage in

Alexander's *De anima* (18.21–25),[41] where Alexander distinguishes between the way in which matter and form are parts of a composite substance and the way in which its material parts are. The latter are 'parts as of (what has a) quantity' (*ta hōs posou merē*), that is, presumably (as Caston's translation suggests), these are parts that have a size and are the result of the division of a continuous object (i.e. a body). Both these features – having a size and being the result of the division of a continuous object – if taken in abstraction from the perceptible features that characterize the objects in question can be seen to describe mere quantities (or rather physical objects only from the point of view of their quantitative determinations).[42]

Whether this cluster of problems arising from the application of the *harmonia*-model as such received specific attention in a separate debate is hard to tell, but certainly the more general issue whether numbers and their principles can exercise a genuine causal function in the structure of reality is a crucial metaphysical issue on which Aristotelian philosophy and Pythagorean-Platonic philosophy essentially diverge. One aspect to take into account in the post-Aristotelian tradition is that, although Aristotle draws relatively neat distinctions between Pythagorean doctrines and Academic doctrines which make numbers and their principles the principles and causes of things that are, he also tends to associate the Pythagoreans and the Platonists in that, despite their divergences, they tend to ascribe to numbers and their principles an ontological status and an explanatory function which they (in Aristotle's view) cannot have. By the time of Alexander, we no longer find a strong and distinctively Pythagorean tradition independent from the Pythagorizing Platonism which had first emerged in the early Academy and continued to develop, with different emphasis, up to Alexander's time.[43] One characteristic feature of this Pythagorizing Platonism is precisely the emphasis on the role of quantities, numbers and their principles in explaining the structure

[41] τὸ γὰρ σχῆμα τοῦ ἀνδριάντος μέρος οὐχ ὡς εἰς τὸ ποσὸν αὐτῷ συντελοῦν τι, ἀλλ' ὡς εἰς τὸ ποιόν, καὶ οὐχ ὡς ἐν τῷ ἀπὸ τῆς ὕλης χωρισμῷ σώζεσθαι δυνάμενον. εἰς δὲ τὰ ὡς ποσοῦ μέρη καὶ εἰς τὰ σωζόμενα μετὰ τὴν διαίρεσιν ἡ προειρημένη τοῦ τε σώματος καὶ τῶν ἄλλων συνεχῶν διαίρεσις. 'For the shape of the statue is a part, though not in a way that contributes something to its size – it contributes to its character instead – and not as something that can persist in separation from the matter. For the division of the body and other continuous objects mentioned above results in parts that have a size and persist after the division' (Caston's translation). I am grateful to Riccardo Chiaradonna for bringing this passage and the issue of its relation to the principle that parts of substances are substances to my attention.

[42] See Arist. *Metaph.* Δ13.1020a7-14 about divisibility and determination as defining features of quanta.

[43] For a reconstruction of the influence of Pythagoreanism on Platonists from Speusippus to Numenius, see Dillon 2014b.

of reality within the framework of *Platonic* philosophy (i.e. within a framework in which the *harmonia*-model has lost that 'materialistic' flavour which Aristotle presents as the hallmark of the old Pythagoreans).

However, there might be reasons to believe that the materialistic trend which Aristotle ascribes to the Pythagoreans is not merely a historical vestige that Alexander has to deal with in commenting on Aristotle's *Metaphysics*. What I would like to suggest is that for Alexander the materialistic trend, while no longer alive in the Platonic tradition, was taken over, albeit with some qualifications, by certain exponents of the Peripatetic tradition. We know, for example, that various versions of the doctrine that the soul is the harmony of the body enjoyed a certain popularity among early Peripatetics.[44] Whether this brought with it the idea that the *harmonia*-model could be generally applied we cannot tell. We have, however, some evidence which allows us to place Alexander's remarks about the limits of the *harmonia*-model within a broader narrative about the Peripatetic tradition and, more generally, about the reception of Aristotle's writings. One trend in this narrative, which I shall not pursue any further here, is the 'Pythagorization' of Aristotle's philosophy and the appropriation of Aristotle's philosophy within the Pythagorean-Platonic tradition.[45] The other trend is the incorporation of Pythagorean elements into Aristotle's philosophy. Unlike earlier Peripatetics and early commentators (such as Aspasius), who were quite willing to borrow elements from the Pythagorean-Platonic tradition,[46] Alexander is rather clear as to the fact that neither the Pythagorean nor the Platonic stance is a genuine option for Aristotle: Alexander depicts the Pythagorean views as intrinsically materialistic – and for Alexander unrefined materialism is as poor an option as transcendental formalism.

In saying this Alexander seems interested in clearly demarcating the boundaries between Aristotle's philosophy and other philosophical traditions, but in taking a clear stance against the materialistic option he might

[44] See Caston 1997 and n. 46. On the materialistic origins of the doctrine of the soul as a harmony, see Sassi 2015.

[45] See, for example, Syr. *in Metaph.* 192.15–29. For some discussion of this trend see Chiaradonna 2013, Bonazzi 2013, and Ulacco 2016.

[46] For an account of the general attitude of the early Peripatetic commentators and, more generally, of Platonic and Peripatetic philosophers in the first century BC as interested in reviving the ancient philosophical debate rather than a specific school of thought anchored to one single authority, see Chiaradonna (unpublished). For some remarks about elements of Pythagoreanism in the early Peripatetics and, in particular, in Theophrastus, see Sharples 1985, section II, and Sedley 1985, 205. More generally on the Peripatetic attitude of Aristotle and Peripatetic philosophers after Aristotle see, respectively, Primavesi 2014 and Huffman 2014b.

also be interested in differentiating his account of Aristotle's philosophy from other 'Aristotelianisms' which (independently of their proponents' intentions) may have been assimilated to Pythagorean philosophy in virtue of the priority accorded to immanent quantities. In particular, Alexander's stance can be better appreciated in the light of a more sophisticated debate internal to the Peripatetic tradition in which a subject-oriented metaphysics (rather than mere materialism) is developed in opposition to the Platonic metaphysics of separate forms. That some such version of Aristotelianism was indeed developed, most of all, by Boethus is fairly uncontroversial, in the light of recent studies.[47] Boethus' Aristotelianism is rooted in his reading of the *Categories*, and in the primacy there accorded to the criterion of subjecthood and the corresponding identification of matter and compounds as primary substances. On Boethus' account, forms turn out to be property-like beings which inhere in their subjects and do not respond to the basic criterion for being a substance; rather, they may turn out to be qualities, quantities or some other kind of accident. Clearly, if one drops the idea that the forms of substances must belong in the category of substance, nothing stands in the way of regarding more or less complex quantitative determinations (possibly among other types of determinations) as forms.

There is some debate as to the sort of categorial specification that Boethus allowed for forms.[48] I do not intend to go into the details of this debate. Rather, I would like to suggest that, independently of Boethus' specific views on this point and possibly independently of his own intentions, there is another sense in which Boethus' (or any other similar) approach to Aristotle's theory of substance could have been – and at some point indeed *was* – taken to emphasize the role of numbers and quantitative determinations in the structure of being. The evidence is sparse, but we can find some hints in Simplicius' commentary on the *Categories*. Simplicius systematically addresses the issue of the order in which the different categories are discussed. In particular, he repeatedly returns to the problem of why the first category to be discussed after substance is quantity. Interestingly enough, the reason Simplicius gives is that in the *Categories* Aristotle takes composite substances to be primary – that is to say, material or corporeal substances, whose basic and primary determination qua corporeal substances is the quantitative determination which comes with their having a body.[49] Note that for Simplicius this does

[47] Rashed 2007 and 2013, Reinhardt 2007.

[48] See Reinhardt 2007 and the discussion thereof in Rashed 2013.

[49] Simpl. *in Cat.* 122.25–30; cf. 120.33–121.3; 157.31–33; 206.19–24; 207.19–21.

not reflect Pythagorean views, at least not without qualification: in fact, for Simplicius this order of the categories is in contrast with the one given by the (pseudo) Pythagorean authority on the matter, Ps.-Archytas. Simplicius emphasizes that according to Archytas quality is the second category to be discussed after substance (121.13 ff.; 156.25–157.2; 157.25–31; 206.8 ff.) and this is because Archytas arranges the categories based on their resemblance to intelligible being (121.20–23) and the forms (122.7–8; 206.15–19).

Boethus' Aristotelianism emphasizes the criterion of subjecthood and, accordingly, the primacy of matter and composite substances as primary substances. Apparently Boethus also thought that one should teach Aristotelian philosophy starting with the *Physics* because natural substances and the natural world are what is better known to us.[50] Simplicius claims that the category that most resembles substance is quantity for those who take substance to primarily coincide with matter and material substances. This view is the one favoured by those who look at things starting from 'the effects' and from 'what is composite' (on 'composite' things see below). Furthermore, this view, according to Simplicius, far from representing the mainstream Pythagorean approach, is rather presented as Aristotle's (122.26; 157.31) approach in the *Categories*. Is this surprising? Probably not. One can hardly underestimate the role of the *Categories* in shaping the image of Aristotle's philosophy starting with the commentators of the first century BC.[51] Bearing this in mind, it would not be very surprising if at some point (certainly before Simplicius) the reading of Aristotle's philosophy that managed to make sense of what the latter was doing in the *Categories* was taken to be Aristotle's own philosophy.

Interestingly enough, Simplicius sketches the full ontological picture which would be compatible with the order in which the categories are discussed in the *Categories* (157.31–158.10; 207.19–26). According to this picture, natural (i.e. material) substances are given together with quantities as their first determinations; these are followed by relatives and, in particular, by relations between quantities (either indeterminate or determinate ratios), which are in their turn followed by the qualities that are the outcome of such ratios. Simplicius adds (158.27–33) that the order in which the *Categories* present the categories was defended by Porphyry, who saw this order as in agreement with Empedocles' cosmogony and with Plato's account in *Ti.* 31c ff. Simplicius' reply to Porphyry is that this order

[50] Philop. *in Cat.* 5.16–18.
[51] For some contextualization of this claim, see Griffin 2015 and 2016.

is adequate as long as one describes generation 'in the effects and in the things that are composite' (159.1: *en tois apotelesmasin kai tois synthetois*), but that it would not be adequate for an account that starts from the causes, in which what is one and simple comes before plurality and composition (158.34–159.8).

If we look at Alexander's analysis of the texts in Sections 4.2 and 4.3, we can see that the full-scale application of the *harmonia*-model in Simplicius is not linked only to the 'materialistic' reading of Pythagorean philosophy which Alexander rejects and to which Simplicius opposes the Platonizing Pythagoreanism of Pseudo-Archytas; rather, the model turns out to be connected to a version of Aristotelianism which Alexander ultimately opposes. In this sense, not only the old Pythagorean doctrines described by Aristotle and the Pythagorizing Platonism still alive at Alexander's time, but also some debates internal to the Peripatetic tradition must be taken into account in order to fully appreciate Alexander's position on the use of the *harmonia*-model and its implications.[52]

[52] In writing this chapter I was supported by the Deutsche Forschungsgemeinschaft (DFG). I would like to thank Riccardo Chiaradonna, Francesco Pelosi and Federico Petrucci for their most generous feedback on a previous version of the chapter.

CHAPTER 5

How to Resist Musical Dogmatism

The Aim and Methods of Pyrrhonian Inquiry in Sextus Empiricus' Against the Musicologists (Math. 6)

Máté Veres

Pyrrhonian Scepticism as presented by Sextus Empiricus is often credited with the defence of unintuitive and unattractive positions for no intellectual gain. A brief exposure to the treatise *Against the Musicologists* (*Pros Mousikous*, *Math.* 6) seems to nurture such a reputation. In this work, Sextus reports arguments in favour of the claims that, first, music does not contribute to a happy life but is rather harmful to its prospects, and second, that music does not even exist. Anyone who remembers hearing a piece of music that filled their heart with bliss will hesitate to buy into the former claim, and most of us would be dumbfounded to hear arguments in earnest for the latter.

The agenda pursued by Sextus in *Math.* 6 is less outlandish than a mere statement of the above two claims suggests. In the very first paragraph, Sextus states that his arguments target music only in the sense of 'a field of knowledge that deals with melodies, sounds, rhythm-making, and the like' (ἐπιστήμη τις περὶ μελῳδίας καὶ φθόγγους καὶ ῥυθμοποιίας καὶ τὰ παραπλήσια καταγιγνομένη πράγματα). In contrast, he does not wish to engage with the musical skill or competence that enables musicians to play various instruments (*hē peri organikēn empeiria*), insofar as such a competence does not rely on the sort of knowledge-claims that a Sceptic opposes (*Math.* 6.1–3).[1]

With this restriction in place, one can get a better grasp of the main claims around which the treatise is organised. Some would argue, as Sextus relates, that a *science* of music – what I shall refer to as 'musicology' – does

[1] To be precise, Sextus makes a distinction between not two but three senses of 'music' (ἡ μουσική) and the corresponding adjective 'musical' (μουσικός). Besides the two proper (κυρίως) and commonly accepted (παρὰ πολλοῖς) senses mentioned above, the Greek adjective can be used rather loosely (καταχρηστικώτερον) to designate success in other artistic endeavours (ἔν τινι πράγματι κατόρθωσιν, cf. Bett 2013, 169 with n. 2). I return to this in the concluding section.

not contribute to a happy life, while others deny that such a science has ever been established. Since the respective beliefs that musicology exists and that it benefits those who have mastered it are fine specimens of dogmatism, all Sextus has to do is to set the naysayers and the believers against each other in good Pyrrhonian fashion. If their accounts balance each other out, he can go on to suggest that reasonable inquirers will suspend judgement as to the truth about these matters, while leaving everyday musical practice intact. *Against the Musicologists* thus lends itself to being read as an attempt to display the Sceptical capacity to motivate suspension of judgement in a specific domain where the Sceptic has detected dogmatic belief.

In what follows, I develop a reading of the treatise along these lines.[2] In Section 5.1, I argue that Sextus' polemical engagement with philosophical musicology sits well with the project of the treatise to which it belongs, and with a plausible understanding of his philosophical position as presented in the *Outlines of Pyrrhonism* (*Pyr.*). Then I turn to the two kinds of arguments that are contrasted by Sextus as being 'more dogmatic' and 'more aporetic' in spirit. After their brief presentation in Section 5.2, explaining the nature of their contrast by pointing to the diverging agendas that they originally served, I give an overview of both as ultimately aiming at *epochē* in Sections 5.3 and 5.4. Finally, in Section 5.5, I push back against readings that take the treatise to present a deviation from the suspensive outlook.

5.1 'Against the Musicologists' and Sextan Pyrrhonism

Against the Musicologists is the last book of Sextus' *Against the Professors* (*Pros Mathēmatikous*, henceforth *Math.* 1–6), a six-book compendium of arguments against those who profess to offer some sort of systematic teaching about various arts (*technai*) or fields of study (*mathēmata*).[3] After its proem (*Math.* 1.1–8), *Against the Professors* registers two ways of combatting dogmatism about the arts. First, it offers a general argument to the effect that nothing is taught or learned, nor is there any field of study

[2] Only a handful of studies have been devoted specifically to *Math.* 6: Riethmüller 1975, Rispoli 1992, La Sala 2010, Bett 2013, Spinelli 2016 (cf. his 2008, 2014). Davidson Greaves 1986 compiles a useful list of correspondences with various accounts of Greek music theory, while de Haas 2020 provides a glimpse at the Renaissance influence of Sextus' treatise.

[3] On *Math.* 1–6 in general, see Russo 1972, VII–XXXVII, Cortassa 1981, Fortuna 1987, Barnes 1988, Desbordes 1990, Hankinson 1995, 226–35, Jürß 2001, Pellegrin 2002, Delattre 2006, Spinelli 2010, Bett 2018, 1–24.

(1.9–40).[4] Second, it delivers six separate series of counterarguments to the dogmatic claims of those who profess knowledge concerning grammar, rhetoric, arithmetic, geometry, astrology, and music.[5] At the end of the day, these two sorts of refutation (*antirrhēsis*) are supposed to bring about the same result, lack of dogmatic views about alleged branches of learning.

Throughout the individual refutation, Sextus states time and again that his polemic is driven by specific dogmatic conceptions of the targeted arts. Furthermore, the resisted notion of an art grounded in some theoretical insight is occasionally juxtaposed to another conception of the same endeavour which is said to be exempt from the same line of criticism. On the basis of these distinctions, scholars have attempted to bring out a uniform notion of arts acceptable to a Pyrrhonian, often by appealing to their usefulness or their comprehensibility in terms of mere appearance-claims, which would allow the Sceptic to embrace some form of these endeavours without buying into their dogmatic underpinnings.[6]

The problems with such an approach are numerous. To begin with, Sextus does not always suggest a sound version of a given art, and even when he does, there is hardly any uniformity in the supposedly acceptable variants.[7] Furthermore, forms of artistic competence that are not eliminated by specific arguments are still vulnerable to the conclusion of the general argument, which denies that any sort of learning ever takes place (*Math.* 1.9, cf. 1.38).[8] Were one to overlook these issues, it would still seem

[4] The general argument is also stated in *Pyr.* 3.252–269 and *Math.* 11.216–243, in the context of arguing against the notion of an art of living (τέχνη περὶ τὸν βίον; cf. *Pyr.* 3.270–273 and *Math.* 11.243–256). This might suggest that the distinction between the dogmatic and the non-dogmatic approach to arts has some affinity with the distinction between the alleged skill relating to living well and the practical criterion followed by the Sceptic (*Pyr.* 1.21–24); on this, see Tsouna-McKirahan 1996, 83.

[5] Sextus refers to this subject matter collectively as the ἐγκύκλια προσηγόρευται μαθήματα (*Math.* 1.7) and as ταῖς ἐλευθέραις τέχναις (*Math.* 2.57). I do not enter the debate whether his presentation reflects the canon of the 'cyclical studies' or 'liberal arts'. The art of dialectic is commonly taken to be excluded from *Math.* 1–6 on the grounds that it was dealt with as part of the argument against philosophy proper (see e.g. Barnes 1988, 56–7, Hankinson 1995, 226, Blank 1998, 85, Spinelli 2010, 249).

[6] See, for example, Desbordes 1990, 175–9, Spinelli 2010, 258–9, La Sala 2010, 261–2, Marchand 2011, 136 n. 100, Corti 2015, 132–43.

[7] Besides the threefold distinction concerning music (*Math.* 6.1–3), Sextus distinguishes between two senses of grammar (*Math.* 1.44, cf. 49), two conceptions of rhetoric (*Math.* 2.5–9, 16–18) and two kinds of astrology (*Math.* 5.1–2). As for his take on arithmetic and geometry – which might or might not have originally formed a single book (see Brochard 2002, 331 n. 3, Janáček 2008a, Russo 1972, VII n. 1, with a rebuttal in Blomqvist 1974; cf. Fortuna 1987, 123 n. 1) – Sextus does not appeal to their 'dogmatism-proof' version, and even their forms that he rejects are quite heterogeneous (see Corti 2015, 134).

[8] On the apparent tension between the two refutations, see Barnes 1988, 60.

problematic to attribute views about demarcation to the Sceptic, or beliefs as to which forms of artistic expertise are useful for life.[9] Most importantly, these attempts fail to pay sufficient attention to the place of *Math.* 1–6 in Sextus' project, and to the division of labour among his different works.

Early on in the *Outlines*, Sextus draws a distinction between the general and the specific account of Pyrrhonism (*Pyr.* 1.6). In the general account, which mostly occupies Book 1, he presents the characteristic achievement of Pyrrhonism, suspension of judgement concerning matters of inquiry, together with an account of the origin and justification of this philosophical outlook, as well as of the practical stance it implies. In the specific account, which takes up the remainder of the *Outlines* (*Pyr.* 2–3), he follows what he takes to be a paradigmatic exposition of philosophy as conceived by his dogmatic opponents, in order to systematically counterbalance their dogmatic tenets with equally persuasive counterarguments, thereby motivating suspension of judgement at each and every turn.

An important link between the general and the specific account is provided by the origin-story of Pyrrhonism (*Pyr.* 1.12, cf. 1.26 and 29). According to this narrative, Pyrrhonians are only a subset of those who initially set out to engage in philosophical inquiry. Prompted by the anomaly in things, men of an inquisitive mind decided to resolve these anomalies by coming to a reason-based decision about the truth or falsity of conflicting appearances. However, their attempts at finding the truth were frustrated, as they have found that to every argument which they have already considered an equally convincing counterargument could be opposed. While some of their fellow inquirers failed to acknowledge the equipollence of the present pool of arguments, or did recognise it but came to despair of ever finding the truth, the first generation of Pyrrhonians realised that the proper reaction is to suspend one's judgement and continue to inquire (cf. *Pyr.* 1.1–4), only to find that they could achieve a tranquil state of mind about the very matters that troubled them.

Given the desirability of the state of suspension, the Sceptic has a reason to match every dogmatic argument with a counterargument of equal persuasive force. The further motivation to extend this practice to the dogmatic views of her fellow inquirers is then supplied by the shared background of all investigators, which makes her aware of their unpleasant epistemic condition, and by the Sceptic's famous claim to philanthropy, that is, her willingness to use any and all argument that would happen to

[9] This is not to deny that *Pyr.* 1 allows for some form of Sceptical expertise, but rather that *Math.* 1–6 is relevant for cashing it out. See Section 5.5 below.

match the persuasive force of another argument that took hold of a philosophical mind (*Pyr.* 3.280–281). In other words, the general account of Pyrrhonism provides the rationale for the specific account: the Sceptic intends to bring any given interlocutor, herself or others, to recognise the equipollence of opposing accounts and to react properly to this recognition.[10]

As a consequence of this methodological division, one should not peruse books belonging to the specific account in search of clues as to the way of life suitable for a Sceptic of his kin. This proviso applies to the attack on the arts, where Sextus not only resorts to arguments stemming from Sceptical sources, but also exploits pre-existing dogmatic disagreements. As an influential reader has suggested, the treatise should be approached as a sort of pharmacy for dogmatism, 'a set or collection of arguments, of differing sorts and strengths, which are to be applied singly or in commixture to rash believers and which are intended to cure the believers of their rash beliefs'.[11] For oppositional purposes, the only thing that matters about an argument is its persuasive force, not its pedigree or the position it was originally meant to establish.[12] Yet any given dogmatic argument repurposed by Sextus, or any given dogma he sets out to oppose, might come with some presupposition or background belief which, if affirmed, would be unacceptable for a Sceptic. Consequently, one should not construe Sextus' remarks about the utility or uselessness of various endeavours as relevant for his personal outlook, as all he does in this context is to report – albeit with a partisan aim – on previous debates that were framed in these very terms.[13]

An anticipated objection to this proposal is that the relevant distinction between the general and the specific account is nowhere made or strongly implied in *Math.* 1–6. The proem of the latter work provides an answer to this objection.[14] In the proem, Sextus makes it rather explicit that he is

10 For a defence of this reading of Sextan Pyrrhonism, see Veres 2020.

11 Barnes 1988, 76 (see also 72–3 and 77), followed by Hankinson 1995, 228, Pellegrin 2002, 21–7, and Marchand 2011, 131–7.

12 Pellegrin 2002, 26, Hankinson 1995, 227. Spinelli 2016, 43–4 makes the same point, adding that his conscious strategy proves that Sextus was not a copyist. Perhaps he means that Sextus was not a *clueless* copyist, which does not go against the claim that he helped himself to vast amounts of dogmatic material in order to make his peculiarly Sceptical points.

13 This point has been made by Pellegrin 2002, 18 n. 13. One should be similarly careful about attributing a welcome notion of τέχνη to Sextus, since he operates with a set of formal criteria that he pries away from protagonists of previous controversies about the existence and capacities of artistic practices. Cf. Barnes 1988, 63–6, Tsouna-McKirahan 1996, 82–4, Pellegrin 2002, 19–20, Bett 2006, 17–21 with n. 7, Blank 1998, xvii–xl.

14 Janáček 1972, 133, argued that the proem is an 'extraneous matter' to the text of *Math.* 1–6, and that this recognition should remove the main obstacle towards reading it as a non-Sceptical work. I agree

carrying over the suspensive agenda to the examination of various arts that have been taken to contribute to the broader project of the search for wisdom. He relates again the story of those who have engaged in philosophy proper, only to be confronted with 'a battle of equal arguments and with the anomalous appearances of things' (ἰσοσθενεῖ δὲ μάχῃ καὶ ἀνωμαλίᾳ τῶν πραγμάτων) they have inquired into, adding that they were then exposed to the same sort of experience with regard to the fields of study discussed in *Math.* 1–6.[15] This formulation reminds us of the *Pyr.* version of the origin story. The same group of people with the same motivational background came to study both philosophy and the arts, and found difficulties that are equally weighty, or perhaps of the very same sort, in both cases (*isas ... aporias*, *Math.* 1.6).[16] By pointing to this experience, and by relating it to the previous encounter with philosophy, the proem supplies the general account, the rationale for combatting dogmatism about the arts, which is the task carried out by the generic argument and the individual arguments contained in the six books that follow.[17]

Sextus' failure to mention philanthropy in the proem does not pose a problem for this reading. One could speculate that, when facing up to the professors of the arts, Sextus was less focused on other-concern, or that the narrative continuity between the *Pyr.* account and the proem supplies the latter with elements that are not explicitly mentioned there.[18] At any rate, even if momentarily lacking in philanthropic motivation, the Sextus of *Math.* 1–6 has a self-standing interest in arguing against the professors. Indeed, the task he sets himself is to select the appropriate arguments (*ta*

with the alternative view of Pellegrin 2002, 11, Spinelli 2010, 256 and 2016, 43. On the proem, see also De Marco 1956.

15 ἀλλὰ τοιοῦτόν τι ἐπὶ τῶν μαθημάτων παθόντες ὁποῖον ἐφ' ὅλης ἔπαθον τῆς φιλοσοφίας. The minority manuscript reading of σοφίας is accepted by Mau but rejected by Barnes 1988, 58 n. 12; see also Blank 1998, 4 n. 1, Pellegrin 2006, 37 n. 6. Pellegrin 2002, 32–4 suggests that Sextus adds insult to injury by allowing for the possibility that the arts might attain truth independently from philosophy. On either reading, Sextus is opposed to those who claim to have progressed beyond ἀπορία on the road to wisdom.

16 Pellegrin 2006, 37–8; but cf. Cortassa 1981, 721–2, Desbordes 1990, 169–70.

17 Recognising the link between the encounter with philosophy, as presented in *Pyr.* 1 and the proem to *Math.* 1–6, does not commit us to a view as to the relative chronology of these works. The latter is better understood in light of the former, but the proem might refer to another version of the *Pyr.* 1 story outlined in a lost work.

18 The other notable omission in *Math.* 1 is that of ἀταραξία, a prominent feature in *Pyr.* 1 and, on that account, the initial motivation for philosophical inquiry. The difference is due to the fact that, while the origin-story in *Pyr.* 1 offers an account of the origin of all of philosophy, the *Math.* 1 version describes the encounter of suspensive philosophers with already existing artistic practices without reference to the conditions that led to their emergence.

pragmatikōs legomena, 1.7) that will prove effective in this fight. In the next section, I discuss the target and the nature of the double argumentation against musical dogmatists.

5.2 Two Dogmas of Musicology

Thus far I have presented *Math.* 6 as an inventory of arguments aimed at curing musical dogmatism. As for its structure, the treatise divides into two main parts, each targeting a type of dogmatic view.[19] In the first part, Sextus rehearses arguments against the belief that knowledge about musical matters is useful for life (6.17–38), and in the second he turns to the existence of musicology, showing that the arguments establishing it are incoherent and unconvincing (6.38–68).[20] In an early remark, Sextus introduces these as 'two forms of the same refutation' (τῆς δὲ ἀντιρρήσεως . . . διττόν ἐστι τὸ εἶδος, *Math.* 6.4), points out their distinct origin, and explicitly contrasts their philosophical character:

> Some have attempted to teach rather dogmatically that music is not a discipline necessary for happiness, but is on the contrary harmful, and to show this by criticizing the things said by musicians and by holding their foremost arguments to be worthy of pulling down; but others, keeping their distance, in a more aporetic manner, from all counter-argument of this kind, thought that in the tossing around of the principal hypotheses of the musicians, the whole of music was also done away with.[21]

The contrast between arguments that are 'more dogmatic' and 'more aporetic' in spirit is not unparalleled in Sextus' works.[22] As a first approximation,

[19] On this structure elsewhere in *Math.* 1–6, see Cortassa 1981, 723, Fortuna 1987, 130–3, Desbordes 1990, 168–9.

[20] Bett 2013, 169 and 173–5, argues that Sextus mistakenly conflates arguments concerning musical performance in the first part with arguments against music theory in the second. On my formulation, both parts of the treatise are concerned with knowledge-claims: see Section 5.4.

[21] *Math.* 6.4–5. οἱ μὲν οὖν δογματικώτερον ἐπεχείρησαν διδάσκειν ὅτι οὐκ ἀναγκαῖόν ἐστι μάθημα πρὸς εὐδαιμονίαν μουσική, ἀλλὰ βλαπτικὸν μᾶλλον, καὶ τοῦτο δείκνυσθαι ἔκ τε τοῦ διαβάλλεσθαι τὰ πρὸς τῶν μουσικῶν λεγόμενα καὶ ἐκ τοῦ τοὺς προηγουμένους λόγους ἀνασκευῆς ἀξιοῦσθαι· οἱ δὲ ἀπορητικώτερον πάσης ἀποστάντες τῆς τοιαύτης ἀντιρρήσεως ἐν τῷ σαλεύειν τὰς ἀρχικὰς ὑποθέσεις τῶν μουσικῶν ᾠήθησαν καὶ τὴν ὅλην ἀνῃρῆσθαι μουσικήν. I quote from the translation of Bett 2018, with occasional modifications.

[22] The strongest analogue comes in Book 1 of *Against the Physicists* (*Math.* 9.12), where Sextus contrasts 'inquiring quasi-dogmatically' (σκεπτόμενοι . . . οἷον δογματικῶς) about god as the most active cause with proceeding more aporetically (ἀπορητικώτερον), which amounts to bringing about an aporia concerning anything being active or affected. Here again, the 'more aporetic' section argues exclusively for non-existence, while the 'quasi-dogmatic' section relies on a wide repertoire of dogmatic views about god as a prime cause. It is also worth mentioning *Math.* 7.28, where Sextus distinguishes between the presentation of the various ways in which dogmatists speak about the

one might try to account for the distinction in terms of the starting-point of the counterarguments. On the one hand, the 'more dogmatic' section manifestly relies on an opposition with dogmatic accounts, first presenting a rebuttal of piecemeal arguments in favour of music's utility, and then of those claims that, according to Sextus, are the most prominent reasons for holding such a view (*tous proēgoumenous logous*). On the other hand, the aporetic section presents only an argument for the non-existence of musicology, without first giving voice to the musicologists. However, since both sections target the same notion of musicology, dependence on dogmatic material does not in itself differentiate them from one another.

Alternatively, one can distinguish the two sorts of refutation with regard to their philosophical pedigree. The aporetic arguments were from the very beginning put forward with a properly Sceptical aim in mind, and their formulation reflects that aim. By contrast, the original proponents of the 'more dogmatic' refutation have themselves argued for a dogmatic view, as mentioned in the passage quoted above, namely, that musicology in some relevant sense harms the prospects of a happy life.[23] Sextus, however, takes the original, dogmatic use of these arguments to be flawed, as in his view they can be used only to induce suspension of judgement about the utility of music. He goes on to suggest that an exhaustive treatment of the targets and the argumentative resources of Pyrrhonian inquiry requires him to report, if only concisely, on both sorts of dogma and refutation. By doing so, he can avoid defrauding those who wish to learn from him the way of effectively resisting musical dogmatism.[24]

That being said, the proper Pyrrhonian objective is the one specified in the aporetic section which, according to Sextus' own summary in the proem, sets out 'to argue that sound and time do not exist' (περὶ τοῦ μηδὲν εἶναι φωνὴν μηδὲ χρόνον, *M* 1.8). These arguments are said to target the foundational hypotheses (*tas archikas hypotheseis*: 6.5) on which dogmatic musicology relies, which is perhaps the reason why these arguments

criterion and the truth, and the aporetic investigation as to whether something existing corresponds to the senses thus distinguished (ἀπορητικώτερον σκεπτόμενοι, εἰ δύναταί τι τούτων ὑπάρχειν). On this passage, see Brunschwig 1994b, 232–3.

[23] I shall discuss the Epicurean origin of the position reported by Sextus in Sections 5.4–5.5. Cf. the back-reference in *Math.* 6.4 to the double argumentation used in *Against the Grammarians* (*Math.* 1), which also heavily relies on Epicurean material.

[24] *Math.* 5.6. ὅθεν καὶ ἡμεῖς ὑπὲρ τοῦ μὴ δοκεῖν τι τῆς διδασκαλίας χρεωκοπεῖν, τὸν ἑκατέρου δόγματος ἢ ἀπορήματος χαρακτῆρα κεφαλαιωδέστερον ἐφοδεύσομεν, μήτε ἐν τοῖς παρέλκουσιν ὑπερεκπίπτοντες εἰς μακρὰς διεξόδους μήτε ἐν τοῖς ἀναγκαιοτέροις ὑστεροῦντες πρὸς τὴν τῶν ἐπειγόντων ἔκθεσιν, ἀλλὰ μέσην καὶ μεμετρημένην κατὰ τὸ δυνατὸν ποιούμενοι τὴν διδασκαλίαν. Cf. Blank 1998, xliii–xliv.

are aptly described as being *pragmatikōtera*, more directly concerned with the topic under investigation (6.38, with Heintze's emendation).[25] The comparative need not imply an overly strong preference on Sextus' side, since both the 'more aporetic' and the 'more dogmatic' arguments are broadly *pragmatikōs*: they both motivate resistance to rash assent to musicological tenets, if slightly different ones.[26]

A striking discrepancy is that, when stipulating his target for the whole treatise, Sextus explicitly associates the kind of musicology he resists with Aristoxenus of Tarentum, the famous music theorist of Pythagorean and Peripatetic leanings. This is surprising for at least two reasons. First, Aristoxenus is an odd suspect for many of the views discussed in *Math.* 6. He is commonly taken to be opposed not only to the analysis of music in terms of mathematical harmony, but also to the idea that there is a correlation between musical structures and ethical dispositions.[27] Second, setting different targets for the two sections would allow Sextus to go on record that he opposes not one but two forms of dogmatism about music; first, the positive dogma that its study is scientifically sound and morally beneficial, and second, the negative one that we should categorically refrain from investigating musicological questions.

[25] Sextus labels arguments pertaining to a specific subject as being πραγματικῶς λεγόμενα (*Math.* 1.7, 5.106, 6.68, cf. 2.28) and those more appropriate for specialised inquiry as πραγματικωτέρας (cf. 1.63). The decision to translate the qualifier as 'an inquiry of a more practical nature' (Bury 1949, 391, cf. 'more practical inquiry' by Davidson Greaves 1986, 157 and 181, and 'betrifft eine praktische Untersuchung' by Jürß 2001, 153) has received considerable criticism (Barnes 1988, 57 n. 9). Some renderings emphasise that these arguments are tailored to the topic at hand: 'une discussion plus technique' (Ruelle 1898, 151); 'le argomentazioni sostanziali', 'una ricerca che è più pertinente all'argomento' (Russo 1972, 5 and 219); 'une recherche qui s'en tient aux faits' (Pellegrin 2002, 64 and 435), 'sachliche, substantielle' (La Sala 2010, 265), 'sachlich orientierte' (Ritoók 2004, 591), or 'mehr auf die Sache bezogene Untersuchung' (Riethmüller 1975, 186); and 'basing ourselves effectively on factual data' (Spinelli 2010, 249); cf. the remark by Bett 2013, 163, that 'It seems to refer to arguments that go to the heart of the matters, or the objects – the *pragmata* – that have been or are about to be discussed'. Others focus on the power and efficacy of these arguments: 'more effective ... investigation, that is, one concerned with music itself, rather than its effects' (Blank 1998, xliv, cf. 64); 'plus efficaces', 'plus capable d'atteindre le coeur même de la question' (Bett 2006, 23); or 'selecting all the counter-arguments that are really effective at demolishing the dogmatic pretensions of the supporters of the liberal arts' (Spinelli 2010, 256).

[26] *Pace* Barnes 1988, 59 and 75; Bett 2006, 20–4.

[27] As pointed out by Bett 2013, 157 n. 4 and 175–6 with n. 32–3. Some readers challenge this view. Thus Provenza 2012 argues that fr. 26 Wehrli shows Aristoxenus as engaged in Pythagorean-style musical therapy, while Rocconi 2012, 76–86 reads the report of Ps.-Plutarch's *De musica*, chapters 31–36 as evidence for his traditional views on the role of musical education in character-formation. Both scholars admit, however, that their reading is not clearly preferable to its alternative. On this, see esp. Barker 2007, 249–59; on Aristoxenus in general, see Barker 1978, Brancacci 1984, Barker 2007, esp. 113–259, Zhmud 2012b.

In response, one might point out two things. On the one hand, the Aristoxenian attempt to ground the science of harmonics in hearing is a good target for the Sextan arguments. On the other hand, those who reject Aristoxenus-style musicology do not thereby form a dogmatic view in a different domain; it is still the very idea of musicology that they claim to have some knowledge about. At any rate, Sextus seems to be looking for a mere figurehead of the project that he opposes without any interest in its details. His carelessness not only makes his procedure less transparent but also diminishes the doxographical value of his presentation. In the words of a prominent scholar of music theory, Sextus 'adds little to our understanding of Greek music – music, for him, was just another subject in which a burden of insupportable, dogmatic lore has accumulated and was in need of removing'; and thus the arguments he gathers together for this purpose 'do not particularly require support from the various technicalities he adduces'.[28]

In other words, music theory does not hold any special significance for a Sceptic, yet it is no accident that it is included among the targets of *Math.* 1–6. Its prominent role in much of dogmatic thought is reason enough to oppose it, and with the material at his disposal Sextus can not only do away with its tenets but also make us sit on the fence about its utility for a life worth living.[29] In the next two sections, I shall present his arguments with this understanding in mind.

5.3 The Non-existence Arguments

The aporetic section takes its departure from a dogmatic definition of musicology, complemented by a rather inconsequential account of music theory (6.39–51). According to the target definition, which adds precision to the initial definition in 6.1, musicology is a field of knowledge concerned with the study of *melos* (melody) and *rhythmos* (rhythm), and thus the proper course of action for a Sceptic is to uproot the dogmatic edifice by arguing that these core notions – as conceived by the dogmatists – are

[28] Rowell 1987, 360. For a different view, see Wersinger 2007, 511–19, who argues unconvincingly for a philosophical link between the notions of musical dissonance and Pyrrhonian disagreement.

[29] Given the anti-dogmatist angle from which Sextus approaches the arts, there is nothing surprising about what Bett 2013, 175, finds 'disappointing', namely, his lack of interest in what one would today recognise as genuinely aesthetic questions. Compare, however, the surprising verdict of Reiss 1934, 183: 'Le traité de Sextus sur la musique n'a pas le caractère d'une dissertation philosophique; grâce à son style, il est plutôt d'une esquisse critique et littéraire.'

inconsistent. Their inconsistency will in turn entail the non-existence of 'music' under the given description.[30]

At this point, Sextus could proceed immediately to argue in support of the claims, first, that *melos* does not exist, and second, that *rhythmos* does not exist. He does not, however, tackle either of these head-on, but rather links them to more fundamental notions, and generates doubts about those instead. On the one hand, he presents *melos* as dependent on the notion of *phthoggos*, which in turn falls under 'sound' (*phōnē*). On the other hand, he points out that *rhythmos* in turn cannot be conceived without a notion of 'time' (*chronos*) already in place, because it consists of *arsis* and *thesis*, which are quantities of time (6.60).[31] On this basis, he goes on to offer arguments to the conclusion that dogmatic thinkers cannot coherently conceive of sound (6.52–58), followed by arguments in the same vein against time (6.59–67).

The arguments against sound are based, as Sextus claims, on the testimony of the dogmatists, but are presented here merely in the form of reminders of their fuller exposition elsewhere.[32] First of all, various dogmatists allegedly held views incompatible with the existence of sound. According to Sextus, the Cyrenaics believed that only *pathē* exist, but sound is not a *pathos* but rather something that brings about a *pathos*; and thus, following the alleged Cyrenaic line, sound cannot be said to exist. Similarly, he maintains that Democritus and Plato 'have done away with' (*anairountes*) every sense-object; but then sound, being 'the proper sense-object of hearing' (*to idion aisthēton akoēs*, as granted already at 6.39), cannot exist on their view (6.53).[33]

[30] 6.38. οἷον ἐπεὶ ἡ μουσικὴ ἐπιστήμη τίς ἐστιν ἐμμελῶν τε καὶ ἐκμελῶν ἐνρύθμων τε καὶ ἐκρύθμων, πάντως ἐὰν δείξωμεν ὅτι οὔτε τὰ μέλη ὑποστατά ἐστιν οὔτε οἱ ῥυθμοὶ τῶν ὑπαρκτῶν πραγμάτων τυγχάνουσιν, ἐσόμεθα παρεστακότες καὶ τὴν μουσικὴν ἀνυπόστατον. The same definition appears at *Math.* 11.186, and it closely corresponds to Aristoxenus, *Harm.* 2.36–38. Cf. also *Math.* 1.255, 7.146 (on Speusippus), and Philodemus, *De musica* 4, col. 34.31–33 and 112.34–36.

[31] He helps himself to these moves partly by pointing to the account of music theory presented before the arguments. This account also includes a reference to the correspondence between musical φθόγγος and ethical characteristics (6.48–51), an idea which does not need to be directly confronted if the divisions underlying it are already done away with.

[32] 6.52: ἐκ τοῦ φωνὴν αὐτοὺς κατὰ γένος ὑπάρχειν, φήσομεν, καὶ τὴν φωνὴν ἀνύπαρκτον ἡμῖν ἐν τοῖς σκεπτικοῖς ὑπομνήμασι δεδεῖχθαι ἀπὸ τῆς τῶν δογματικῶν μαρτυρίας. On this section and the possible cross-references, see especially Bett 2013, 177–80.

[33] For Sextus' presentation of Democritus' views, see *Math.* 7.135–141, cf. *Pyr.* 1.213–215; of Plato's, *Math.* 7.141–144; on Cyrenaic epistemology, see *Math.* 7.190–200. The same point about sound being a proper sense-object is exploited by the arguments attributed at 6.55 to a lost work. These arguments allegedly showed the non-existence of the soul, which entails the non-existence of the senses and their proper sense-objects, and thus that of sound as well.

The same would follow from the claim, not attributed to anyone in particular, that 'sound is conceived of neither as a completed nor as a substantial thing' (ἡ φωνὴ οὔτε ἐν ἀποτελέσματι οὔτε ἐν ὑποστάσει νοεῖται), but rather as something 'that comes to be in time' (ἐν γενέσει καὶ χρονικῇ παρεκτάσει); since something that comes to be, says Sextus, does not yet exist, sound will be found to be non-existent as well (6.57). Similarly, if one were to be guided by dogmatic arguments, one would have to face the disagreement between Stoic arguments for the corporeality of sound and the Peripatetic arguments for its incorporeality (6.54),[34] or deal with the inability to conceive of sound as either short or long (6.56), as already established in the book *Against the Grammarians* (*Math.* 1.124–30).

The section ends with an appeal to further considerations presented elsewhere (6.58), leaving the reader with the impression that the arguments mentioned in this subsection are not only unconvincing but also rather derivative. Instead of making his case at length, Sextus seems to require his reader to work out various details on her own. On a charitable reading, one could understand Sextus as consciously basing his present task of refutation on successful applications of his Sceptical capacity in related contexts; thus, if he has indeed managed to raise suspicion about fundamental matters elsewhere, the immediate implausibility of the local arguments – or the lack thereof – is arguably less of a concern.[35]

Similarly, the subsection concerning the non-existence of time is presented as the recapitulation of arguments presented in another context. At 6.61, Sextus announces that he will restate the arguments he has already made elsewhere, but only up to a certain extent (*epi poson*). He might very well have in mind the discussion of time in Book 2 of *Against the Physicists*.[36] Thus he argues that, on several counts, one cannot accept any of the opposing views about time – whether it is limited or unlimited (6.62), whether it is divisible or indivisible (6.64–67); and also, that various dogmatic conceptions, for example, that time is composed of parts other than the present, are incompatible with the conception of time as existing (6.63, cf. 66–67).[37]

[34] On this see Bett 2013, 179 with n. 37.

[35] Indeed, he seems to assume familiarity not only with arguments presented in earlier books (compare his remark at *Math.* 1.160 that he will postpone the discussion of ποδός until *Math.* 6), but also with those presented in other works. Perhaps Sextus had a roadmap laid out for his continuous demolition job all along.

[36] The argument in *Math.* 10.169–247, and its relationship to *Pyr.* 3.136–150, has been analysed by Bobzien 2015, 275–92. At 292 n. 43, she points out that the presentation in *Math.* 6.62–67 is closer to the *Math.* 10 version (esp. 189–199) than to *Pyr.* 3 (esp. 140–146). See also Warren 2003.

[37] At *Math.* 6.66, as well as at *Math.* 10.197, Sextus attributes this latter argument to Timon of Phlius.

If one is tempted by any of Sextus' arguments, one will be drawn towards conclusions of the following sort: if either sound or time does not exist, a science of music does not exist either; but sound and/or time do not exist, and thus a science of music does not exist. Sextus must be propounding these arguments against a view concerning the nature of music, according to which it is not merely related to sound and time – which is a rather trivial claim – but can be accounted for in terms of properly grasped notions of sound and timing. Given such a view, the conclusion that these notions are incompatible with other tenets held by dogmatists entails that the very same dogmatists could not have convincingly established a branch of musicology on their basis.

This raises another problem. It is *prima facie* unclear how these arguments are meant to bring about a state of *aporia* in a sense compatible with Sextus' more familiar goal of *epochē*. It seems that, by considering the aporetic arguments, one is meant to arrive at the conclusion – and thus, perhaps, the belief – that the core notions of musicology, and thus musicology itself, are non-existent (*anyparktos, anypostatos, asystatos*). Similar considerations have prompted various interpreters to assume that one can find in Sextus remnants of a previous stage of Pyrrhonism which embraced the conclusion that no view can be defended.[38] However, if one reads *Math.* 1–6 in light of *Pyr.*, it becomes clear that Sextus employs aporetic argumentation in the service of suspension of judgement.

Quite often in the specific account of *Pyr.*, Sextus argues for the non-existence of a thing under a given dogmatic description. This amounts to saying that the dogmatic account on offer is incoherent, or that nothing can be firmly asserted about the matter at hand, with the implication that one should avoid acquiring a dogmatic belief by rashly assenting to the proposed notion.[39] This conclusion does not entail the non-existence of the thing *tout court*, which would itself be a dogmatic view. Thus the Sextan argument to the effect that the criterion of truth is *anyparktos* covers only dogmatic accounts of the

[38] On such a dogmatising variant of Pyrrhonism, attributed to Aenesidemus, see Woodruff 1988, esp. 100–6, Bett 2006, 28–32 (partially withdrawn by Bett 2013, 167–8). These readings rely on considerations similar to those proposed by Janáček 1972, 41–3, 87–9, 132–3, who argued that the Sextus of *Math.* 1–6 is using a pre-Sextan sort of ἀντίρρησις, not as a means to ἐποχή but as an end in itself. Cf. also his 1994/2008, 351.

[39] For a detailed defence of such a reading, see Schofield 2007, 283–303, who shows that Sextus takes aporetic arguments either to engender ἐποχή in themselves, or to do so by counterbalancing dogmatic accounts. See also Decleva Caizzi 1992, 307–13, Pellegrin 2006, 39–41, Polito 2014, 94–5; cf. Fortuna 1987, 130–3. On Sextus' understanding of ἀπορία, see Castagnoli 2017.

criterion under discussion.[40] He argues along the same lines that there is no indicative sign, which he explicitly presents as an argument to counterbalance the dogmatic account of such a sign, leading to equipollence as a result (*Pyr.* 2.103); and he carefully explains that the non-existence and inconceivability of signs is equivalent to claiming that signs are not accurately apprehended (*Pyr.* 2.123).[41]

This accords well with Sextus' understanding of the equivalent denominations of his philosophical movement. In *Pyr.* 1.7, he describes the state of *aporia* in terms quite similar to what suspension of judgement is supposedly like: in such a state, 'one is raising puzzles and investigates everything' (*peri pantos aporein kai zētein*), 'not being able to give assent and to choose as a result' (*amēchanein pros synkatathesin ē arnēsin*). It is true that, for whatever reason, the aporetic language predominates in *Math.* 1–6, at the expense of any significant mention of *epochē* outside of the proem.[42] It is perhaps not implausible to explain this away as merely a choice of terminology that reflects the specific task of the treatise: offering suggestions as to how one should bring about the desired state, the details of which have been sufficiently explained on a previous occasion.

5.4 The Utility Arguments

I have argued in the previous section that, even if Sextus does not set out the dogmatists' case before presenting the aporetic arguments, the state of indecision that he intends to bring about is compatible with, or even equivalent to, suspension of judgement about the existence of musicology. Turning to the 'more dogmatic' section, we are faced with a difficulty concerning not the format of the presentation but rather the domain in which these arguments apply.[43] On the one hand, the discussion of the utility of knowledge concerning matters of music exhibits the oppositional arrangement that one usually expects from Sextus. On the other hand, it is puzzling that suspension of judgement about this question would somehow contribute to the demolition of dogmatic musicology. An appealing

40 *Pyr.* 2.79–80; see similar considerations about, for example, the truth, the sayables, and statements (*Pyr.* 2.109).

41 Cf. *Math.* 8.159–161, where the purpose of the counterargument about signs is explained as that of bringing the investigation into equilibrium and suspension. Similarly, the arguments for the inconsistency of dogmatic notions of time and for the non-existence of time are both taken to lead to ἀπορία (Bobzien 2015, 281–2, 289–90). Another way to explain the tension away is to emphasise that the non-existence claims are mere appearance-claims (Riethmüller 1975, 189–90).

42 As pointed out by Janáček 1972, 87, the only occurrence, at 2.99, is philosophically irrelevant.

43 On this section, see Blank 1998, xlii–xliv, Bett 2013, 168–75.

suggestion has been that, since an art is by definition useful, arguing against the usefulness of musicology amounts to arguing that no art of musicology exists.[44] After an overview of the section, I will point to another, though compatible, suggestion.[45]

As a first approximation, one might take the section to divide naturally into arguments in favour of (6.7–18) and against (6.19–37) the utility of music. However, this rough division is inaccurate, since Sextus accomplishes the task of refutation in two successive stages. First, he contests claims 'that are customarily babbled around by many about music' (τὰ ὑπὲρ μουσικῆς παρὰ τοῖς πολλοῖς εἰωθότα θρυλεῖσθαι, 6.7), and then he comes up against what he takes to be the principal argument (*proēgoumenos logos*, 6.29) of the dogmatists. The resulting division between the first and the second round of refutation (7–28 and 29–37, respectively) cuts across the simple oppositional divide mentioned above and reflects Sextus' method of first addressing specific proposals and only then narrowing in on the bone of contention.

In the first round, he catalogues a number of stories familiar from Greek cultural and literary history that allegedly testify to the power of music. Thus we learn that Pythagoras advised an *aulos*-player on what tune to play in order to bring a group of drunken youth back to sobriety (6.8), and that the raging Achilles knew that he could calm himself down by playing the right notes on his lyre (6.10). These stories allege that knowledge about the peculiar powers of musical tunes allows the protagonist to manipulate human behaviour. The very same idea explains the practice of military music by both the Spartan and the Athenian army (6.9), or the fact that musical guardianship was thought to be appropriate for guarding the virtue of women like Clytemnestra while their husbands were away (6.11–12).[46] In sum, the usefulness of music is generally recognised, as is shown by its widespread use in various social contexts (6.18).[47]

[44] Barnes 1988, 74–5.

[45] Spinelli 2010, 258, suggests that Sextus relies on these arguments because the arts, unlike philosophy, claimed to be useful for life. Yet the claim that philosophy is useful is not only not unheard of (cf. *Math.* 9.41), but is in fact the Epicurean position which these arguments were originally meant to support.

[46] The story about Pythagoras is also reported by Iamblichus, *VP* 111–112, and by Quintilian, *Inst.* 1.10.32. Philodemus' *De musica* differs in mentioning a female *aulos*-player (4, col. 42.39–45), while Galen, *PHP* 5.6.21 (= *CMG* 5.453.2–6 Müller) attributes the story to Damon, and Ps-Plutarch, *Mus.* 1146F to Aristoxenus. See Spinelli 2016, 302–5. The stories about Achilles and Clytemnestra come from Homer (*Iliad* 9.186–189 and *Odyssey* 3.265–271 respectively), while the claims about the Greek military use of music appear in Ps.-Plutarch, *Mus.* 1140C, cf. Philodemus, *De musica* 4, col. 72.43–73.2.

[47] Sextus also reports on debates about the relative merits of old and new music (6.14–15) and of poetry and music (6.16–17), which have little significance for the progression of the argument.

The underlying idea, according to Sextus, is that these stories provide evidence for the view that, for the purposes of ethical transformation, music is preferable to philosophy:

> If, they say, we approve of philosophy for imparting self-control to human life and suppressing the passions of the soul, we approve of music much more, because instead of ordering us around rather forcefully, it uses a certain enchanting persuasiveness to achieve the same results as philosophy.[48]

The underlying assumption, according to Sextus, is that musical notes are by nature (*physei*) of a certain character – for example, sobering or encouraging, calming or consoling. This is then denied on various grounds: not only that the same sound can be produced by more than one cause – the relevance of which is unclear – but, more importantly, because the same sound can have different effects on different subjects, or on the same subject at different times (6.19–20). The denial is then followed up by the suggestion that, even if notes were such-and-such by nature, it would not be enough to establish that they are thereby useful for life. On the proposed alternative, their actual effect is more diversion than moderation.[49] Once the music is over, we return to our previous state of mind, without as much as a hint of ethical progress. The unnerved soldiers, the irate Achilles, or the drunken youth were only momentarily distracted from their troublesome state of mind (6.24–25). Nor does music encourage chastity, as famous examples of misbehaving wives testify (6.26). Most importantly, Pythagoras, who was mistaken in the first place to have engaged with the intoxicated, admits by his conduct that the musician is better suited to the task than the philosopher (6.23) – an objection that loses sight of the fact that it was the philosopher, not the musician, who knew what to do.

The underlying concern that one should not outsource the job of philosophy to the ill-suited discipline of music is most probably that of an Epicurean thinker.[50] In giving the counterargument, Sextus copies

[48] *Math.* 6.7: εἴπερ τοίνυν, φασί, φιλοσοφίαν ἀποδεχόμεθα σωφρονίζουσαν τὸν ἀνθρώπινον βίον καὶ τὰ ψυχικὰ πάθη καταστέλλουσαν, πολλῷ μᾶλλον ἀποδεχόμεθα τὴν μουσικήν, ὅτι οὐ βιαστικώτερον ἐπιτάττουσα ἡμῖν ἀλλὰ μετὰ θελγούσης τινὸς πειθοῦς τῶν αὐτῶν ἀποτελεσμάτων περιγίνεται ὧνπερ καὶ ἡ φιλοσοφία. The translation in Bury 1949 ('we should rather more admit music') is perhaps based on Bekker's conjecture of ἀποδεξόμεθα, implying the stronger claim that one should do music *rather than* philosophy.

[49] *Math.* 6.21: εἶτα κἂν τοιαῦτα ᾖ τὰ τῆς μουσικῆς μέλη, οὐ διὰ τοῦτο καὶ ἡ μουσικὴ βιωφελὴς καθέστηκεν. οὐ γὰρ ὅτι δύναμιν ἔχει σωφρονιστικήν, καταστέλλει τὴν διάνοιαν, ἀλλὰ ᾗ περισπαστικήν. On the construction of this passage, see Shorey 1916.

[50] On Epicureanism in *Math.* 6, see Gigante 1981, 180–6, Rispoli 1992, Blank 1998, Delattre 2006 and 2007, Blank 2009, 233.

a characteristically non-Sceptical statement into his refutation, namely, that 'it is contrary to our belief' (παρὰ γὰρ τὴν ἡμετέραν δόξαν τὸ τοιοῦτο γίνεται) that sounds by nature have a certain sort of effect. Then he draws an analogy with the mistaken notion that thunder is a divine epiphany; as the Epicureans have maintained (*kata phasin Epikoureiōn paides*), it is a superadded belief (*all' hyph' hēmōn prosdoxazetai*: 6.19–20) that renders musical units or meteorological phenomena ethically or theologically significant.[51] Furthermore, the inserted Epicurean tenets are contrasted to the view, championed by Plato, that musical harmony correctly describes the state of the philosopher's and the musician's soul.[52] This is allegedly the reason why Plato describes the aging Socrates as turning to the study of music under the guidance of Lampon.[53] The authority of Plato on this matter is explicitly contrasted with that of Epicurus, who thought that such an enterprise does not contribute to the pursuit of happiness.[54]

At this point, Sextus turns to what *proēgoumenōs legetai*, that is, to the essential points needed to make the Sceptic's case.[55] This turns out to be a conjunction of five propositions, so that if any of them is correct, the usefulness of musicology for a happy life is vindicated. Unsurprisingly, Sextus – or his Epicurean source – claims to rebut each conjunct. First, one might argue that the possession of musical skill (*mousikē empeiria*)[56]

[51] On the thunder example, see Epicurus, *Ep. Pyth.* 100.

[52] For an extensive treatment of the Platonic account, see Pelosi 2010; see also Schofield 2010. The Platonic approach was further developed by various Stoic thinkers, with the crucial difference that they understood both τέχνη and ἐπιστήμη to be grounded in increasingly firmer grasps of theoretical principles deriving from sense-perception, which made their conception of the arts vulnerable to Academic objections against the apprehensible impression (see Cicero, *Acad. post.* 20–22; 31; 87; 91). On the privileged position of musical τέχνη in Stoicism, see Long 1991, Barker 2001, Scade 2017, Woodward 2010.

[53] *Math.* 6.13: Οἵ τε μέγα δυνηθέντες ἐν φιλοσοφίᾳ, καθάπερ καὶ Πλάτων, τὸν σοφὸν ὅμοιόν φασιν εἶναι τῷ μουσικῷ, τὴν ψυχὴν ἡρμοσμένην ἔχοντα. Καθὸ καὶ Σωκράτης καίπερ βαθυγήρως ἤδη γεγονὼς οὐκ ᾐδεῖτο πρὸς Λάμπωνα τὸν κιθαριστὴν φοιτῶν, καὶ πρὸς τὸν ἐπὶ τούτῳ ὀνειδίσαντα λέγειν ὅτι κρεῖττόν ἐστιν ὀψιμαθῆ μᾶλλον ἢ ἀμαθῆ διαβάλλεσθαι. As for the story about Socrates and Lampon, one might point to *Menexenus* 236a, which mentions Lamprus as teaching Socrates; while Lampon is mentioned by Plutarch, *Pericles* 6.2 (154A). The story told in *Phaedo* 60d of Socrates first composing poetry in prison might also be relevant here. See also *Euthydemus* 272b-c, mentioning Metrobius the harpist.

[54] *Math.* 6.27: καὶ μὴν <οὐκ> εἰ [οὔτε] οἱ περὶ τὸν Πλάτωνα μουσικὴν ἀπεδέξαντο, ῥητέον [οὐ] πρὸς εὐδαιμονίαν αὐτὴν συντείνειν, ἐπεὶ καὶ ἄλλοι μὴ λειπόμενοι τῆς τούτων ἀξιοπιστίας, καθάπερ οἱ περὶ τὸν Ἐπίκουρον, ἠρνήσαντο ταύτην τὴν ἀντιποίησιν, λέγοντες τοὐναντίον αὐτὴν ἀσύμφορον εἶναι καὶ ἀργήν, φίλοινον, χρημάτων ἀτημελῆ.

[55] Compare Sextus' use of the adjective to refer to 'criterion' in the logical sense (*Pyr.* 2.16, *Math.* 7.34), or when disregarding details only interesting to the specialist (*Math.* 9.418; 10.306; 2.9; 3.65; 5.3). Cf. Bobzien 2015, 280. It is also used for the Sceptic's own position, as opposed to the specific account, in *Math.* 7.1.

[56] Barnes 1988, 70 points out that it is a synonym for the relevant τέχνη.

increases the pleasure of listening to music. But on the contrary, it is not only the case that the pleasure deriving from music is not necessary for life, but also that the expert musician gets the same amount of it as a non-musical being does (6.31–34).[57]

Second, one might argue that musical education is a prerequisite of moral excellence. However, one could just as well make the case 'for the contrary, namely, that music might induce us to resist the striving after virtue' (ἀνάπαλιν γὰρ ἀντικόπτει καὶ ἀντιβαίνει πρὸς τὸ τῆς ἀρετῆς ἐφίεσθαι: 6.35). The third conjunct is met by a rather laconic response. Some might argue, we read, that the elements (*stoicheia*) of music and philosophy are identical, but it does not follow that music is therefore properly said to be useful (6.36). As for the last two arguments, the rebuttals are increasingly short. Pythagoreans claim that, given the harmonious order of the universe, the knowledge of musical theorems brings knowledge of the universe as well, but 'this is shown to be wrong by a variety of proofs' (*poikilōs deiknytai pseudos*) and does not contribute to happiness (*makariotēs*: 6.37); while the claim that melodies (*melē*) affect the soul has already been dismissed (*ibidem*, referring perhaps to 6.28).

It seems fairly clear that the arguments in this section derive from an Epicurean attack on Pythagorean, Platonising, and perhaps Stoic ideas about the utility of musical knowledge for philosophical purposes.[58] In order to explain how Sextus might relate to such material, it is worth returning once again to the proem, where he contrasts his suspensive motives with the agenda of Epicureans who mounted disturbingly similar 'objections against the fields of study' (πρὸς τοὺς ἀπὸ τῶν μαθημάτων ἀντίρρησιν). According to Sextus, they did so from differing dispositions (*diathesis*): while Epicureans concluded that the arts 'do not contribute to the attainment of wisdom' (μηδὲν συνεργούντων πρὸς σοφίας τελείωσιν, 1.1), the Pyrrhonians would have never subscribed to such a claim, as it is a dogmatic one (*dogmatikos gar ho logos*: 1.5).

[57] The only, rather feeble, reason given to believe so is that the behaviour of uneducated children and non-rational animals indicates their enjoyment of music (6.32). While stories of toddlers soothed by lullabies and dolphins swimming closer to ships to hear the musicians play are rather amusing (see e.g. Euripides' *Electra* 435), they do not convince us either way about the relative pleasures of the educated and the non-educated.

[58] The most plausible candidate is Book 4 of Philodemus' *De musica* (Delattre 2007), organised around the presentation and refutation of arguments by the Stoic Diogenes of Babylon. See, for example, Abert 1899, 37–8, Wilkinson 1938, Gigante 1981, 214, Asmis 1991, 80–1 (who also mentions Zeno as a possible source), Rispoli 1992, Delattre 2006, 52–60. For some doubts, see Fowler 1984, 254–5, Bett 2013, 171, Spinelli 2016, 306–7. I see little support for the suggestion by Riethmüller 1975, 185 n. 6 that these arguments were familiar to Sextus from an earlier Sceptical source.

Epicurus did in fact argue that, since the only way towards human happiness is through philosophy (for philosophy is the only 'useful' art), vigorous attempts to master any other discipline would merely distract us from the salvation within our reach. Thus he explicitly urged Pythocles to flee from traditional education and promoted his own lack of traditional education (*apaideusia*) as an example worth following.[59] On a charitable reading, this applies only to the professional engagement with arts: one should not take it as one's priority to familiarise oneself with the details of artistic theory, or to achieve a level of competence by continuous practice, in place of practising philosophy. Should the opportunity arise, the Epicurean would nevertheless derive pleasure from artistic performances or from intelligent sympotic discussions.[60]

Sextus understands Epicurean *apaideusia* rather differently. He claims that Epicurus went out of his way to attack well-educated men in order to hide his own ignorance; thus he violently criticised Plato, Aristotle, and especially Nausiphanes, a pupil of Pyrrho and a teacher of the young Epicurus himself. In order to present himself as a self-taught and self-made philosopher (*autodidaktos . . . kai autophyēs philosophos*), he denied having learned anything from Nausiphanes (*Math.* 1.2–3). Sextus' remark is clearly *ad hominem* and points not only to an ongoing family feud between Epicureans and Pyrrhonists but also to an effort to represent the Pyrrhonist as less of an enemy of common culture than she might seem.[61]

Having pointed out that his attitude is uncharitable and self-serving, one should also mention that Sextus helps himself to a further point. Epicureans are, after all, dogmatisers, who have completely missed the suspensive potential of their arguments. Sextus can explain this by pointing out that they were misled by their own motivated reasoning. Thus they have found themselves with a view about the utility of the arts for wisdom and the happy life (see *Math.* 1.270; 6.4, 34, 37), and having such a view

[59] On the value of philosophy, see *Ep. Men.* 122. The advice to Pythocles comes at *Ep. Pyth.* 6: Παιδείαν δὲ πᾶσαν, μακάριε, φεῦγε τἀκάτιον ἀράμενος; on Epicurus' lack of education, see Cicero, *Fin.* 1.26 and 71–72; see also Plutarch, *Non posse* 1094D-E, Athenaeus, *Deipnosophistae* 13.588A, Cicero, *Tusc.* 5.116–117, and perhaps *Ep. Pyth.* 85.

[60] Plutarch, *Non posse* 1095C-D, attempts to catch Epicurus in a contradiction in this regard: despite his profession of ignorance about these matters, Epicurus claims that only the wise will correctly discuss poetry and music (cf. *Ep. Pyth.* 120). But there is no actual contradiction. Cf. Asmis 1991, 76–7, Blank 1998, xxii and 2009, 219–20. For a classification of Epicurean pleasures, see esp. Celkyte 2017, 61–70.

[61] On Epicurus' admiration for Pyrrho's διάθεσις (Diog. Laert. 9.64 = Antigonus of Carystus fr. 2), see Sedley 1976, 137; cf. Fortuna 1987, 127–8. On the relationship between early Epicureans and Pyrrhonians, see also Warren 2002, esp. 25 n. 56. On the Sceptical διάθεσις, see also Diog. Laert. 9.70, *Math.* 11.1, *Pyr.* 1.187 and 2.10; cf. Blank 1998, 74.

blocks the possibility of further inquiry. One might sit on the fence concerning the existence of musicology while at the same time taking Epicurus' word for its lack of utility; but then someone who has achieved the proper attitude with regard to the former question might still fail to be a Pyrrhonian inquirer. Sextus, then, does a great service to his reader by appropriating these arguments and showing that they are in fact compatible with his suspensive project.

5.5 Sextus on Music: A Form of Scepticism

In the previous sections, I have defended the compatibility of Sextus' arguments against the arts with a plausible reading of the Sextan project in general, and briefly analysed the two sorts of arguments he uses against musicology in particular. The reading I have proposed helps us better understand *Math.* 6 in its own terms. Sextus argues for the non-existence of musicology in order to counterbalance the arguments in its favour, and seizes upon a set of Epicurean arguments in order to bring about suspension of judgement concerning the utility of such an art. As a result, he can arrive at the coherent position that one cannot make firm assertions about the existence of such a science, nor about whether its existence would be desirable. This is compatible with the Pyrrhonian agenda outlined in *Pyr.* 1, and can perhaps be seen as a further step in the continuous refutation of dogmatism across the board.

At the same time, my proposal is relevant for the overall interpretation of *Math.* 1–6. According to an influential reading, the treatise at large shows signs of Sextus' philosophical identity crisis, the most important evidence for which allegedly comes from *Against the Musicologists*. On the one hand, he sometimes speaks in an Epicurean voice, drawing a distinction between useful and useless arts, while at other times he urges his reader to suspend judgement across the board. On the other hand, even his Sceptical arguments are ill-suited to their purpose: they are too strong and in effect commit Sextus to the dogmatic belief that musicology does not exist.[62] By showing that the two 'voices' of *Math.* 6 are compatible and that they aim at the same suspensive outcome, I have explained away the main motivation for either sort of incoherence reading of *Math.* 1–6.

[62] The first charge was pointed out by Barnes 1988, 72–3, who also proposed various ways of dealing with Sextus' so-called 'schizophrenia' (including the one I have presented). The second charge was added by Bett 2006, 21–2; cf. Desbordes 1982, 55.

However, the emerging Sextan critique of the ethical and epistemic credentials of musicology invites further remarks. First of all, the view presented by Sextus conflicts with the attitude towards the arts in early Pyrrhonism: based on at least one strand of tradition, Pyrrho and his disciple Timon were just as hostile to traditional *paideia* as Epicurus seems to have been.[63] Arguably, Sextus' overall presentation of Pyrrhonism testifies to his effort to reformulate it as a position that accords with ordinary life to a much higher degree than any other philosophical option available. It is in this spirit that he claims, in the proem to *Math.* 1–6, that Pyrrhonians are well educated, broadly experienced, and indifferent to the opinion of the masses – a claim that might signal a significant departure from Pyrrho's position.[64]

This passage seems to give licence to revisionary readings with varying degrees of ambition. To begin with, some argue that this in itself is a refutation of any reading of Sextus according to which he propagates a radical form of Scepticism.[65] Others go even further and argue that, by this stage in his intellectual development, Sextus has abandoned Scepticism for a form of empiricism about justification.[66] These readings, however, read more into the text than it allows for. The Sextus of the *Outlines* insists that the Sceptic returns to the ordinary practices she is familiar with from her pre-suspensive life, and that insofar as these include appearances about technical competences, the Sceptic will be able to practice some arts and crafts (*Pyr.* 1.24, cf. 237).[67] Sextus hastens to assure his reader that, once the instances of illicit belief have been removed, suspension of judgement will leave everything as it is, and his assurance is compatible with more and less radical readings of his genuinely Sceptical project.

One might nevertheless object that the Sextan arguments in *Math.* 1–6 do not cover every form of artistic practice. When it comes to *Math.* 6, it is

[63] See Diog. Laert. 9.69 and 100; 10.2; Aristocles *apud* Eus. *Praep. evang.* 14.18.1–4 and 24; Timon *apud* Athenaeus, *Deipnosophistae* 13.610B. See Lévy 2009, 95–6.

[64] *Math.* 1.5: πεπαιδεῦσθαι καὶ πολυπειροτέρους παρὰ τοὺς ἄλλους ὑπάρχειν φιλοσόφους ἔτι καὶ <ἀ> διαφόρως ἔχουσι πρὸς τὴν παρὰ τοῖς πολλοῖς δόξαν· καὶ μὴν οὐδὲ δυσμενείας χάριν τῆς πρός τινας (μακρὰν γὰρ αὐτῶν τῆς πραότητός ἐστιν ἡ τοιαύτη κακία). This point is explicitly made in contrast to the Epicureans, and thus it is somewhat surprising to find Delattre 2006 arguing that Sextus has a 'réelle sympathie' towards the Epicureans.

[65] Blank 1998, 80; cf. Spinelli 2016, 43.

[66] Thus we find Janáček 2008b arguing that *Math.* 1.5 is the voice of 'der alte Sextos' (351), who has learned to trust 'die volkstümliche συνήθεια' (355). For a classic statement of the empiricist reading, see Brochard 2002, 345–91; see also a remark in Spinelli 2010, 259–61.

[67] On the practical criterion, see Tsouna-McKirahan 1996. The arts posed a special problem for any Sceptical position: 'Accepter les arts, ou au moins certains d'entre eux, entrenait la risque nullement négligeable d'être pris dans l'engrenage de la connaissance. Les refuser, c'était s'exposer à la critique dogmatique accusant le scepticisme de rendre la vie impossible' (Lévy 2009, 106).

especially striking that Sextus distinguishes not two but three senses of *mousikos*, mentioning that it can be used loosely (*katachrēstikōteron*) in ordinary speech. One could offer the following example: when one encounters a beautiful painting of a horse, only to recognise that its painter represented the tedious detail of foam around the horse's mouth with unusual finesse, one would not hesitate to declare that this artwork is very 'musical' indeed. This loose notion seems to invoke a significant artistic concept, the ability to understand and appreciate art, which comes with cognitive and even ethical connotations that are less innocent than the second sense, the simple 'know-how' of music.[68] However, there is no reason to think that its inclusion is more than a pedantic remark by Sextus. As we have seen, the third sense does not contribute to the discussion of music throughout the treatise, and it is unlikely to pick out a sense in which the Sceptic *qua* Sceptic might use the term.[69] Sextus perhaps had a source in front of him which used the threefold distinction, and he merely reproduced it for reasons of completeness.[70]

As for the more general objection that Sextus seems to accept some forms of artistic expertise, I have given three reasons to think that it does not bring non-Sceptical commitments. First, on Sextus' official line, reliance on appearances about the arts is compatible with suspension of judgement. Second, even if the specific argument against, say, music leaves some forms of music untouched, it comes on top of the general argument which is intended to undermine every form of teaching and learning. Finally, Sextus understands the Sceptic's task as the ongoing refutation of newer and newer expressions of dogmatism. In his experience, reason, if anything, is not harmonious: it formulates opposing arguments of equal persuasive force at an astounding rate. Consequently, it might be that the counterarguments employed on one occasion do not target some tenet that will be refuted by another series of arguments later on. This in turn suggests that *Math.* 1–6 is not going to enrich the notion of dogmatism-proof expertise allowed for by *Pyr.* 1.

In sum, the Sceptic might attend musical performances, she might even be moved by music, and discuss its effects on her, but she will not give 'assent to non-evident tenets investigated in the sciences' (τὴν τινι πράγματι τῶν κατὰ τὰς ἐπιστήμας ζητουμένων ἀδήλων συγκατάθεσιν:

68 On this notion, see Halliwell 2012.

69 Even if Sextus claims at *Pyr.* 1.191 that the Sceptic speaks ἀδιαφόρως ... καὶ καταχρηστικῶς; cf. *Math.* 8.129.

70 For reports on similar distinctions employed by dogmatists, see *Pyr.* 3.75 and 119; *Math.* 8.129 and 400.

Pyr. 1.13) – the science of musicology included. She will be ready to fight assertions concerning music that go beyond mere appearance, but the counterarguments she makes use of will not reveal anything about her personal convictions. All one can surmise from the Sceptic's polemics at any point in time is that she finds fault with a certain form of dogmatism, which does not allow for the inference that whatever is left untouched by the arguments on that occasion is *ipso facto* acceptable from a Pyrrhonian point of view.[71]

[71] I thank the editors, Federico M. Petrucci and Francesco Pelosi, for the conference invitation and for their comments on the written version, and Laura Castelli, Aiste Celkyte, Riccardo Chiaradonna, Carlos Lévy, David Machek, and Maria Michela Sassi for helpful comments and suggestions. While preparing and revising this chapter, I was supported first by the DFG–FOR 2311 project and then by the Swiss Government Excellence Scholarship programme.

CHAPTER 6

Shifting Epistemological Perspectives in Ptolemy's Harmonics

From the Science of Sound to the Study of Music

Andrew Barker

In the opening words of the first sentence of his *Harmonics*, Ptolemy tells us what the science of *harmonikē* enables us to grasp and understand. It is 'the differences between sounds (*psophoi*) in respect of high and low pitch' (Ptol. *Harm.* 3.1–2), and this specification serves, in effect, as a definition of the science. In his commentary on the passage, Porphyry quotes two other definitions which he has found in existing technical writings. 'Some people', he says, 'define it as "the knowledge that discerns the nature of that which is attuned (*tēs tou hērmosmenou physeōs*)", others as "the skill of discernment directed to intervallic melody (*hexin theōrētikēn tou diastēmatikou melous*) and its attributes" – that is, the melody which is especially designated as "attuned" (*hērmosmenon*)[1] . . . ' (Porph. *Harm.* 6.4–6). He then quotes Ptolemy's own definition, and he apparently expects readers to take the view that its tenor is so different from the others that Ptolemy and the other writers cannot have been addressing the same intellectual enterprise. He hastens to assure them that this is not the case. 'The definitions', he asserts, 'seem to apply to the same thing'.[2]

But it is abundantly clear that they do not, and part, at least, of Porphyry's attempt to justify his assertion is patently inadequate. 'To say "the difference between sounds in respect of high and low pitch" is no different from saying "the nature of that which is attuned" or "intervallic melody". For it is from differences in respect of high pitch and low that

[1] Porphyry adds this explication to emphasize that the kind of μέλος in question, the 'intervallic' kind, is specific to music, whereas the μέλος of speech is not intervallic but 'continuous' (for Porphyry's discussions of the distinction see Porph. *Harm.* 9.34–10.27, 83.1–84.29).

[2] Or perhaps 'to amount to the same thing', εἰς ταὐτὸ . . . συντείνειν (6.9–10). Massimo Raffa, in his note *ad loc.*, reminds us, correctly, that attempts to reconcile apparently conflicting positions adopted by earlier intellectuals are thoroughly characteristic of Neoplatonist writers, and of Porphyry in particular (Raffa 2016a, 707).

what is attuned is put together, and it [*scil.* that which is attuned] is also designated as "intervallic melody"' (Porph. *Harm.* 6.13–16). The argument is plainly broken-backed; although the attuned melody (*to hērmosmenon melos*) and the intervallic melody (*to diastēmatikon melos*) are indeed formed from sounds that differ in pitch, their scope by no means embraces all sounds that differ in pitch, many of which are incapable of being incorporated into any sort of musical melody. There is in fact nothing in Ptolemy's definition or in its sequel in the rest of his first chapter from which we could confidently infer that the sounds with which his science concerns itself are exclusively or even primarily those involved in music.

Readers in the ancient world would of course have been astonished to be confronted with a work that announced itself as a treatise on *harmonikē* and yet turned out to have nothing to do with music at all. If Ptolemy's first chapter left them wondering whether his treatise might indeed be of that unexampled and alarming sort, they would have been reassured, on reaching chapter 2, by its allusions to the 'harmonic *kanōn*' (i.e. the monochord) and to the errors of Pythagoreans and Aristoxenians (which could be guaranteed to have involved disagreements on musical matters, even though Ptolemy here says nothing to that effect). But so far as his explicit statements reveal, Ptolemy's perspective in this chapter and the next remains as extensive as it was in chapter 1. It is not until chapter 4 that he begins, gradually and almost imperceptibly, to narrow the focus of his attention, to the extent that by the time this chapter is complete and we are launched on chapter 5, we can see that he is unambiguously concerned, after all, not with sounds of each and every kind but with musical sounds and no others.[3]

My main project in this chapter is to consider the way in which this shift of perspective is negotiated. One might argue that no substantial 'negotiation' is necessary, since in moving fairly directly from a discussion of the natures of sound and pitch to a discussion of the concords, Ptolemy is merely following an established practice, one which neither he nor his precursors and successors saw any need to justify. Similar sequences do indeed turn up quite often elsewhere, and authors regularly shift from the first of these topics to the second without explaining the rationale behind the transition; examples can be found in the Euclidean *Sectio canonis*, for instance, in an essay on the *Timaeus* by Adrastus of Aphrodisias and in

[3] Cf. Raffa 2016a, 246 n. 26: 'Con questo capitolo Tolemeo passa dal campo dei suoni in genere (ψόφοι) a quello dei suoni utilizzabili in musica (φθόγγοι).' Quite so: our question is how he conducts the transition; and we shall also find it relevant to enquire whether or not the change of focus involves any substantial alteration in Ptolemy's epistemological stance.

another by Aelianus 'the Platonist', and again in a passage of Boethius where the author is almost certainly ventriloquising Nicomachus.[4] But neither Boethius nor the writer of the *Sectio*, nor Adrastus or Aelianus so far as we know from the substantial surviving remains of their works, had announced, as Ptolemy has, that the topic to which his science is devoted is 'the differences between sounds in respect of high and low pitch'; they address the general class of such differences merely to gain an entrée into the issues about musical relations which are their central concern. As it turns out, much the same is true of Ptolemy, but in specifying the subject of harmonics in the way he does at the beginning of his treatise he sets himself a task which the other writers have no need to tackle. He evidently owes his readers some explanation of the fact that his perspective has now so dramatically narrowed.

An explanation of a sort can be excavated from 1.4, but Ptolemy does not draw attention to its role in the sequence of his thought, and its relevance is easily missed. It is in two parts. First, after distinguishing 'continuous' (*synecheis*) from 'discontinuous' or 'divided' (*diōrismenoi*)[5] unequal-pitched sounds (9.29–10.14),[6] he writes as follows (10.14–18):

> But the former are foreign to harmonics, never providing anything that is one and the same, so that contrary to what is proper to the sciences, they cannot be circumscribed by a boundary (*horos*) or a ratio; while the latter are at home in harmonics, being bounded (*horizomenoi*) by the limits of the equal-pitched parts, and measured against one another (*parametroumenoi*) by the ranking order of their excesses.

We shall return to some of the details embedded in these remarks. What matters most in the first instance, as Porphyry recognises in his commentary *ad loc.* (*Harm.* 85.16–26), is that what Ptolemy calls 'continuous unequal-pitched sounds' are disqualified by their indeterminacy from

[4] *Sect. can.* 148.3–149.24; Adrastus *ap.* Theon, *Exp.* 50.5–52.9, Aelianus *ap.* Porph. *Harm.* 33.16–36.3, Boethius *Inst. mus.* 1.3–8.

[5] Ptolemy here substitutes the participle διωρισμένος for the adjective διαστηματικός ('intervallic') used in this context by Aristoxenus and most other writers. Massimo Raffa suggests that the change is motivated partly by his wish to keep his vocabulary 'il più possibile "neutro" – nel senso di "acustico", non "musicale" – in tutta la trattazione fisico-propedeutica di questi primi capitoli' (Raffa 2002, 284). I think this suggestion is probably correct.

[6] In Ptolemy's usage, an 'unequal-pitched sound' is one that changes pitch in the course of its duration. If it is 'continuous', it changes pitch constantly, never coming to rest on any determinate pitch; if it is 'discontinuous', it moves through a series of steps from one determinate pitch to another, holding itself steady on each of the pitches (which thus constitute a series of 'equal-pitched parts') and moving between them silently and instantaneously, without slurring. Writers on harmonics had repeatedly drawn a distinction of this sort from at least as early as Aristoxenus (*Harm.* 13.7–15.14); it may even have originated with Archytas, half a century earlier (see Porph. *Harm.* 57.24–5).

consideration by the sciences, and *a fortiori* from consideration by harmonic science.[7] Discontinuous unequal-pitched sounds, by contrast, present sequences of clearly delimited and distinguishable pitches; and since differences in pitch are quantitative – or so Ptolemy has argued in 1.3 – the relations between their constituent pitches can be specified in the precise, quantitative form that the sciences demand.

This, then, is part of the explanation; one large class of sounds in which differences of pitch are present has been eliminated from the enquiry, not, however, on musical grounds but for much more general reasons, on account of the conditions that must be met by anything that is to come under scientific scrutiny. Continuous unequal-pitched sounds are simply incapable of meeting these conditions, and harmonic science must therefore focus exclusively on unequal-pitched sounds of the discontinuous kind. But we still need to know why the science's scope is immediately restricted still further. From this point onwards, Ptolemy shows no interest in relations between pitches in discontinuous sounds other than those that have a role in musical constructions. Yet those that have no such role may be equally determinate and no less capable of being specified in precise quantitative terms. On what grounds, then, can Ptolemy justify his neglect of them?

The rest of the explanation we are looking for emerges piecemeal, not so much in statements bearing on the issue directly but through implicit connections between several different passages. One unambigous statement on its own, however, enables us to take the first step. He has already told us (10.12–14) that each individual component of a discontinuous unequal-pitched sound stays on the same pitch throughout its duration; and after dismissing the continuous kind from his agenda, leaving only those that are discontinuous, he adds: 'And indeed we might now call such sounds "notes" (*phthoggoi*), since a note is a sound that maintains one and the same pitch' (10.18–19).

This way of describing a note agrees in its essentials with descriptions found in many other sources and is reminiscent in particular of statements made by Aristoxenus in Book 1 of the *Elementa harmonica*: 'A note is the incidence of the voice on one pitch; for it is when the voice appears to rest at one pitch that there seems to be a note capable of being placed in

[7] Cf. Aristox. *Harm.* 86.6–8: δεῖ γὰρ ἕκαστον τῶν ἐν τῇ μουσικῇ καθ' ὃ πεπέρασται κατὰ τοῦτο τιθέναι τε καὶ τάττειν εἰς τὰς ἐπιστήμας, ᾗ δ' ἄπειρόν ἐστιν ἐᾶν, 'For everything in music must be specified and assigned to its place in the sciences in accordance with the respect in which it is determinate, and insofar as it is indeterminate it must be left aside'. (In the last clause here I read ᾗ with Macran, in place of the MSS reading εἰ.)

a harmonically attuned melody'.[8] The rather different nuances of Ptolemy's description and Aristoxenus' would repay close examination and comparison, but I must not be diverted from the task in hand and will postpone reflections on this alluring topic for another occasion. For present purposes the important point is that while Ptolemy's statement introduces overtly musical terminology for the first time in his treatise and effectively gives notice that musical issues will be – at least – *among* those under scrutiny in the sequel, it by no means guarantees that all the relations between the 'notes' that are to be scrutinized will be musical ones. Let us recall that the subject of harmonics was initially specified as 'the differences between sounds in respect of high and low pitch' and observe that it is not the sounds that constitute the science's subject-matter but the relations between them indicated by Ptolemy's word 'differences'. Let us further agree that sounds which 'maintain one and the same pitch', and no others, are capable of standing in specifically *musical* relations to one another. But in many cases the relations between pairs of pitches are musically unacceptable, and Ptolemy has not yet explained why these non-musical relations should not also fall into the territory of harmonics.[9]

The next part of the text, which completes the chapter, is worth quoting in full.

> Hence each note by itself has no ratio, since it is identical with itself, whereas a ratio is a relation, and holds in the first instance between two notes. In cases where they are unequal-pitched, when they are compared it makes a ratio from the quantity of the excess (*ek tou posou tēs hyperochēs*);[10] and it is in these that the unmelodic and the melodic now become apparent. Melodic notes are those which in conjunction with one another are pleasing (*euphoroi*) to the hearing, and unmelodic notes are those that are not. People also describe those that implant a homogeneous (*homoios*) impression in the ears as 'concordant' (*symphōnoi*), deriving the term from the

[8] *Harm.* 20.16–19, with the supplement first proposed by Meibom and accepted by all later editors except Da Rios. Her alternative proposal is more economical, but not (I think) syntactically satisfactory. That Aristoxenus is not satisfied that what he says here is an adequate definition of a note becomes clear in Book 2, at 45.10–18 (cf. also 59.10–16). On the issues involved, see especially Gibson 2005, 44–8, 148–9, and cf. Barker 2007, 183–92.

[9] Cf. Raffa 2002, 284 n. 141. Many commentators, he says, have missed the fact that we find here 'il passaggio dal dominio dell'acustica – che pertiene alla fisica pura – a quello della percezione di ciò che *può essere considerato* musicale' (Raffa's italics). The sounds under discussion have attributes which make them *capable* of being correctly considered as musical, but they will actually *be* musical, properly entitled to be treated as musical notes, only insofar as they are related to other notes in special ways which Ptolemy will go on to explore.

[10] I shall try to clarify this rather tortuous expression when we consider aspects of 1.5.

> most beautiful (*kalliston*) of sounds, the voice (*phōnē*), and as 'discordant' (*diaphōnoi*) those that do not. (10.19–28)

One point to notice about these remarks is that in saying that a single note by itself has no ratio, and that ratios first appear in the relation between any two notes of unequal pitch, Ptolemy implicitly reminds us that the science is essentially concerned with the relations between notes, not with each note as such, and alerts us at the same time to the importance he will attach to ratios as his account of the science develops. And the passage has two other particularly striking features. First, in setting out the criteria by which he distinguishes the pivotal musical attributes introduced here from one another – distinguishing melodic from unmelodic and concordant from discordant – he does not characterize them in straightforwardly objective terms. The distinguishing feature of melodic relations between notes is that they seem pleasing to our hearing, and of concordant relations that they implant or impress a 'homogeneous impression' in or on our ears. For the present we need only bear this point in mind; its relevance will become clear later. Secondly, the terms in which the perceived qualities of these musical relations are portrayed are not merely descriptive; they carry unmistakable evaluative implications. Melodic relations are those which are 'pleasing' and concords are distinguished from discords by making a 'homogeneous' – that is, a smooth and undifferentiated – impression on us, evidently to be reckoned more agreeable than its opposite, which is presumably rougher and more diversified. The voice is said to be the 'most beautiful' of sounds, and in offering this apparently irrelevant remark and pointing out (correctly) the etymological link between the words *phōnē* and *symphōnos*, Ptolemy may be dropping a hint that the concords, correspondingly, are the most beautiful of musical relations. These are slight indications, but they at least suggest to the reader that in progressing from the domain of pure acoustics to that of harmonics – that is, in narrowing our focus from the study of sounds in general to issues concerned exclusively with musical melody – we are simultaneously moving from an enquiry that is entirely innocent of evaluative considerations to one in which they have a significant part to play. These hints are amply confirmed in subsequent chapters, especially in 1.5 and 1.7; and the introduction of considerations which may well be reckoned subjective, and are certainly evaluative, would seem to mark Ptolemy's adoption of a set of epistemological commitments which are not only new but also seem thoroughly problematic. Can such considerations have any place in an enquiry purporting to be a rigorous, objective and empirically testable contribution to scientific knowledge? As a first reaction we would probably contend that they cannot, but it remains to be seen whether Ptolemy can find any way of anchoring judgments of these sorts in more solid foundations. He does not address this issue directly and explicitly, however; insofar as a response is to be found in his text it has to be disinterred from propositions primarily concerned with questions of other sorts. My own approach to it will be correspondingly indirect, and for the present we shall simply continue to observe the way in which Ptolemy develops his themes as the discussion proceeds.

In 1.5 Ptolemy continues to focus explicitly on perceptual impressions, excluding from consideration all concords other than those that sense-perception (*aisthēsis*) recognises as such (11.1–5). At the same time evaluative judgements move to centre stage in the construction of his arguments, as we see in a set of propositions which he borrows approvingly, so he says, from the Pythagoreans.

> Just as there are two principal species of relation between notes of unequal pitch, that of the concords and that of the discords, and that of the concords is the more beautiful (*kallion*), so there are two principal classes of difference between unequal numbers; one is the class of those known as 'epimeric' and 'number to number', the other that of the epimorics and multiples,[11] which is better (*ameinōn*) than that of the former, because of the simplicity of the comparison (*kata tēn haplotēta tēs parabolēs*). (11.10–16)

A little later he goes on to register approval also of the Pythagoreans' association of the octave with the ratio 2:1, the fifth with 3:2, and the fourth with 4:3. In asserting these correspondences, he says, they are behaving very rationally (*logikōteron . . . poiountes*), 'because the octave is the most beautiful (*kallistē*) of the concords and the double ratio [i.e. the ratio 2:1] is the best (*aristos*) of the ratios' (11.19–21).

Ptolemy's contention that the octave is the 'most beautiful' or 'finest' of the concords is evidently grounded in some aspect of the guise in which it presents itself to our sense of hearing. The features that earn it this high aesthetic ranking must be connected with the 'homogeneity' attributed at 10.27 to the impression created by a concord; we may reasonably guess that

11 'Epimeric', 'epimoric', and 'multiple' are names given to classes of ratio. In a multiple ratio, the greater term is a multiple of the smaller. In an epimoric ratio the greater term is equal to the smaller plus a unit fraction of the smaller (by 'a unit fraction' I mean any fraction in which the numerator is 1 and the denominator is an integer greater than 2, e.g. ¼). In Ptolemy's work and often elsewhere, every ratio that is neither epimoric nor multiple is classed as epimeric, though certain other writers make further distinctions within this class and label the ratios of only one group within it as epimeric.

the octave's supremacy will be due to its being the most homogeneous of them all. But before we can test this hypothesis, which will involve reconsidering the precise meaning of the phrase 'homogeneous impression' (*homoian antilēpsin*) in that passage, we need to investigate Ptolemy's grounds for holding that multiple and epimoric ratios are 'better' than the epimerics, and that the best of them all is the ratio 2:1. The importation of evaluative assessments into the domain of arithmetic as well as that of harmonics may well strike modern readers as strange, perhaps as completely inappropriate; but there can be no doubt that this is what Ptolemy is doing, whether or not he is correct in implying that the same step had already been taken by earlier writers in the Pythagorean tradition.

Here is Ptolemy's reasoning. The class of epimoric and multiple ratios is better than that of the epimerics, 'because of the simplicity of the comparison, since within this class, in the case of the epimorics the excess is a simple part [*scil.* of the smaller term], and in the case of the multiples the smaller term is a simple part of the greater' (11.15–17). In their purely arithmetical aspect, these statements are clear and correct. The 'excess' (*hyperochē*) to which they refer is the amount by which the greater term of the ratio exceeds the smaller. All epimoric ratios, taken in their lowest terms, have the form (n+1):n. Hence the excess is in all cases 1, and this will necessarily amount to a 'simple part' – that is, a unit fraction such as ¼, ⅛, and so on – of each of the terms.[12] Multiple ratios are defined as those in which the greater term is a multiple of the smaller, and the fact that the smaller term is a simple part of the greater is merely the other side of the same coin. Neither proposition, nor any other proposition of a similar sort, is true of epimeric ratios, those of the form (n+m):n where m is greater than 1. There is no element in ratios such as 7:5, 17:13 and the like which in every case amounts to a simple part of any of the ratio's other elements.

In a sentence which we glanced at earlier (10.21–22), we were informed that when two notes are compared with one another, a ratio is created 'from the amount of the excess' (*ek tou posou tēs hyperochēs*). We need now to work out what exactly this means; in so doing we shall also come to see how it relates to the notion of 'simplicity of comparison' and why this is relevant to the evaluative ordering of ratios and intervals. Ptolemy does not tell us explicitly how the proposition is to be understood, but the answer can be inferred from the way he uses it in particular cases. In 1.5 he explains

[12] The proposition is in fact true by definition (see n. 11 above). This is why the ratio 2:1 does not count as an epimoric, despite having the form (n+1):n. In this ratio the greater term is equal to the smaller plus the whole of the smaller, not a simple part of it.

why the octave is the most beautiful of the concords and the double ratio is the best of the ratios. The octave is the most beautiful, he says, 'on account of being closest to equality of pitch', and the double ratio is the best 'by being the only one in which the excess is equal to that which is exceeded' (11.22–24). The first part of this explanation raises further problems, since two notes an octave apart are obviously not 'closer to equality of pitch' – in the straightforward sense that one might naturally assign to the expression – than those related in the intervals of a fifth or a fourth. This minor enigma will be demystified as we proceed.

The second part of the explanation is significantly developed in 1.7, where Ptolemy sets out his own account of the ratios of the concords in general, and – crucially for our purposes – of the octave in particular; it differs, in fact, only marginally from the one attributed to the Pythagoreans in 1.5. His starting point, he says, is the same as theirs: we should assign equal numbers to notes of equal pitch, and unequal numbers to those of unequal pitch, since 'that sort of thing is immediately obvious'. It follows from this starting point, he continues, that the differences between notes of unequal pitch should be 'measured against one another' (*parametreisthai*) by their closeness to the equalities. And 'it is immediately apparent that the double ratio is the closest to this equality, since it has an excess equal to and the same as the term that is exceeded; and of the homophones the most unitary and beautiful is the octave,[13] so that we should fit to it the double ratio' (15.18–27). A few lines later he assigns ratios to the fifth (3:2) and the fourth (4:3), but on the basis of arguments of a rather different sort which we need not pursue (15.29–16.6). Considerations of the kind that concern us re-emerge a few lines later, where Ptolemy sets out the most important of the principles governing his constructions of the 'melodic' intervals, those that are not concords but are nevertheless 'pleasing to the hearing' and which can constitute individual steps of a well-formed musical scale.

> Next after the epitritic ratio [4:3], the closer to equality are those that are put together to constitute it, and in which the excesses are commensurable (*symmetroi*), that is, the epimoric ratios that are smaller than those ones [*scil.* those of the fifth and the fourth]; and following the concords in excellence (*kat'aretēn*) are the melodics (*emmeleis*), such as the tone and those which, when put together, constitute the smallest of the concords. Hence to these we should fit the epimoric ratios smaller than the epitritic.

[13] The 'homophones', in Ptolemy's usage but not those of most other writers, are the octave and its multiples; he defines the term ὁμόφωνος at 15.10–12, explaining that it applies to these special concords because when the two notes are played at the same time they convey to our hearing the impression of a single note.

> Among them, those that most nearly make divisions into halves will for the same reason be the more melodic (*emmelesteroi*), as are all those in which the differences (*diaphorai*) comprise larger simple parts of the terms that are exceeded, since they too are closer to the equal, just as the half is closest of all, then the third, and so on for each of the others. (16.12–21)

We are now in a position to give a clear answer to one of the questions raised above. When Ptolemy refers to a ratio or an interval as being 'closer to equality', he does not mean that the terms of the ratio are more nearly equal to one another, or that the notes bounding the interval are more nearly equal in pitch. He means that the amount by which the terms of the ratio differ, the 'excess' (a word replaced by 'difference' in the passage just quoted), is more nearly equal to the smaller term, while also being 'commensurable' (*symmetros*) with them both. The sense of the latter condition is that the excess or difference in such a ratio is an integral factor or unit fraction of each term, by which they can therefore be 'measured', and – as we have seen – this guarantees that the ratio will be epimoric (cf. 30.9–14 with 32.1–3).

As to the question why the octave is 'better' than the other concords, Ptolemy has made two remarks which, together with his arithmetical propositions, point fairly clearly to the feature he has in mind. He has said both that the octave is 'the most unitary and beautiful', and that it is the most beautiful 'on account of being closest to equality of pitch'. When the two notes under consideration are actually equal in pitch, they are identical and in that sense completely 'unitary'. When they are 'closest to equality of pitch' without being actually equal, one would therefore expect them to be 'the most unitary', as Ptolemy says. Just what this means becomes intelligible in the light of the way in which ancient writers regularly described a concord, that is, as a relation formed by two notes which, when sounded simultaneously, blend together in a mixture so thoroughly integrated that our hearing can discern neither of them individually. The octave might thus be described as the limiting case of a concord, one in which the two elements are immersed in one another to the fullest possible extent short of complete identity.

As the next step in our enquiry we need to find out what exactly it is that induces Ptolemy to contend that the 'better' ratios, those 'closer to equality and with commensurable excesses', are to be linked directly with the 'more beautiful' intervals, those placed higher in the ranking of intervals 'in respect of excellence' (*kat'aretēn*), so that the ratios in the arithmetical hierarchy line up, one to one and in the same order, with the intervals in its acoustic and musical counterpart. Here if anywhere, perhaps, it might be possible to find an answer to the question we raised earlier about the credentials of an approach that depends so heavily on evaluative and apparently irreducibly subjective considerations. In the absence of an answer, it will be hard to put much faith in the reliability of Ptolemy's general methodology, which in other respects seems to offer an innovative and largely convincing solution to problems raised repeatedly by earlier theorists about the rival claims of reason (*logos*) and sense-perception (*aisthēsis*) as authoritative criteria of truth in the field of harmonic analysis.[14] Ptolemy brings the two criteria together by deriving the details of systems of attunement from strictly 'rational' – that is, mathematical – premises, and then submitting them to the judgment of the ear. The operations conducted in this second phase, with the help of meticulously designed instruments, seem to be intended as genuine experimental tests; the theoretically derived conclusions will finally be accepted only if the tests confirm their credentials.[15] But if the judgments of the ear are merely expressions of each individual's – perhaps idiosyncratic – tastes and prejudices, constructions which one person perceives as musically acceptable may grate on the ears of another, and tests of this kind will carry little evidential weight. How, then, can Ptolemy justify his association of perceptual judgments about the greater or lesser beauty of intervals with a hierarchy of mathematical (and therefore objectively determinable) relations between the terms of numerical ratios? Since he offers no explanation in the context of 1.5 and 1.7, where the reader is evidently expected to accept the correspondence between them without further ado, he presumably assumes that it is embedded in considerations that have already been discussed and established; and this does indeed turn out to be the case.

Most of the key passages are right back at the beginning, in 1.1, where Ptolemy is discussing the credentials of judgements made on the basis of sense-perception (*aisthēsis*) and the relations between them and those made on the basis of reason (*logos*). Like many philosophers from Parmenides and Plato onwards, and like many of the mainstream 'Pythagorean' musical theorists, he places considerable emphasis on the senses' unreliability. They deliver only rough approximations to the truth: those of different people present different results, and even those of a single person faced repeatedly with the same phenomenon will perceive it differently on

[14] See in particular Ptolemy's overall judgments on the work of Aristoxenus and that of the Pythagoreans in 1.2, together with the discussions of Ptolemaïs and Didymus quoted at Porph. *Harm.* 22.22–28.26.

[15] These remarks present Ptolemy's position in a radically simplified form; I have pursued the matter in much greater detail in Barker 2000a.

different occasions. Hence if the sense of hearing, or indeed any other of the senses, is to play a part in harmonic science, 'it needs in addition the teaching of reason, as it were as a stick to lean on' (3.3–20).

As a first step towards explaining what he means by this, Ptolemy offers an analogy:

> Thus just as a circle constructed by eye alone often appears to be accurate, until the circle formed by means of reason induces the eye to recognise the one that is really accurate,[16] so if some specified difference between sounds is constructed by ear alone, it will commonly, in the first instance, seem to be neither smaller nor greater than it should be; but when the difference constructed in accordance with its proper ratio has been attuned alongside it, it will often be convicted of not being so, as by means of the comparison the hearing recognises the more accurate as legitimate, as it were, by contrast with the bastardy of the other. (3.20–4.7)

Neither sight nor hearing, then, can safely be relied on to make sound judgements, on its own, in cases of these kinds. I say 'of these kinds' because it's unlikely that Ptolemy would have made precisely parallel contentions, for instance, about judgements concerned with attributes (of sound or of anything else) which he took to be purely qualitative. In such cases perceptual judgements may indeed be in some respects unreliable and insecure, but they do not seem to be susceptible to authoritative correction in the light of judgements that Ptolemy would have conceived as the work of reason. The essential feature shared by the examples he presents here is that their defining characteristics, 'being a circle' and 'being such-and-such an interval between sounds', can both – at least in Ptolemy's opinion – be interpreted as *mathematical* characteristics and defined in clear-cut mathematical terms. A construction formed in accordance with the mathematical or 'rational' criterion will, we are assured, be 'legitimate' (*gnēsia*), whereas one formed on the basis of unaided sense-perception will be a 'bastard' (*nothos*).

What is more, if sense-perception compares the two, it will recognise the 'legitimacy' of the mathematical construction and will accept its superior credentials. As Ptolemy remarks at the end of the chapter, in such a context the sense of hearing serves as a 'maid-servant' of the 'theoretical and rational part of the soul' (5.6–8, cf. also the characterisation of sight and hearing and their relation to mathematical reason at 93.11–12). But it emerges in the course of Book 1, as a central tenet of Ptolemy's

[16] That is, through the use of an instrument such as the compasses, which has been designed by the application of reason to produce accurately drawn circles.

methodology, that there may be circumstances in which hearing will not meekly accept the conclusions at which reason has arrived, and that when that happens the testimony of hearing carries the greater weight. Reasoning, after all, can be conducted on erroneous principles or set out from mistaken assumptions, and human reasoners are not immune from making logical errors. Ptolemy asserts that harmonic science has the task of demonstrating that judgements of the relevant sort made on the basis of hearing, at any rate those that 'most people' would make,[17] will in all cases agree with those of reason; there is no quarrel or incompatibility between them (5.13–15). But this will hold water only in cases where the reasoning is sound, and the demonstration can only be achieved by subjecting reason's conclusions to empirical tests, submitting them to the judgements of hearing through procedures involving the meticulously designed experimental instruments which Ptolemy later describes. In principle, at least, reason's conclusions may sometimes fail the tests and must be rejected; and it turns out that this is in fact the case with conclusions to which reasoning – presumably flawed in one way or another – had led some of Ptolemy's predecessors. Thus certain conclusions drawn by Archytas must be rejected because they conflict with the evidence of sense-perception (30.15–17, 32.3–15); so too, for similar reasons, must those of Didymus (68.15–69.12).[18]

There must, then, be something about the relation between hearing and reason which ensures that when 'most people' bring their hearing to bear on judgements reached purely through sound reasoning, the two criteria will be in perfect agreement. In this connection we may note in particular Ptolemy's triumphant peroration at the end of 1.15, at 37.5–20, where he insists that even the 'most musical' of listeners, having constructed on the appropriate experimental instrument the divisions of the octave to which pure mathematical reasoning has led him, would see no need to alter any of them by even the slightest amount. So we must enquire into the nature of this relation; and we must also ask how, if at all, the agreement between hearing and sound reasoning is connected with the correlation between 'better' ratios and 'more beautiful' intervals with which we have been concerned.

The hunt for answers to these questions takes us back to the opening chapter. At 4.10–15, Ptolemy points out that when sense-perception is used to make a (quantitative) comparison between two items, it is unlikely to be

[17] Presumably this qualification is intended to rule out of court judgements made by a minority of people whose sense of hearing is seriously flawed or anomalous.

[18] On the thesis propounded here and the tests to which reason's conclusions are to be subjected, see Barker 2000a, 230–58.

mistaken if it is required to judge only whether one of them is larger or smaller in the relevant respect than the other. Much the same still holds if it is trying to quantify the difference in cases where the excess of one over the other consists in a larger 'part' – that is, a larger unit-fraction – of each of the items compared. But when the excess amounts to a smaller part of each, sense-perception will be less reliable in judging by how much the one exceeds the other; and as the excesses become progressively smaller parts of the things compared, so it becomes harder to make reliable perceptual comparisons.

We'll consider shortly why this is so; Ptolemy offers an explanation and works through some examples at 4.15–5.2. But first we need to be clear about the way in which his thesis should be understood, and we can shed some light on this by slightly adapting the examples he uses. First, given a straight line of a certain length, it's easy to construct one that is simply longer or shorter than it and to judge the success of our construction by eye alone. Secondly, it's also quite easy to judge whether we have successfully constructed a line such that the excess of the longer over the shorter length is a large unit-fraction of the latter.[19] The largest unit-fraction is one half, and if the difference between the two lengths is half the length of the shorter, it follows that the length of the shorter is two-thirds of the length of the longer. The ratio of the longer to the shorter will therefore be 3:2. Thirdly, the next unit-fraction in order is one third. If the excess is one third of the length of the shorter, the shorter must be three quarters of the length of the longer, where the corresponding ratio is 4:3; if it is one quarter, the shorter will be four fifths the length of the longer, so that the ratio is 5:4; and so on for all the successive unit-fractions and the corresponding epimoric ratios.

At 5.2–3 Ptolemy returns from his visual examples to the domain with which he is really concerned, assuring us that what applies in the examples he has provided applies equally when we are dealing with sound and hearing. If we take this conclusion back to the material we examined earlier, we can immediately see that the sequence of relations which the unaided ear finds progressively more difficult to identify is exactly the same as that which it finds progressively less beautiful (and in the case of intervals smaller than the perfect fourth, progressively less 'melodic'); and it

[19] It will also be a relatively large unit-fraction of the longer, and Ptolemy does not say here that its relation to the shorter length matters more than its relation to the longer. But we have found in our examination of later passages that – at least in the context of relations between the pitches of sounds – it is the relation between the excess and the smaller term of a ratio that Ptolemy treats as defining the ratio and hence the size of the interval.

corresponds also to the arithmetical sequence in which the ratios proceed, step by step, from better to worse. Hence there is a direct correlation between the ease with which our hearing assesses the relation between the pitches of two notes and the extent to which it strikes us as beautiful. It is easier to identify the interval between two notes confidently and accurately when it is, for instance, a perfect fifth, than to do so when it is – or we think it is – a minor third in the ratio 6:5, or one of the possible epimoric approximations to half a tone.[20] Our purchase on intervals of the latter sort is more inclined to error and hence more infected with uncertainty; we can offer no guarantee that the interval which our hearing identifies as a true minor third, for example, is in fact exactly the appropriate size. In Ptolemy's opinion, if we have more confidence in our assessment when we judge that an interval we hear is a perfect fifth than we do in the case where we take it to be a minor third, we are fully justified in doing so.

Why, then, are the intervals we identify more easily and reliably exactly the same as those which we consider more beautiful? It may be easier to find an answer if we try first to clarify the way in which Ptolemy conceives the process of 'comparing' two items so as to identify the difference between them. The explanation he presents at 4.15–5.2 involves complexities which we do not need to unpick in detail; a simplified version, tailored to engage directly with the issues that concern us here, will be enough. In comparisons between the lengths of two lines, if the excess of the one over the other amounts to half the length of the shorter, so that the ratio between the two lengths is 3:2, we can establish that this is really so by imagining that we are laying the excess alongside the shorter line twice over, much as one might use a one-metre ruler to measure a two-metre length.[21] Conceived in this way, the comparison involves just two steps, and according to Ptolemy the risk of error is therefore small. But when the excess is a smaller fraction of the shorter length, the number of steps in the comparison increases, and the risk of error (which presumably is always present to some extent, though in the two-step comparison it is virtually negligible) correspondingly accumulates.

Let's assume that this explanation is adequate for cases where we are comparing the lengths of lines. Since Ptolemy assures us that the same

[20] At 24.10–14 Ptolemy states the thesis, endlessly reiterated by mathematical theorists, that 'neither the ratio 9:8 [that of the whole tone] nor any of the other epimorics can be divided into two equal ratios', and he goes on to say, correctly, that the ratio of an exact half-tone (if there were such a ratio) would fall somewhere between 17:16 and 18:17.

[21] Except that our 'measurement' cannot involve any material accessories or instruments. For Ptolemy's purposes at this stage of the argument, the judgements must be made by eye alone.

holds true in the realm of sound and hearing, it should be possible to envisage comparisons between the pitches of sounds in a directly comparable way. But at least at first glance, this seems to present insuperable difficulties. To apply the analogy directly in a case where we are judging whether a given interval is a perfect fifth, we would apparently need to decide, on the basis of hearing alone, whether the difference between the two pitches (the 'excess' of the one over the other) is exactly half the 'size' of the smaller of them, thus confirming that the ratio between the two pitches is 3:2. But this makes no sense. The difference between two pitches or notes is an interval, and an interval cannot amount to any fraction of a note. Hence the analogy breaks down in irretrievable conceptual confusion.

I do not think that the objection is conclusive, even though what seems to be the most promising response to it appears – at first sight – to break down in a rather similar way. Let us review the way in which Ptolemy envisages the auditory and mental processes involved when we hear and compare the pitches of sounds. When a sound reaches our ears, what we encounter, in its material aspect, is a disturbance or movement in the air. What we perceive as the sound's pitch is, from that perspective, the speed (or as Ptolemy sometimes puts it, the 'tension' or 'intensity') of its movement; and the difference between two perceived pitches is the amount by which one speed or degree of intensity exceeds the other. So far there is no confusion. On the other hand, when we consult our experience of what we hear, and refer to the difference between two pitches as an interval (*diastēma*), we are likely to be conceiving it along more or less Aristoxenian lines, as something like a distance between two points. But this creates a problem: if what we perceive as pitches are really speeds or intensities of movement, they are not points, and the difference between them is not a distance.[22] Hence if we force the Aristoxenian conception of an interval into a framework in which a sound's pitch is not conceived as a point but as a degree of speed or intensity, we are indeed bound to generate nonsense.

There is no need, however, or so I shall argue, to suppose that Ptolemy meant his analogy to be construed in this way, and given his resolute hostility to the idea that an interval can coherently be conceived as a quasi-linear distance, it would be more than a little surprising if we found that this was what he intended. His analogy with relations between lengths can in fact be given a coherent interpretation, and when viewed from that perspective it implicitly reveals something interesting about the mental and

[22] See especially *Harm.* 21.9–20.

perceptual processes which, in his view, underlie our assessments of what we call the 'sizes' of intervals. When we hear sounds and attend to their musical aspects, and more particularly to those of the relations between them, what presents itself within the field of our consciousness is obviously connected very intimately with physical events taking place in the world outside us, and in the organs of our auditory apparatus. But equally obviously, these physical events are not, in any straightforward sense, identical with the experiences impressed on our consciousness. No one would contend that a pitched sound is represented in our experience *as* an aerial movement travelling at such-and-such a speed, or as a wave of such-and-such a frequency. When events of a certain kind impinge on us from outside, the phenomena of which we become consciously aware, which those events have somehow generated or into which they have somehow been transformed, are utterly different in kind from their physical causes or counterparts. (Much the same can be said, for example, about the relation between the colour of a physical object, as we perceive it, and the events in the material world that underlie this experience.) Ptolemy says nothing about the processes (which must, I suppose, be both physiological and psychological) that mediate the transition from the 'objective' event to the 'subjective' experience of it; even nowadays, I don't think that either scientists or philosophers would claim to have succeeded in penetrating all their mysteries.

The important point here, however, is that Ptolemy's treatment of pitch-relations simultaneously reflects the fact that the realms of physical events and of conscious experience are significantly different, and draws attention to the ways in which they are indissolubly linked with one another. After his foray into issues in acoustics in 1.3, he says little or nothing more about the relevant physical events as such. What he takes forward from that investigation is the fundamental conclusion that the differences between pitches of sounds – which are advertised at the outset as the focus of his whole enquiry – are differences of a quantitative sort. More specifically, as becomes clearer in 1.4, if the pitches of two sounds differ, the difference between them is a relation between two quantities, and can therefore be expressed as the ratio between two numbers. Hence from this point on, Ptolemy can put on one side the strictly material aspects of what I have called the 'physical' events involved, and represent them simply in terms of numbers and ratios of numbers.

Thus although, when we hear a sound with a determinate pitch, its pitch does not figure in our consciousness in a quantitative guise, it is indeed in that guise that it must initially have registered on our organs of hearing. When we hear two differently pitched sounds in succession and recognise the difference between them as some specific musical interval, we are not consciously aware of it as a ratio between two quantities or numbers; but somewhere in us, below the threshold of our awareness, our perceptual faculties must not only have registered the two quantities as such, but must also have calculated the ratio between them. As I have sometimes put it elsewhere, what's in play here is a sort of subconscious mental arithmetic.

When Ptolemy asserts that one ratio is 'better' than another, his proposition evidently applies at an 'objective' level and states what he takes to be an arithmetical truth. The 'simplicity of comparison' which he picks out as the attribute of a ratio that is responsible for its excellence is also among the ratio's objective features; it could not otherwise perform its explanatory function, and Ptolemy in any case explicates the expression 'simplicity of comparison' in purely arithmetical terms. But we must not confuse this 'simplicity of comparison' with the relative 'ease' with which, in I.I, we are said to assess certain quantitative differences through sense-perception alone. There is unquestionably a close connection between them, and the features of the items compared which make some such assessments easier than others are indeed arithmetical. But 'simplicity' (*haplotēs*) is an attribute that 'simple' things have in their own right and in that sense objectively, whereas in representing one perceptual judgement as 'easier' (*procheiroteron*) and another as 'more difficult' (*chalepōteron*), Ptolemy plainly means that the task in which we are engaged as perceivers, in our attempts to identify the relation between two sounds, is more demanding and arduous in the latter case than it is in the former. Its relative arduousness *depends on* an objective feature of the relation, but is itself a feature of our own perceptual engagements with it. Hence insofar as it is not a feature intrinsic to the relation in question, we may reasonably describe it as 'subjective'.

Yet it is clear from the reflections we have been pursuing that the assessments which are said to be easier or more difficult cannot be directed to items present in our conscious experience, since we are not perceptually aware of the quantitative relations with which they are concerned. The comparisons must indeed take place at some stage of the perceptual process that brings the sounds and the relation between them to our attention, but must do so in a phase of the process of which we are not directly aware, and whose conclusions about the relation are epistemologically prior to those presented to our consciousness. There is in fact nothing to which the 'ease' or 'difficulty' of the comparisons can attach, except to the workings of the 'subconscious mental arithmetic' to which I alluded above.

As a reconstruction of the picture that Ptolemy's statements presuppose, this hypothesis looks quite promising. There is one question, however, to which I have suggested two possible answers without choosing between them. But it is important to make the right choice here, since if we fail to eliminate the possibility which, I suppose, seems superficially the more appealing, we shall leave the hypothesis open to damaging objections. The question is this: What is the relation between, on the one hand, our ears' reception of the movements travelling through the air at certain speeds, together with the 'subconscious mental arithmetic' that identifies the ratio between the two speeds, and on the other the conscious experience of pitched sounds and intervals that somehow – but how? – arises from them? I have hinted above at the two possible answers that suggest themselves. The first is that the relation is causal: the auditory phenomena presented in our experience are distinct from and caused by the events and quasi-computations taking place below the threshold of our consciousness. In that case we are to envisage two parallel sets of events or processes, of which one is generated by the other; and it is a mode of generation in which the quantitative characteristics essential to the cause are not transmitted to the effect.

But this cannot be what Ptolemy had in mind, and the reason why it cannot is vividly brought out by Porphyry in his commentary on 1.3. Here he launches a long and vehement attack on the main conclusion that Ptolemy reaches in this passage – that is, the conclusion that the differences between pitches are quantitative – and on the reasoning by which that conclusion has been reached.[23] He sharply distinguishes Ptolemy's position from his own, which is that although the differences between the items causing our experience of pitch-differences are indeed quantitative, the differences that we consciously perceive – that is, the differences between pitches, by contrast with the differences between speeds – are not; they are differences of quality (see especially Porph. *Harm.* 61.9–14). He clarifies this position further in a later passage, where despite his commitment to a qualitative conception of pitch, he insists that Ptolemy's quantitative comparisons of pitches are nevertheless, with one slight modification, entirely legitimate.

[23] Porph. *Harm.* 43.23–67.14, especially 58.5–61.15. For discussion see Barker 2015, 22–7, and the notes *ad loc.* in that volume and in Raffa 2016a.

> But one must realise that even though the differences between sounds in respect of height and depth are qualities, there is nothing to prevent us from giving an account of notes in terms of quantity, on the grounds that these differences arise from (*epiginestai*) the quantity of what underlies them. (Porph. *Harm.* 88.1–5)

Porphyry's view is essentially the same as the one we proposed to attribute to Ptolemy in our first attempt at answering the question we raised. Since Porphyry represents Ptolemy's position as radically different from his own and vigorously denounces it, this first answer cannot be right unless Porphyry is badly mistaken.

But he is not mistaken. Ptolemy's arguments in 1.3 turn in large part on observations about the causes of sounds and of variations in their attributes. But the conclusion to which they are directed is not about the *causes* of differences of pitch but about what these differences *are*, and the statement with which he summarises his view on the issue is unambiguous: 'For these reasons it appears that the difference between sounds in respect of height and depth *is* some form of quantity' (8.15–17). This chimes perfectly well with a passage in 1.4 that we have reviewed already, 10.18–28, where sounds of equal pitch, now identified as 'notes' (*phthoggoi*), are said to be related to one another in certain ratios; when they are compared, the 'quantity of the excess' produces the ratio in question; and those among them which, when conjoined with one another, are pleasing to perception are 'melodic' (*emmeleis*). What is significant in this is that the subject under discussion remains the same throughout; the items of which one exceeds the other by some quantity, and which stand to one another in a numerical ratio, are identical with the items called 'notes'; and it is these notes again of which those related in certain ratios are agreeable to perception and are thereby qualified as melodic. Then the quantitative relation between two speeds of aerial movement is not something different from and causally related to the phenomenon we experience as a pleasing melodic interval; it is the very same thing. The difference lies in the ways in which we have represented it, first in the form in which it exists objectively in the physical world, and secondly in the form in which we are consciously aware of it.

This brings us, at last, to a viewpoint from which we can see why Ptolemy is able to correlate so readily the perceived beauty of a musical interval and the 'simplicity of comparison' that characterises the corresponding ratio. When he asserts, much later in the *Harmonics*, that sight and hearing are the only senses capable of judging their objects by the standard of beauty (*to kalon*), we find that it is because they are 'of all the senses the ones most closely allied to the ruling principle (*to hēgemonikon*)', and more specifically because they are the 'servants' of mathematical reason and the 'rational part of the soul' (3.3.93.11–94.1). At this point we have already been told that *mathēmatikē*, which comprises all the mathematical sciences (but here especially harmonics and astronomy), is itself focused on what is beautiful; it is indeed, says Ptolemy, 'not limited to the theoretical understanding of beautiful things (*theōrias* . . . *tōn kalōn*) . . . but includes at the same time the demonstrative exhibition (*endeixis*) of them and the concern for them (*meletē*) which arises out of the very act of understanding' (93.6–10). Sight and hearing pick out for us, in a vivid sensory mode, the relations in which beauty can be found, and it is then the task of mathematical reason to identify the quantitative counterparts of these relations and to explain the admirable features of them in which their beauty ultimately consists.

Thus our perception of the octave as the most beautiful of the concords, because it is 'nearest to equality of pitch', is simply an audible representation of the arithmetical fact that the excess of the larger term of its ratio over the smaller is equal to the smaller term (11.21–24). Similarly, the 'homogeneity' of the impression made by concords on the hearing (10.25–28), which qualifies them as more beautiful than discords (11.12), is an audible reflection of the fact that the relation between the terms of their ratios is mathematically 'simpler' and is easier for sense-perception to assess than that between the terms of any other epimorics (as well, of course, as all the epimerics).

Any doubts we may initially have entertained about the legitimacy of Ptolemy's transition from an acoustic to a musical enquiry should by now, I submit, have been finally laid to rest. Differences of pitch, according to Ptolemy, are quantitative; they are identical with the ratios between the speeds or intensities of movement that constitute sounds, in cases where the pitch of each sound is steady throughout its duration; and these sounds are entitled to be called 'notes'. When such movements impinge on our organ of hearing we experience them as notes, not as movements, and the relations between them not as ratios but as intervals; we perceive intervals as concordant or discordant, melodic or unmelodic, and we evaluate them as more or less beautiful. They are also subject to evaluation when they are considered in their 'objective' guise, as ratios; some ratios are better and some are worse, and the criteria according to which they are better or worse cohere perfectly with those according to which the corresponding intervals are perceived as more or less beautiful. Finally, Ptolemy reveals in 3.3 that the mathematical sciences themselves are ultimately concerned with the investigation of what is beautiful, and that it is the task of hearing (in harmonics) and sight (in astronomy) to assist them in their enterprise. It thus emerges that there is, after all, no distinction to be drawn between the enquiry into differences in pitch, announced at the beginning of the *Harmonics*, and the enquiry into musical relations to which the bulk of the treatise is in fact devoted. Whether Ptolemy's correlation of perceptual and mathematical modes of evaluation is enough to give his account the objectivity proper to a science is another matter. To settle the question we would need to burrow further into his discussions, to try to establish whether he has actually demonstrated, or merely assumed, that the link he claims to have established between perceptible musical beauty and objective mathematical considerations guarantees that everyone (or everyone with adequate musical sensibilities) will in fact agree on which intervals and sequences of intervals are beautiful, on which intervals are more beautiful than others, and on which intervals have nothing beautiful about them and are therefore alien to music. These contentions seem counter-intuitive, and it is not at all clear to me that Ptolemy has found a persuasive way of putting such doubts to rest. But I must leave readers to wrestle with these conundrums for themselves.

CHAPTER 7

Musical Imagery in Clement of Alexandria and Origen

The Greek Musical World Revised and Accepted

Francesco Pelosi

Music has a very special place in the Christian literature of the first centuries. The Church Fathers' works include countless references to music, which range from observations on practical topics, such as instructions for an appropriate Christian musical culture, to notions concerning theoretical issues, such as the role of music for intellectual and spiritual training. For the sake of clarity, Christian references to music can be broadly grouped under four categories: (1) the theory and practice of liturgical song; (2) the role of music in Christian education; (3) the criticism of pagan musical culture; (4) the use of musical notions and images for exegetical and apologetic purposes.[1] While the first topic is mainly (albeit not exclusively) of interest to historians of music, the other themes deserve serious consideration by scholars of early Christian thought, as well as by anyone interested in the relationship between music and philosophy in Antiquity. An overall and detailed study of the above-mentioned topics in the works of the first Christian writers is still missing, though the importance of the references to music in ancient Christian literature has not passed unnoticed by scholars. In this chapter I shall address some of these many references by analysing topics that mainly pertain to the third and the fourth aforementioned points. At the centre of my analysis there are some musical images and notions in Clement of Alexandria's and Origen's works, whose treatments of musical

[1] For this classification, together with an assessment of its usefulness and limits, see McKinnon 1987, 1–11, which provides the most exhaustive collection of Christian references to music. Other important studies on musical topics in the writings of early Christian authors are Gérold 1931, Skeris 1976 (with a special focus on the figure of Orpheus), Stapert 2007 (with comparisons between pagan musical culture and the musical thought of early Christianity) and Kramarz 2016, 359–402 (particularly, on Christian writers' stances towards the ethical view of music). On music in early Christian worship, see Kraeling-Mowry 1957, Gelineau 1962, Smith 1962 and Foley 1996. On the Christian attitude towards dance and pantomime specifically, see Bermond 2001 and Webb 2008a.

topics provide some prime examples of the important role of music in early Christian thought. In analysing this musical imagery, my main aim will be to throw light on its Greek background – that is, the music theory and the philosophical thought on music that developed in Greece from the early Classical age onwards. This pagan legacy shapes Clement's and Origen's musical imagery: as I shall show, important clues as to Clement's and Origen's attitude towards pagan culture, as well as their apologetic and exegetical strategies, emerge from their references to music, which represent an important and underexplored part of the intellectual enterprise through which these Christian writers build up a new philosophical and theological identity.

Broadly speaking, the patristic attitude towards pagan music is characterised by condemnation. The contexts, practices and instruments of ancient Greek musical culture are the target of harsh criticism. Oddly enough, this contentious attitude is not generally linked to the definition of the practice of Christian musical culture, as one would expect,[2] but is rather part of a broad theoretical development leading to the complex Christian stance on pagan culture. From this point of view, the Christian criticism of myths, notions and figures associated with the world of Greek music is an important part of the debate between Christianity and paganism. It is all the more interesting when it implies the adoption, in a suitably revised form, of those very aspects that are eyed suspiciously and criticised – as we shall see, in particular, in relation to Clement. Despite the fact that the Christian attitude towards pagan music is generally critical, many ideas and notions characterising the Greek musical tradition enter Christian literature and significantly contribute to defining the identity of Christian life and thought. First of all, many Christian authors embrace and develop the idea – a mainstream one throughout Antiquity, rooted in Pythagorean and Platonic theories – that music can promote intellectual and spiritual amelioration, as both an ethical tool and an auxiliary science on the road to knowledge.[3] Moreover, they explore at length the use of musical notions and images for exegetical and apologetic purposes: notions such as *harmonia*, *symphōnia* and *epōidē* – just to mention a few – as well as many musical

[2] One emblematic case is the criticism of pagan instruments, which is not related to the practice of psalmody and sacred music, that is, *a cappella* performances (with the notable exception of Joan. Chrys. *In Ep. I ad Tim. Hom.* 14.3–4, an exception that proves the rule; see McKinnon 1987, 3–4). On the Jewish and Christian criticism of instrumental music, see Kraeling-Mowry 1957, 315.

[3] Just to limit ourselves to the two authors dealt with in this chapter, the ethical role of music is acknowledged by Clement in *Paed.* 2.4 (see below, pp. 156–7), while the idea that music, as one of the sciences preparatory to philosophy, has a place in the study propaedeutic to Christianity is expressed by Origen in his *Letter to Gregory* (*Ep. ad Greg.* 1).

instruments and musical myths borrowed from pagan culture, appear, in an adequately reinterpreted form, in the description and explanation of crucial aspects of Christian doctrine. Far from playing a merely decorative role, these references to music are based on a deep knowledge of the musical culture they stem from and play an important role in the philosophical and theological contexts they appear in. In view of this, it is hardly an overstatement to say that the use of musical notions and images is a significant part of the strategies deployed by early Christian thinkers in order to establish a strong Christian identity on firm philosophical foundations. The intellectual endeavour through which Christians constructed distinct philosophical doctrines, by means of a complex relationship of continuity and discontinuity with Hellenic thought, has been described in detail (Karamanolis 2013, Boys-Stones 2001). An analysis of musical notions in early Christian works, in relation to the Greek culture they come from, can contribute a further piece to this puzzle, while at the same time widening our knowledge of the relationship between music and philosophy in the early centuries of the Common Era.

The chapter consists of two parts of unequal length: the first and longer one is devoted to the analysis of some musical images in Clement's *Exhortation to the Greeks*, while the second part focuses on Origen's use of the image of a well-tuned instrument as an expression of the deep consistency between all parts of Scripture. As I am primarily interested in the impact of the Greek reflection about music on Christian thought and in its adaptation, I shall dwell at length on Clement's *Exhortation to the Greeks*. This text figures prominently among the apologetic works imbued with Hellenic notions (including many musical notions) and offers a unique vantage point on the Christian appropriation of Greek musical imagery. As we shall see, Clement's definition of the Word as the New Song, far from being only a rhetorical device, is used to express the supremacy of Christ's message, against the competing view of Hellenic culture. Interestingly, this operation is conducted through methods and notions that characterise the Greek, and especially Platonic, use of musical images in philosophical contexts, so that Clement's use of musical images provides a new angle on his Platonism. Clement's illustration of the cosmological function of the New Song gives further evidence that he aligns himself with a well-established philosophical tradition of exploitation of musical notions for philosophical purposes (from the Pythagoreans to Philo), when he uses musical notions to illustrate crucial aspects of Christian thought. The second part of the chapter offers an incursion into the field of Origen's musical analogies that raises some significant questions on both the general topic of musical imagery in Christian literature and the specific issue of the role played by musical notions in biblical exegesis, within the framework of Origen's philosophical theology. Origen's use of the image of a well-tuned instrument to explain the inner concord of the Scriptures provides some important insights into central aspects of Origen's thought, such as his hermeneutic approach to the sacred texts and his attitude towards pagan philosophy.

7.1 Clement

Among Christian writers, Clement of Alexandria stands out as the first to pay special attention to music, by discussing a broad spectrum of topics – from musical practices to the philosophical implications of some key musical notions – which lead to the core of his attitude towards pagan culture and his theoretical commitment to demonstrating the superiority of Christianity.

In the *Paedagogus*, which provides guidelines for leading an appropriate Christian life, the whole fourth chapter of the second book is devoted to defining the music that Christians should allow at banquets. By adopting a moralising view on music, which echoes the Greek (especially Platonic) criticism of some musical practices and elements,[4] Clement offers believers some instructions for identifying a musical culture that is suited to the Christian lifestyle. Moreover, through an allegorical reading of *Psalm* 150, opposing the peaceful music of the divine *Logos* to the warrior music of the instruments that inflame passions and encourage fighting (*Paed.* 2.4.41–42), Clement suggests that at the basis of the new Christian musical culture there lies an innovative way of conceiving music and its role in human life, in the light of the divine dimension associated with it. Hence, despite the fact that the focus of *Paed.* 2.4 is relatively narrow, insofar as it specifically concerns musical practices in social contexts, a distinctive feature of Clement's approach to music emerges in these pages: the adoption of some characteristic aspects of Greek musical culture – such as its ethical

[4] Among the most striking similarities with Plato's thought on music, it is worth mentioning Clement's selection of instruments, with the rejection of the *aulos* and the acceptance of the *syrinx* for shepherds (*Paed.* 2.4.41, cf. Pl. *Resp.* 399c-d), the banishment of all visual and auditory stimuli that may have negative effects on the soul (*Paed.* 2.4.41.3; a cornerstone in Plato's reflection on the educational role of music; for some observations concerning the negative impact of both visual and auditory stimuli, in the same vein as *Paed.* 2.4.41.3, see Pl. *Resp.* 401b-d), and his disapproval of those *harmoniai* which do not have an edifying moral impact (*Paed.* 2.4.44.5, cf. Pl. *Resp.* 398d-e).

perspective on music – and their adaptation within a competing view of music and of its relationship with philosophy.

This approach characterises extensive passages of the *Exhortation to the Greeks* (*Protrepticus*) and some scattered references to music in the *Stromata* and represents an interesting and understudied aspect of Clement's complex attitude to Greek culture. The main features of this attitude are widely known. Clement plays a pivotal role in the cultural debate, which developed in Alexandria from the second century onwards, about whether and to what extent Christians must strike a compromise with pagan culture. His contribution to this debate tends to mitigate the Christian mistrust of pagan culture in general, and in particular of Greek philosophy and sciences (including music). Fully conversant with Greek literature and philosophy, and committed to addressing well-educated people imbued with Greek culture, Clement frequently resorts to topics and literal quotations borrowed from Hellenic sources. Far from being only a rhetorical and persuasive device, this lively and constant debate with the pagan literary and philosophical sources highly contributes to shaping Clement's own thought, through an approach that implies both the criticism and adoption of elements from the pagan world.[5] As I shall illustrate, Clement's use of musical notions and images, simultaneously characterised by a break and a degree of continuity with pagan musical culture, plays a noteworthy role in defining his stance towards Greek culture and his view of the relationship between Christianity and pagan philosophy.

At the centre of my analysis there are the musical images and notions used in the first chapter of the *Exhortation to the Greeks*. Through this work – a key text in the apologetic and parenetic literature of early Christianity – Clement appeals to non-Christian cultured Greeks with the aim of persuading them that the acquisitions of pagan culture need to be revised (i.e., emended or completed) in the light of Christ's message. The role played by musical topics within this strategy is remarkable, as we shall see in the following paragraph. In exploring this rich musical imagery, my main aim is to illustrate the Greek musical landscape from which the images and notions that Clement employs come from, so that his use of musical topics can be fully evaluated against the background of his general strategy of criticism and adaptation of Greek

[5] On Clement's attitude to Hellenic culture, see Van den Hoek 2005, 72–5, 80. For the related and fundamental topic of Clement's thought on the relationship between philosophy and Christian theology, see Osborn 1957, Lilla 1971, Osborne 2010, 271–81, Boys-Stones 2001, 189–94. For Clement's role in dispelling the distrust harboured by the second-century Christian community in Alexandria towards the sciences, and music in particular, see Gérold 1931, 88–9.

culture.[6] In particular, I shall concentrate on two pairs of images that are introduced and widely exploited by Clement in the first chapter of this work: (a) Christ as Orpheus and the Word as the New Song; (b) the cosmic harmony and man as a musical instrument.

7.1.1 Christ-Orpheus and the New Song

In the Christian tradition the figure of Orpheus appears both in literary passages and in iconographical sources.[7] In Clement's *Exhortation* it is at the centre of one of the most powerful 'musical' representations of Christ: the image of Christ as Orpheus. As a first step in the analysis of this complex and intriguing analogy, it is important to point out that, in describing Christ by means of a figure drawn from the Greek mythological repertoire, Clement widely exploited Orpheus' musical traits:[8] in *Protr.* 1.4.1 Orpheus' musical power – in particular his ability to tame wild animals – is used analogically to describe and explain Christ's power. The image is introduced by a rich musical section, aimed at outlining a sophisticated comparison between the 'old' (pagan) music and the 'new' (Christian) music, that is, Christ's redeeming Word. In this preparatory section some crucial views on Greek musical culture emerge, and the foundations are laid for the subsequent development of the Christ-Orpheus image. Before getting to the core of the analogy between Christ and Orpheus, let us analyse how this powerful image is fashioned.

References to music are used from the very beginning of the *Exhortation*. The work opens with an astonishing immersion in Greek musical mythology, where four mythical musicians – Amphion, Arion, Orpheus and Eunomos – and their musical marvels burst onto the scene (*Protr.* 1.1.1). Orpheus is not in the foreground here: the spotlight is on Eunomos, the Locrian musician credited with an extraordinary duet with a cicada. As the

6 A detailed study of the links between Clement's references to music and ancient Greek musical culture is provided by Cosgrove 2006; however, Cosgrove professedly focuses on Clement's treatment of 'actual' music, that is, musical practices and the notion of heavenly music, and deals with Clement's use of musical images only insofar as it casts some light on these aspects (256 n. 3). The role of the musical notions and images in Clement's apologetic strategy is emphasised by Costache 2014, 36–7.

7 Christian representations of Orpheus appear, for example, in the catacombs of St. Peter and Marcellinus, and the catacombs of St. Domitilla in Rome. On the Christian iconography of Orpheus and its relationship with the literary sources, see Skeris 1976, 146–56, and Roessli 2014 and 2008.

8 Later Christian writers were to develop the comparison between Orpheus and Christ on the basis of another aspect of the myth: Orpheus' descent into the underworld. See Irwin 1982, 55–6 and Jourdan 2010, 81.

story goes, Eunomos was playing the *kithara* and singing at the Pythian games, when one of the strings of his instrument snapped; at that moment, a miracle happened: a cicada flew on the crossbar of the instrument and replaced the missing string with its voice.[9] Traditionally, the core of the story had been the praise of the extraordinary power of Eunomos, able to enchant the cicada and elicit its help. In Clement's version, however, the values conveyed by the traditional account are completely overturned through a refined shift of the emphasis from the extraordinary ability of the musician to the differences between the cicada's song and Eunomos' song, and the superiority of the former over the latter. Eunomos delivers his performance in the heat of the day, surrounded by the cicada's song. The competition between Eunomos' song and the cicada's chorus takes place as a contest within the contest: the cicada's song, addressed to God and not governed by any laws (*autonomon ōidēn*), is better than Eunomos' songs/laws (*tōn Eunomou ... nomōn*), as Clement highlights (*Protr.* 1.1.2–3). In underscoring the differences between the two songs, Clement clearly suggests a new perspective on the marvellous event. According to him, in emphasising Eunomos' musical skills and the cicada's impossibility to resist the power of his music, the Greeks have completely misunderstood the meaning of the story. In particular, what has escaped the Greeks is the fact that both the cicada's actions – flying and singing – were performed purposely (*hekōn ephiptatai kai aidei hekōn*), not under the influence of Eunomos' music. In Clement's view, the relationship between Eunomos and the cicada is completely reversed: far from being enchanted by Eunomos' song, the cicada spontaneously puts its song at Eunomos' service, obeying its own rule (*autonomos*). Significantly, Clement points out that it was Eunomos who attuned himself to the cicada's song (*tou tettigos tōi aismati harmosamenos ho ōidos*): in a sense, it is Eunomos who is charmed by the cicada's song, not the other way round.

As has been noted, Clement's revised interpretation of Eunomos' story gives us some insight into his strategy of appropriation and exploitation of the pagan background: Greek philosophy – Eunomos' song – acquires full meaning when it is attuned to, and perfected by, God's Word (Stapert 2007, 51). It should also be noted that the transformation of the pagan myth of Eunomos into the Christian parable of the cicada occurs through some interesting twisting of the meanings originally conveyed by the story, according to an operation of 'turning upside-down Greek values' that has

[9] *Protr.* 1.1.2–3. Cf. Anon. *Anth. Pal.* 9.584, Paul. Silent. *Anth. Pal.* 6.54, Conon *ap.* Phot. *Bibl.* 186.131b, Greg. Naz. *Ep.* 175.2.

been identified as characteristic of Clement's strategy in this work (Van den Hoek 2005, 74–6 and 92). Let us focus on what I regard as the central variation in Clement's version of the story: the fact that at the basis of the cicada's act there is a spontaneous impulse, instead of some kind of enchantment, as is implied in the traditional version of the myth. This point is raised again, at the end of the story, and expressed as a more general criticism of the Greek belief in the effects of music on animals: 'how in the world is it that you have given credence to worthless legends, imagining brute beasts to be enchanted by music?' (*Protr.* 1.2.1, transl. Butterworth). What Clement impugns here is a significant aspect of Greek thought on the pervasive and magical power of musical sounds: the conviction, often expressed in myth, that even animals and inanimate objects are moved by music. The four musicians mentioned at the very outset of the *Exhortation* embody these beliefs on the musical conditioning of animals and things, as their deeds concern the musical enchantment of animals and objects (by means of music, Amphion moved the stones forming the walls of Thebes; Arion, a dolphin; Orpheus, animals and trees; and Eunomos, the cicada).[10] It would be rash, however, to conclude that Clement rejects Greek thought on the fascinating power of music and its symbols. As his reading of Eunomos' story shows, a completely different interpretation of the Hellenic musical imagery can be given: a reading that transforms the Greek musical world into a valuable repository of images and notions for expressing Christian content. This is exactly the kind of operation that Clement performs in the following pages of the first chapter, where he embraces the fundamental Greek idea that music is a powerful instrument of persuasion, including the conviction that it has some sort of magical power, but then reinterprets it in the light of the Christian message.[11]

With a plot twist, which foreshadows the comparison of Christ to Orpheus, Clement presents Christ in the guise of Eunomos. At *Protr.* 1.2.3–4 Christ is called 'this Eunomos of mine' (ὁ Εὔνομος ὁ ἐμός): that is, a Eunomos who does not sing the *nomos* of Therpander, nor the *nomos* of

[10] On these four figures and the prominent role of Eunomos in *Protr.* 1.1, see Halton 1983, 178–80, 193–4 and Stapert 2007, 49–51.

[11] It is telling that Clement accepts the idea that music enchants animals and conditions their behaviour in a passage of the *Paedagogus* where he rejects those instruments that are more suitable for animals than for men, and, among men, for those who are more unreasonable (*Paed.* 2.4.41.1–2). The crucial aim in the first pages of the *Exhortation* is not to deny the enchanting power of music nor to question the idea that it has an impact on the natural world, but rather to contend that the fountainhead of this power is the *Logos*. In fact, as we shall see, Clement recovers the idea of the enchanting power of music and of its effect on animals by saying that the New Song (i.e. the *Logos*) fascinates the most terrible brutes: human beings (see below, p. 162).

Capion, nor a Phrygian, Lydian or Doric *nomos* – in short, who does not sing old songs, but 'the eternal *nomos* of the new harmony' (τῆς καινῆς ἁρμονίας τὸν ἀΐδιον νόμον). Thus, the creation of the Christ-Eunomos image occurs through a double move: on one hand, the rehabilitation of Eunomos as an extraordinary musician – a move which probably implies the recovery of the positive etymological meaning of the name Eunomos, 'good *nomos*' (Lugaresi 2001, 252); on the other, the replacement of the musical tradition to which the figure of Eunomos belongs with completely different content. The *nomos* of Christ-Eunomos is good insofar as it is different from the traditional *nomoi* of the Greeks: it is the New Song of the heavenly Word (*logos ouranios*). This passage presents the first definition of Christ in musical terms and the first occurrence of the notion of New Song (*āisma kainon*), which is key to the first book of the *Exhortation* (see below, pp. 163–71). Before analysing this notion, let us explore Clement's overturning of the values traditionally linked to the musical myth in order to see how this strategy leads to the analogy of Christ as Orpheus.

A crucial move in this project is the unmasking of the deceptive and coercive use that mythical musicians make of their musical powers. The idea that the musical deeds of those famous musicians have an illusory quality to them already emerged from Clement's re-reading of Eunomos' story, but in that case the emphasis was on the misleading interpretation of the event as it is given in the myth (*ho mythos bouletai*). However, at *Protr.* 1.3.1 the criticism is openly levelled at the musicians' use of their musical powers: the Thracian, the Theban and the Methymnian – that is, Orpheus, Amphion and Arion – are 'impostors' (*apatēloi*), and their music is an excuse to outrage human life by leading men to idolatry and limiting human freedom. The magical power of this deceiving music performed by the three mythical musicians is strongly emphasised here: we are told that they used sorcery (*goēteiai*) and that they enslaved men by means of songs and enchantments (*ōidais kai epōidais*). It is worth noting that the beguiling character of one of these musicians – significantly, Orpheus – is particularly emphasised, albeit in somewhat ambiguous terms: at the beginning of the work, Orpheus is introduced as *sophistēs* – with the term bearing the double meaning of 'skilful' (in his art) and 'cheat'.[12] Then Orpheus, who in a few pages will soar to represent Christ, is here

[12] See Halton 1983, 179–80; Roessli 2002, 506 and n. 2. Among those passages that might have suggested to Clement the definition of Orpheus as a sophist, Eur. *Rh.* 924 and Pl. *Prt.* 315a-b, 316d are usually mentioned. The misleading character of certain kinds of music also emerges at *Paed.* 2.4.40.2, where Clement speaks of 'those who are surrounded by the sounds of the instruments of deceit' (τοῖς τῆς ἀπάτης ὀργάνοις περιψοφούμενοι).

described as an impostor, whose music makes men slaves by acting as a sort of magic spell.

As has been convincingly argued, this criticism is but the first step in a strategy which includes – after the condemnation of some of Orpheus' traits, as these emerge from the Greek tradition – an operation of 'transposition' and 'appropriation' of those very traits, in order to apply them to Christ.[13] As we shall see, both the image of a fascinating musician and the notion of a music that acts as magic are fully exploited in Clement's definition of Christ in musical terms: Clement's response to the pagan world of musical deceitfulness and dangerous enchantments is not a silent word nor a music without allure, but rather the charming song of the *Logos*.

Interestingly, Orpheus' redemption and his transformation into Christ have their starting point in an aspect which is strongly called into question at the outset of the *Exhortation*: the impact of music on animals and inanimate things. After having stressed the difference between the Greek mythical musicians and Christ (*Protr.* 1.3.1), Clement praises Christ's capacity to tame 'the most intractable beasts, men' (*Protr.* 1.4.1: τὰ ἀργαλεώτατα θηρία, τοὺς ἀνθρώπους). In Clement's rereading of the Orpheus myth, each animal comes to exemplify human characters: birds are unstable men, snakes are deceptive men, lions are passionate men, pigs are pleasure-loving men and wolves are rapacious men. Even inanimate things, like stones, correspond to human types – specifically, to 'men without reason' (*hoi aphrones*) – while a further category includes those who are so sunken in ignorance that they are more insensible than stones. All these 'most savage beasts, and all such stones the heavenly song of itself transformed into men of gentleness' (*Protr.* 1.4.3, transl. Butterworth). The New Song makes men out of wild beasts and stones by giving them the truest life. The musical enchantment of Greek mythology becomes a humanising act: listening to Christ-Orpheus' Word means letting human wildness be charmed away (*Protr.* 1.4.3–4). Those who do not undergo this musical redemption are described through another evocative image, as 'those serpents whose ears are closed to the enchanters'.[14]

[13] A description of Clement's reworking of the figure of Orpheus as consisting of three steps – opposition, transposition and appropriation – has been set out by Jourdan in her extensive and detailed analysis of the Christian reception of the Orpheus myth (2010, see also Jourdan 2008). Cf. the alternative interpretations of Skeris (1976, 146) and Roessli (2002, 506–7), which emphasise respectively the ambivalence of the figure of Orpheus and his negative traits in Clement's *Exhortation*.

[14] *Protr.* 10.105.4–106.1: 'With good reason, therefore, have you been likened to those serpents whose ears are closed to the enchanters. "For their hearth," the Scripture says, "is after the likeness of the serpent, even like an adder that is deaf and stoppeth her ears, who will not give heed to the voice of

Two points are worth emphasising in this description of Christ as Orpheus. First, Christ-Orpheus' musical power is analogous to the one ascribed to the mythical Greek musicians: it can move beasts and stones, and does so by enchantment, but – and this is the second relevant point – the content of Christ-Orpheus' song completely reshapes the meaning of this charming power. Instead of the deceptive and enslaving elements of Orpheus' music, the song of Christ conveys the truthful content of the *Logos* and, in captivating the listener, actually makes him free.[15] At the basis of the image of Christ-Orpheus at 1.3.2–1.4.4 there lies the idea of a music that conquers without enslaving; a music that frees, thanks to its fascinating content of truth.[16] This leads us to the theme of the Word as the New Song.

As we have seen, the notion first emerges at *Protr.* 1.2.4, where it describes Christ-Eunomos' song, in opposition to the traditional Greek *nomoi*. Although the concept of a New Song occurs in many passages of the Old Testament, Clement's analysis of this notion greatly contributes to extending the expressive power of the concept by emphasising in particular its enchanting potential and the special temporal dimension of newness/eternity that characterises it.[17] It is worth noting that, immediately after having stressed the originality of the New Song, Clement describes it

charmers." But as for you, let your wildness be charmed away' (transl. Butterworth. Ἄρα οὖν εἰκότως ὡμοίωσθε τοῖς ὄφεσιν ἐκείνοις, οἷς τὰ ὦτα πρὸς τοὺς κατεπᾴδοντας ἀποκέκλειστα. "Θυμὸς γὰρ αὐτοῖς," φησὶν ἡ γραφή, "κατὰ τὴν ὁμοίωσιν τοῦ ὄφεως, ὡσεὶ ἀσπίδος κωφῆς καὶ βυούσης τὰ ὦτα αὐτῆς, ἥτις οὐκ εἰσακούσεται φωνῆς ἐπᾳδόντων." Ἀλλ' ὑμεῖς γε κατεπᾴσθητε τὴν ἀγριότητα). The image of the deaf serpent, which is drawn from *Ps.* 58.4–5, expressly quoted by Clement, also occurs in *Strom.* 7.16.102.3. On the closure of the ears that hinders moral and spiritual transformation, see *Protr.* 10.89.3. On the taming action of the *Logos*, see *Paed.* 3.12.99.2 and the definition of the *Logos* as 'all-taming' (πανδαμάτωρ) in the *Hymn to Christ the Saviour* (l. 12), at the end of the *Paedagogus*.

15 Cf. *Protr.* 1.5.4, where the expression 'truthful music' (ἀληθεῖ . . . μουσικῇ) describes David's music, and *Protr.* 1.4.1, where the New Song is characterised as being 'in consonance with truth' (συνῳδὸς ἀληθείας).

16 From this perspective, the sharp distinction that Skeris (1976, 152, 155) observes in *Protr.* 1.1 between the figure of Orpheus as founder of the mysteries and as mythical singer – the former being rejected by Clement, while the latter is used in the comparison to Christ – does not seem entirely convincing to me. On one hand, Clement does not distinguish between the form and content of Orpheus' music when describing Orpheus' deceptiveness at 1.3.1; on the other hand (and most importantly for us), the content of Orpheus' music is exactly what determines the forms and limits of its effects (just as the revolutionary content of Christ-Orpheus' music is what determines its exceptional effects).

17 Another original aspect of Clement's treatment of the notion is the identification of the New Song with Christ, whereas other Christian writers simply consider it to be the song addressed to God by man (Lugaresi 2011, 261 n. 3). For some occurrences of the notion of New Song in the Old Testament (ᾆσμα καινόν, ᾠδὴν καινήν in the Septuagint), see, for example, *Ps.* 32.3 (quoted by Clement in *Paed.* 2.4.43.3), 39.4, 95.1, 97.1–3, 143.9–10, 149.1. In the *Exhortation*, the notion also appears at 1.4.4, 1.6.1, 1.6.3, 1.6.5, 1.7.3. For an attempt to identify the source of Clement's concept of New Song, see Brigham 1962.

through a quotation from the old pagan world (*Protr.* 1.2.4). The effects of the New Song are compared to those of the drug poured into wine by Helen in *Od.* 4.221: 'Soother of grief and wrath, that bids all ills be forgotten'. The quotation is not surprising in itself, for it is characteristic of Clement's rhetorical strategy to resort to Greek literature as a means to introduce a new and crucial concept of the Christian message, in order to emphasise its originality.[18] Nonetheless, it is worth paying special attention here to the notion that the Homeric quotation introduces: the concept of *pharmakon*. A 'drug' has been added both to Helen's wine and to the New Song, but the *pharmakon* of Christ's Word is 'truthful'.[19] As the notion of enchantment, the idea that the New Song acts as a *pharmakon* stresses its 'compelling' character and confirms that, in describing it, Clement widely resorts to the Greek tradition on the psychagogic and therapeutic effects of music. This is further confirmed by the insistence on the idea that the Word is a form of enchantment, which reappears later on in the work – at 11.115.1–2, where the exhortation is to trust in 'God's enchantment' (*tēi epōidēi tou theou*) – and by the comparison of the fascinating power of God's voice, expressed by the Scriptures, to the Sirens' call, in a passage of the *Stromata* (2.2.9.6–7).[20]

As both the image of Christ-Orpheus and the notion of a New Song illustrate, Clement's adaptation of the Greek musical landscape to the Christian scenario is based on a refined elaboration and appropriation of some ambiguous and potentially negative elements characterising Hellenic thought on music: in particular, the rich imagery concerning the overwhelming power of music. In describing Christ and his Word by means of the alluring impact of music – a cornerstone in Greek speculation on music – Clement is claiming for the Christian message those very seductive aspects that characterise the competing view of Hellenic culture, turning the weapons of pagan culture against it, as it were, according to an apologetic strategy that has been highlighted by scholars in relation to other fields of early Christian thought (Karamanolis 2013, 127). This strategy is designed to 'tame' the ambiguous elements of the culture that has to be defeated and to put them at the service of a new doctrinal content

[18] See Irwin 1982, 53 and Van den Hoek 1996.

[19] 'There is a sweet and genuine medicine of persuasion blended with this song' (transl. Butterworth, γλυκύ τι καὶ ἀληθινὸν φάρμακον πειθοῦς ἐγκέκραται τῷ ᾄσματι).

[20] See also *Strom.* 6.11.89–90, where Clement says that it is possible to order the *ēthos* and enchant our desires (*katepaidontes hēmōn to epithymētikon*) through music. Regarding the Sirens, the complexity of Clement's operation in comparing the fascination of their song to the appeal of God's voice in *Strom.* 2.2.9.6–7 becomes evident in the light of *Protr.* 12.118.2–4, where the Sirens' song comes to exemplify the allure of vulgar music by contrast to God's song.

in order to compete with the culture in question on an equal footing. It seems to me that some remarkable similarities are to be found here with Plato's sophisticated strategy of endowing the philosophical word with 'magical' and 'musical' powers in order to overcome various seductive forms of expression, including music. In many passages of his work, Plato deals at length with the seductive power of the musical culture of his own day, which represents a serious threat to his educational projects. He is well aware that the allure of poetry and music, and their power to condition behaviour, must be overcome by employing analogous means: that is, a *logos* endowed with the enchanting and persuasive power traditionally ascribed to music and poetry. Notions such as *epōidē* ('enchantment') and *pharmakon* ('drug') – just to mention two concepts that find direct parallels in Clement's treatment – are fully exploited by Plato in order to describe the capacity of the philosophical *logos* to condition human behaviour.[21]

In the framework of this comparison between Plato's and Clement's strategies, I would now like to focus on another image set out in the *Exhortation* as a representation of the New Song. At *Protr.* 1.2.3 the 'heavenly Word' is described as 'the true champion, who is being crowned upon the stage of the whole world'.[22] The image of a contest between the old and the New Song on a cosmic stage, powerfully evoked in a few words, echoes those Platonic passages where the philosophical word competes against the poetic word for the education of citizens in the ideal city.[23] As in Plato's reflection, the negative allure of bad music must be overcome by another kind of music: the New Song of Christ in Clement, the 'musical' word of the legislator-philosopher in Plato.[24]

21 Cf., for example, *Phd.* 77d-78a, *Men.* 79e-80b, *Resp.* 595a-b, *Tht.* 148e-151d; see Pelosi 2010, 26–8 and 2015.

22 Transl. Butterworth, ὁ γνήσιος ἀγωνιστὴς ἐπὶ τῷ παντὸς κόσμου θεάτρῳ στεφανούμενος. The definition of the *Logos* as 'the genuine competitor' recalls the definition of the cicada as Eunomos' 'ally in the contest' (συναγωνιστήν) at *Protr.* 1.1.3: that is, the role played by the cicada, in the traditional interpretation of the story, where the true competitor is Eunomos. As the cicada is the real competitor in the myth, when rightly interpreted, on account of the fact that its song appeals to God, so Christ/Eunomos is the true competitor on the stage of the world because his song is the Word. On the dramatic dimension of the *Logos* in Clement, see Lugaresi 2008, 489–509 and 2011, 251–4.

23 See Pl. *Resp.* 398a-b, and esp. *Leg.* 817b6-c1: 'So we are poets like yourselves, composing in the same *genre*, and your competitors as artists and actors in the finest drama, which true law alone has the natural power to "produce" to perfection (of that we're quite confident)' (transl. Saunders).

24 Obviously, the parallels I have drawn here must be considered within the framework of Clement's Platonism, on which, see Lilla 1971, Butterworth 1916, and Van den Hoek 2005, 77–8. More generally, on Platonism and Christian thought, see Waszink 1957 and Boys-Stones 2001, 151–202.

In Clement's reflection, however, the opposition between pagan and Christian music is distinctly outlined in terms of old *versus* new, and the song of Christ is invariably characterised by the quality of newness: a quality that Plato would hardly have stressed as the principal quality of the 'music' of philosophy, since according to his conservative view of music newness carries a decidedly negative meaning. In order to better appreciate how Clement describes the newness of Christ's song and the strategies it implies, let us return to the first occurrence of the notion of New Song at *Protr.* 1.2.4. In introducing the concept, Clement presents an idea that is as fascinating as it is puzzling: Christ's song is new, while being eternal. The antithetic concept expressed by the phrase 'the eternal *nomos* of the new harmony' (τῆς καινῆς ἁρμονίας τὸν ἀΐδιον νόμον) is not explained here, but Clement returns to the issue later on in the text. At 1.6.3 Clement seems to be aware that the quality of newness, so keenly highlighted by him as a distinctive feature of God's Song, might be misunderstood; he therefore devotes a paragraph to explaining how the newness of the divine song must be properly grasped. The 'redeeming song' (τὸ ᾆσμα . . . τὸ σωτήριον) is not new in the same sense as a tool or a house can be new; in a way, it is eternal because, as the Scriptures say, Christ (the Song) was generated 'before the morning star' (*Ps.* 109.3) and 'in the beginning was the Word (Christ), and the Word was with God, and the Word was God' (*Io.* 1.1). The newness depends on the truthfulness of the content conveyed by this song (*Protr.* 1.6.3: 'But error is old, and truth appears to be a new thing'): Christ's song is new because it is the truthful word of the incarnated Christ and it is eternal, at the same time, because it is the song of the *Logos*, which is the pre-existing *nomos*.[25] Behind this sharp definition of the sense in which the newness of Christ's song must be understood, we can see another sophisticated operation at work, which consists in turning upside down the central values in the Greek intellectual tradition about music: Clement redeems the notion of newness, generally viewed with suspicion by the Greek champions of the ethical view of music (especially Plato).

[25] See Halton 1983, 193, Van den Hoek 2005, 75–6, and Costache 2014, 47–9. Cf. *Protr.* 1.7.3: 'This is the New Song, namely, the manifestation which has but now shined forth among us, of Him who was in the beginning, the pre-existent Word' (transl. Butterworth, τοῦτό ἐστι τὸ ᾆσμα τὸ καινόν, ἡ ἐπιφάνεια ἡ νῦν ἐκλάμψασα ἐν ἡμῖν τοῦ ἐν ἀρχῇ ὄντος καὶ προόντος λόγου). On the idea that as far as God is concerned, the present amounts to eternity, see *Protr.* 9.84.3–6, where Clement explains the expression 'if today we hear His voice' by borrowing the Platonic image of time as an image of eternity and saying that today is 'an image of the everlasting age'. The double temporal nature of the *Logos*' song is further emphasised at *Strom.* 7.16.102.3 (*tou kainōs men legomenou, archaiotatou . . . aismatos*).

7.1.2 The Cosmic Harmony and Man as an Instrument

In expressing its enchanting and salvific power, the New Song also accomplishes a cosmological function: in *Protr.* 1.5.1–4 – a passage packed with technical musical notions and evocative images – Clement describes at length how the Word-song has harmonised the opposite elements of the universe. Like the other passages analysed so far, this account is imbued with notions drawn from Greek musical culture. To begin with some terminological remarks, we can note that, in describing how the *aisma kainon* organised the universe melodiously and tuned the dissonance of the elements, so as to bring the whole cosmos in harmony with it (*Protr.* 1.5.1), Clement uses notions such as *emmelōs*, *diaphōnia*, *symphōnia* and *harmonia*, which are fundamental terms in the vocabulary of Greek music theorists. Furthermore, he uses other concepts, whose musical nuances are less evident to us but were probably easily detectable by the learned reader to whom the work was addressed: for example, *enteinō* and *aniēmi*, which in the Greek sources describe the tension and slackening of the strings, and *malassō*, which is used both in ethical passages on music and in technical accounts to mean the slackening of the strings and the psychological effects produced by certain kind of music.[26] Besides revealing Clement's acquaintance with the technical vocabulary of ancient Greek music, this impressive use of technical musical notions offers some hints as to Clement's use of concepts and paradigms typical of Greek philosophical and musical writings. In particular, *Protr.* 1.5.1–4 bears traces of two closely related ideas that are widely attested in the Greek sources: the notion that the structure of the universe is based on the same proportional relationships as those underlying musical phenomena and the well-known concept of heavenly music.[27] The relationship between the cosmic order and musical structures is a crucial aspect of the intersection between music and philosophy throughout the history of Greek thought on music, from

[26] For a detailed analysis of the Greek music theory at the basis of the passage, see Raffa 2017. Clement's good command of the most technical aspects of Greek musical culture is also testified by other passages, such as *Strom.* 6.11.88.1, where he speaks of *harmoniai* and *genē*, quoting Aristoxenus. Evidence of Clement's familiarity with Greek musical and poetic forms also comes from the Classical-style composition he provides, at the end of the *Paedagogus*: the *Hymn to Christ the Saviour*.

[27] These notions emerge elsewhere in Clement's work. The idea that the study of music concerns harmonic proportions, together with the observation that astronomy studies divine entities and their *symphōnia*, is featured at *Strom.* 6.10.80.2–3. The notion of heavenly music appears at *Strom.* 5.6.34.9, where Clement says that the sun imparts the light to the planets, 'according to a sort of divine music' (κατά τινα θεῖαν μουσικήν). On the notion of heavenly music in Clement, see Cosgrove 2006, 276–82.

the Pythagoreans to Aristides Quintilianus. The Greek influence aside, in his conception of a cosmological action of the *Logos* resulting in the harmony of the universe, Clement finds an antecedent in Philo, whose speculation on the cosmological function of the *Logos* and notion of universal harmony (see Lévy's chapter in this volume) are clearly echoed in Clement's theory. One example of the layering of influences in *Protr.* 1.5.1–4 is offered by the passage where Clement describes the *Logos*-song as 'stretched from the centre to the circumference and from the extremities to the centre' (ἀπὸ τῶν μέσων ἐπὶ τὰ πέρατα καὶ ἀπὸ τῶν ἄκρων ἐπὶ τὰ μέσα διαταθέν), in such a way as to harmonise the whole universe (*Protr.* 1.5.2). As has been noted, the passage presents literal analogies with Philo *De Plant.* 9, where musical notions, though, do not appear. At the same time, it is reminiscent of the most famous account in Greek philosophical literature combining music and cosmology: the creation of the world soul in Plato's *Timaeus*, where notions drawn from music theory play a pivotal role. In particular, *Protr.* 1.5.2 closely recalls the passage where Plato describes how the world soul, after its creation, is woven 'from the centre to the extremity of the heavens' (ἐκ μέσου πρὸς τὸν ἔσχατον οὐρανὸν) so as to envelop the whole body of the cosmos (*Ti.* 36e2-3).

Without entering the specific debate concerning the possible background to this passage,[28] it is important to note that Clement's approach here, based on establishing relations among different fields – the *cosmological* role of the *Logos*-song is closely linked to its *ethical*, *psychological* and *soteriological* effects – by way of musical notions recalls a method of investigation well attested in the Greek sources, where music is often at the centre of enquiries that draw connections between different domains. The closest parallel to Clement, both in time and space, is the work of Ptolemy, whose harmonic investigations include attempts at explaining how the fundamental principles governing the musical field are also essential in other domains – such as that of human souls and the movements of the heavens – and provide clues as to the relation between cosmology, astronomy, ethics and psychology (*Harm.* book 3).

However, despite the massive use of notions and forms of conceptualisation drawn from the Greek world, Clement once again marks his distance from Hellenic musical culture by specifying in a conclusive remark that the

[28] The literal analogies between *Protr.* 1.5.2 and Philo *De Plant.* 9 have been highlighted by Lilla 1971, 209–11 and Van Winden 1978, 208–9. Costache 2014, 38 n. 62 (*contra* Stapert 2007, 52–3) warns against the risk of exclusively emphasising Plato's influence on Clement's musical cosmology, while overlooking the influence of Philo. On music in Platonic cosmology, see Petrucci's and Demulder's essays in this volume.

song by which the *Logos* accomplished its cosmological plan is 'not in accordance with Thracian music' (οὐ κατὰ τὴν Θρᾴκιον μουσικήν) but 'in accordance with the fatherly purpose of God' (κατὰ δὲ τὴν πάτριον τοῦ θεοῦ βούλησιν), like the music emulated by David.[29] In this underlining of the differences between the Greek musical culture and the new music of Christianity, at the end of an account that heavily relies on notions borrowed from the pagan world, we have further confirmation of Clement's overall strategy in the *Exhortation*, which is characterised by a complex balance of criticism, manipulation and appropriation of the Hellenic legacy.

The recurring theme of the opposition between the old pagan music and the new Christian song also characterises the last image I shall explore: the representation of man as an instrument in God's hands, which Clement illustrates immediately after his description of cosmic harmony. At *Protr.* 1.5.3 we are told that God's *Logos* 'scorned those lifeless instruments of lyre and harp' (λύραν μὲν καὶ κιθάραν, τὰ ἄψυχα ὄργανα, ὑπεριδών). Instead of using them, the *Logos* harmonised the world with the microcosm – that is man, including both body and soul – by the power of the Holy Spirit and played this many-voiced instrument. The representation of man as an instrument in the *Logos*' hands is followed by a quotation, whose source is unknown – 'For thou art my harp and my pipe and my temple'[30] – and by Clement's interpretation of it. Finally, the concept of the man-instrument is combined with the crucial idea that mankind was created in God's own image: the Lord fashioned man 'a beautiful, breathing instrument, after His own image' (καλὸν ὁ κύριος ὄργανον ἔμπνουν τὸν ἄνθρωπον ἐξειργάσατο κατ' εἰκόνα τὴν ἑαυτοῦ), and 'He Himself is an all-harmonious instrument of God, melodious and holy' (αὐτὸς ὄργανόν ἐστι τοῦ θεοῦ παναρμόνιον, ἐμμελὲς καὶ ἅγιον, *Protr.* 1.5.4). The opposition between the traditional musical scenario and the new musical world introduced by the *Logos* is expressed in this passage through the effective contrast between the 'lifeless instruments' (*apsycha organa*) and the 'breathing instrument' (*organon empnoun*), that is man – with *empnoun* carrying the double meaning of 'alive' and 'with the breath in it', as in the case of a wind instrument.[31] In spite of this contrast, pagan themes, together with

[29] This 'Thracian music' clearly recalls Orpheus' music. For the hypothesis that David acts as a *trait d'union* in Clement's comparison between Orpheus and Christ, see Irwin 1982, 55, 59.

[30] According to Butterworth (1919, n. *ad loc.*), it may come from an early Christian hymn; however, the notion may have been inspired by passages such as *Ps.* 56.8–9 and especially 1 *Cor.* 6.19, where the image of man as a temple of the Holy Spirit appears.

[31] See Skeris 1976, 131. The idea that the *Logos* creates 'living instruments', by making men the truest instruments of all, subtly recalls the idea, introduced in the description of Christ as Orpheus, that the *Logos*-song animates inanimate things, like stones, bringing them to (the true) life. See *Protr.* 1.4.4:

Christian concepts, contribute to shaping the image of the man-instrument in this passage. In particular, the Christian criticism of organology is combined here with the idea, widespread in ancient Greek sources, that the constitution of the human being (the soul, the body, or both) has some analogies with musical structures and with the related analogy between man and cosmos (the so-called microcosm/macrocosm theory), via music. Let us delve more deeply into Clement's reception of these themes.

Clement's dismissal of the Greek organological scenario at the beginning of the passage leads us to a fundamental and complex strand of Christian thought on music: the analysis of musical instruments. This analysis includes both a fierce criticism of pagan instruments and an allegorical interpretation of instruments, of the sort which features prominently in the *Psalms*.[32] A Clementine passage in which these two strands and their interplay clearly emerge is *Paed.* 2.4.41.4–42.3, where an allegorical reading of *Ps.* 150.3–5 is provided (Lugaresi 2011, 249). As Clement explains, when the *Psalm* says 'praise God with the *psaltērion*' and 'praise him with the *kithara*', what these two instruments stand for, respectively, are the tongue and the mouth; and when the *Psalm* says 'praise him with the strings and *organon*', what *organon* and strings mean, respectively, is the human body and its nerves, through which it has received a harmonious tension. As in *Protr.* 1.5.3, the image evoked here is that of the man-instrument, and its expressive power is used to mark the difference with the Greek organological scenario: man is a 'peaceful instrument' (*eirēnikon … organon*), whereas the Greek instruments, largely used in war to inflame passions, are 'warlike instruments' (*polemika organa*).[33] Greek musical culture is apparently dismissed here, along with its warrior instruments. However, the image of the man-instrument outlined in these passages bears traces of the Greek doctrines of the musical structure of the world, both as a microcosm and as a macrocosm – a doctrine which

'See how mighty is the new song! It has made men out of stones and men out of wild beasts. They who were otherwise dead, who had no share in the real and true life, revived when they but heard the song' (transl. Butterworth). The musical instrument as a representation of the saved man also appears at *Strom.* 6.11.88.3, where redeemed humanity is portrayed as a *kithara*, 'played for faith by the Word' (κρουόμενος εἰς πίστιν τῷ λόγῳ) – the latter being significantly depicted, through another musical image, as Apollon *mousēgetēs*. On man as a wind instrument in the hands of God, cf. *Gen.* 2.7, where God blows into man to give him life, as though he were a wind instrument.

[32] It is interesting to note Clement's remarkable role in the history of the Christian approach to organology, as one of the first apologists to grasp the importance of providing an allegorical interpretation of instruments, as shown by *Paed.* 2.4.41: see Gérold 1931, X, 125–6, 130.

[33] *Paed.* 2.4.42.1–2. The Greek instruments mentioned here by Clement are the *salpinx*, the *syrinx*, the *pēktis*, the *lyra*, the *aulos*, the *keras*, the *tympanon* and the *kymbalos*.

characterises the history of Greek thought on music, from the earliest evidence to the latest writings.[34] Plato's contribution to this area is remarkable and can be summarised in two main themes, both providing some clues concerning the background to Clement's imagery: first, Plato's investigation of the close affinity between the structure of the world soul and the constitution of the human rational soul, on account of their both being created according to harmonic proportions (*Ti.* 35a-36d, 41d-42a); second, his frequent use of musical images and notions (such as the strings of an instrument and their tension) in ethical and psychological analyses, as a representation of the different components of the soul.[35] As in the case of the other musical images used in *Protr.* 1.1, an investigation of the Greek images, notions and theories which might have influenced Clement in his use of the man-instrument image in the *Exhortation* provides further evidence that Greek musical culture and philosophical thought on music constitute an essential, if controversial, point of reference for the construction of Clement's rich musical imagery.

7.2 **Origen**

Musical images and notions abound in Origen's work too. In some cases, there are evident analogies with Clement's musical imagery. At *Cels.* 5.33, for example, a 'musical' representation of Christ appears: Christ is presented in the guise of a chorus-leader (*chorostatēs*), guiding the whole world (Skeris 1976, 83); again, at *Cels.* 8.67, Origen introduces the notion of heavenly music through the image of the divine choir (*theios choros*): the choir of the planets and the stars raising a hymn of praise to God, together with just men. Further parallels concern the notion of enchantment, which Origen uses to define the taming effect of God (*apo tōn tou theou epōidōn*) on 'human beasts', as well as the effect of the Scriptures on evil, and the Scriptures themselves (*Philoc.* 12).

[34] The earliest appearance of a theory entailing the idea that music is in the human body – in particular, the concept that harmonic ratios are at the basis of the development of a viable embryo – within the framework of a microcosm-macrocosm doctrine, is to be found in the Hippocratic treatise *On Regimen*, probably dating from the late fifth/early fourth century BC (see Pelosi 2016). For late occurrences of similar notions, see Ptol. *Harm.* 3.4.95.11–16 and Aristid. Quint. *De mus.* 3.18.117.-18–118.28, 3.23.124.5–26.

[35] See, for example, the harmonisation of the spirited and the rational elements of the soul, as though they were two strings of an instrument, at *Resp.* 411a-412a, and 441e-442a, and the definition of justice as the harmony between the notes of a musical scale at *Resp.* 443c-e. The analogy between the nerves of the human body and the strings of an instrument used by Clement in his allegorical reading of *Ps.* 150, at *Paed.* 2.4.41.4–42.3, is foreshadowed by Plato in *Phd.* 98c-d and *Ti.* 74b, where the tension and relaxation of the nerves is described through the verbs used to describe in technical terms the tightening and the slackening of the strings (*epiteinō* and *aniēmi*).

Instrumental allegories are also employed: for example, in the *Homilies on Joshua* Origen compares the words of the Apostles and the Evangelists to the sound of the trumpet by borrowing the powerful image of the Gospel as a trumpet introduced by Clement in *Protr.* 11.116.2–3.[36]

In the following pages, I shall focus on a musical image, and the concepts related to it, in order to illustrate a crucial point in Origen's hermeneutic approach to the Scriptures: the inner concord and unity of the scriptural message. The Scriptures are compared to a well-harmonised musical instrument, or, more precisely, to the consonant layout that characterises the instrument's arrangement. As I shall show, the crucial concept at the basis of the comparison is the notion of concord (*symphōnia*). This is a key concept in Greek musical theory and practice: usually defined as the perfect combination of two different sounds – whether played simultaneously or in succession – *symphōnia* represents a fundamental principle for melodic structures; as such, it lies at the centre of theoretical analyses and performances. But the great import of this notion in the Greek sources goes well beyond the musical field, in the strict sense. Thanks to the particular acoustic impression that it produces and the mathematical expression by which it is described, *symphōnia* has remarkable philosophical implications, especially as far as the relationship between multiplicity and unity is concerned: not surprisingly, it is widely employed by ancient Greek philosophers in the description and explanation of various phenomena, as well as in argumentative passages (Pelosi 2014). In approaching Origen's use of *symphōnia* to express some key aspects of his theology and hermeneutics, it is important to bear in mind that he is writing in the wake of this Greek tradition, which fully exploits the expressive power of the musical concept to investigate some crucial philosophical issues. From this perspective, it is possible to fully appreciate how Origen borrows and further expands the argumentative potential of the term *symphōnia*, whose philosophical implications are as interesting as its technical meaning in music theory.

7.2.1 The Scriptures as a Well-Tuned Instrument and Their Inner Consonance

The notion of *symphōnia* is introduced in the first paragraph of the sixth chapter of the *Philocalia*, where the point at issue is the exegesis of the term

[36] *Hom. Jes. Nav.* 7.1, where the *tubae ductiles* – in Rufinus' translation – represent the 'praedicationis magnificam coelestemque doctrinam'.

'peace-maker' (*eirēnopoios*), which appears in *Matth.* 5.9.[37] As a third meaning of the word – the first two are not illustrated – Origen mentions the exegete of sacred texts, namely the one who establishes 'the concord and the pax of the Scriptures' (συμφωνίαν καὶ τὴν εἰρήνην τούτων), by demonstrating that what might seem like a contradiction actually is not. At the end of the paragraph, the musical notion is expanded: the Scriptures sound like a *diaphōnia* 'to those who have not ears to hear', but, in point of fact, they possess *symphōnia*.[38]

In the second paragraph, the musical analogy expressing the intrinsic cohesion of all parts of the Scriptures becomes more detailed and the image of the instrument is introduced. The Scriptures are compared to instruments such as the *psaltērion* or the *kithara*, which are made up of different strings, each producing different sounds that seem to have no similarity to one another; owing to this apparent dissimilarity, the strings seem 'discordant' (*asymphonoi*) 'to one who is not acquainted with music' (*tōi amousōi*). Analogously, those who are not able to hear God's harmony in the Scriptures think that the Old Testament is at variance with the New, that the Prophets are at variance with the Law, that the Evangelists are at variance with one another, and that each Apostle is at variance with the Gospel, with himself, and with the other Apostles. On the contrary, 'one who has been educated in God's music . . . will produce the sound of God's music, which has taught him to pluck the strings at the appropriate

37 The *Philocalia* is an anthology of excerpts from Origen's writings, whose composition has been ascribed, not uncontroversially, to the Cappadocians Fathers Basil of Caesarea and Gregory of Nazianzus (Harl 1983, 19–41; McLynn 2004, 32–33). *Philoc.* 6.1–2 derives from the second book of Origen's *Commentary on Matthew*. The use of the notion of *symphōnia* in *Phil.* 6.1–2 has resonance with other passages of Origen's work: for example, *Comm. in Matth.* 14.1, where the concept of *symphōnia*, meaning both agreement and musical concord, is analysed through examples drawn from the Scriptures (Skeris 1976, 85–8, 140); *Comm. in Io.* 10.42.290, where Origen criticises the Gnostics and Marcionites for not respecting the *symphōnia* of the Scriptures, and *Philoc.* 8.3, where the notion of *symphōnia* appears in the description of the process by which man passes from being multiple – that is, being separate from God, as a sinner – to being one with/in God. Clement too exploits the concept of *symphōnia* to some extent: for example, at *Protr.* 9.88.3, to describe the unity of the Christians under the guidance of the *Logos* (significantly represented in musical terms as a 'chorus leader', χορηγός); and *Strom.* 6.11.88.5 and 6.15.125.2–3, where *symphōnia* illustrates the inner cohesion of Scripture, analogously to *Philoc.* 6.1–2.

38 . . . δόξαν μὲν ἐχόντων διαφωνίας τοῖς μὴ ἔχουσιν ὦτα εἰς τὸ ἀκούειν, τὸ δὲ ἀληθὲς συμφωνότητα. συμφωνότης is a *hapax*, clearly implying the opposite of διαφωνία; an alternative explanation is that συμφωνότητα derives from a mistaken reading of a form of συμφωνέω (Harl 1983, 316 n. 2). 'To those who have not ears to hear' recalls *Lc.* 8.8 ('Whoever has ears to hear, let them hear'). It is interesting to note that, while ears must be well open in order to grasp the *symphōnia* of the Scriptures, Origen recommends that we keep them closed to 'the sounds of the theatres and the indecent songs' of the actual music (*In Gen. Hom.* 3.5). On Origen's attitude to spectacles, see Lugaresi 2003, 658–61; on his criticism of dance, Bermond 2001, 131–8.

time':[39] the strings of the Law and the strings of the Evangelists, which are in *symphōnia*; the strings of the Prophets and the strings of the Apostles, which produce the same sound; and the strings of the Evangelists that are in concord with those of the Apostles. This 'musical' exegete 'knows that the Scriptures, as a whole, are God's only musical instrument, perfect and harmonised' (ἓν γὰρ οἶδεν τὸ τέλειον καὶ ἡρμοσμένον ὄργανον τοῦ θεοῦ εἶναι πᾶσαν τὴν γραφήν): an instrument 'that produces one saving melody out of different sounds' (μίαν ἀποτελοῦν ἐκ διαφόρων φθόγγων σωτήριον τοῖς μανθάνειν ἐθέλουσι φωνήν).

As this summary of the passage shows, the comparison between a well-tuned instrument and the Scriptures is essentially based on their both being made up of parts, whose hidden relationship creates a *symphōnia*. The key aspect in the organological illustration is the inner arrangement of the musical instrument: that is, the reciprocal relationships between its strings. It is important to note that, in *Philoc.* 6.2, this focus on the notion of *symphōnia* serves a twofold purpose: firstly, it expresses the intrinsic coherence of the Scriptures;[40] second, it makes the hermeneutic point that a learned approach to the sacred texts is needed.[41] As a bridge between these two aspects, there is the implied idea that the *symphōnia* of the Scriptures, while essential, is far from obvious.

Regarding the first point, by comparing the Scriptures as a whole to the arrangement of an instrument, characterised by the *symphōnia* between different sounds, Origen does not only suggest that the Scriptures possess an inner coherence, beneath the surface of their apparent (multiple and even inconsistent) meanings, but also defines certain features of their deep consistency: as a *symphōnia*, the Scriptures possess a unity that comes from a differentiated multiplicity, and it is within this very unity that each element finds its inmost meaning. Furthermore, the analogy suggests that the key to grasping the consistency of the Scriptures lies within the Scriptures themselves, as it is the very arrangement of an instrument that explains its *symphōnia*. This leads us to the second previously aforementioned point: the fundamental work of the exegete in bringing to light the *symphōnia* embedded in the Scriptures.

At the very outset of the paragraph, the hidden nature of musical *symphōnia* is highlighted: the relationship between the different sounds is

[39] ὁ πεπαιδευμένος τὴν τοῦ θεοῦ μουσικὴν ... ἀποτελέσει φθόγγον μουσικῆς θεοῦ, ἀπὸ ταύτης μαθὼν ἐν καιρῷ κρούειν χορδάς.

[40] On the various terms Origen uses to underscore the inner consistency of the Scriptures, including *harmonia* and *symphōnia*, see Ramelli 2011, 349–50.

[41] Cf. *Cels.* 3.74 and 7.11, where the need for a skilful exegete is also emphasised.

not self-evident and escapes the *amousos*, 'who does not understand the *logos* underlying the musical consonance' (μὴ ἐπισταμένῳ λόγον μουσικῆς συμφωνίας). The lack of an 'epistemic' approach is equally stressed with regard to 'those who do not know how to hear God's harmony in the sacred Scriptures' (οἱ μὴ ἐπιστάμενοι ἀκούειν τῆς τοῦ θεοῦ ἐν ταῖς ἱεραῖς γραφαῖς ἁρμονίας). These remarks clearly suggest that perceiving the *symphōnia* produced by both a musical instrument and the Scriptures requires some sort of preparation. Just as perception of musical *symphōnia* requires a capacity to grasp unapparent analogies within the perfect system represented by the arrangement of the instrument, in order to understand the consistent Scriptural message we must interpret the Scriptures with the Scriptures by connecting apparently unrelated passages and concepts.[42]

The 'musical' preparation of the exegete is all the more important since he plays an active role in making the inner concord of the Scriptures resonate for others. Within the analogy of *Philoc.* 6.2, this active role is emphasised by the verb ἀποτελεῖν, which is thrice repeated to indicate the *production* of a sound (Harl 1983, 312). More specifically, the verb is used to define the activity of the exegete in the sentence 'he will produce a note of God's music' (ἀποτελέσει φθόγγον μουσικῆς θεοῦ), where his role as a 'performer' is further stressed by the idea that from this divine music he has learned to 'pluck the strings' (*krouein chordas*) of the biblical books at the appropriate time. Hence, besides being a 'peace-maker', the exegete turns out to be a '*symphōnia*-maker', for he is able to perceive the consonance that lies behind the apparent inconsistency of the Scriptures and make it resound.[43]

At this point, some conclusions can be drawn on the general import of the musical image featured at *Philoc.* 6.1–2 within Origen's thought. The hermeneutic point made through that musical image captures some fundamental aspects of Origen's approach to the sacred texts, namely his belief in the deep consistency and unity of the scriptural message and in the need

[42] The need to grasp the similarity between sounds, beyond their apparent dissimilarity, in order to perceive the inner consonance of an instrument can be compared to the need to study the similarity between words (the *homoiai phōnai*) or concepts, which is an essential step on the path to the spiritual meaning of the Scriptures in Origen's hermeneutics (Harl 1983, 141–2; Ramelli 2011, 350). Another interesting image designed to express the idea that the key to interpret the Bible lies within the Bible itself is featured at *Philoc.* 2.3, where the Bible is compared to a house consisting of many locked rooms, whose keys are placed randomly before the doors.

[43] On the link between peace and consonance/harmony, see also Clem. Al. *Strom.* 4.6.40, where the notion of 'understanding the world's harmony through its contradictions' is mentioned as one of the meanings of 'peace-maker'.

for a skilful interpreter able to make this cohesion clearly emerge. These aspects play a crucial role in Origen's construction of a philosophical theology and in his endeavour to advocate the philosophical respectability of Christian teaching, as demonstrated by his dogmatic and apologetic works: the treatises *On First Principles* and *Against Celsus*.

Hermeneutic topics are at the centre of the fourth book of *On First Principles*, which stands out as a rich summary of Origen's exegetical approach and as a fundamental piece of early Christian hermeneutics.[44] Origen stresses the deep cohesion of the Old and New Testaments, written under the inspiration of the Holy Spirit, and argues for the need to seek out the deepest meaning of the Scriptures beneath the surface of their literal – sometimes incoherent – meaning. Origen thus argues that the sacred texts, from which all theological and philosophical knowledge derives, have an inner coherence and intelligibility. As suggested by the comparison with a well-harmonised instrument at *Philoc.* 6.1–2, the harmony of the Scriptures is presented here as an intrinsic feature, which does not depend on our capacity to grasp it, as it is the result of the Scriptures' being pervaded by divine inspiration through and through.[45] As in *Philoc.* 6.1–2, where the musical analogy implies the idea that the key to grasping the *symphōnia* of the Scriptures lies within the Scriptures themselves, in the treatise *On First Principles* Origen stresses that the sacred texts themselves teach us how to understand their content (*Princ.* 4.2.4).

From an apologetic point of view, the crucial idea conveyed by the notion of scriptural *symphōnia* – that the Scriptures are characterised by a deep harmony, which can be fully grasped through a correct hermeneutical approach – is central to Origen's response to the pagan attack on Christianity. In his most important apologetic work – the *Against Celsus* – Origen undermines Celsus' criticism, which emphasises the untrustworthy and inconsistent character of the scriptural content, by underlining Celsus' defective approach to the sacred texts, incapable of attaining their true meaning. In this counter-attack, designed to dispel the charges of inconsistency and vindicate the intellectual legitimacy of Christianity, a fundamental part is played by allegory: an exegetical technique with

44 On the place of the hermeneutic treatment of *Princ.* 4 in the overall structure of the work, see Behr 2017, xlvi–liv.

45 *Princ.* 4.1.7. The idea that the Holy Spirit extends throughout the entire body of the Scriptures – *per omne corpus eis extenditur*, διατείνουσα εἰς πάσαν αὐτήν – can easily be translated in the musical terms used in *Philoc.* 6.1–2, as the extension throughout an entire system is exactly what defines the best *symphōnia*, that is, the octave, whose name in Greek musical theory is διὰ πασῶν (χορδῶν) – literally 'through all (the chords)'.

a long history in the Hellenic philosophical tradition, adopted and reinterpreted by Origen in the light of his view of the Scriptures as a coherent and self-consistent whole (Ramelli 2011). Within the analysis set out in this chapter, it is notable that where Origen explicitly lays claim to the Christian right to interpret the sacred texts allegorically in search of the truest meaning of the Scriptures, he once again resorts to musical vocabulary: at *Cels*. 4.17, reacting to Celsus' attack on the allegorical readings of Scripture, Origen affirms the Christians' right to give a 'consistent explanation which harmonizes and agrees (συνᾳδούσης καὶ συμφωνούσης) in all respects with the Scriptures inspired by the divine Spirit dwelling in pure souls'.[46] The notion of *symphōnia* – a concept adopted by Greek philosophers as one of the most powerful expressions of the unity and rationality underlying music and, by analogy, other phenomena – is for Origen a powerful means of affirming the wholeness and truthfulness of the Scriptures, not least against the charge of incoherence and irrationality levelled by pagan philosophers.

[46] Transl. Chadwick. Cf., at *Cels*. 4.51, Celsus' remark on Jewish and Christian allegories: 'they connect with some amazing and utterly senseless folly ideas which cannot by any means be made to fit (ἁρμοσθῆναι)'.

CHAPTER 8

Plotinus on Music, Rhythm, and Harmony

Alexandra Michalewski

8.1 Introduction

In *Enn.* 6.3(44).16,[1] where Plotinus establishes a cartography of what should be ranked among qualities and what belongs to the world of substances, he indicates that there is a 'double music' – just as there is a double arithmetic, geometry or astronomy – drawing inspiration from analyses of *Republic* 7. On the one hand, there is sensible music, which manifests itself through the sound of the singer and of an instrument, and which makes the soul incline towards the sensible world. On the other, there is intelligible music, which directs the soul towards the intelligible and that which is beyond any sound. A few lines further on, Plotinus compares the practice of sensible music to that of *praktikai aretai*, which confine the activities of the soul to the requirements of the political life, that is, to the general care of the life of the soul-body composite. This presupposes that the other music is analogous to the purificatory virtues that lead the soul to the contemplation of the intelligible. Nevertheless, to fully understand this opposition, one must consider the general context of the treatises on the genera of being, in which Plotinus endeavors to emphasize the distance between the intelligible, the only true essence (*ousia*), and the sensible, which is only a set of qualities. Indeed, if the sensible has only a homonymous relationship with the intelligible, from which it derives, their separation does not imply a total break. The deficiency that Plotinus indicates both in acts of conventional virtue and in the sensible arts is indeed their 'other-directedness', to use an expression of J. Wilberding.[2] But in other contexts, Plotinus shows that, just as some virtues related to the composite, that is, civic virtues, can prepare the soul for its ascent to the intelligible, certain arts related to the sensible, such as music, likewise serve to prepare the soul for its ascent towards the

[1] *Enn.* 6.3(44).16.13–32. [2] See Wilberding 2008.

intelligible realm. However, if one examines *Enn.* 1.3(20), addressing the role of sensible music in the soul's ascent to the intelligible realm, Plotinus appears to have relatively little to say on the matter. This third treatise, according to the Porphyrian order, follows *Enn.* 1.1(53) entitled 'What Is the Living Being? And What Is Man?'. Identifying the properly human dimension of human beings, that is, that which connects them to the intelligible realm, as opposed to the *zōon*, the part that is subject to passions and emotions, is the first step in Plotinus' philosophical programme. The next treatise, *Enn.* 1.2(19), which is devoted to the analysis of political and purificatory virtues, lays out the various stages that are required for the soul to return to its principle, and *Enn.* 1.3(20) examines the three natures that are most apt to ascend to the intelligible (the *mousikos*, the *erotikos* and the *philosophos*). In this context, the experience of music is presented as a transitory step in the ascent of the soul to the intelligible realm and, ultimately, to the One.

Plotinus' engagement with the Platonic tradition concerning music is in fact rather limited. While in the *Republic* and the *Laws*, Plato addresses at length the importance of choosing appropriate melodies and choreographies, as an essential part of his reflection on politics, these concerns are hardly touched upon by Plotinus. He does not detail which kinds of melodies or rhythms are conducive to the softening of the senses, to courageous deeds, or to virtue.[3] Music is no longer conceived as a collective experience, but instead – and above all – as a stage in the soul's solitary progress towards the recovery of its original, essential nature.[4] On the one hand, from the very early treatises on, Plotinus states that the perception of harmonies and rhythms is conducive to the understanding of intelligible harmony. On the other, however, he gives only marginal attention to issues such as the nature of harmony itself – the mathematical reflection on numerical relations. To a certain extent, his approach to music is an expression of what has been identified as a 'de-mathematization' of Plato's thought.[5] Although Plotinus does point to the definition of the soul as a musical harmony in *Timaeus* (36a-37a) and to the role of numerical proportions in its generation, these are only allusive references. Nor does he explicitly articulate the link between music and its 'sister science', astronomy[6] – the importance of which as a pedagogical practice also remains unmentioned in the treatises. Plotinus thus departs

[3] According to Porphyry, *Plot.* 14, 'Plotinus had a complete knowledge of geometry, arithmetic, mechanics, optics and music, but was not disposed to apply himself to detailed research on these subjects'.

[4] Jankélévitch 1998, 38. [5] Chiaradonna 2014. [6] Plato, *Republic* 7.530d8.

from the general reading of Plato developed in the imperial era, which is exemplified in chapter 7 of the *Didaskalikos*, among other sources. In this passage, Alcinous discusses the role played by 'the theory of mathematics' (*hē tou mathēmatikou theōria*), which he defines as a subdivision of theoretical philosophy, together with theology and physics. For him, the purpose of mathematics is to sharpen the mind and to help develop mental precision. Music and astronomy are part of the mathematical training in that they each contribute to the exercise of a specific sense:

> For even as the eyes are naturally suited to astronomy, so is the sense of hearing to harmony; and even as in applying our minds to astronomy we are led from visible objects to invisible and intelligible essence, so in listening to harmonious sound we in the same way transfer our attention from things audible to what is contemplated by the mind itself.[7]

On the one hand, Plotinus simplifies the analyses devoted to music as a preparatory discipline to the contemplation of the transcendent realm, but, on the other, he draws on examples taken from the arts of rhythm (namely dance and music) to illustrate key aspects of his cosmology and of causal processes. The rhythm of human choreographies provides an insight into the cosmic order, its harmony and its regularity. But this image is also used to point to astral causality, as well as to the relationship between the individual soul and the body which depends on it. Together with music, the art of dance (whether individually practiced, as in pantomime, or collectively, as in the case of choral dancing) follows a numerical pattern, and it is ruled by rhythm, that is, 'the order of movement', as stated in book 2 of Plato's *Laws*.

Beyond the simple evocative use of musical or choreographic rhythms to illustrate causal processes, Plotinus attaches great importance to the very notion of rhythm (*rhythmos*). The concept of rhythm runs through Plotinus' metaphysics and cosmology insofar as – and this is what this paper proposes to examine – it expresses the dynamism and productive power of intelligible realities. First of all, we will discuss the role that Plotinus confers on music in the ascent of the soul to the intelligible. Sensible music, when regulated according to measure and proportions, is a manifestation of a higher order, stemming from the intelligible world to which the soul itself, in its highest dimension, is always connected. Secondly, we will see how the notion of harmony, understood as the perfect unity of a multiplicity, which is at the heart of the process by

[7] Alcinous, *Didaskalikos* 7.161.37–41.

which the soul gradually becomes aware of its intelligible nature, is also used by Plotinus as an image of the causal relationships between the different levels of reality. This will lead us to see how the concept of harmony is, in a way, subordinated to that of rhythm, which is at the very foundation of the generative power of the Forms.

8.2 Music and Sensible Beauty

At the beginning of *Enn.* 1.3(20), commenting on *Phaedrus* 248d3, Plotinus establishes that the natural dispositions of the *mousikos* are twofold and complementary.[8] On the one hand, the musician has an emotive and reactive temperament; on the other, he naturally seeks beautiful things:

> One must consider the musician as easily moved and excited by beauty, but quite incapable of setting himself in motion on his own, while quick to be dragged by random images that are, so to speak, impressed upon him; and just as fearful people are quick to react to noises, so the musician is to sounds and their inherent beauty; always avoiding what lacks harmony and unity in songs and rhythms, he seeks instead rhythmic proportion and appropriate sounds.[9]

As V. Jankélévitch notes, following Ficino, the Plotinian *mousikos* has an inner disposition – or 'flair', as it were – that allows him to perceive beauty before he can fully apprehend it.[10] For the music-lover, to be defined as an emotional being signifies that the dominant part in him is the lower, irrational soul. His emotive nature causes him to shun discordance and disharmony and seek harmonious sounds instead. The musician differs from the philosopher in that, while easily moved by the beauty of harmonious sounds, he is incapable of initiating his ascension towards essential beauty.[11] Therein lies his weakness: he is dependent on external *stimuli*, on the impressions caused by random objects on his senses (*ek tōn tychontōn hoion ektypōn*).[12] His soul is not capable of spontaneously setting itself in motion and returning towards the superior principles of the universe. Of the three natures that are best disposed to turn towards the intelligible – the musician, the lover, the philosopher – only the philosopher is naturally disposed to detach himself from the sensible in order to contemplate the

[8] As Gourinat 2016, 99, notes, in this treatise the term *mousikos* is not employed in the general sense of 'friend of the muses', that is, a cultivated person, but more specifically to designate the lover of music and dance – not necessarily the professional musician, but also the amateur who practices music or simply appreciates it.

[9] *Enn.* 1.3(20).1.22–28, my translation. [10] Jankélévitch 1998, 34. [11] *Enn.* 1.3(20).1.22–23.

[12] On the meaning of τυχόντες, see Gourinat 2016, 110–11.

intelligible. By contrast, the lover and the *mousikos* need, first, the impulse of sensible beauty and, second, an education, in order to turn towards intelligible beauty. There are several stages in this education. The first one consists in comprehending that harmonies perceived by the senses are only a trace of the higher, intelligible harmony. Once the musician has been moved by sensible harmonies, he will dissociate them from their sensible shell and thus apprehend the beauty of harmonious measures and rhythmic proportions:

> After perceiving the sensible sounds, rhythms, and figures,[13] he is to be guided as follows: by discarding the matter of those things upon which such measures and proportions supervene, he is to be led to the beauty that reigns over them. He is to learn that this was the source of his transport – that is, the intelligible harmony and its inherent beauty, or the universal beauty, not just some particular beauty, and he has to internalize the philosophical notions. It is from this starting point that he is to be taught to believe in what he still does not know to be in his possession. What these arguments consist in will be discussed later on.[14]

There are three elements in particular that the musician seeks: (1) harmony, that is, consonant arrangements of sounds; (2) rhythmic proportion, which lies in the arrangement of long and short; (3) the appropriateness of figures (*schēmata*) – be it musical figures or choreographic figures set to music. This triad, which is inspired by *Republic* 3.413e, was to become a main tenet of Middle-Platonic thought.[15] According to Plotinus, by seeking order and measure, the musician is willing to order his own soul, which is the first step in the process of purification by which the individual soul gradually arrives at its intelligible origin. In this chapter, Plotinus remains quite elliptic and does not give precise details about the steps of this ascensional process. In the next one, however, studying the case of the lover, who, like the musician, is initially moved by sensible beauty, he introduces the role played by the practice of civic virtues. To order one's soul, to give measure to the emotions that come from the living being, corresponds to what Plotinus calls the practice of the civic virtues, which are themselves

[13] As Gourinat notes (note *ad loc.*), it is difficult to determine whether σχήματα designates the 'figures' of sound – this rather enigmatic expression may refer, as in *Laws* 2.660a, to a certain rhythmic arrangement – as the context would indicate or, more generally, the dance figures executed to the musician's tune.

[14] *Enn.* 1.3(20).1.28–35, my translation.

[15] The triad has often been read in terms of the Pythagorean tradition associating musical intervals and harmony as an expression of mathematical proportions. See Plato, *Laws* 2.654e-655a and Theon, *Exp.* 11.12–13.

a propaedeutic to the acquisition of the purificatory virtues.[16] This entire progression through the degrees of virtues shows the processes implemented so that the soul may detach itself as far as possible from its alienating concern with the sensible world and direct its attention towards its higher dimension, living in accordance with the intelligible. From harmonious sounds, the musician's soul is to ascend to the apprehension of a loftier beauty; from visible beauties, the lover's soul is to progress to the apprehension of the beautiful as displayed in righteousness and honest behavior. Perceptible proportions, measures and harmonies, thus point to a superior harmony, and ultimately to the measured order of intelligible Forms. Now, what enables the soul's ascension is that its higher dimension has never actually left the intelligible realm. This is why, before considering its collective or political aspects, Plotinus primarily conceives of music as an individual experience, that of the soul's return to its primordial origin. In the case of the musician and of the lover, the perception of sensible beauty can be seen as a starting point permitting the ascent towards the intelligible.[17] When the soul perceives sensible harmony, what makes it capable of recognizing it as such is a pre-existing and higher harmony in the intelligible world. According to Plotinus, what Plato calls 'recollection' is the achievement of this relational activity of the soul, ultimately leading it to the full recognition of its intelligible nature.[18] In *Enn.* 2.9(33), Plotinus actually pits the musician's aesthetic emotion against the crudeness of the Gnostics, who fail to see through sensory beauty and recognize the traces of the original and intelligible perfection. Only those who are aware of

[16] In the previous treatise, *Enn.* 1.2(19), Plotinus studied the scale of virtues. Briefly speaking, according to Plotinus, the four cardinal virtues of *Republic* 4 are to be found on two levels in the soul. On the lower level, they manifest themselves as the civic or political virtues, and their role is simply to discipline the soul, whereas on the superior level, they are no longer linked to the exercise of a practical activity, but are identified with contemplative activity. The latter are the virtues of the philosopher, who strives to achieve the goal of 'becoming like god', as stated in the *Theaetetus*. Thus, courage, as a cathartic virtue, in the upper dimension of the soul, does not consist in performing an act of bravery, but is 'freedom from affection, according to the likeness of that to which it looks, which is free from affection by nature', *Enn.* 1.2(19).6.25–27. By prioritizing the levels of virtues (civic and cathartic), Plotinus articulates the different definitions of virtue that Plato gives in the *Republic*, where their role is to lead the lower and desiring parts of the soul to obey the upper part, and in the *Phaedo*, where the virtues are defined as the purifications of the soul. For more on this, see O' Meara 2003, 40–4; Wilberding 2008, 380–5; Cooper 2012; Noble (forthcoming).

[17] *Enn.* 6.7(38).6.3. See Emilsson 1988. The interpretation of the sense-perception process in Plotinus is a very delicate question which has been subject to much debate in secondary literature. This problem goes far beyond the limits of the present paper. I merely indicate that, in his latest book, Emilsson 2017 has nuanced his previous reading, according to which the soul activates innate concepts in every act of sense-perception.

[18] On Plotinus' interpretation of recollection, see Chiaradonna 2019 and Michalewski 2021.

the higher harmonies and numbered measures of the intelligible can be moved by harmonious sounds in the sensible world and be led, via this experience, to the recollection of truth.[19] This insensitivity of the Gnostics with regard to the beauty of the sensible world is the corollary of their inability to elaborate a theory of virtue, of its acquisition and of the process of the purification of the soul, as pointed out in *Enn.* 2.9(33).15.

Music, then, is mainly significant as a stepping stone – most importantly considering where it may lead the souls. What really matters is the contemplation of what is 'there' (*ekei*). If we follow Porphyry's classification, the treatises lay out the various stages of the soul's ascent towards the higher principles. Plotinus demonstrates in *Enn.* 1.1(53) that human nature is essentially intelligible; in *Enn.* 1.2(19), he shows how the virtues could work as milestones in the soul's cathartic progress; in *Enn.* 1.3(20), the methods of ascent are adapted to different natures; finally, in *Enn.* 1.4(46), Plotinus concludes with a musical analogy to illustrate the way in which, in a sense, the body can serve as an instrument of the soul. He compares the individual soul's relation to the body to a singer using his instrument for accompaniment.[20] Though the lyre was once useful, the soul of the sage sings a better song without the accompaniment of the body. This higher kind of music is played without the mediation of instruments, just as the activities of the higher part of the soul are exercised without the body.[21] When the soul reaches the intelligible realm, the body, which is a mere instrument of the soul, is cast aside as it now practices a higher kind of activity, without accompaniment.[22] Plotinus' comparison of the body to a lyre recurs throughout the treatises: for instance, in *Enn.* 2.3(52).13, Plotinus notes that a sick body is an impediment to the soul's activities, just as a poorly strung lyre affects the musician's performance.[23] In a way, these last lines of *Enn.* 1.4(46) indicate that the supreme goal of music, while relying on the sensible, is to lead the soul of the *mousikos* to grasp the order and rationality that structure and lay beyond perceivable sounds, and to gradually detach his soul from sensible exteriority.

19 *Enn.* 2.9(33).16.40–47: 'They feel a kind of disturbance and come to a recollection of the truth (εἰς ἀνάμνησιν ἔρχονται τοῦ ἀληθοῦς)'. Unless otherwise indicated, I refer to Armstrong's translation.
20 *Enn.* 1.4(46).16.24–29. Cf. Hadot 1997, 175–6.
21 On the silence of the soul as it separates itself from the body, see *Enn.* 5.1(10).12.14–20.
22 On this, see Chrétien 1997, 37–8.
23 *Enn.* 2.3(52).13.45–47.

8.3 Musical Images and Their Use

There is a reason why music represents such a privileged example of the use of sensible beauty as a step towards the soul's contemplation of its own interiority: harmony is that which makes most visible the unity and internal structuring of multiplicity, in other words, the simultaneously unifying and productive activity of Forms. In passages where harmony is not addressed as such, but as part of a discussion on music, Plotinus employs related images to illustrate various types of regulated correlations and proportions. In a more general context, such as the opening chapters of *Enn.* 1.6(1), the imagery of harmony and consonance serves to express the participation of sensible things in the intelligible Forms.[24] Elsewhere, the images evoke the harmonious arrangement of various parts, either in an individual body or in the body of the universe, but also the correspondences between individual souls and the bodies that are the most suitable to receive them.[25] In the treatises on providence, Plotinus adapts a traditional Stoic model to his perspective as he repeatedly invokes images of harmonious unity to express the universal sympathy between the various parts of the world.[26] Finally, as will be discussed below, the motif of musical harmony illustrates the impassibility of incorporeal beings.

For Plotinus, the rhythms of dance and the ordered measures of human choreographies serve as illustrations of the order and regularity of the universe.[27] This becomes truly obvious in *Enn.* 4.4(28).33, in which the image of dance is omnipresent. Plotinus, in this chapter, highlights the harmonious correspondence between the arrangement of celestial movements and the sublunary state of affairs. This accordance is compared, at the beginning of the chapter, to the one between the movements of dancers and the musical accompaniment.[28] Through this, Plotinus exemplifies the

[24] See Darras-Worms 2007, 159. [25] *Enn.* 1.9(16).1.5–7.

[26] *Enn.* 2.3(52).12.32; 3.2(47).2.29–33; 16.37–47; 17.59–64; 4.4(28).8.55–57. On this, see Clark 2016, 106–9.

[27] Many studies from secondary literature have been devoted to the Neoplatonic critique of the imitative arts, especially the critique of theatre and pantomime insofar as they exalt the passions. My perspective here is different. My aim, in this chapter, is to show how Plotinus, in some contexts, without making an axiological judgment on the nature of artistic representations, uses them to philosophically illustrate certain aspects of his philosophy. For a detailed study of images related to pantomime in Neoplatonism, and in particular its uses in Plotinian cosmology, see Sheppard 2017.

[28] *Enn.* 4.4(28).33.5–12: '[. . .] according to every figure of the heavenly circuit there is a different disposition of the things which it governs, as if they were performing a single ballet in a rich variety of dance-movements. In our ballets, too, there is no need to mention, since they are obvious, the external elements, the way in which piping and singing and everything else which joins in contributing to the total effect of the performance change variously at every movement'. The formulation 'in our ballets' (ἐν ταῖς παρ' ἡμῖν ὀρχήσεσι) could indicate that Plotinus was acquainted

concomitance of and parallelism between these celestial motions and mundane events. But, from line 11 on, the image of dance also serves to illustrate something else: the deep unity of the heavenly body, compared to a unique, single dancer. Indeed, borrowing Plato's imagery of the choral dance of the stars from *Timaeus* 40d, Plotinus transposes this image into a comparison with a solo dancer: the dance of the heavenly body is the dance of a single living entity,[29] the courses of the stars being analogous to the movements of the dancer's limbs, each involved in the general dance.[30] After having described the activity of the performer, whose movements must conform to the requirements of the ballet, Plotinus indicates that the choreography of the performer is accomplished, so to speak, automatically. Then, quite intriguingly, he gives an account of the dance from the performer's perspective and states that his intention is focused on something else (ἡ μὲν προαίρεσις τοῦ ὀρχουμένου πρὸς ἄλλο βλέπει). In this passage, Plotinus points out that the dancer who is concentrated carries out his choreography without paying attention to each of his steps as he is performing them.[31] According to J. Wilberding, in this passage, Plotinus exemplifies a case of 'automatic action' and 'emphasizes that an action that is not preferred (*proēgoumenon*) does not produce a conscious perception'. The heavenly bodies, like the artist, 'execute these motions in such a way that they are not preferred, and this is precisely the kind of sensible activity that is compatible with their perpetual contemplation, since it does not draw their attention to the sensible world'.[32] The dancer does not think consciously of the execution of steps, as a result of his perfect mastery of his art, and focuses his attention on something else.[33] The movements of the

with these spectacles. On this, see Schlapbach 2018, 143–4, who studies also the reappraisal of this comparison between the theatrical drama and the workings of the universe by Augustine.

29 The pantomime (ὄρχησις) is a mimetic dancing performed by a single dancer (for the classification of ὄρχησις in the scale of arts, see *Enn.* 5.9(5).11.1–6).

30 For a comparison of the dancer's anatomical movements in this passage of Plotinus and in Galen's treatise, *De sanitate tuenda*, see Webb 2008a, 67.

31 *Enn.* 4.4(28).33.17–25: 'The dancer's intention looks elsewhere (πρὸς ἄλλο βλέπει); his limbs are affected in accordance with the dance and serve the dance, and help to make it perfect and complete; and the connoisseur of ballet can say that to fit a particular figure one limb is raised, another bent together, one is hidden, another degraded; the dancer does not choose to make these movements for no reason, but each part of him as he performs the dance has its necessary position in the dancing of the whole body'. Plotinus here does not specify what the object of the dancer's concentration may be. According to Webb 2008b, 57, who has devoted a study to the pantomime from the performer's perspective, πρὸς ἄλλο may be referring 'to the story and the character'.

32 Wilberding 2008, 388.

33 According to Wilberding 2008, 388–9, this case of 'automatic action' carried out by the astral dancer can serve as a model for the action of the wise man who, while directing his intellect towards the intelligible order, is at the same time engaged in the sensible world.

celestial bodies are not presented as deliberate ones, but as being produced automatically; and just as music accompanies the dancer's gestures, world events are linked to the movements of the stars. However, this parallelism does not imply that the celestial motions exert mechanical (in that they do not operate upon sensible things) or deliberate causality.[34] Yet, in the same way as certain dance figures are associated with particular feelings such as fear or joy, certain configurations in the heavenly motions can also be correlated with particular events in the passive regions of the universe. The image of the dance thus serves to highlight two main elements, the first being the regulated correspondence between the celestial motions and the world's events; the second being the nature, both spontaneous and necessary – and at any rate, *infra*-voluntary – of the heavenly motions.

The numbered rhythms of dance illustrate the kind of necessity that governs not only the celestial motions, but also the souls' descent into bodies. In *Enn.* 6.7(38), Plotinus resorts to the image of choral dancing in order to remind us that procession is always a global activity, and that individual souls do not independently descend into their respective bodies. In chapter 7 of the same treatise, Plotinus notes that, when an individual soul is about to animate a particular body, it follows the traces laid out by the universal soul, submitting itself, as it were, to the organizing principle of the universe, 'as the dancer does to the dramatic part given him'.[35] Only through an awareness of the intelligible realm, in its entirety and its numbered harmony, can one apprehend the relation of particular entities to their distinctive intelligible principles. Among the rhythmic metaphors developed to illustrate the regulated activity of incorporeal realities, that of dancing in a circle is worth mentioning: music, with its rhythmic patterns imitating the harmony of the intelligible world, sets the soul on its path back to its source – and once the soul has begun to look towards its principle, this contemplation is evoked in terms of dancing. For instance, in *Enn.* 6.9(9).8.37–45, Plotinus compares the One to a coryphaeus, with the individual souls dancing around him like a choir:

> But we desire it, so we are around it. And we are always around it but do not always look to it; it is like a choral dance: in the order of its singing the choir keeps round its conductor but may sometimes turn away, so that he is out of their sight, but when it turns back to him it sings beautifully and is truly with him; so we too are always around him – and if we were not, we should be totally dissolved and no longer exist – but not always turned to him; but

[34] See Guitton 1933, 97. [35] *Enn.* 6.7(38).7.16–17.

> when we do look to him, then we are at our goal and at rest and do not sing out of tune as we truly dance our god-inspired dance around him.

The soul's dance around its principle echoes, in turn, the ordered unfolding of the divine intellect according to the intelligible number, which itself precedes numerical multiplicity. As discussed in *Enn.* 6.6(34), the essential and intelligible number, prior to the quantifiable and the measurable, is what underlies the inner structure of the divine and intelligible realm. Plotinus employs the images of the circle and the sphere in order to evoke this unfolding of the intelligible world according to the substantial number. Conversely, the beginning of *Enn.* 2.2(14) indicates that the circular motion of the heavenly body originates from a movement of mimetic tension towards the divine intellect. As S. Slaveva-Griffin notes, 'the dancing scenes in the *Enneads* are literary metaphors of the harmonious universe, but at a deeper level, there is a certain literalness to them that conceptually reveals the inherent ontological roles of substantial number in the structure of the intelligible. This ontological movement of number, which organizes the *kosmos noetos*, originates and directs the circular cosmic dance of intellect and soul'.[36] Images derived from rhythmic arts thus work as a complement to the actual discussion of the nature of such arts, as they express the mimetic tension of generated entities towards their generating principle – whether it be the motions of the stars imitating the structure of the divine intellect, or the individual soul's return to its origin.

At the end of this overview of the passages in which Plotinus illustrates the causal relationships between the different ontological levels using images borrowed from the art of dance, we see that the notion of rhythm occupies an important place. My hypothesis is that if the rhythm of music or dance is an example preferred by Plotinus to illustrate cosmological processes, the very notion of *rhythmos* has an even broader scope. Referring to the origin of what, from a unity, guides the organized and structured development of a multiplicity, *rhythmos* plays a role similar to that of numbers. Just as it is necessary to distinguish between the arithmetical number and the intelligible number, which is at the very root of the organization of intelligible Forms,[37] I hypothesize that it is possible to detect in the texts of Plotinus a distinction between the rhythm found in sensible harmonies and an intelligible rhythm at the source of the regulated deployment and productive power of intelligible realities.

[36] Slaveva-Griffin 2009, 119; see also Chrétien 2001.

[37] *Enn.* 6.6(34).9.35–39.

8.4 Rhythm and Harmony

According to the classification of arts established in *Enn.* 5.9(5).11, music is located at the bottom of the hierarchical order, which goes from the arts of imitation to the arts that are fundamentally turned towards the intelligible order – such as geometry or, to move even higher up the scale, wisdom (*sophia*). That being said, imitative arts do not form a homogenous category. While dance and pantomime are modeled on the sensible order alone, this is not necessarily the case for music or sculpture. There is a kind of music that is patterned after intelligible music.[38] Through its harmonic regularities and its measured numbers, it helps the soul begin its progress towards the realm of principles. Now the very phrasing of the passage in *Enn.* 5.9(5).11 concerning the place of music in the hierarchy is somewhat a textual crux. The HS2 edition omits the interpolated clause in line 11, which is interpreted as a redundancy or an added gloss, a choice that can be traced back already to Mueller and Bréhier. In both HS1 and HS2, the end of the sentence is established as follows, with the reading ἀριθμὸν (*arithmon*, literally, 'number') at line 13:

HS1:

[10] Καὶ μὴν καὶ μουσικὴ πᾶσα περὶ ἁρμονίαν ἔχουσα καὶ ῥυθμόν – ᾗ μὲν περὶ ῥυθμὸν καὶ ἁρμονίαν, ἔχουσα τὰ νοήματα – τὸν αὐτὸν τρόπον ἂν εἴη, ὥσπερ καὶ ἡ περὶ τὸν νοητὸν ἀριθμὸν ἔχουσα.[39]

HS2:

[10] Καὶ μὴν καὶ μουσικὴ πᾶσα [περὶ ἁρμονίαν ἔχουσα καὶ ῥυθμόν ἡ μὲν] περὶ ῥυθμὸν καὶ ἁρμονίαν ἔχουσα τὰ νοήματα τὸν αὐτὸν τρόπον ἂν εἴη, ὥσπερ καὶ ἡ περὶ τὸν νοητὸν ἀριθμὸν ἔχουσα.

And certainly all music, since the ideas which it has are concerned with rhythm and harmony, would be of the same kind, just like the art which is concerned with intelligible numbers.[40]

[38] The premises of this double conception of music are laid out in Plato's *Symposium* 187e. See also *Laws* 655a (where music is defined as a present given by the gods to order the behavior of men).

[39] Igal translates as follows: 'Puesto que toda musica versa sobre la armonia y el ritmo, aquella parte de la musica que estudia intelectivamente el ritmo y la armonia està allà por el mismo titulo que lo està el arte que estudia el numero inteligible'.

[40] *Enn.* 5.9(5).11.10–13, HS2, transl. Armstrong slightly modified.

If we accept the HS2 text, as it is generally the case in contemporary translations, the sentence implies that the art of music is to be linked to another *technē*, previously evoked in the chapter, that consists in connecting the visual perception of symmetrical relations and proportions, as presented in living beings, to the intelligible measures that lie at the source of all symmetry. The sentence, then, would align music, which is concerned with rhythm and harmony, with another *technē* dealing with intelligible numbers. This implies that not all music is an imitation of the sensible order; instead, insofar as it deals with numerical order and measure, music is indeed linked to the intelligible world, and thus expresses its rationality. Now, at line 13, following older editions,[41] Bréhier adopts the reading ῥυθμὸν (*rhythmon*, literally 'rhythm'):[42]

> Καὶ μὴν καὶ μουσικὴ πᾶσα περὶ ἁρμονίαν ἔχουσα καὶ ῥυθμόν τὰ νοήματα, τὸν αὐτὸν τρόπον ἂν εἴη, ὥσπερ καὶ ἡ περὶ τὸν νοητὸν ῥυθμὸν ἔχουσα.
>
> Il faut en dire autant de la musique qui réfléchit sur le rythme et l'harmonie: elle est analogue à celle qui a pour objet le rythme intelligible.

If one were to adopt this reading, this would be the only mention in the treatises of an 'intelligible rhythm', in the literal, non-figurative sense. In my view, however, Bréhier's interpretation should be met with reservations. How should we understand that sensible music is 'analogous' to its intelligible paradigm? I would argue instead that the two *technai* invoked in the passage have the same relationship to the intelligible, and that Plotinus is establishing a comparison between two distinctive kinds of art, not between an intelligible *technē* and its imitation in the sensible world. Aside from editorial concerns, it seems to me that ῥυθμός and ἀριθμός here hardly differ in meaning: both define intelligible rhythm as number. To be concerned with intelligible rhythm is to practice mathematics. The music of the sensible world does not equal the true kind of music, utterly dedicated to the art of number and rhythmic proportions.[43] When composed according to the principles of mathematics, music does not rank among the imitative arts of the sensible realm but rather among the arts

41 Those by Perna, Creuzer, Mueller, and Bouillet. Harder also adopts this reading.

42 This is also the reading in MS Q (*Marcianus Graecus* 242) in the **z** family and in mss. **A, F, E** in the w family.

43 See Jankélévitch 1961, 172. An alternative to such a conception of music, in which the musical sounds are the expression of a transcendent, superior order, can be found in the essay by Wolff 2015, which seeks instead to articulate the essence of music in terms of a purely sensible internal order. Wolff understands the art of music as capable of creating a kind of autonomous universe, governed by its own dynamics and not derived from any pre-existing harmony.

directly modeled on the intelligible order. This kind of sensible music, which expresses intelligible measure and harmony of a higher, intelligible, music, is precisely the one capable of setting the soul in motion towards the recollection of its authentic nature. The soul itself is 'number and harmony', as defined in *Enn.* 6.6(34).16, a passage echoing the Pythagorean tradition, as well as Plato's discussion of the mathematical and harmonic structure of the soul in *Timaeus* 36a-37a.[44]

Another passage in *Enn.* 5.8(31) – immediately preceding *Enn.* 5.9(5) in the Porphyrian order – offers further insight into the issue of intelligible rhythm. In the opening lines of the treatise, Plotinus employs the hapax *arrhythmistos*. This term, extremely rare in the philosophical lexicon, is borrowed from Aristotle[45] – and in fact had hardly ever appeared in philosophical writings ever since, apart from its use in Alexander of Aphrodisias' *Quaestio* 1.10, on the issue of the material nature of celestial bodies.[46] In this deliberately aporetic discussion, Alexander asks whether the substrate of celestial bodies can be called 'matter'. He develops arguments *pro* and *contra*, playing on two distinctive meanings of the word 'matter', each designating distinctive cosmological functions. If, on the one hand, matter is defined as the substrate of the contraries (μόνον τὸ ἔσχατον ὑποκείμενον τῶν ἐναντίων), then the celestial bodies cannot be said to have 'matter'.[47] If, on the other, matter is defined as 'the ultimate inarticulate substrate' (ἔσχατον ὑποκείμενον ἀρρύθμιστον καθ' αὑτό) – or, to quote from Marwan Rashed's translation, 'le dernier substrat inorganisé par soi'[48] – then they can be considered as having 'matter'.

At the beginning of *Physics* 2, Aristotle starts his enquiry on the different meanings of '*physis*'. One of the possible meanings of the term is nature as matter, as defended by Antiphon. It is in this doxographical context that the adjective *arrhythmistos* is employed.

> Some people think that the nature and reality of a thing which is due to nature is the primary constituent present in it, something unformed in itself

[44] This definition of the soul, Plotinus notes, should be clearly distinguished from erroneous conceptions of the 'soul-harmony': the passage of *Enn.* 4.7(2).8[4] intends to outline an authentic, Pythagorean definition of the soul as harmony, which is the only correct one, distinguished from erroneous readings of it. Following those misleading interpretations, to define the soul as harmony would be to consider the soul as a bodily entity or as the result of a certain bodily disposition; but such a conception of the soul-harmony, Plotinus notes, necessarily implies the prior existence of another soul, from which the individual soul would derive its unity – thus paving the way for the Third Man Argument. On this issue, see Baltes and d'Ancona Costa 2005, and Longo 2009, 187–91.

[45] *Metaph.* 1014b28 and *Ph.* 2.1, respectively.

[46] Alexander, *Quaestio* 1.10. See, on this, Rashed 2007, 183–4.

[47] Alexander, *Quaestio* 1.10.20.29.

[48] Alexander, *Quaestio* 1.10.21.2.

> (*arrhythmiston <on> kath' heauto*). Thus in a bed it would be the wood, in a statue the bronze. It is an indication of this, says Antipho, that if you bury a bed, and the decomposition gets the ability to send up a shoot, what comes up will not be a bed but wood: this seems to show that the disposition of parts customary for beds and the artistry (τὴν κατὰ νόμον διάθεσιν καὶ τὴν τέχνην) belong only by virtue of concurrence, and that the reality (*ousian*) is that which persists uninterruptedly while being affected in these ways.[49]

According to Antiphon,[50] nature consists in the substrate, not in the form of things, the latter necessarily holding a secondary position in relation to matter. In his translation of the passage, G. Romeyer-Dherbey chooses to treat the ἀ- not as denoting a lack but rather as indicating the primordial and original nature of the matter;[51] he thus translates *arrhythmistos* as 'affranchi de tout *rythmos*' and 'libre de structure' so as to remind us that, according to Antiphon, *physis* is the primitive core of things, which precedes the form, and which exists in natural beings as well as in artificial ones. The example of the bed that is buried in the ground and, by decomposing, ends up producing more wood, clearly shows not so much the superior status of *physis* over *technē* but rather the anteriority of *to arrhythmiston* over the form. This example illustrates the distinction between that which possesses a durable *ousia* – for instance, wood – and composite entities, deriving their arrangement (*diathesis*) from human convention or art – for example, a bed. In his commentary *ad loc.*, Simplicius suggests an alternative reading of the phrase, '*kata nomon diathesin*':

> Some write the 'formal construction' (*kata rhythmon*) instead of the 'conventional construction' (*kata nomon diathesin*) – which is more comprehensible, since the shape is called 'form' (*rhythmos gar hē morphē legetai*).[52]

Simplicius admits that he prefers the second option, *kata rhythmon*, which he finds clearer and more appropriate, while also reminding us that *rhythmos* might mean 'form'. The equivalent meaning of 'form' and '*rhythmos*' is acknowledged by Aristotle himself. In *Physics* 7, he opposes what is deprived of form to what 'has been completely shaped or arranged into a structure (τὸ μὲν γὰρ σχηματιζόμενον καὶ ῥυθμιζόμενον)'.[53] What he stresses here is the fact that we do not name individual realities after their material causes, but rather define them according to their form. And in two

[49] *Ph.* 2.1.193a9-17, transl. Charlton.

[50] Benveniste 1966, 332, thinks that this term was coined by the sophist Antiphon and borrowed by Aristotle.

[51] Romeyer-Dherbey 1985, 95–7. [52] Simplicius, *in Phys.*, 275.5. [53] Arist. *Ph.* 7.2.245b9-10.

doxographical passages of the *Metaphysics*,[54] in which Democritus' theories are mentioned, *rhythmos* is presented as a synonym of 'form'.

This overview of the uses of *arrhythmistos* and of *rhythmos* helps understand why, at the beginning of *Enn.* 5.8(31), Plotinus employs this term. At the beginning of chapter 1, Plotinus reminds us that the origins of sensible beauty are to be found in the structuring and ordering power of form. Beauty manifests itself in a work of art when the raw material is shaped into form, which ultimately expresses the unity of the intelligible order. Plotinus gives, as an illustration, the example of two blocks of stone, one shaped by the artist and the other shapeless.

> Let us suppose, if you like, a couple of great lumps of stone lying side by side, one shapeless and untouched by art (τοῦ μὲν ἀρρυθμίστου καὶ τέχνης ἀμοίρου), the other which has been already mastered by art and turned into a statue of a god or of a man, of a Grace or one of the Muses if of a god, and if of a man, not just of any man, but of one whom art has made up out of every sort of human beauty. The stone which has been brought to beauty of form by art will appear beautiful not because it is a stone – for then the other would be just as beautiful – but as a result of the form which art has put into it.[55]

The carved block has received a form given by the sculptor, insofar as he has mastered a *technē* linking him to the intelligible. This is why the work is beautiful: it is not an imitation of the sensible world, but an expression of the intelligible realm mediated by the sculptor. By contrast, the raw block of stone is utterly devoid of *rhythmos* – but not because it is formless, since it does possess a certain quality, insofar as it is a certain type of stone. Rather, it is *arrhythmistos* as it does not partake in *technē*. The form in the sensible realm is inferior to the Form which remains in the intelligible – the generating principle being always ontologically superior to generated realities: 'For a thing is weaker than that which abides in unity in proportion as it expands in its advance towards matter' (Καὶ γὰρ ὅσῳ ἰὸν εἰς τὴν ὕλην ἐκτέταται, τόσῳ ἀσθενέστερον τοῦ ἐν ἑνὶ μένοντος).[56] The formula 'that which abides in unity' (*tou menontos en heni*) is the definition of eternity

[54] Arist. *Metaph.* 985b14; 1042b16.

[55] *Enn.* 5.8(31).1.7–15. This is a striking example of Plotinus' assimilation of Aristotle's writings; when evoking an untouched block of stone, Plotinus naturally employs a rare term, with only two occurrences in Aristotle's texts. This is actually not the only time that Plotinus retrieves rare terms or hapaxes of Aristotle's. Another instance is to be found in the opening of *Enn.* 3.8(30), in which Plotinus associates the adjective *ellogos* to its antonym *alogos*. This is a clear echo of a doxographic passage in the *Metaphysics*, in which Aristotle refers to Eudoxus' classification of the heavenly spheres. I am grateful to Victor Gysembergh for drawing my attention to this passage.

[56] *Enn.* 5.8(31).1.26–27.

given by Plato in *Timaeus* 37d6 – a passage that Plotinus discusses in *Enn.* 3.7(45).6, defining eternity as life that abides in unity, always standing in and being directed towards the One. What remains in eternity, that is, in the intelligible realm, is superior to what is manifested in the sensible world, which is a weaker and inferior kind of form.

Before returning to a further account of the example of the two blocks of stone, Plotinus illustrates his theory of intelligible causality through an evocation of music – a metaphor perhaps motivated by the notion of *rhythmos* presented in the previous pages:

> Every original maker must be in itself stronger than that which it makes; it is not lack of music which makes a man a musician, but music, and music in the world of sense is made by the music prior to this world (οὐ γὰρ ἡ ἀμουσία μουσικόν, ἀλλ' ἡ μουσική, καὶ τὴν ἐν αἰσθητῷ ἡ πρὸ τούτου). But if anyone despises the arts because they produce their works by imitating nature, we must tell him, first, that natural things are imitations too.[57]

Nature is an image derived from the intelligible and its productions are regulated according to models, the *logoi*, derived from the transcendent Forms. Art does not imitate nature, but nature and art both imitate the intelligible. No more than music imitates nature but instead imitates an intelligible music from which it derives, Phidias' art is not inspired by the sensible but is also derived from the intelligible. Sculpture is an art privileged for showing the emergence of Form in matter. Thus, this progressive and regulated deployment of the order amongst the lower levels is that of a *rhythmos*, source of an intelligible unity, which reaches all the way to the sensible.

In this passage, Plotinus highlights the instrumental role of the artist: the actual source of all sensible music is intelligible music, as performed by the musician. The musician only translates intelligible harmonies into sensible form; he is not the source of harmony, he only mediates and interprets the pre-existing harmony of the intelligible world.[58] This view is often stressed by Plotinus. For instance, at the end of *Enn.* 1.6(6).3, in a suggestively alliterative passage, he indicates that harmonies of sound originate in soundless harmonies (Αἱ δὲ ἁρμονίαι αἱ ἐν ταῖς φωναῖς αἱ ἀφανεῖς τὰς φανερὰς ποιήσασαι).[59] The causality of intelligible harmony is immobile,

[57] *Enn.* 5.8(31).1.30–34.

[58] On this definition of the artist that deprives him of a (strictly speaking) creative role, see Chrétien 1997, 95–6.

[59] *Enn.* 1.6(6).3.28–29. On this passage and on Plotinus' re-appropriation of this motif, already to be found in Heraclitus, see Darras-Worms 2007, 160–1.

like the causality of Forms, insofar as they are immutable and perfect realities. In *Enn.* 3.6(26).4, dealing with the impassibility of incorporeals, Plotinus resorts again to a comparison in order to express the complete impassibility of the soul. The soul is a form, and as such, impassible. By its mere existence, it causes effects. In this, the soul is comparable to the harmony that causes the strings of a lyre to vibrate: the soul is the cause of the passions that affect the composite entity, without, however, being affected itself. In the same way as harmony causes vibration without vibrating itself, the passive part of the soul causes the motions that are associated with passions without being moved. The effect is on the strings, that is, on the sensible part of man but not on harmony itself. Now, if it were not for the prior harmonic relations in the intelligible world, the musician could not produce anything, even if the musician so desired:

> The causes of the movement are like the player, and the parts on which the affection makes its impact might correspond to the string. For in the case of playing an instrument, too, it is not the tune which is affected, but the string; the string, however, would not be plucked in tune even if the player wished it, unless the tune said that it should be.[60]

The musician contemplates and knows the proportions, the order, and the true measures of the intelligible, which he, in turn, translates into melodic sounds. He has a part in *rhythmos*, just as Phidias imposes *rhythmos* on the shapeless stone: *rhythmos* is the informing, configuring principle, bringing form to the shapeless weakness (*astheneia*) of matter.

Prior to any configuration, then, is the existence of a primary rhythm, at the source of the harmonious and eternal unfolding of the Forms themselves. This inner pulsation of the eternal, intelligible world is regulated by the essential number that governs the internal development of the intelligible hierarchy.[61] Each Form, in turn, manifests a generative power that is linked to that of all other Forms. In a way, one could say that rhythm, understood as a substantial number, is the source of harmony, which itself consists in the power to order and unify the multiple. What sensible harmonies reveal,

[60] *Enn.* 3.6(26).4.48–53: Τὰ δὲ αἴτια τοῦ κινῆσαι ἀνάλογον τῷ μουσικῷ· τὰ δὲ πληγέντα διὰ πάθος πρὸς τὰς χορδὰς ἂν τὸν λόγον ἔχοι. Καὶ γὰρ κἀκεῖ οὐχ ἡ ἁρμονία πέπονθεν, ἀλλ' ἡ χορδή· οὐ μὴν ἐκινήθη ἂν ἡ χορδή, εἰ καὶ ὁ μουσικὸς ἐβούλετο, μὴ τῆς ἁρμονίας τοῦτο λεγούσης. The very same image, that is, the musician's subordination to the fixed, numerical proportions of intelligible harmony, is similarly used in *Enn.* 4.7(2).8^4.20–21, in order to demonstrate that the soul, as an incorporeal entity, cannot possibly consist in a synthesis of discrete elements, according to the vulgar understanding of harmony. In the same way as the strings of a harp cannot be tuned of their own accord, the body is incapable of conferring unity upon itself.

[61] *Enn.* 6.6(34).9.35–42.

therefore, is the existence of numbered relations and proportions, which, in their turn, manifest the structuring, configuring, and generative power of the Forms, which ultimately derives from the One.[62]

In *Enn.* 1.6(6).1, Plotinus indicates that, although beauty is expressed by harmony, it cannot be reduced to a sum of harmonious proportions. More than being the unity of a multiplicity, it reveals itself in a single, pure tone – just as, visually, it reveals itself in primary color or in a flash of lightning. This critique of the definition of the beautiful as *symmetria*, as relayed, notably, by the Stoic tradition, is a kind of leitmotiv in the *Enneads*. According to Plotinus, to define beauty only in terms of the proportion of various parts is to deprive it of its essential and constitutive element: life. Here, Plotinus does not follow Polyclitus' canonic model, which defines the beautiful statue in terms of the commensurability of its parts with one another, as well as with the whole. As J. Laurent notes, Plotinus considers the classical ideal of beauty as a balanced arrangement of various parts to represent an extension of the Stoic postulate stating that the world is composed of various corporeal parts.[63] For Plotinus, beauty stems from the primordial unity, which is also the principle of intelligible life. Stoic corporealism is therefore inadequate for thinking properly about the very nature of life, which is in the truest sense intelligible – all the rest is just a by-product. Together with beauty, life is the primary manifestation of the supra-essential One. In *Enn.* 6.7(38).22, Plotinus underlines that if it were deprived of the illumination of the One, the divine intellect would remain inert (*argon*),[64] incapable of awakening the desire of the soul. Life, even in its imperfect, sensible manifestations, is always more beautiful than an inert design, however balanced and well-proportioned it may be. A trace of this vitalism can be found in the priority that Plotinus gives to rhythm over symmetry and harmony. This point has been noted by F. Ravaisson, who remarks that, for Plotinus, *eurhythmia*, in a sense, precedes symmetry. However, he seems to overextend this relation when he writes:

> The Greeks said what Vitruvius repeated when applying it to architecture: beauty has two parts, symmetry and eurhythmy, and the latter is superior to the former. (. . .) But symmetry is not sufficient for beauty. Plotinus, whose life reflects movement, said that more is necessary. Movement is grasped through time and number. This is what the word eurhythmy says.[65]

[62] *Enn.* 1.6(6).3.31–33. See Darras-Worms 2007, 160.
[63] Laurent 2011, 59. On this, see also Chrétien 1990, 320–1.
[64] *Enn.* 6.7(38).22.11. See Laurent 1992, 158.
[65] Ravaisson 1933, 81–2: 'Les Grecs disaient ce qu'a répété Vitruve en l'appliquant à l'architecture: la beauté a deux parties, la symétrie et l'eurythmie, celle-ci supérieure à celle-là (. . .). Mais la symétrie

In fact, Vitruvius considers a masterpiece of architecture to be achieved when it shows both symmetry and *eurhythmia* – the latter appearing as the visible expression of the former.[66] Plotinus, instead, prioritizes the rhythmic dynamics of form over the static balance of symmetry.

At the end of this study, we may note the following points. According to Plotinus, sensible music, through the order and structure it expresses – and which derives from intelligible music, which is purely order and proportion – constitutes a first step for the individual soul in its ascent towards its origin. If, in a way, Plotinus, unlike the Middle Platonic exegetes, leaves aside the mathematical treatment of musical harmonies, he still considers music to be an art based on numbers. In the meantime, he develops a stylistic register of images related to music and the rhythmic arts to show the causal links between the different ontological levels. In this context, it appears that the notion of rhythm occupies a central place in his cosmological architecture. It is only through a consideration of the intelligible as a numerically ordered whole that one may apprehend the participation of singular things in their intelligible paradigms and the descent of individual souls into bodies – this is what the imagery of rhythmic dance expresses, as an illustration of the measured harmony of all intelligible beings. The measured unfolding of the harmony of Forms is, in turn, dependent on an essential principle of unity, derived from the simplicity of the One – a primordial rhythm informing the multiplicity of the intelligible world. The irreducibility of beauty to a mere harmony may, in the end, be due to its fundamentally rhythmic nature, as it reveals the principle of unity that underlies every measured and consonant arrangement.

ne suffit pas à la beauté; il y faut de plus, a dit Plotin, la vie de laquelle témoigne le mouvement. Le mouvement s'estime par le temps et par le nombre. C'est ce que dit le mot eurythmie.'

[66] Vitruvius, *De architectura* 1.2.3. Gros 2006, 272, defines *eurhythmia* as follows: 'une scansion satisfaisante de tous les éléments rythmiques – colonnes, ouvertures, vides et pleins – observables à la périphérie d'un monument; c'est ce qui explique que l'eurythmie soit souvent liée chez Vitruve à la notion de *species* ou d'*aspectus*, et plus précisément à celle de *commodus aspectus*.'

CHAPTER 9

Porphyry's Commentary on Ptolemy's Harmonics

Questions of Philosophic and Scientific Identity

Harold Tarrant

9.1 Introduction

Any volume that sets out to examine the relationship between philosophy and music in Antiquity should have a place for Porphyry's *Commentary on Ptolemy's Harmonics*. Porphyry is known to us primarily as a philosopher, born around AD 234,[1] and he is usually thought of as a pupil of Plotinus, and thus perhaps as the second of the 'Neoplatonists'. However, he did not join Plotinus' circle until he was thirty years old, after a long period of study in Athens with Longinus, for whom he retained considerable respect as his chief mentor. He left Plotinus and Rome only six years after joining him, and at that time Plotinus, whose intellectual powers were already diminishing, had only months to live. Moreover, Porphyry's expertise seems to have covered a much broader range of subjects, including matters that may have seemed too 'philological' for Plotinus,[2] given his much quoted opinion of Longinus (*Plot.* 14), and others that engaged with scientific or medical opinions just as seriously as with philosophic ones,[3] with the short study *To Gaurus: On How the Embryo is Ensouled* being actually found within the Galenic corpus.[4] For this reason the present chapter will aim to challenge the assumption that Porphyry, *in this work*,

[1] See Barker 2015, 1–3, for a summary of what we know of Porphyry's life.

[2] I think for instance of the *Homeric Questions*, and to a lesser extent of works like *On the Styx* and *On the Cave of the Nymphs*.

[3] Besides this commentary, we may possess another that engaged with Ptolemy, an *Introduction to the Tetrabiblos*, which Greenbaum (2016, 266–70) has recently argued to be correctly attributed to Porphyry; Greenbaum 2018 also demonstrates how fruitful it can be to consider this work alongside others when determining Porphyrian doctrine. I subjected long passages from this work and others in the corpus to stylistic tests examining their use of everyday vocabulary, and while it would never have been expected to seem wholly typical of Porphyry I found nothing that would have made his authorship improbable.

[4] Note that it is only soundly reasoned scholarly consensus that attributes this work to Porphyry, though it is clear from its differences on the key issues that it cannot be by Galen.

can be referred to as a 'Neoplatonist' or 'pupil' of Plotinus, and to try to consider how he sees his own role here.

As for the *Commentary on Ptolemy's Harmonics*, it comes across largely as an exercise in harmonic theory, but with two passages of exceptional philosophic interest that Barker (2015, 16–27) highlights, namely 11.1–15.29 and 43.23–67.14. In most respects it looks like a normal ancient commentary on a respected author, consisting of a short introduction, with discussion of the text lemma by lemma. It has a significant gap, in that book 1, section 16 of Ptolemy's text is left without extant treatment, probably because of damage to that part of the scroll, while the text as a whole breaks off after Book 2, section 7. One may also feel that the commentary becomes more routine as it progresses, with much less comparative material. More importantly, it presents a significant question that may commonly arise when one is considering how musical theory and philosophy borrowed either language or ideas from one another in Antiquity: is one dealing with a musical or a philosophic text? Is it even legitimate to expect that any clear distinction between the two is appropriate? What we can say, perhaps, is that in the author's mind the text that he is interpreting was a text by a *mousikos*,[5] and it may well be implied that he is not a *mousikos* himself. But exactly how does Porphyry see himself in this work and to what end does he here believe he is contributing?

It is easy to raise questions about the kind of intellectual persona that Porphyry is building up in several of his works. At one level one may express concern that he seldom seems to write as a follower of Plotinus, except in the *Life of Plotinus* which dates from late in his life (fourth century), long after Plotinus has made his escape from this world, and in the *Sententiae*, a work that engages constantly with Plotinus, seemingly alluding to passage after passage.[6] Many works, however, among them the present commentary, engage with and build on much earlier material in a very different way from Plotinus' rather distant scholarship,[7] and emphasise his credentials in areas with which Plotinus was undoubtedly familiar but only indirectly concerned. Commentary itself might well have seemed

[5] See 15.6, 16.32, 20.8. All references that do not mention a work are to Porphyry's *Commentary on Ptolemy's Harmonics*.

[6] See particularly Brisson 2005; statistical studies have also shown the *Sentences* to be closer to Plotinus in the use of non-technical vocabulary than any other work of Porphyry.

[7] For the most part Plotinus is reluctant even to name his predecessors, let alone to specify and quote individual works, preferring to consider their theories independently from historical contexts and their literary exposition. It is as if he were influenced by Plato's own caustic remarks about persons who converse through other persons' voices (ἀλλοτρία φωνή, 347e3) rather through their words (*Protagoras* 347c3-348a6).

a rather 'philological' activity to Plotinus, especially commentary on texts that he might not have regarded as philosophic in any case. So first there is the question that others, including Andrew Smith (1974; 2010, 235–6), have paid close attention to: how far should Porphyry be viewed as a '*Neo*platonist'?[8]

But in the work on harmonics there is another question even more fundamental than this, that of whether Porphyry identified himself a Platonist at all. It is a question that one would not ask in relation to the *ad Gaurum*, for example, bearing in mind that it employs the twin strategy of using both philosophic argument and the authority of Plato (largely the *Timaeus*) to support its conclusion that the embryo is only ensouled at birth.[9] In the present commentary, however, speaking of Plato's theory of hearing, he says at 46.24 that 'all the Platonics as a single group'[10] (*apaxaplōs*) have misunderstood the Platonic definition of sound. Clearly Porphyry is not numbering himself among the 'Platonics' at this point, and that is the normal word for somebody who aspires to be a Platonist teacher. Though another sense seems to apply rather to those who interpret Platonic texts, including persons associated with other schools,[11] Porphyry is himself interpreting Plato at this point, so he would have to be included in this sense. One need not doubt his respect for Plato, whose *Timaeus* is quoted as a text of some significance (46.5–13, 92.16–18) and referred to elsewhere (115.29, 161.2, 163.7).[12] But the *Timaeus* was an authority for the Pythagoreans as for Platonists, other Platonic works do not receive anything like the same attention, and a wide range of other authors are also quoted. Porphyry's regard for Aristotle's *Categories* is shown by quotations at 41.14–27 and 43.1–6; the *De anima* is quoted at 47.15–23, 49.16–21 and 52.15–17; and the suspect *De audibilibus* is quoted at 50.15–27, 67.24–77.18. Given Porphyry's conviction that Ptolemy has benefitted from the works of Plato and Aristotle in particular (38.5–7), this use of Plato and Aristotle can be seen as merely good practice.

8 Gerson 2013, 30–3, objects to the label 'Neoplatonist' much more generally, largely because the term has been used pejoratively and Plotinus was not an innovator, but that is not my point here.

9 Plato is mentioned some thirty times, Aristotle twice (12.2–3), Pythagoras only once, and then only in relation to 'Numenius and those who interpret the hidden meanings of Pythagoras' (2.2), persons who are opponents in this particular work. Note that the assumption of Plato's authority here also marks Gaurus as a Platonist.

10 I feel that Barker's translation here, 'virtually all', is far too weak.

11 An obvious example is the Trypho who is described as a 'Stoic-cum-Platonic' at *Plot.* 17; Aelian is the only person specifically referred to as a 'Platonic' in our commentary (91.12, 96.7), and that involves a work in which he interpreted aspects of the *Timaeus*. It also involves a contrast with 'Adrastus the Peripatetic', who had also been interpreting the *Timaeus*.

12 The *Philebus* is also referred to at 78.10.

However, there are plenty of musical and mathematical authors who are quoted, especially in the early parts of the work, including Ptolemais, Didymus on both Pythagorean and Aristoxenian 'music' in chapter 2, but also using Aristoxenus himself and 'Archytas'[13] for the Pythagorean side in the absence of any writings of Pythagoras himself; also Dionysius the musical writer (37.17–21 or 24 [Raffa and Barker respectively]). Quotations from other philosophic authors include Democritus (32.10–16 = A126a DK) and Heraclides (30.3–31.26 on Xenocrates; cf. with Raffa and Barker 32.23–33.4).

It is therefore legitimate to ask whether we can confidently say that being a Platonist is part of Porphyry's persona in this work; and if an affirmative answer should somehow be warranted, might it be that being a Pythagorean is a bigger part?[14] Furthermore, how does his engagement with Ptolemy's *Harmonics* contribute to this persona? What is it that he is doing here, and what is this study contributing to his philosophic concerns? A philosopher with leanings towards Plato and Pythagoras would be expected to have a concern for all branches of mathematics, and the attention given to harmonics in Theon of Smyrna's *Expositio* demonstrates the importance of such theory *for Platonism*.[15] This interest was likely to be highly theoretical, involving the kind of 'music' that Plato's *Republic* included in the advanced education required for the guardians, the twin sister of astronomy as Plato there conceived it, and answering rather to the name of 'harmonics'. However, Porphyry called Ptolemy a *mousikos* in relation to his contribution to harmonics. So the Greeks did not regularly make the distinction between a 'musical' and a 'harmonic' expert, and Porphyry makes it clear that harmonics was widely viewed as one of a number of branches of music (5.21–25), indeed as the primary branch insofar as it studied what was primary, like notes and intervals (5.26–6.1).[16] It is 'music' in this theoretical sense that was deeply rooted in the Platonic tradition, and its place there is due primarily to the *Timaeus*.

[13] Including both dubious (32.1–4 from *On Wisdom*) and generally accepted (56.5–57.23 = Archytas fr. 1, cf. 81.7–11) material; cf. 93.6–17 = fr. 2.

[14] I am not here asking whether he conforms better with our definition of a Platonist than with our definition of a Pythagorean, and I allow, with Centrone 2000 and 2015, that it is extremely difficult to propose criteria by which the two can be safely separated in the early centuries of the Roman Empire. One might profitably consult Centrone 2000 and 2015 on such issues. It is how Porphyry conceived of himself, whether more generally at this time, or at least for this project.

[15] See Petrucci 2018b for Theon's being first and foremost a Platonist philosophy, and regularly putting Plato before recent mathematical science.

[16] As noted by O'Meara 2005, 132.

For philosophers, no dialogue was more important in early imperial times than the *Timaeus*.[17] In this dialogue the ongoing motions of the universe are entrusted to a world-soul structured according to harmonic principles, and the most valuable part of us humans is similarly structured, so much so that our structure benefits from the observation of the cosmic motions so as to restore the harmonic patterns by which we too operate. Harmonious motions become central to the relation between human being and cosmos. A double result follows from this: harmonic science becomes vital to those who ally themselves either with the philosophy of the author or with the school to which the protagonist himself belonged. Platonists and Pythagoreans alike claimed allegiance to the views expressed by 'Timaeus'.[18] Lucian's character 'Pythagoras' (*Vit. auct.* 3–5), besides placing great emphasis on mathematical education, attributes shapes that affect their movement to the four elements as at *Timaeus* 53c-57c, accepts some kind of theory of recollection and the transmigration of souls (the latter explicit at *Timaeus* 41e-42c), and postulates a divinity that is number, mind and harmony (recalling the world-soul at *Timaeus* 35b-37c). At this time differences between the schools became somewhat blurred, and there are a number of figures about whose ultimate allegiance scholars tend to argue. For now, however, let us note that Alcinous, often taken to be the paradigmatic Middle Platonist for the convenient reason that we do not actually know anything about him aside from what he wrote, includes music in his *Republic*-based discussion of the mathematical sciences, and mathematics according to his treatment becomes part of *theoretical* philosophy, which also embraces theology and physics. Music there transcends

17 For wider audiences capable of literary discrimination, including the audiences of Lucian or Maximus of Tyre, *Phaedrus* could have been far more familiar, and this may explain why the *Timaeus* seems under-represented in the papyrus record.

18 Here I think of Cicero's dedication of his translation of the *Timaeus* to the Pythagorean P. Nigidius Figulus, and of Posidonius' exegesis of the *Timaeus* for specifically Pythagorean purposes (F85 = Sext. Emp. *Math.* 7.93). Presumably the author of the work attributed to Timaeus Locrus must have been a Pythagorean indebted to the *Timaeus*. Philo, whose debt to the *Timaeus* was immense, was perhaps surprisingly described as a 'Pythagorean' by Clement of Alexandria (*Strom.* 1.15.72.4, 2.19.100.3), and as for Numenius (on whom see also n. 24 below) I take it that it was not simply Clement's peculiarity (*Strom.* 1.22.150.4) nor that of Eusebius (*Praep. Evang.* 9.6.6, 9.7.1, 11.9.8–11.10.1, 14.4.16) which suggested that Numenius' preferred description of himself was as a 'Pythagorean', given his view of Plato as 'not superior to the great Pythagoras, though perhaps not inferior' (*Praep. Evang.* 14.5.2 = fr. 24.19–20). He allows that Plato was influenced by Socrates but claims that Plato knew Socrates himself had been dependent upon Pythagoras (14.5.7 = fr. 24.57–59). This shows Numenius rejecting the line espoused most obviously by Apuleius (see *De Platone* 1.3.186–187, and Apuleius, *Expositio* 14, Stover 2016, 110) that Plato's works combined independent Socratic and the Pythagorean-Eleatic traditions, seeing Plato as combining the Pythagorean with the Platonic *manner* rather than two (or three) different strands of doctrine. Nicomachus was perhaps a more regular Pythagorean, but his use of the *Timaeus* (27d, 35a etc.) is well brought out by Dillon 1977, 354.

the ear and is directed to *to enharmonion* – a probable allusion to *Republic* 7.530d6-7 (*Didask.* 161.34–37). Music, in the ordinary sense of the word, plays no part.[19]

9.2 'Harmony' in Other Porphyrian Works

From no other work in the Porphyrian corpus could one easily deduce the author's fondness for the study of reason through harmony. The vocabulary of harmony (any word commencing with ἁρμονὶ-)[20] is sparsely spread across the different works. Apart from a reference to Simon the harmonic theorist (3) there are just three occurrences in the *Life of Pythagoras*, two in chapter 30 and one in 39. A single occurrence in *On the Cave of the Nymphs* (29) alludes to the harmony of Heraclitus' bow (B51 DK), and five occur in an extended analogy at *Sententiae* 18.9–18. The single reference in the fragmentary *Philosophy Drawn from Oracles* occurs within an oracular quotation (147.2), while two occur in Porphyry's comments on *Iliad* 4.4 and 19.386. Of seven references in Proclus' reports of Porphyry's *Timaeus* commentary,[21] most concern the Platonic world-soul, where such language is hard to avoid. Here the interesting phrase *harmonikoi logoi*, suggesting a 'harmony of reason', occurs three times, but it occurs nowhere else in Porphyry and is in fact typical of Proclus, so we are dealing with his language rather than Porphyry's. The vocabulary of music (*mousikē*) is even more sparsely distributed, with only five independent occurrences, of which just two (*Life of Pythagoras* 33 and 42) clearly use it for the production of sound-sequences rather than for poetry or abstract theory.

Hence musical harmony occupies very little space outside the commentary on Ptolemy, so that he does not ordinarily write even as a philosopher with special harmonic interests. That does not, however, mean that he has no place for harmony in his philosophy. In his biography of Pythagoras (39) he appears to assume that the kind of pleasure that is taken in just and beautiful things is not only free from unpleasant consequences, but also 'like some harmony of the Muses'; furthermore, it claims that Pythagoras

[19] This should not be taken as questioning the ability of Platonism at this time to make use of music in its more ordinary sense and to have it contribute usefully towards one's moral education, on which one should consult Sheppard 2005 and Demulder in this volume. Sheppard (151) uses Iamblichus *De Mysteriis* 3.9, as well as Porphyry's inclusion of remarks by Theophrastus regarding music as the release from troubles at 65.13–15, as evidence that Porphyry himself accepted a therapeutic role for music in its ordinary sense.

[20] Though the verb ἁρμόζειν occurs several times, it seems to be used generally for X fitting Y, and so not in specifically musical contexts.

[21] One in fr. 46 on 29e2-4, and the remainder in fr. 69 on 35b4-6.

could charm away his disciples' physical and psychical ailments by means of rhythms, tunes, and incantations (30), and also that he could, unlike normal human beings, hear the universal harmony, understanding the entire harmonious relationship of the heavenly spheres and the heavenly bodies associated with them. While it is here Pythagoras who is seen to bring musical harmony and philosophy together, elsewhere it is the assumed Pythagorean speaker of Plato's *Timaeus*. Porphyry was not at liberty to deny the fundamental harmonic structure of the world-soul, the harmonious heavenly movements for which it was responsible, or the relation between such harmonies and the best condition of the human soul, but Proclus implies that, when offering exegesis of Timaeus' monologue, he went to some lengths to demonstrate that the soul fills all the cosmos with harmony (*in Ti.* fr. 69.1–8). Porphyry also gives harmony a role not demanded by the text, making it the first of three things whose presence can make generated things good, the others being symmetry (or 'proportion': Runia 2008) and order.[22] Thus harmony is fundamental to the design of the universe by the creator, who 'brings all things to completion with a view to the completion of others or of wholes'.[23] The only question is whether 'harmony' in such passages is a genuine musical term or an indication of abstract mathematical principles. This non-musical sense that sometimes applies to the noun *harmonia* is still more a feature of the verb *harmozein*.[24]

Ordinarily, then, Porphyry's introduction of harmony into his theory is prompted by his debts to Pythagoras and 'Timaeus'. In *Sententiae* 19, however, he wants to show that our physical sensory organs, in the course of sensation, are liable to be affected by passive change, but not the incorporeal soul, which responds with its own action. The perceiver is treated as analogous to a musician playing a stringed instrument, with the soul corresponding to the internal harmony located in the musician's mind, without which he would be powerless to perform; and the body to the strings themselves, which are tuned with an *immanent* harmony. The mind's internal harmony is active, controlling the musician's ability to play musically, while the strings undergo externally produced change.[25] It is

[22] Τὴν ἁρμονίαν καὶ τὴν συμμετρίαν καὶ τὴν τάξιν, fr. 46.6 = Procl. *in Ti.* 1.366.16, and see Runia 2008, 228.

[23] συντελεῖ γὰρ ἅπαντα ὁ θεὸς πρὸς ἁρμονίαν τῶν ἄλλων ἢ καὶ ὅλων (*Homeric Questions on the Iliad* 4.4).

[24] There are some 14 matches to the pattern ἁρμοζ– in works other than the commentary on Ptolemy, and 19 others to the pattern ἁρμοσ– (of which some relate to other related terminology).

[25] The passage appears to show much engagement with the outline and refutation of the notion that the soul itself is a harmony at *Phaedo* 85e-95a. Hence the soul is directly compared with harmony

doubtful, however, whether Porphyry seriously wants to teach us anything relevant to musical practice in such a passage.

9.3 Some Background to Porphyry's Exegesis

The relationship between Porphyry's *Commentary on Ptolemy's Harmonics* and its background began to interest me in the early 1990s when working on Thrasyllus. I have wondered ever since whether it might be an earlier work of Porphyry reflecting the time before he came to study at Rome with Plotinus, thus representing an interest that was later all but abandoned. However, it is difficult to produce a reasonable relative or absolute chronology of Porphyry's works, and commentaries are such that they are reused and perhaps updated at any time when the teacher is helping his classes to investigate the same body of texts.[26] In such circumstances it is always possible to add or subtract material as one's views or one's didactic priorities change. One result of this, of particular significance for this Porphyrian commentary, is that a commentary may never be finished. We have only occasional examples of ancient running commentaries on the whole of a work of Plato, two from Olympiodorus, and one each from Hermias and Damascius. Olympiodorus' *On the Alcibiades* becomes curiously thin as one reaches what he himself regards as the climax of the work at 133a-c, while Hermias' efforts are certainly much briefer as one passes beyond Socrates' Palinode. With others, I have always tended to assume that the later pages of Proclus' running commentary on the *Timaeus* are lost, apart from a snippet in Philoponus about matter and an Arabic fragment on 89–90. My own palinode reaches a different conclusion.[27] The running commentary stops quite naturally at 44d2; it does so because that is where Iamblichus' running commentary had stopped before him for reasons given at 3.356 (= Iamblichus fr. 88 Dillon), and because Porphyry had stopped even earlier. Book 5 is remarkably thin on the earlier material for which Proclus would normally have relied on Porphyrian testimony.

My distinct impression is that the ancient commentators were concerned above all to ensure that the earlier pages of a text were read with

within the musician, but it cannot be identified with the kind of harmony that could be said to inhere within the musical instrument itself.

[26] It is now believed that Proclus' commentaries on the *Republic* and *Timaeus* refer to one another, and different versions of the same teacher's lectures can be found recorded by different pupils, if often altered by them. Ammonius' lectures on the *Categories* and Damascius' on the *Phaedo* would be examples.

[27] See Tarrant 2017a, 1–11.

the required care by the pupil, more being entrusted to them as their familiarity with the text concerned increases. After a certain point the teacher might be ready to offer a series of hermeneutic essays of a type known from Proclus *On the Republic* and from Calcidius *On the Timaeus*. That does not mean that all unfinished running commentaries from Antiquity never were finished, but rather that references to a philosopher's *hypomnēmata* or *exēgēseis* cannot be presumed to be referring to complete running commentaries.

So (i) in the case of Porphyry's commentary on Ptolemy we should not be surprised that coverage dwindles as the commentary goes on and the text breaks off halfway through Ptolemy's second book (Barker 2015, 7–9), and (ii) in the case of Aelian's *Exegesis on the Timaeus* (Εἰς τὸν Τίμαιον ἐξηγητικά) to which Porphyry refers there can be no presumption that a running commentary was ever intended, for the title would better fit 'interpretative essays on the *Timaeus*'. The subject matter of the long extract (33.19–37.5), concerned principally with the way in which the striking of the air determines the pitch of the sound, and using the dimensions of the *aulos*, both length and the width of the bore, as its primary example, really does not sound like material suitable for a standard philosophical running commentary, being ill designed to explain any details of the *Timaeus* itself; yet it might indeed have belonged in a so-called 'Special commentary' aimed at tackling particular issues. So also the shorter fragment (96.8–15), which deals with traditional harmonic terminology relating to *symphōniai*. The term itself is found only at 67c2-3 and 80a5-6, not in the popular material concerning the world-soul at 35a-36b; and whereas the construction of the world-soul involves only the intervals of the fourth and fifth, Aelian's discussion of six or more 'concords' and his distinction between the simple (fourth and fifth) and the compound ones are beyond the needs of somebody simply intent on explaining the passage. One may add that Aelian is never mentioned by Proclus, which is a little surprising if he had written a standard running commentary.

9.4 How Does Porphyry Situate His Work?

This leads on to my main topic: the nature of the intellectual tradition from within which Porphyry approaches his exegetical task. To begin with, one might ask why he should be tackling such a recent author as Ptolemy anyhow. It is easier to see why he wants to interpret Plato, Aristotle and Homer, and plenty of others were already engaged in the exegesis of such gifted authors whose Greek was becoming less accessible to the Greek speakers of the Roman Empire. One might think of Ptolemy as a strange choice, and it would seem unnecessary for him to help his pupils or readers understand Ptolemy's language in the same way that one might help with obscure texts like the *Timaeus* or *Categories* or with outmoded or riddling language. Nor is Ptolemy treated as inspired, or especially authoritative, or above criticism. Presumably Porphyry chose to interpret texts for which he had some special affinity, and which he considered valuable when correctly understood. Presumably he also perceived that they had acquired a high reputation, with the result that there was no shortage of interested persons with the leisure to participate in the circle reading them. What one cannot affirm is that Porphyry wanted to be regarded as a follower of Ptolemy in the same way that commentators on the *Timaeus* usually sought to be regarded as followers of Plato – or of the Pythagoreans taken to be Plato's source.

In this regard one may plausibly make appeal to Porphyry's polymathy. The fact that he chose to study with Longinus suggests that his interests were already broad, and accordingly we find that his works covered a very broad range of topics – so much so that it is tempting to regard it as not really representative of the author. Porphyrian polymathy involved literary, philosophic, scientific and religious matters, and demonstrates his thirst for almost any knowledge in the Greek tradition. In writing these works he used a wide variety of sources, often naming them, and almost always naming them in this commentary. Yet polymathy does not necessitate that one commentates on all kinds of text that one is proficient in.

What is perhaps clearest is that Porphyry aspired to be a *philosopher* rather than some sort of scientist or technical thinker. As a philosopher he is most interested in the philosophies of the fourth century BC or earlier, so that he seems especially devoted to ancient wisdom either in philosophic prose or in verse. But he is prepared to acknowledge that technical subjects, such as music, medicine and the like, were inclined to make progress particularly when their natural empirical inclination was tempered with an adequate grasp of theory. Perhaps this is why he chooses to comment on comparatively recent works of science and on ancient works of philosophy and poetry. The division might be seen as mirroring that between the Pythagorean (theoretical) and Aristoxenian (empirical) approaches to harmonics, of which the former is obviously Porphyry's favourite (as it would be for Platonists and Pythagoreans alike). And the one time when Porphyry's philosophical aspiration emerges most clearly in the *Commentary on Ptolemy's Harmonics* is where he elaborates on Ptolemy's statement (*Harm.* 3.3–5) that hearing and reason (*logos*) are the 'criteria' of *harmonia*. This requires him to embark on a long discussion of *ancient* theory of how *sensation* and reason are the twin criteria of form (11.4–15.28),[28] temporarily abandoning the particular focus on hearing.[29]

Porphyry's rather radical preference for reason over sensation underlines his personal commitment to a certain type of philosophy rather than to technical and scientific studies *even as handled by Ptolemy*, and to the ancient over the more recent. But to what kind of philosophy is he committed? If one had only our extant collection of texts, without supporting background evidence, it might have been quite difficult to work out from them what Porphyry's precise school allegiance was. If in fact we look at many of the more recent theorists used as sources that should be no surprise, since there is a similar problem with a number of these authors too. In this commentary there is Thrasyllus, arranger of the Platonic but also of the Democritean corpus, who seems to have used Democritus' *Pythagoras* to illustrate the philosophic life in the same way as he used Plato's dialogues set in the final weeks of Socrates' life for this purpose. Is it possible that he held Pythagoras, Democritus, Socrates and Plato all to be equally worthy of emulation? Evidence in Porphyry's *Life of Plotinus* 20–21 suggests that Thrasyllus thought of himself as belonging equally to the Pythagorean and Platonic traditions. He is also regarded in the *Commentary on Ptolemy's Harmonics* as worthy of citation on both philosophic and harmonic matters, but we should not forget that it was his astrology that had most to do with his position as Tiberius' court intellectual. Similar ambiguities are found in the figures of Numenius and Cronius who feature prominently in *On the Cave of the Nymphs*, some sources listing them among Pythagoreans, and others among Platonists.[30]

[28] Note 11.5 and 11.30 (οἱ παλαιοί); 13.13 (τὰ τῶν παλαιῶν συγγράμματα); examples of 'ancient' writers referred to in this passage include Aristotle, Archytas and the Stoics (11.21–24); if I am correct (Tarrant 1993, 114; 124) there are allusions to the sixth and seventh *Epistles* (323d3, 341c7-d1) ascribed to Plato at 12.19–20 and 14.4–5 respectively; some variation of the Platonic Theory of Recollection also lurks in the background at 15.1–28, but Plato is not actually named. From the early imperial period Thrasyllus is the only named source (12.21), chosen it seems more for the way in which he expressed ancient theory about *logos* than for anything original that he added.

[29] Even Ptolemy's definition of harmonics, of which Barker, in this volume, affirms that 'There is in fact nothing in Ptolemy's definition, or in its sequel in the rest of his first chapter, from which we could confidently infer that the sounds with which his science concerns itself are exclusively or even primarily those involved in music', does at least confine his subject matter to sounds.

[30] Numenius (on whom see also n. 19) is often regarded as a Middle Platonist, but I find no clear evidence that he would have regarded himself as a Platonist, since the term *Platōnikos* could signify any Platonic interpreter. This applies to both philosophers in Porphyry (*Plot.* 14), to Numenius at fr. 43 des Places (Iamblichus), and similarly at Proclus *in R.* 2.96.10–15 Kroll (= Numenius T21 Leemans; see also T4–5); Cronius is referred to as a 'Platonic' by Syrianus (*in Metaph.* 109.11 Kroll

What I wish to argue here is that it is Porphyry's feeling of allegiance to the Pythagoreans that best explains the commentary on Ptolemy, repeating my earlier claim (Tarrant 1993, 109) that there is nothing specifically *Neo*platonic about it.[31] But if it should be to the Pythagoreans rather than to Plotinus *or Plato* that he feels allegiance when writing this work, then a lively interest in theoretical harmonics can be virtually taken for granted. For as we have seen in Section 9.2 it is when he interprets Pythagoras and 'Timaeus' that Porphyry affords the most central place to universal harmony, a harmony actually *audible* to Pythagoras (*Life of Pythagoras* 30). It is central there to both physics and ethics.

9.5 The Philosophic Core of the Commentary

While much of surviving Porphyry has a distinct Pythagorean leaning, the commentary on Ptolemy is a special case. Harmonic science was a branch of mathematics, and to the Pythagoreans the essence of the world in which we live was itself mathematical. The goodness of the world was exhibited in its harmonic functioning that depended upon its mathematical foundation. The same could be said of *some* Platonists, but one can again appeal to Alcinous as an example of a Platonist for whom this does not seem to be true. Ultimately this meant that for Pythagoreans harmonics and physics were not separate sciences, and talk of harmony and dissonance by physicists was therefore not purely a metaphor. Hence, although harmony in one sense is something heard, and thus to some extent something judged by the hearing, its more important judge is *logos*, as one might expect of a mathematical science. In response to Ptolemy's statement at *Harm.* 3.3–5 that harmony's criteria are hearing and reason, the former regarding the matter and the passive experience and the latter regarding the form and the cause, Porphyry feels the need to embark upon a lengthy discussion of the twin roles of sensation (no longer just hearing) and of *reason* in the apprehension of all sensible things: and hence presumably of the entire sensible world. Both are considered as faculties and as processes that are capable of grasping form (*eidos*).

= Kronios 14 Lakmann). The order in which authorities are listed in Numenius fr. 36 may be helpful: Pythagoras leads, the Platonic Myth of Er comes next, and Homer, Orphics, and Pherecydes follow. At fr. 24.19–20 Plato is described as 'not superior to the great Pythagoras, but still perhaps not inferior to him'. The 'perhaps' gives a hint of Pythagoras' superiority, while fr. 24.62–67 gives a suggestion that Plato's strategy was flawed.

[31] What I do not wish to repeat is any sustained attempt to show that the language is somehow at odds with that of Plotinus and the mature Porphyry (see Tarrant 1993, 109 n. 2), as I believe that Chase 2010 and Lautner 2015 have adequately refuted this.

The straight dichotomy of form and matter might seem to remind us of Aristotelian physics rather than any other kind, but it soon becomes clear when he employs the Stoics and the Pythagorean Archytas too that nothing specifically Aristotelian is implied for Porphyry (11.22–26), and that he thinks that he is dealing with widespread ancient theory (cf. 11.33). Some of them, states Porphyry (11.32–12.2), thought that reason judged the substance (*ousia*) while sensation judged rather things that had been made substantial (*ousiōmena*) involving the *enmattered* form. The idea that substance is not enmattered and can be investigated as it is apart from matter sounds Platonic, though this is not explicitly stated. Their position on harmony would accordingly be that sensation judges what is harmonised rather than harmony itself, as 'what's harmonised differs from harmony in the same way that what's numbered differs from number', the former being in each case involved with matter (12.3–5). There is no attempt to affirm or deny the correctness of this, nor any suggestion that it results in differences in the way that harmonic science is pursued. Porphyry is championing an ancient philosophical approach to the subject, but his auditors or readers are not being encouraged to choose between approaches.

What follows now is a discourse on *logos* and its role not simply as judge of things sensible but also as their cause, claiming that it is thanks to the power of *logos* that things in this world display their formal attributes. In this sense *logos* appears not just as a judge of that form (considered as a function within us as judges), but also as its origin (considered as a function within the divine). Admittedly there were two fundamental senses that would be encountered routinely in harmonic texts, one indicating the *ratios* that apply to the musical intervals, and the other to the human reason that examines them. The former are organisational principles of sounds, the latter the organisational principles by which we try to understand them. Porphyry, however, is by no means satisfied with two senses. He starts by enumerating several senses in which *logos* is used, clearly drawing on traditional material, but on material that Theon had seen as Peripatetic rather than Platonic.[32] He begins with two facets of its

[32] Gersh 2017, 205, draws attention to the comparison but fails to mention that Theon presents two lists, one allegedly in the Peripatetic tradition at 72.24–73.11 and another in the Platonic tradition (and firmly rooted in the dialogues), which mentions only silent discursive thought, its outward expression through the voice, the enumeration of parts of the whole, and analogy. Theon's Peripatetic list includes equivalents of all of Plato's, but also mentions the sense used in banking, definitional and syllogistic senses, seminal *logos* and the *logos* of the form, all of which appear in Porphyry's list. His Platonic list, then, looks rather like an oblique criticism of an excessively long list

role in nature: as seminal principle and as the coordinator of nature's own activities. There would seem to be a distinction here between whatever it is in the seed that is responsible for the shape that it will grow into, and whatever it is within what lives that organises its motions (commonly seen as soul in Antiquity). It applies also to mathematical ratio or to a banker's percentage,[33] and to the relationship implied in analogies (12.6–10). Primarily, however, it applies to something that determines the relationships and measures out the natural totality of things, a *logos* that imports form into matter and one of which human reasoning is a mere imitator (12.10–14).

Porphyry is building his account to a climax here, and readers familiar with the *logos* that Philo's creator employs for the construction of the world will not be surprised that we now meet the divinity that employs this *logos* and reasoning (*logismos*) 'just like a sacred knowledge (*epistēmē*) and thought-process (*dianoēsis*)'.[34] The phrase 'god that is leader of the whole' may sound like an allusion to the sixth Platonic letter (*Ep.* 323d),[35] but the words are matched exactly in Philo,[36] who often also substitutes the *Epistle*'s 'all' for 'whole',[37] and Philo traces such language back to Pythagorean treatments of the heptad, and in particular to Philolaus.[38] It is highly likely that he knows the text of the *Epistle* (quoted by Clement and Origen for instance), but thinks that 'Plato' is here indebted to

found in a source, possibly Adrastus or Thrasyllus. For Theon, Porphyry too would be straying beyond the bounds of Platonism. On Theon's lists, see Petrucci 2012a, 382–3.

33 The language of banking (τραπεζιτικά), including totalling (συμψηφισμός) and counting up (συγ- or ἀνα-κεφαλαίωσις) occurs in a parallel discussion of human and cosmic *logos* inspired by *Ephesians* 1.10 in Origen (frr. *in Eph.* 6), which I cannot discuss in detail here.

34 The terms *logismos* and *dianoēsis* count against Plotinian influence, for see *Enn.* 3.2.14, where the former is dissociated from the work of the providential organising principle, even though things are as reasoning would have demanded. Porphyry is here closer to Ptolemy's own epistemology (*On the Criterion* 22.3–10), where he postulated a *dianoetic* element at the peak of the heavens to match the dianoetic faculty in the human head, though Philo too has a creator able to διανοεῖσθαι (*Opif.* 19, 26 and 82) following the *Timaeus* (32c8, 39e9, 74c6, 76c7), which also gives him *logismos* (30b1, b4, 33a6, 34a8; cf. *Opif.* 26).

35 τὸν τῶν πάντων θεὸν ἡγεμόνα τῶν τε ὄντων καὶ τῶν μελλόντων, τοῦ τε ἡγεμόνος καὶ αἰτίου πατέρα κύριον, *Ep.* 323d2-4, quoted verbatim by Clem. *Strom.* 5.14, Orig. *C. Cels.* 6.8, Eus. *Praep. evang.* 11.16.2, 13.13.26.

36 *Spec. Leg.* 4.176: ὁ τῶν ὅλων ἡγεμὼν θεός; also found without θεός at *Somn.* 148, and with other minor variations at *Mos.* 2.169; similar variants occur in Josephus: Against Apion 2.185, and Eusebius: *Praep. Evang.* 7.10.3 (and 8.8.19 quoting *Against Apion* 2.185), *DE* 4.1.4, *Vit. Const.* 1.24.

37 I.e. πάντων or (τῶν) συμπάντων for τῶν ὅλων: *Opif.* 75, 135, *Cher.* 127, *Quod deus* 19, *Mig.* 62, *Mut.* 45, 127, *Mos.* 1.318, *Spec. Leg.* 1.32.

38 At *Opif.* 100 Pythagoreans are said to liken the heptad to τῶι ἡγεμόνι τῶν συμπάντων, and shortly Philolaus fr. 20 will be quoted: ἔστι γὰρ ἡγεμὼν καὶ ἄρχων ἁπάντων, θεός, εἷς. However, much the same quotation is attributed to the later Onatas (fr. 140.21 Thesleff) and by Lydus to an unnamed Tarantine rhetor (*de Mensibus* 2.11).

Philolaus, so quite where Porphyry's source is deriving this language from is uncertain.

The kind of language that we found in Philo is repeated in a number of other authors, including the Pseudo-Aristotelian *De mundo* (399a30-31: 'the leader and generator of all' – *ho pantōn hēgemōn te kai genetōr*), whose words come close to those of Justin Martyr (*Apol.* I 21.5: the leader and begetter of all' – *ton hēgemona kai gennētora pantōn*); the Platonists Plutarch and Atticus;[39] the sophist Dio (12.27: 'particularly the leader of all' – *malista tou pantōn hēgemonos*); and the Jewish historian Josephus (2.185: 'god that is leader of the whole' – *theon men hēgemona tōn holōn*).[40] It is often connected with *logos* in Philo, and in a variety of ways,[41] though Eusebius goes so far as to identify not god but god's *logos* with 'the leader and chief of all' (*Demonstratio Evangelica* 4.7.4: *ho kathēgemōn kai prostatēs hapantōn tou theou logos*). The widespread appeal of this language under the empire is important in so far as it suggests a single force in charge of one totality that operates as a coordinated whole. It suggests harmony in a metaphorical if not in an aural sense. *Logos* is naturally associated with the organisational principles of such harmony.

Returning to Porphyry, we learn that 'in accordance with this *logos* nature makes provision for every type of thing in the cosmos' (12.18–20). Assuming his awareness of the allegedly Platonic passage, which postulates a 'father' of its leader-god, we may deduce that we are talking of a divinity at the summit of the physical world rather than a transcendent one, but some kind of mind nevertheless, whereas nature appears rather to be a power that only acts in accordance with this *logos* without doing so cognitively. At no stage do we feel that this is a real digression, for this *logos* seems to be very much akin to a cosmic harmony, fundamental to the design and operation of the universe in which we live – a design to be revealed in the way that we see it and in the way that we hear it. What Porphyry describes is indeed a harmony of reason. The *Timaeus* and its harmonically ordered world-soul seems to be always in the back of his mind without its ever coming to the surface, and he avoids any statement

39 Plut. *De Is. et Os.* 371A: ὁ τῶν ἀρίστων πάντων ἡγεμὼν καὶ κύριος Ὄσιρις is intelligence and reason in soul; Atticus fr. 6.11 = Eus. *Praep. evang.* 15.6.11: ταύτην (*scil.* τὴν ἀρίστην αἰτίαν) ἡγεμόνα τῶν πάντων.

40 While a Jewish parallel for the language can be found in LXX *Maccabees* 4.2.22, it only concerns intelligence's leadership within us. In this regard it provides no more help than Isocrates (*Nicocles* 9, *Antidosis* 257: ἁπάντων ἡγεμόνα λόγον).

41 See particularly *Conf.* 59, *Mig.* 174, *Fug.* 103, *Somn.* 276, *Spec. Leg.* 4.92, *QGen.* 2.34a.

that would tie this theory too closely to any one of the traditional schools, Platonic, Pythagorean, or otherwise.

Porphyry identifies this *logos* with what Thrasyllus had called 'the *logos* of the forms', presumably on account of its embracing all the design-principles that the divinity embedded within the universe as part of the creative process. Thrasyllus failed to outlive his sponsor Tiberius, and was thus a slightly older contemporary of Philo who lived to represent his people before Caius Caligula. Nothing tells us that Thrasyllus adhered to the same *philosophy* as Philo (who does not use that phrase), but they would have shared certain characteristics of their age in general, as well as being difficult to associate with any one school in particular. The question naturally arises as to whether Thrasyllus had not been the inspiration behind the whole of this discussion of *logos* so far, in which we have detected parallel material in Philo and Theon. I have argued (Tarrant 1993, 108–36) that this had in fact been the case. Editors[42] unsurprisingly only identify 12.22–28 as a 'fragment' of Thrasyllus, and indeed the implication behind Porphyry's words seems to be that he is only now breaking into direct quotation, mentioning Thrasyllus' phrase for describing this *logos*, and going on to give his description of its operation. But if it is Thrasyllus' description of *this supreme logos*, then he must have had approximately the same concept of a universal *logos* as Porphyry had been describing from 12.10 onwards, but the stronger verbal echoes are rather with 12.7–8, as the following comparison with 12.22–23 will show:

Table 9.1

λόγος καὶ ὁ φυσικός, ὅ τε τῆς <u>σπερματικῆς δυνάμεως</u> καὶ ὁ κατὰ τὴν σύνταξιν <u>τῶν αὐτῆς τῆς φύσεως ἐνεργειῶν</u>. (12.7–8)	ὁ τῶν εἰδῶν λόγος, ὥς φησιν ὁ Θράσυλλος, <u>συνεσπειραμένος μὲν ἐν τοῖς σπέρμασι</u> . . . ἐξαπλούμενος δὲ . . . <u>κατὰ τὰς ἑκάστης φύσεως ἐνεργείας</u>, . . . (12.22–23)
Also natural *logos*, both that of the seminal power and that which deals with the coordination of the activities of nature itself.	The *logos* of the forms, as Thrasyllus calls it, encapsulated in seeds . . . but unfurling . . . with each of the activities of nature, . . .

[42] So Barker and Raffa, as well as Düring.

This *logos* in the supreme sense of the word had been said by Porphyry at 12.13 to be 'imitated as it were (*hōsper*) by the reasoning (*logismos*) in the soul'. In the passage assumed to be taken straight from Thrasyllus the qualificatory *hōsper* is no longer present, possibly meaning that Porphyry saw something more metaphorical in this imitation than Thrasyllus had done, though another metaphor is softened by *hōsper* within the Thrasyllan passage at 12.22 (συνεσπειραμένος ἐν τοῖς σπέρμασι καὶ ὥσπερ ἐγκεκρυμμένος). The *logos* is present by imitation in (a) the study of the crafts, (b) the actual products of the crafts, and (c) the calculations of discursive thinking and wisdom, in accordance with which intelligence forms an impression of just what a thing is and defines and establishes its essence. At this point there is a more nuanced parallel with the earlier material, this time between 12.18–20 and 12.25–26, the earlier passage involving the creative understanding and discursive planning[43] of the cosmos-managing divinity, which brings form *into the physical world*; and the later one involving the cognitive wisdom and discursive thinking of human calculation that can *extract form from it*. The passages run as follows:

Table 9.2

ᾧ χρῆται λόγῳ καὶ λογισμῷ καθάπερ ἱερὰν ἔχων ἐπιστήμην καὶ διανόησιν ὁ τῶν ὅλων ἡγεμὼν θεός, καὶ καθ' ὃν ἡ φύσις ἕκαστα . . . παρέχεται. (12.18–20)	καὶ τῷ τῆς διανοητικῆς φρονήσεως καὶ σοφίας λογισμῷ, καθ' ὃν ὅ τι ποτ' ἐστὶν ὁ νοῦς ἐπισφραγίζεται . . . (12.25–26)
This is the *logos* and reasoning that the god and leader of the whole uses as though he had a sacred knowledge and thought-process, and in accordance with which nature makes provision for everything.	and in the reasoning of cleverness of thought-process and of wisdom, in accordance with which the intellect (*nous*) fashions an impression of just what something is . . .

[43] It is not uncommon for an element of planning to be captured by the verb διανοεῖσθαι, as in a passage at *Tim.* 39e which had been much discussed from the time of Numenius (fr. 22) until that of Plotinus (e.g. *Enn.* 3.9.1) and Amelius (tackled by Proclus at *in Ti.* 3.103.18–32); both of these had postulated separate intellects responsible for the contemplative and the planning functions at that point; it seems likely that Porphyry (who refers to his detailed discussion of the psychogony of the *Timaeus* later in the work, 115.30–116.1), or possibly his source, had the *Timaeus* in mind in our passage but resisted making too obvious an allusion to it, preserving the appearance of one who writes from the point of view of philosophy more widely.

What is noticeable here is not an exact matching of terms, but (a) the double structure of the calculation (*logismos*)[44] involved in each case, and (b) the clause introduced by *kath'hon* that indicates what happens under the guidance of that calculating power. In general the language of the accepted quotation from Thrasyllus is quite rich, especially in verbs and adjectives, a tendency that had been present already in the immediately preceding lines. This richness involves a considerable list of words found only once or not at all in Porphyry outside the discussion of this lemma, as I have previously noted (Tarrant 1993, 109 n. 2). In the passages quoted, however, what is most significant is that the terminology of *dianoia* (i.e. anything beginning with *diano-* or *dieno-*) is totally absent from the rest of this work.

The similarity of language perhaps confirms that Porphyry was drawing on Thrasyllan *material*, even though this would have involved paraphrase rather than exact quotation.[45] However, one receives no clear indication of where Thrasyllan quotation and paraphrase stops, even though a small percentage[46] of quotations later in the text are marked with the author's name at both beginning and end.[47] While editors all see the quotation of Thrasyllus as ending at 12.28,[48] the following sentence (καὶ γὰρ ὁ ὁρισμὸς ...) does not begin with any of the particles and connectives most likely to be found at the end of quotations, these being *men* (13 out of 35 cases), *de* (10 or 11),[49] *oun* (7–8), and *dē* (5).[50] For this reason I should maintain that the likeliest place for the quotation to end is before the phrase 'So then, for these reasons and others like them' (διὰ μὲν δὴ ταῦτα καὶ τὰ τούτοις ὅμοια) at 13.12–13, using two particles often used for closing a quotation plus a reference to what has just been said (*dia tauta*), another common technique. Furthermore, Porphyry makes it clear that nothing

44 Note that this term is a natural one for use in mathematical contexts and in contexts involving discursive reasoning rather than contemplative thought, but that it is often used of the reasoning used by the demiurge for planning things in a certain way in Plato's *Timaeus* 30b4, 33a6, 34a8, 36e6.

45 Porphyry has already rejected Ptolemy's tendency to borrow directly from other authors without mentioning their names (5.7–15), so it is natural to think of the first mention of Thrasyllus' name to come where direct quotation begins.

46 A close look at significant quotations between the end of the present lemma and p. 100 in Düring's edition shows that the author is again named (or otherwise identified) at the end of the quotation about 25 per cent of the time. About 30 per cent more are marked by a reference to what has been said (24.4, 24.22, 31.26, 32.5, 33.5, 47.24, 51.1, 58.1, 92.19, 93.18). Occasionally a quotation can end with a new lemma (52.17) or with the introduction of another author or text to be cited (31.26, not in Düring but in both Barker and Raffa; 78.21, 96.7).

47 This does not apply to Thrasyllus' fragments taken from a work *On the Heptachord* (or some similar title) at 91.16–92.8 and 96.19–20 with 24–25 (= T15a and T15b).

48 There is much more disagreement over Thrasyllus fr. 15b (p. 96).

49 Depending on editors at p. 96.

50 γὰρ occurs only once in these same 35 cases.

that he has just argued is original to him, by adding 'things that the writings of ancients are full of'. The lines 12.29–13.12 had been explaining the references to our logical processes towards the end of the accepted quotation of Thrasyllus, and if Porphyry goes on to say that this sort of thing is nothing original to him, then his own well-documented interests in logic cannot be used to credit him personally with such a passage of logic.

The whole discussion from the sentence beginning at 12.6 until 12.28 had been conducted without reference to the cause (*to aition*), which as 12.5–6 and 13.12–14 make clear was one of the two principal intentions of the intervening passage, the other being to establish the connection with the form (*eidos*). The closest that one had come there is the reference to the 'god and leader of the whole', where the original Platonic epistle had also spoken of the father of that 'leader *and cause*' (*hēgemonos kai aitiou*), as Thrasyllus and Porphyry must have known.[51] The notion of cause is reintroduced only in the discussion of our own reasoning processes after the acknowledged Thrasyllan passage. Here demonstration, unlike definition that is concerned simply with the form (13.2–6), goes about 'calculating additionally (*epilogizomenē*) the cause of their [*scil.* the two terms in the conclusion of the syllogism][52] being bound together' (13.7–8). Reference to binding down an opinion by the calculation of a cause is another Platonic feature (see *Meno* 98a), yet besides the statement at 13.13 that the writings of the ancients are full of such things, we are finally told at 13.13–14 that the purpose of the passage has been to show how the criterion of *logos* in humans is 'everywhere' associated with form and cause respectively.

Both this passage and the following passage on the way in which sensation extracts the form from matter by means of several stages (13.21–14.14) offer important clues concerning the kind of metaphysical and epistemological theory that influence Porphyry here. We said above that harmonic theory usually makes *logos* embrace either organisational principles of sounds or the organisational principles by which we try to understand it. Porphyry has treated *logos* in the wider sense, but after the section treating cosmic organisation and various forms of human imitation of it, he proceeds to treat the way in which we come to understand it

[51] One way this might have been relevant would be if Porphyry or his source had identified that 'father' at *Ep.* 323d with the demiurge and the 'leader and cause' with the Platonic world-soul, to which *logos* in the sense of harmonic ratios is famously central (*Tim.* 35b-36d).

[52] The example given is: (premise 1) all that is heavy is carried downwards; (premise 2) earth is heavy; hence (conclusion) earth is carried downwards. Its being heavy is here seen as the 'cause' for earth's being carried down.

through the study of form. The stages are (1) an internalising response (*antilēpsis*), (2) opinion-giving processes (*doxastikē hypolēpsis*) including the naming and recording of the thing perceived, (3) a process of image-construction undertaken by the imagination (*phantasia*), (4) the placement of the form in the soul as a concept (*ennoia*), (5) the transformation of the securely founded concept into knowledge (*epistēmē*), and (6) the sudden emergence of intelligence (*nous*) 'like a light kindled from leaping fire'. The final stage is a simple quotation of the seventh Platonic *Epistle* (341c7-d1), and that it is intelligence that so arises is deduced by comparison with 344b3-7 (*mogis* ... *exelampse* ... *nous*).[53] I have already discussed the passage (Tarrant 1993, 120–34), with more concern for the possibility of continued Thrasyllan influence. Here, however, one needs to consider rather what the material, whether borrowed or original, can tell us about Porphyry's exegesis here. It contributes little to the picture of *logos* and sensation as criteria, and the description of the process only uses the term *logos* for the mind's internally recorded discourse (13.28). It has thus been adapted for the present purpose, not designed for it.

Attempts to show dependence upon Plotinus make more of this epistemology than of anything else in the commentary. This is strange when one considers Mueller's observations that this is a 'highly Aristotelian account of judgement' and that 'the mechanism [of abstraction of the form] is purely Aristotelian.'[54] Nevertheless, while Gersh allows that the Neoplatonists were the 'primary legatees of the Pythagorean tradition', he goes on to affirm that Porphyry here 'sharpens the emphasis upon reason with a more explicitly Platonic epistemology'.[55] This leads him to attempt to analyse the epistemology of 13.15–15.28 in terms of the Plotinian hypostases of intellect and soul in a manner that seems to take Plotinus' influence as a given, with no consideration of whether the Porphyrian features that he draws attention to might also have been present in Longinus or in the Platonism of the two previous centuries.[56] In fact, apart from the passage

[53] Note here the reference to the means by which the spark of intelligence is achieved: rubbing together (like sticks) names, descriptions, sights and perceptions. These relate to name, description and image at 342b2, which are one influence behind the stages two and three in Porphyry's epistemology.

[54] Mueller 1990, 479. Cf. Chiaradonna 2017, 45–7, who speaks of 'the aristotelianizing doctrine of abstraction developed in the *Commentary on Ptolemy's Harmonics*'.

[55] Gersh 1992, 141 and 143.

[56] Gersh 1992, 147–9; it seems pointless, for instance to draw attention to the presence of a material intellect, when it had been present in Aristotle *de Anima* 3.4–5, with the term θύραθεν (13.18) applied to its superior counterpart at *Gen. an.* 736b28 etc., and with the expression ὑλικὸς νοῦς already found in a report of Aristocles' view (fr. 42) and common in Alexander of Aphrodisias. The basic distinction was already present in Plutarch, *De Iside* 374E-F. A similarly uncritical approach is

about external and material intellect (13.17–19),[57] where the theory and language is Peripatetic, our passage is notable rather for the fact that it does not express itself in hypostatic terms, *nous* being an element of cognition ('intelligence' or 'intellection', 14.5, 12) rather than an entity.

Raffa is also constrained by the belief that Porphyry is indebted to Plotinus, which prevents him from assenting to Romano's idea that the *Commentary on Ptolemy's Harmonics* was in some way inspired by Porphyry's association with his teacher of mathematics, Demetrius,[58] in which case a pre-Plotinian date, at least for most of the material, would have seemed likely. While the work of a Demetrius is cited by Porphyry at 92.25 and 95.1, Raffa is also deterred by the thought that Porphyry had addressed this commentary to one Eudoxius rather than to Demetrius.[59] Evidence produced of Plotinian influence seems to me to be remarkably thin given the size of the Plotinian corpus that Porphyry has transmitted to us. Raffa claims that in both Porphyry and Plotinus the notion of a perceptual grasp (*antilēpsis*) is separated from the bare act of sensation attributable to the sense organs themselves, whereas in Alexander the senses themselves are spoken of as if they were responsible. Yet the notion that something other than the senses was responsible for such a perceptual grasp is explicit in theory known to Sextus Empiricus. Take the following:

> τοίνυν οὐ δύνανται καθ' αὑτὰς αἱ αἰσθήσεις κρίνειν τἀληθές. συνθέσεώς τε δεῖ καὶ μνήμης πρὸς ἀντίληψιν τῶν ὑποκειμένων, οἷον ἀνθρώπου, φυτοῦ, τῶν ἐοικότων.

taken in claiming that 'There seems to be one allusion to such an [*scil.* Chaldaean] oracle in a passage comparing the intellect's approach to being to the leaping of a spark [at 14.3–6] although the reference is admittedly fleeting' (147). The only thing required to explain the spark imagery is that it is an exact five-word quotation of *Epistle 7* 341c-d, and the Chaldaean Oracles appear not to have acquired scriptural status for Porphyry.

57 This passage is an *addendum*, designed only to justify the term 'psychical matter' above. I would not regard any of 13.12–21 as dependent on the Thrasyllan *logos*-theory, to which our attention is returned in 13.21. Note that the perfect participles ὑποβεβηκώς (13.16) and ἐπαναβεβηκώς (13.17 and 18) are very rarely found in conjunction, but twice in Porphyry (also at *Isagoge* 4.17). The former was rare until the first century AD, but common in Nicomachus and Origen, while the latter was rare until Clement, Sextus Empiricus, Origen and Alexander of Aphrodisias. The terms occur just twice each in Plotinus (*Enn.* 3.5.9.18, 6.3.10.23; 2.9.1.22, 6.9.5.13). In Porphyry the latter term is found eight times (not counting the two in anon. *Parmenides*-commentary). Porphyry himself should be credited with this terminology.

58 See Raffa 2016a, lvi–vii; Romano 1979, 111. Proclus names Porphyry's teacher at *in R.* 2.23.14–15, and we hear from Eusebius (*Praep. Evang.* 10.3.1) that a geometrician Demetrius moved in the same circles as Porphyry and Longinus.

59 Raffa 2016a, xlvii, talks of 'dedication' rather than address, but this is inaccurate. Any expectation that such a work would be addressed to a respected teacher rather than to a valued pupil or interested friend is misguided.

> Hence the senses, of themselves, are unable to judge the truth. There is a need for composition and memory for the perceptual grasp (*antilēpsis*) of underlying things, e.g. human, plant, etc. (*Math.* 7.346)

So Porphyry's notion of a perceptual grasp that *follows* sensation did not depend on any innovation of Plotinus. Furthermore, the perceptual grasp in question is that of form in matter (or *qua* matter), which Porphyry has already given to sensation *to judge* (11.31; 12.1). It is entirely natural that the perceptual grasp should arise *as a result of* the sensation's judgement. Again, Plotinus in the passage quoted by Raffa (*Enn.* 4.5.8.22–23) did not rigidly separate the perceptual grasp from sensation, for he says rather 'sensation will be the soul's perceptual grasp through organs assimilated to the things grasped'.[60] Sensation is not other than the perceptual grasp here, and the precedent that we need for Plotinus' making the soul responsible for it, via the sense organs, is none other than *Theaetetus* 184c-d. Plotinus' theory is routine. Porphyry's is more interesting.

Another thing that we lack in Plotinus is the desire, evident in Porphyry through the numbering of stages (13.24; 29) or the repetition of a preposition,[61] to set out the way the cognitive process functions through a series of discrete steps, as in Stoicism (particularly Zeno's well-known manual illustration in Cicero *Acad. post.* 144 = *SVF* 1.66), or less obviously in *Epistle 7* (342a-b, 344b), which does nevertheless number five elements of cognition, name, description, image, ordinary cognition, and 'the fifth' of which a few have intelligence (*nous*). Since Porphyry quotes 341c-d concerning *nous*, one should notice that the first three correspond rather closely to stages 2a, 2b and 3 in Porphyry. However, the earlier stages are also somewhat reminiscent of the kind of transition from sensation through naming and recording, to notions that involve reasoning, and on to knowledge that Cicero gives to Lucullus (*Acad. post.* 19–22).

Raffa's comparison with Plotinus continues beyond the perceptual grasp to stages 2 and 3 without any remarkable claims, but he makes more of Porphyry's comparison at 15.10–22 between the roles of sensations and reason with those of king and messenger. Though the senses had often attracted the language of giving messages, so that this aspect of the

[60] ἡ αἴσθησις ψυχῆς ἀντίληψις ἔσται δι' ὀργάνων ὁμοίων τοῖς ἀντιληπτοῖς. See Raffa 2016a, xlviii n. 58.

[61] Particularly διὰ μὲν . . . (14.6) followed by διὰ δὲ . . . (14.7; 8; 10); also μετά (13.27; 29; 14.11).

comparison is unremarkable, Plotinus (*Enn.* 5.3.3.39–45) has extended the comparison to include that between *intelligence* (*nous*) and our king (cf. Philo, *Mut.* 112–113), but of course Porphyry is treating *logos* and sensation, not *nous* and sensation. Had Porphyry's comparison, then, been an adaptation of Plotinus? Given that by the time Plotinus' treatise 5.3 was written Porphyry had already departed for Sicily, it is theoretically possible that the influence is quite the reverse, but the whole issue is complex. Plotinus' passage is not so unexpected. In the Platonic and Aristotelian tradition, human reason or intelligence is that element within us that has most authority and capacity to rule.[62] But then (a) it is not thought of as ruling the senses in particular, and (b) the term 'King' would not normally be applied to its being 'ruler'. Porphyry not only innovates in using the term 'King', but also envisaging a king who has *complete and accurate* foreknowledge of all that goes on in his kingdom, even though he is confined within his royal palace.[63] This is a very strong claim for the power of *logos*, but it is an even stranger claim to make about any earthly monarch, so was there any special king that Porphyry had in mind?[64] Could it have been some kind of divine 'king'?[65] One such 'King' whose status was debated between Ammonius' pupils Origenes and Plotinus was that of *Epistle 2* 312e-313a,[66] but it is hard to see how it could explain anything in Porphyry's text. And any reference to so strange a king during Porphyry's stay at Rome would surely have provoked laughter: for 'King' was Amelius' name for none other than Porphyry himself, because Porphyry's own Syrian name 'Malchus' had meant 'king' (*Plot.* 17). Regardless of such complications, there is far more in the Porphyrian passage to explain than there is in the Plotinian one, and no appeal to a Plotinian precedent could possibly suffice.

62 For reason as κυριώτατον see Pl. *Ti.* 90a2, cf. Arist. *Protr.* fr. 7 = Iambl. *Protr.* 73.14; for its being ἀρχικώτερον Arist. *Protr.* fr. 7 = Iambl. *Protr.* 71.26–72.9. For intelligence as ἀρχικώτατον see Max. Tyr. *Or.* 6.5.

63 Note 15.11–12: πάντα προειληφότι καὶ προειδότι ἀκριβῶς καὶ ἔνδον παρ' ἑαυτοῦ ἐν τοῖς οἰκείοις βασιλείοις διατρίβοντι; also 15–16 προεγνωκὼς ἅπαντα, and ὁ λόγος πᾶσαν τὴν τῆς αἰσθήσεως ἀντίληψιν εἰδὼς εὑρίσκεται.

64 Previously (1993, 139–41) I related this strange comparison to the divine powers afforded to Tiberius through his association with Thrasyllus, but this would reduce Porphyry to an unthinking copyist with no motivation of his own.

65 There is one mythical 'King' to whom early imperial Platonism credits such supernatural knowledge, including foreknowledge, while confined within his dwelling, and that is the sleeping Kronos in Plutarch's *De Facie* (941F-942A) and *De Defectu* (420A), who knows in his dreams all that Zeus plans. He even has *daimones* who act in the role of messengers, but Plutarch mentions only their announcing the prophecies of Kronos to others, not their keeping Kronos informed.

66 On this debate see now Tarrant 2017b.

9.6 Where (and What) Are the Intelligibles

Reference to Platonic metaphysics is what is required to resolve the most important aspect of the chronology of this work, that of whether it is, at least for the most part, a pre-Plotinian or a post-Plotinian exercise. At some time during his stay with Plotinus (approximately AD 263–9) Porphyry was persuaded to abandon his previous view and allow that the intelligibles (*ta noēta*) were embraced within intellect (*nous*) itself (*Plot.* 18). Hence it would be worth examining whether there are any clues about Porphyry's position on intelligibles and on intellect when writing on Ptolemy. We have said quite a bit about *nous* already, observing that its normal use is epistemological and not as any kind of metaphysical hypostasis. The passage that distinguishes a material from an external *nous* (13.17–19) may look like a potential exception, but, as we have seen (above, n. 56), it is Aristotelian in character and not without parallel in Middle Platonism. We have also noted in this regard that *logos* rather than Plotinus' *nous* plays the role of king at 15.10–17, so that if anything were being hypostasised it would be *logos*. Indeed *logos* and forms are very closely related, not least in Thrasyllus' use of the term 'the *logos* of the forms' (12.21).

When we discuss the intelligibles, however, overt statements on their nature and whereabouts are lacking. Of relevant Platonic terms, *eidos* is regularly employed for *immanent* form, while *idea* is totally absent from the work except at 79.21 in an unrevealing quotation of Aristoxenus, so that we are reliant on the terminology connected directly with the term that appears in the debate over intelligibles (*noēta*). There are no interesting cases of the noun *noēsis* or of the verb *noein*,[67] while the adjective *noētos* occurs only at 14.27, 16.33–17.31 often, 27.15, and 62.3.[68]

Let us give Barker's translation of 14.22–28, modifying the words italicised:

> It [*scil.* judgement] is made accessible to each individual in himself [*kath'-heauton*, not an expression of place] and communicable to the multitude through perception, when the voice takes up the image in the soul to articulate it in speech, and as it were adjusts (*epharmozousēs*)[69] it to the

[67] The noun is found only at 97.23; the verb occurs at 36.20 and 37.2 (both in Aelian), 79.16 (in Aristoxenus: the line is missing in Barker), 80.3 ('notice'; 'understand' in Barker), 121.17/22 (mathematical uses in the imperative).

[68] This final case may be ignored, as it occurs within a fragment of Theophrastus, dealing with the Pythagorean understanding of the melodic accuracy of the human voice, which attributed it to 'intelligible numbers'.

[69] This term is not even a metaphor here; I count fifty-nine cases of the verb in Plotinus and Porphyry, and they never concern sound except later in this work where five out of seventeen cases do so.

> archetypal forms themselves and the things that participate in them in matter. Thus, once again, the image of things that exist is brought, through hearing, *out of an intelligible into a perceptible <form>*, just as it is also through sight when someone writes the words down.

Here spoken and written speech is thought of as an expression of form that is somehow attuned to an archetypal form (*archetypon eidos*) as well as to its physical instantiations. This is the only case of a reference to an 'archetype' in the work, though the general idea of an archetype that produces several copies is present in the few lines before the quotation (14.14–22). Yet it must be remembered that Plato himself did not speak of his intelligible ideas as 'archetypes'. It is otherwise clear that the form is sometimes disengaged from matter, and Chiaradonna (2007, 47) speaks of such disengagement as 'his (direct realist) abstraction theory'. Being a realist about something that starts off being enmattered seems at odds with Platonists' usual insistence that only intelligible Ideas are fully real, and it would scarcely seem Platonic that form should migrate between enmattered and matter-free existences in this way, even if soul may do so. Reason, also immaterial (18.1; 10), encounters form as freed from matter (11.11–19), and the cognitive processes that start with sensation try to make the judgement immaterial (13.24). Presumably this form that is recovered from the material realm and rendered immaterial, however 'real' it may be or become, cannot be archetypal in any meaningful sense, but it remains unclear how the archetypal form is conceived, and indeed whether Porphyry saw any quasi-location for it at all. One might suggest that it should be located within the supreme *logos* used by the god and leader of all at 12.18–20, but one then has to ask whether that *logos* is located within him. Does a god really 'use' (*chrētai*) something that is actually a part of himself?

At 27.14–15 the manuscripts tell us that it is rather sophistic to speak of the *form* of a musical note only, and thus to postulate that it is something intelligible (σοφιστικώτερον ὂν τὸ λέγειν τὸ εἶδος μόνον φθόγγου καὶ νοητὸν οὕτως ἀπολιπεῖν αὐτό).[70] We are clearly not speaking of intelligible Ideas in the Platonic tradition, but of the theoretical approach to music usually branded 'Pythagorean'. It would be difficult to regard notes, even as so conceived, as 'not outside mind'.

[70] Published texts agree in emending to καὶ <τὸ> νοητὸν, but Barker's translation has 'to leave it as something merely intelligible', and his note expresses some perplexity. I see no reason for the supplement.

This brings us to the passage where the term 'intelligible' occurs most frequently, but here it must be immediately stated that Porphyry is responding to a case of it within the relevant lemma (Ptol. *Harm.* 3.8–14) where Ptolemy had referred to 'things intelligible through sensation'. At 16.33 it is stated that Ptolemy knew that there were also rational acts of comprehension independent of sensation, 'the kind involving the intelligibles',[71] but was saying that reason needed sensation for a grasp of sensible objects. This then leads to a discussion of the use of the term 'intelligible', introduced at 17.11 and concluding at 17.31. The special sense of the word involves things that differ in their very substance (*ousia*) from sensibles, all bodiless intelligibles and those that are not bodies, and he notes that discussion 'among the ancients' was about 'intelligibles' in this sense. No special mention is made of Plato. A different sense covers everything that the intelligence can detect and comprehend, including everything sensible and everything of the sensible type even if too small for the senses to perceive it. Again, a special sense of intelligible will cover things grasped by intelligence not sensation, including things too small to be sensed. Porphyry prefers to posit the most general sense of intelligible at 17.23–26. The term will here apply to anything that can be grasped by reason (*logos*), 'which the ancients more generally called intelligence (*nous*) too'.

This establishes that the term 'intelligible' will be used in this study rather broadly and in a sense that any non-skeptic school could find a use for. There is no hint of a special affinity with Plato or Platonism that will get in the way of his adopting an appropriate approach to the text that he interprets. The idea that no intelligible is outside intelligence (*nous*) is totally alien to this discussion, both because of the concept of intelligibles employed and because of the non-hypostatic treatment of *nous* itself. In my view it is alien to the commentary in a way that it could never have been allowed to become after his moment of conversion in Plotinus' school, particularly if Porphyry had been using his treatment of harmonics in order to prepare students for the study of Plato. And furthermore it would seem that Porphyry saw the kind of discussion about intelligence and its own special objects that flourished within the Plotinian school as being essentially a thing of the past: belonging rather to the ancients. Porphyry cannot be writing here as a Plotinian convert. And if he is not a Plotinian convert, then he did not have to be a Platonist either.

[71] It is difficult to deny that a comma should appear at the end of the final line of Düring's page 16, but neither Barker nor Raffa print one in the Greek; Barker's translation has one.

9.7 Conclusion

So what are Porphyry's allegiances as he writes here? The commentary *never* looks like a Neoplatonic exercise, and many of the debates that arise from Ptolemy's text would seem unusual material for a Neoplatonist's attention unless there are signs that the author is trying to make them relevant to some higher project. There are ways in which the commentary coheres with Porphyry's wider theory detectable in his mature works, making it profitable to employ it for the reconstruction of an overall Porphyrian attitude to harmony. Thus Gersh (2017) can successfully use it in a metaphysical study that brings in harmony elsewhere in the corpus, but he finds 'more nuanced' (208) material on harmony outside the commentary, with chapters 13 and 16 of the overtly Platonist *ad Gaurum* being 'most interesting' (216–217). Likewise Chiaradonna (2007) can use it profitably in explaining *Sententiae* 42. There can be no complete disconnect between the products of different stages of Porphyry's career.

In explaining Ptolemy the commentary makes no use of Ptolemy's other works, not even the brief *On the Kriterion and the Hegemonikon*. It draws on several sources connected with Pythagoreanism and/or the *Timaeus*, but none that we should closely associate with Plotinus. The fact that Porphyry tackles Ptolemy's *Harmonics* at all is best explained on the assumption that he feels an affinity with a moderate version of Pythagorean harmonics, and by the fact that in book 3, which his commentary never reaches, Ptolemy had extended his treatment of 'harmony' to include both those harmonies that are found in the human soul and in the cosmos.[72] After all, Porphyry sees Ptolemy as a staunch opponent of the Pythagoreans' Aristoxenian rivals (16.31–32), and therefore as offering support for the Pythagorean cause. Even when he wrote the *Life of Plotinus* Porphyry's selection of material from Longinus placing Plotinus in the tradition of Thrasyllus, Moderatus, Numenius and Cronius, a tradition that had discussed the principles of Pythagoras (unequivocally) and of Plato as he thought (*hōs edokei*, *Plot.* 20.72), and his comments upon that material (*Plot.* 21.1–9), showed his respect for that predominately Pythagorean tradition. Porphyry's works make further reference to these figures.[73] This picture

[72] See Feke 2018, 98–112.

[73] Thrasyllus is cited *In Harm.*, and found once in *Intr. Tetr.*; Numenius is central to *Cave of the Nymphs*, and cited also in *ad Gaurum* and in fragments of *On Powers of the Soul*; Cronius is also cited in *Cave of the Nymphs* and in *On the Styx* fr. 1; Moderatus is cited in *VPyth.* and the fragment on three Ones (236F = Simpl. *in Phys.* 230.34–231.24).

also conforms well with Porphyry's account of the good side of whichever Origenes is referred to at *Contra Christianos* 39:[74]

> For he constantly engaged with Plato and with the writings of Numenius, Cronius, Apollophanes and Longinus, Moderatus, Nicomachus and the celebrated men from the Pythagorean school, . . .

The list (at least if one excludes the two Stoics) names those Greek authors dear to Origen whom Porphyry too found congenial – beginning with Plato but continuing chiefly with those whom one could associate with Pythagorean leanings.[75] Origen is being praised for his intellectual commitment to the same tradition of religious philosophy that Porphyry would be proud to be associated with. Thrasyllus, the one to feature in our commentary, is not here mentioned. Perhaps Origenes took no interest in him, or perhaps (if our commentary was written earlier) he no longer excites the mature Porphyry.

Given that the kind of debts to Plotinus that Raffa (2016a) suspected have little substance, and that even if odd points of influence were substantiated they might result from later additions to the commentary, I have no difficulty in accepting Romano's (1979) suggestion that the work was at least started soon after its author's studies with the mathematician Demetrius, and thus in all likelihood before he arrived in Rome, before he converted to the doctrine that the intelligibles are not outside the intellect, before his metaphysics became hypostatic, and before Amelius' calling him Basileus might have caused embarrassment at the analogy involving *logos* as omniscient king.

Regardless of its date, I associate the Porphyry of the *Commentary on Ptolemy's Harmonics* with the Pythagoreans rather than the Platonists, even if this association fell well short of the kind of commitment that would be expected of the leading Pythagorean teacher of an organised school. A certain tendency towards eclecticism and the harmonisation of key philosophers entailed few restrictions on the presence of a good deal of Peripatetic and Platonic material. I can see two objections to a generally Pythagorean outlook, but both are easily answered. First, Porphyry's epistemology at 15.4–28 presupposes a theory of recollection whereby *logos* actually has some kind of foreknowledge of everything that sensation

[74] Clearly a Christian, but that does not preclude his being the figure referred to in the *Life of Plotinus*; the distinction may in fact be a misguided one (see Ramelli 2018), though in some contexts it is nevertheless useful.

[75] While we do not know who Apollophanes was, the phrasing (Ἀπολλοφάνους τε καὶ Λογγίνου) suggests to me that he was more closely associated with Longinus than with others on the list.

will tell it. However, (a) obvious Platonic allusions are absent from this passage, and (b) the theory was popularly credited to Pythagoras anyway.[76] Second, Barker (2015, 47–52) has argued that an important purpose of the work is to prepare pupils for the reading of Plato's *Timaeus*. There is a certain plausibility in this thesis, and no denying that Porphyry is already intensely interested in the *Timaeus*, but even so it cannot indicate an allegiance to Plato rather than to Pythagoras, for the existence of the work attributed to Timaeus Locrus complicated the attribution of much of the doctrine, and the mathematics of the work was especially liable to be associated with Pythagoras.[77] A Platonist has to be interested in many works besides the *Timaeus*; a Pythagorean can choose which he wants to appropriate for Pythagoras and which he can safely ignore.

Postulating that Porphyry is here writing primarily as one of Pythagorean inclination has one particularly welcome consequence: it makes it less important to distinguish between the goals of his harmonics and his natural philosophy, for the Pythagorean natural world has mathematics and harmony at its roots, so that studying harmonics is integral to the study of the natural world and the power that controls it. It may be thus for some Platonists too, but mathematics was usually a less direct concern insofar as we may judge, and physics was generally secondary to metaphysics. If the languages of music and of philosophy often converge in this text, and most obviously in the discussion of *logos*, it is because there simply was no boundary between Pythagorean music and Pythagorean physics.

[76] See Lucian, *Vit. auct.* 3; Pythagoras' alleged memory of previous lives, accepted by Porphyry *VPyth.* 26, was obviously a factor.

[77] E.g. the shapes of the four elements at Lucian, *Vit. auct.* 4, cf. Aetius *Plac.* 2.6.5. Other doctrines too, particularly those relating to soul, were likely to be credited to Pythagoras and Plato in common (e.g. Aet. *Plac.* 4.7.2, 4.7.5, 4.9.10, 5.20.4).

CHAPTER 10

The Music of the Virtues in Late Ancient Platonism

Dominic J. O'Meara

10.1 Introduction

Late ancient Platonists, from Iamblichus in the late third century to the last philosophers of Alexandria in the mid-sixth century, generally conceived of philosophy as consisting of a range of sciences, including both the theoretical sciences (physics, mathematics and metaphysics or 'theology') and practical philosophy (ethics, 'economics' and politics). This range of sciences constituted a hierarchy in which the practical sciences were seen as subordinate to the theoretical sciences, themselves arranged in a scale going in ascending order from physics up to mathematics and culminating in metaphysics.[1] This hierarchy represented a progression in the study of philosophy, moving from the lower (practical) to the higher (theoretical) sciences. But it also expressed relations of priority and posteriority obtaining between the sciences themselves. Thus late ancient Platonists claimed that the mathematical sciences, as theoretical, had a paradigmatic status and function in relation to lower, practical sciences such as ethics.

We might take the following two statements as examples of this claim. The first can be read in Iamblichus' *De communi mathematica scientia*:

> [T1] [Mathematics] contributes to ethics in that it contains the rational principles of the virtues and reveals the mathematical forms as paradigms of friendship, for instance, or of happiness, or of some other of the greatest goods. It also presents mathematical paradigms of all in life, such as fertility or infertility, productivity or dearth, and all such things. Hence we should make use of mathematics everywhere, as providing a preliminary sketch of philosophy in these paradigms.[2]

Iamblichus' claims are stated more fully and clearly by Proclus in his *Commentary on Euclid's Elements*:

[1] For an overview and references, see O'Meara 2003, 50–60.

[2] Iamblichus, *Comm. math.* 56.8–16.

> [T2] [Mathematics] perfects us for ethical philosophy by instilling order and harmonious living in our characters; it furnishes the gestures, songs and dances appropriate to virtue by which, as we know, the Athenian Stranger [Plato, *Laws* 654d ff.] wishes those who are to share in ethical virtue (*ēthikēs aretēs*) to be perfected from their childhood onwards; it presents the proportions that characterize the virtues – now in numbers, now in movements, now in musical consonances (*symphōnois*) – and shows up by contrast the excesses and deficiencies (*tas hyperbolas kai tas endeias*) of vice, thereby helping us to make our characters measured and ordered. For this reason Socrates in the *Gorgias* [508a], when reproaching Callicles for his unordered and dissolute life, says 'you are neglecting geometry and geometrical equality'.[3]

The mathematical sciences include music, which, with the other mathematical sciences (arithmetic, geometry, astronomy), contributes, as we can see from these passages, paradigms to ethics. But what precisely is this contribution? In what way is music paradigmatic, or provides paradigms, for ethics? In the following pages I would like to explore these questions in order to reach a more detailed view than that suggested in the succinct statements made by Iamblichus and Proclus.[4]

However, before exploring the paradigmatic relation obtaining between music and ethics, we will need first to take account of a wider context, the view that, according to these late ancient Platonists, both music and the virtues display a hierarchy of levels. I will thus begin with an account of the various levels of music (Section 10.2) and then offer a brief overview of the scale of virtues (Section 10.3), before attempting (in Section 10.4) to coordinate the levels of virtue with the levels of the music so as to see in more detail what it might mean for music to have a paradigmatic function for ethics.

10.2 The Hierarchy of Music

In his fifth essay on Plato's *Republic*, Proclus distinguishes between four kinds, or levels, of music according to Plato.[5] I will describe these kinds starting with the lowest, although Proclus himself follows the reverse order

[3] Procl. *in Eucl.* 24.4–17, transl. Morrow slightly modified.

[4] For discussion of Plotinus and Porphyry on the subject of music, see the chapters by Michalewski and Tarrant in the present volume.

[5] Procl. *in R.* 1.57.8–60.6. Sheppard 2005 has drawn attention to and discussed this text. See also Moro Tornese 2010, ch. 4. Other hierarchies of kinds of music can be found in late ancient Platonism, for example in Theon of Smyrna (see Hadot 2005, 71 n. 30; Petrucci 2012a, 344–6), in Proclus (*in Alcib.* 204–205) and in Boethius (see Gersh 1996, 41–5). Of course, no attempt can be made here to discuss Plato's own views on music and its relation to ethical education, on which see Pelosi 2010.

and starts with the highest. Here, then, is the lowest kind of music, as Proclus presents it:

> [T3] [This kind of music] educates the character by means of harmonies and rhythms which lead to virtue, discovering which harmonies and rhythms can educate the passions of the souls and mould the soul with excellent character traits in all actions and circumstances, and which ones, opposite to these, put souls out of tune by tightening or loosening them and leading them to disharmony and lack of rhythm. And this you might say is the educational music which is ordered by the statesman, in conjunction with gymnastics, to which the Socrates of the *Republic* is looking when he discussed [398d ff.] harmonies and rhythms.[6]

Music of this kind educates the irrational part of the soul, 'tuning' it through appropriate sounds which are structured by means of harmonies and rhythms. It is audible music and is, according to Proclus, the subject of Book 3 of Plato's *Republic*.

This type of music is inferior to a second, higher kind of music, which Proclus describes as follows:

> [T4] [This kind] leads up from perceptible harmonies to the imperceptible beauty of the divine harmony. For this kind of 'musician' too loves beauty, just like the lover, although the latter is reminded of beauty by means of sight while the former is reminded by means of hearing.[7]

The higher kind of music leads to intelligible knowledge. Stimulated at first perhaps by audible music, it becomes in fact a theoretical knowledge of purely intelligible harmonies, of intelligible forms. Proclus identifies this music with the mathematics discussed by Plato, in Books 6–7 of the *Republic*, which is described as leading away from perceptible objects to knowledge of immaterial objects (the Forms).[8] It corresponds to music as defined by Nicomachus of Gerasa (i.e. a purely theoretical knowledge of the relations [ratios] between numbers).[9] Following Nicomachus,[10] I will refer to this science of the relations between numbers as 'harmonics'. 'Harmonies', here, are specific ratios between numbers, in particular the consonances of the octave (2:1), the fifth (3:2) and the fourth (4:3).

6 Procl. *in R.* 1.59.20–60.1. I use Sheppard's translation (2005) of the first part of this passage.

7 *in R.* 1.58.28–59.3 (Sheppard's transl.).

8 Plato, *Resp.* 510c-e. Plato's image of mathematics as leading away, or 'drawing' (ὁλκός, *Resp.* 521d3) as if a drawing rope, is recalled by Proclus in relation to this kind of music (*in R.* 1.60.3). On the difference between music in this context in Plato and music as part of the educational programme of *Republic* Book 3, see Pelosi 2010, 115.

9 Nicomachus, *Intr. arithm.* 1.3.6.2–3; Proclus, *in Eucl.* 36.1.

10 Nicomachus, *Ench.*; see Proclus, *in Eucl.* 34.16; O'Meara 2005, 132–3.

Two yet higher kinds of music are distinguished by Proclus: a music inspired by the gods, by the Muses, in the souls of poets (Proclus refers for this to Plato's *Phaedrus* 245a), and, highest of all, the 'music' with which Plato identifies philosophy itself in the *Phaedo* (61a). On this last level, the true philosopher is the highest 'musician' in being assimilated to god, to Apollo, celebrating the gods and, like a god, bringing order to human affairs.[11]

In short, we can speak of the following four kinds of music, which I list in ascending order: audible music (M1), which, through ordered sounds, can mould the irrational passions in human souls; theoretical music (M2), 'harmonics', which is a mathematical knowledge of the relations between numbers and which brings human reason to knowledge of intelligible realities; divine inspiration (M3) in the souls of poets; and finally 'music' as the life of the gods (M4), in which the philosopher can share by assimilation to the divine. In examining the paradigmatic relation between music and ethics in Section 10.4 below, I will concentrate on the two lower kinds of music, audible (M1) and theoretical (M2) music, as they may relate to different kinds or levels of virtue.

10.3 The Hierarchy of Virtue

The hierarchy of levels of virtue, as conceived by late ancient Platonists, has been discussed quite often in modern studies,[12] and I might be permitted to limit myself here to recalling some of its major features so as to prepare the way for the coordination between kinds of virtue and kinds of music to be attempted in Section 10.4.

The late ancient Platonist theory of a hierarchy of levels of virtue was stimulated by Plotinus' distinction, in *Ennead* 1.2, between the 'political' virtues which he found defined in Plato's *Republic*, Book 4, and 'higher' virtues described as 'purifications' in Plato's *Phaedo* (69c). The 'political' virtues bring rational order to our passions in our lives as souls living in bodies, whereas the 'higher' virtues separate soul from material preoccupations and allow it to live the purely immaterial life of reason. Porphyry, in his *Sentences* (ch. 32), added two further levels to Plotinus' scheme, distinguishing Plotinus' 'higher' virtues into 'purificatory' and 'intellectual' (called 'theoretical' virtues by later Platonists), even if Plotinus himself

[11] Procl. *in R.* 1.57.8–58.27.

[12] An overview can be found in O'Meara 2003, 40–9; the source texts are collected and presented in Saffrey and Segonds' introduction to Marinus, *Vita Procli*, LXIX–C.

did not think that purification as a process was a virtue,[13] and adding 'paradigmatic' virtues as models of the lower levels of virtue, even if Plotinus did not think that the models of virtues were virtues.[14]

Iamblichus was responsible, it seems, for the addition of yet more levels to Porphyry's four-level scheme, adding, as inferior to the 'political' virtues, the levels of 'natural' (i.e. inborn) virtue and 'ethical' virtue (i.e. virtues acquired purely by training, in animals and small children), and, as superior to the 'paradigmatic' virtues, the 'theurgic' virtues. Thus the complete scheme included the following levels in the scale of virtues: (V1) natural; (V2) ethical; (V3) political; (V4) purificatory; (V5) theoretical; (V6) paradigmatic; (V7) theurgic. This elaborate scheme varies somewhat in the accounts of it that have come down to us.[15] As in the case of the hierarchy of types of music, I will be concerned mostly with the lower levels of the scheme.

10.4 Music and the Virtues

Natural virtues (V1) are simply given to us with birth and thus are not such as to be open to the possibility of being acquired or not. This possibility begins with the next level in the scale of virtues, 'ethical' virtue (V2), and so we can begin with this level in order to see what role music might play in its acquisition.

10.4.1 Ethical Virtue

This virtue (V2) is acquired simply by the behavioural training that can be given to animals or small children. It seems that it is to this kind of virtue that Proclus is referring where he speaks, in the first part of the passage quoted above (**T2**), of children being perfected in 'ethical virtue' by audible music (M1). Proclus refers us to the account of this ethical education through music that can be read in Plato's *Laws*. The association of audible music with the education of the young in ethical virtue is also made in Proclus' description of audible music as the lowest level of music in passage **T3**, where he refers this time to Plato's prescriptions for musical education in the *Republic*, Book 3. The appropriate rational structures, expressed in specific harmonies and rhythms of audible music, can mould the irrational passions of the young into moral characters, whereas inappropriate music can have the opposite effect, stimulating irrational passions and producing

[13] Plot. *Enn.* 1.2.4. [14] Plot. *Enn.* 1.2.6.13–18. [15] See note 12 above.

vicious behaviour.[16] These passions relate to the irrational aspects of the soul and correspond to 'spirit' (*thymos*) and 'desire' (*epithymia*) in Plato's division of the soul into three parts (reason, spirit and desire) in the *Republic*. An example of the use of music so as to control desire was given by the Platonists of Alexandria, who tell the story of how Pythagoras had used music to cure a youth of his erotic passion.[17] And Iamblichus tells us that Pythagoras sang to his disciples, sometimes accompanied by the lyre, it seems, to cure their souls of irrational passions.[18]

10.4.2 Political Virtue

The 'political' virtue (V3) which Plotinus found defined in Plato's *Republic* Book 4 is not reducible to the mere moulding of passions in children by the imposition of rational order from outside by others (parents, teachers, trainers), since the order is imposed internally, by reason exercising its rule over the irrational aspects of the soul. Late ancient Platonists assimilated this 'political' virtue to the ethical virtue defined in Aristotle's *Nicomachean Ethics*, Book 2, as a disposition of the soul which is the mean between excess and deficiency in passions and actions. We can find traces of this assimilation already in Plotinus and in Porphyry.[19] Proclus seems to be referring to it in the second half of passage **T2**, where he speaks of vices in terms of 'excess' and 'deficiency'. The adoption of Aristotelian ethical virtue (as a mean between excess and deficiency) in Platonism can already be found in Platonist authors of the second century AD, most significantly, for our present purposes, in Nicomachus:

> [T5] Those [numbers] which are said to be opposites to one another, the superabundant and deficient, are distinguished from one another in the relation of inequality in the directions of the greater and the less; for apart from these no other form of inequality could be conceived, nor could vice (*kakia*), disease, disproportion, unseemliness, nor any such thing, save in terms of excess and deficiency. For in the realm of the greater there arise excesses, overreaching and superabundance, and in the less need, deficiency, privation, and lack; but in that which lies between the greater and the less,

[16] As Francesco Pelosi has pointed out to me, in Plato the emphasis is not so much on the rational structures brought to ethical education by music, but rather on music as reproducing ethical dispositions, on which see Pelosi 2010, ch. 1.

[17] On this story, see Sheppard 2005, 151–3.

[18] Iamblichus, *VP*. 15.35.16–36.7; Proclus, *in Alcib.* 194, gives gymnastics the role of educating desire and music that of educating spirit, describing this as 'contributing somehow to political virtue as a whole'. On musicotherapy in late ancient Platonism, see Sheppard 2005, Moro Tornese 2015.

[19] See O'Meara 2013, 50–4.

namely the equal, are virtues, wealth, moderation, propriety, beauty and the like, to which the aforesaid form of number, the perfect, is most akin.[20]

In rewriting Nicomachus' handbook, Iamblichus develops at greater length the comparison between equality, excess and deficiency in numbers and the virtues as means between excess and deficiency by integrating more material taken from the corresponding parts of Aristotle's *Nicomachean Ethics*.[21]

However, for the Neoplatonist philosophers of Late Antiquity, the most important source suggestive of a relation between mathematical, in particular musical structures and political virtue is the text in *Republic* Book 4 where Plato defines the four cardinal virtues:

[T6] [Moderation] is more like a consonance (*symphōnia*) or harmony than the others we have considered hitherto.[22]

As compared with other virtues, practical wisdom (*phronēsis*) and courage, which are the virtues of particular parts of the soul (wisdom the virtue of reason, courage the virtue of spirit, 431e10-432a1), moderation involves all three parts of the soul, when reason rules the other parts, spreading through the entire octave (*dia pasōn*),[23] making all parts of the soul 'sing in unison' (432a2-3). A little later, comparing the soul to a stringed instrument, Plato describes the harmonious unity of soul as justice:

[T7] And justice was in truth, it appears, something like this. It does not lie in a man's external actions, but in the way he acts within himself, really concerned with himself and his inner parts [. . .] he orders what are in the true sense of the word his own affairs well; he is master of himself, puts things in order, is his own friend, harmonizes the three parts [of the soul] like the limiting notes of a musical scale, the high, the low, the middle, and any others there may be between. He binds them all together, and himself from a plurality becomes a unity. Being thus moderate and harmonious, he now performs any action, be it about the acquisition of wealth, the care of his body, some public actions, or private contract [. . .][24]

Plato's comparison between the virtues of the soul and musical consonance is developed, for example, by Aristides Quintilianus[25] and in greater detail

20 Nicomachus, *Intr. arithm.* 1.14.36.9–37.3, transl. D'Ooge, slightly modified. See also 1.23.65.8–16.
21 Iamblichus, *in Nicom.* 32.25–33.17.
22 Pl. *Resp.* 430e3-4, transl. Grube. On this text and on the following one (**T7**), see Pelosi 2010, 184–9.
23 Modern translators (e.g., Grube) do not find in this expression a technical reference to the octave, as Plato's ancient readers sometimes did, as we will see below.
24 *Resp.* 443c9-e4.
25 *De musica* 3.16 (conveniently available in translation in Barker 1989). See Long 1991, 113–4.

by Ptolemy in his *Harmonics* in terms of the theory of three consonances, the octave, the fifth and the fourth. Thus the virtues of desire (Ptolemy lists moderation among these) relate to the consonance of the fourth, whereas the virtues of spirit relate to that of the fifth, a consonance which is nearer to the best consonance of all, that of the octave. Justice, Ptolemy declares, the greatest disposition of the soul, is the consonance of its parts:

> [T8] For the fifth is closer to the octave than is the fourth, since it is more consonant, due to the fact that the difference between its notes is closer to equality [. . .] Our soul is also divided in another way, into the rational, the spirited and the desiring part [. . .] Thus there will be three species of virtue belonging to the desiring part, as in the consonance of the fourth: moderation in contempt for pleasures, self-control in the endurance of deprivations, and shame in the avoidance of what is disgraceful. There will be four species of virtue belonging to the spirited part, as in the consonance of the fifth: gentleness in refusal to be stirred up by anger, fearlessness in refusal to be perturbed by the anticipation of what is dreadful, courage in contempt for dangers, and steadfastness in the endurance of hardships. The seven species of virtue belonging to the rational part will be acuteness [. . .], cleverness [. . .], shrewdness [. . .], judgement [. . .], wisdom [. . .], practical wisdom [. . .] and experience [. . .] In souls it is natural for the intellectual and rational parts to govern the others, which are subordinate and they [i.e., the former] need greater accuracy in the imposition of correct ratio, since they are themselves responsible for the whole or the greater part of any error among the others. The best condition of the soul as a whole, justice, is as it were a consonance between the parts in themselves in their relations to one another, in correspondence with the ratio governing the principal parts.[26]

Ptolemy's *Harmonics* was read by late ancient Platonists. Porphyry wrote a commentary on it.[27] And Proclus, in explaining Plato's assimilation of the virtue of moderation to the octave in the *Republic* (432a2-3), makes use of Ptolemy's harmonic elaboration of Plato's comparison between the virtues of the soul and the three types of musical consonance:[28]

> [T9] For if indeed reason, as ruling both [spirit and desire] and responsible for their reverting to it and becoming obedient to it, includes the principle of the measure which it has given to the others, then moderation, as starting from reason, ending with desire, through the mediation of spirit, would thus

[26] Ptol. *Harm.* 3.5, transl. Barker (1989), slightly modified.

[27] See Barker 2015. However, Porphyry's commentary on Ptolemy's *Harmonics*, as we now have it, does not reach as far as 3.5 (**T8**).

[28] Winnington-Ingram, in Festugière 1970, vol. 2, 194 does not notice Proclus' use of Ptolemy. The use of Ptolemy's works in the later Neoplatonist schools is a subject which requires further research. We still have access to Proclus' use and critique of Ptolemy's *Almagest* in his *Outline of Astronomical Hypotheses*.

be a harmonious octave made of three terms, reason, spirit and desire. Of these three, spirit as intermediary constitutes in one respect a consonance of the fourth and, in another, a consonance of the fifth: a fifth in the consonance of reason with spirit, a fourth in the consonance of spirit with desire. But the Pythagoreans called the latter '*syllabē*' as not being a perfect consonance, whereas the fifth is more of a consonance than it.[29] So spirit is to be granted as having a greater consonance in relation to reason than desire has in relation to spirit, even if the distance between the latter two terms is lesser than that between the former two, for the latter two [spirit and desire] are just strivings (*orexeis*), whereas the former two are reason and striving. Thus the consonance of spirit with reason is greater, even if the distance between them is greater, than that between spirit and desire, even if the distance between them is lesser. For as has been said also before [at 211.18–20], by nature spirit likes to ally itself with reason and prefers to fight on the side of reason, rather than on the side of desire, when these two are in conflict. Therefore consonance is to be ascribed more to the relation between spirit and reason than to the relation between desire and spirit. But we should say that the consonance constituted by all these intervals is the octave, which again the Pythagoreans named the 'most perfect' of all consonances.[30] And this consonance is indeed truly so. For of all consonances it alone has this in particular (this Timaeus tells us),[31] that the movements of faster sounds are caught up when they cease by those of the slower sounds, and in doing this they join the beginning to the end and produce one movement which quietly ceases in going from the fast to the slow. Since then only the octave is this kind of consonance, it alone is appropriate to the one harmony of soul, which pervades all of the parts of soul, which binds the motions of the lower parts with those of the higher, which naturally harmonizes the tensions of the latter with the slacking of the former, truly making one life out of many.[32] With this digression, we have shown how Socrates could say that moderation is a harmony of the octave.[33]

Ptolemy (in **T8**) assigns the consonances (intervals) of the octave, fifth and fourth to the virtues of the particular *parts* of the soul, reason, spirit and desire, whereas justice is the consonance of the soul as a whole. However, here Proclus assigns the fifth and fourth to the *relations* between parts of the soul and the octave to *moderation* in the sense that it harmonizes the three parts of the soul. The middle part of the soul,

[29] See Festugière 1970, vol. 2, 195 (Winnington-Ingram, referring to Nicomachus).
[30] See Festugière 1970, vol. 2, 194–5 (Winnington-Ingram, referring to Nicomachus).
[31] Pl. *Ti.* 80a-b. On this text see Pelosi 2010, 172–80.
[32] See Pl. *Resp.* 443e1 (**T** 7): 'from a plurality becomes a unity'.
[33] Procl. *in R.* 1.212.20–213.29 (my translation makes use of that published by Festugière [1970] and his corrections of the Greek text).

spirit, represents, in its relation to reason, the interval of the fifth, and in its relation to desire, the fourth, since the fifth is more of a consonance than the fourth and spirit is nearer to reason than to desire, as being the ally of reason in controlling desire. Fifth and fourth united make up the octave, the most perfect of the consonances. So does moderation unite the various diverging parts and motions of the soul and make for the soul one life out of many.

Indeed, according to Proclus, both moderation and justice are octaves, the former being an 'integrating' consonance, the latter a 'discriminating' consonance. This is information we can derive from Damascius' lectures on the *Phaedo*. In these lectures, Damascius came back to the comparison between the four virtues of Plato's *Republic* and consonant intervals and asked how the virtues could be consonances. In one version of his lectures he is reported as saying:

> [T10] Moderation is harmony, and so is courage, inasmuch as it causes spirit to yield to reason, but to dominate desire. But how about justice, the essence of which is the pursuit of one's own functions? The answer is that justice is discriminating consonance, as moderation is integrating consonance;[34] justice seeks its own in such a way as to keep each thing distinct, yet common to all. Moderation, then, is consonance between the controlling and the controlled, justice between the rulers and the ruled. But in what sense is practical wisdom harmony? As the consonance, Proclus says, between the knower and the known.
>
> However, since practical wisdom, too, is a virtue (seeking what is right and avoiding what is wrong, and apprehending good and evil as distinct kinds by an act of cognition that is also appetitive), it is better to view it as belonging to the sphere of action, and to make it harmony in the sense of consonance between the givers and receivers of benefits.[35]

The first part of this text, ending with the reference to Proclus, probably reports Proclus' views, as set out in his (lost) commentary on the *Phaedo*, to which Damascius adds ('However [. . .] it is better') his own qualifications, as is his practice in the commentary.[36]

We find the same arrangement (Proclus' views, followed by Damascius' critical comments) in the report of another version of his lectures on the *Phaedo*:

[34] See Plato, *Statesman* 282b7: 'And there were, we agreed, two great kinds of expertise in every sphere, that of integration (συγκριτική) and that of discrimination (διακριτική)' (transl. Rowe, slightly modified).

[35] Damascius, *in Phd.* 2.55 (transl. Westerink, slightly modified).

[36] See Westerink's introduction to his edition, 10–11, 16–17.

[T11] In what way is virtue a harmony? Let us grant that moderation could be the octave, in so far as it links desire to reason with spirit as the middle term. But how about courage? Its one aspect, gentleness, could be the fifth, being a relation between reason and spirit; the other, daring, the fourth, since it belongs to spirit and desire.[37] What to say, however, of justice, which is rather a discriminating force? We can view it as communion without confusion. And what to do with practical wisdom, which is a quality of reason alone? It is a consonance in so far as it is knowledge, and knowledge is a consonance between the cognitive faculty and its object.

Some corrections: (1) practical wisdom, too, should be viewed as a virtue, the one by which we elect what is good and shun what is evil; (2) practical wisdom and courage can also be identified with the octave, since each of the virtues extends through the whole of tripartite soul, bestowing its own specific quality on the entire soul; (3) though it is true that practical wisdom is more especially the formative principle of reason and courage of spirit, it should be noted that moderation is similarly peculiar to desire, imposing a certain restraint on its shamelessness and looseness; (4) each virtue is not only common to the whole, spanning the entire soul, but in each part by itself there is also a harmony and a musical proportion, which coordinates the manifold contrary strivings (*orexeōn*) of each several part.[38]

From the first part of this passage we can see, by comparison with **T10**, that Damascius is reporting Proclus' views. In the second part of the passage, Damascius rejects his predecessor's account and supplies a 'better' explanation. According to this, practical wisdom is not adequately viewed merely as a cognitive relation, since it has to do with action and is directed to obtaining the good and avoiding evil: it is an appetitive cognition (**T10**).[39] Furthermore, all four virtues (not just moderation and justice) are consonances of the octave, extending through all parts of the soul, each giving something specific to the whole soul. So is moderation specific to desire, while also concerning all parts. Finally each virtue is a consonance in each part of the soul, since each part includes a multiplicity of opposing strivings which virtue harmonizes. In these brief lecture notes, Damascius effectively deconstructs the exegetical constructions of his predecessors: all four cardinal virtues are 'octaves' in the sense that they all concern the whole soul, and not just one part or another, giving to the whole specific moral qualities, each part of the soul being itself not one, but a multiplicity of strivings,

[37] See the passage in Ptolemy (**T8**) for the virtues of spirit. [38] Damascius, *in Phd.* 1.371–372.

[39] See Aristotle, *Nicomachean Ethics* 6.2.1139a22-24; 6.5.1140b4-6.

which requires a structure harmonizing it and thus allowing it to have (as Proclus had said, in **T9**, following Plato) a life which is one.

What might one conclude from these discussions of Plato's assimilation of cardinal virtues to musical intervals, with regard to the relation between music and 'political' virtue in late ancient Platonism? What is most striking is the importance given to knowledge of music as harmonics, as a theoretical knowledge (M2), in connection with 'political' virtue (V3). Nicomachus and Ptolemy provide this theoretical knowledge, which concerns the formal structures allowing for the acquisition of 'political' virtue. 'Political' virtue involves the use of reason, and reason's rule of the soul will require knowledge including harmonics. Harmonics will provide the structures to be used in audible music (M1) for training the irrational parts of soul ('ethical' virtue). Thus we may conclude that 'political' virtue will be nurtured by harmonics on the level of reason, which will learn this knowledge from, and also perhaps express it in, audible music (M1), a knowledge which is itself the means for imposing reason's rule on the irrational parts of the soul.

10.4.3 The Higher Virtues

In speaking of reason as possessing a knowledge, harmonics (M2), which it uses in producing audible music (M1) so as to control the irrational in soul (V2), we have been speaking of the virtue of reason as a 'political' virtue (V3). But this rational virtue, as 'political' (i.e. practical wisdom), must derive its knowledge from purely theoretical knowledge (theoretical wisdom) which will include harmonics as a pure mathematical science. Thus we can say that the philosopher who reaches complete knowledge of harmonics, as a pure mathematical science, has reached 'theoretical' virtue (V5), in which case the grasp of the science of harmonics (M2) *is* theoretical virtue (V5). Proclus describes in **T4** the ascent to this knowledge which is theoretical virtue. The transition to theoretical virtue (V5) from political virtue (V3) is mediated by purificatory virtue (V4). In the case of music, we can suppose that this purification takes place when reason learns to turn away from the rational patterns expressed by audible music to the purely intelligible ratios which they express and which make up the knowledge of harmonics. In singing hymns to his gods,[40] the Platonist philosopher could practice an audible music which would lead up, beyond sounds, to a purely intellectual activity, a knowledge which, as harmonics, could be said to be

[40] On the singing of hymns in late ancient Platonism, see Van den Berg 2001, ch. 5, 4.

an inaudible, intellectual song.[41] More precisely, the philosopher, in knowing the science of harmonics, is projecting in mathematical thought the essential rational principles (*ousiōdeis logoi*) which are the sources of mathematical concepts, which are innate, constituting as they do the nature of soul, and which themselves image higher, divine principles.[42]

Going up higher on the scale of virtues, we find in Proclus (**T5**) a stage where the true philosopher, by assimilation to the life of the gods through theoretical virtue, shares in the life of the gods, in particular that of Apollo, thus sharing in divine harmony, in the 'song' of the gods (M4).[43] At this stage, the philosopher goes beyond theoretical virtue and moves in the direction of yet higher levels of the virtues, paradigmatic (V6) and theurgic (V7). We might take as an example of the 'song' of the gods the intellectual hymns sung by Apollo in praise of his father Zeus, a song imitated by the philosopher.[44] A further example of an intellectual song sung by divinities might be that sung by the Fates in the myth of Er in Plato's *Republic*.[45] The Sirens also sing in the myth of Er, a song which Proclus describes as follows:

> [T12] For if, as [Plato] said, [the Sirens'] movement is harmonic, they must possess by essence harmonic ratios, as [Timaeus] also says.[46] And if they are carried around, they are themselves certain kinds of circles, as Timaeus also says.[47] And if each of them emits one voice and one tone, they are in all respects intellectual in essence, using simple, non-composite activities, not like our souls which reason and guess in one way or another so as to know beings. And again, if they complete one single harmony, they all dance together, as it were, around one choir-leader, the world-soul.[48]

For Proclus, the 'song' of the Sirens in Plato's myth is not audible but purely intelligible. It is not made up of a multiplicity of sounds harmonized with each other, but each divinity 'sings' one simple, non-composite activity, one 'tone' in unison with that of other divine beings. Both the multiplicity of audible music (its variety of sounds) and the conceptual multiplicity of harmonics (its variety of ratios) in the thinking practiced by

[41] Intellectual, soundless hymns of the ascending soul are mentioned by Proclus, *Exc. Chald.* fr. 1 (end). I omit here the harmony of the spheres, inaudible to us but audible to exceptional souls such as that of Pythagoras, on which see O'Meara 2007.

[42] Proclus, *in Eucl.* 36.20–25; on this see O'Meara 2005, 136.

[43] On this divine life, see Proclus, *in R.* 1.177.15–23.

[44] Proclus, *in R.* 1.57.12–15.

[45] Proclus, *in R.* 2.249.28–251.17.

[46] Plato, *Ti.* 36a.

[47] Plato, *Ti.* 36c.

[48] Proclus, *in R.* 2.238.11–20, discussed by Moro Tornese 2010, 196.

human rational souls give way to greater unity in the music of the gods, where the many becomes more and more one.

10.5 Conclusion

The paradigmatic function which music can have in relation to ethics might be described consequently as follows. Audible music can be used to influence and shape the passions, the irrational aspects of soul's relation to the body, by imposing rational order on soul through the use of specific harmonies and rhythms. This use of music was set out, for the late ancient Platonist, by Plato in his prescriptions in the *Republic* and in the *Laws* as to which kinds of music (in singing and dancing) should be used in the moral education of the young. This rational order could be imposed by others (parents, teachers) on immature children who would acquire thereby good moral characters, 'ethical' virtue. On a higher level of virtue, 'political' virtue, reason imposes this order from within on spirit and desire by means of the knowledge it can have of the principles of rational order, also perhaps using this knowledge for shaping audible music in the education of others (**T3**). The principles of rational order are found originally in a pure mathematical knowledge of the relations between numbers, 'harmonics'. Harmonics thus contains the models of the rational order used to structure an audible music which can provide moral education. The philosopher who fully possesses the theoretical knowledge of harmonics may be said to have reached the level of theoretical virtue. But here 'higher' music, harmonics, is no longer a paradigm or model of virtue, but is identical with theoretical virtue. However, the true philosopher will not stop in reaching this theoretical virtue, but will seek to take part in divine life, in the life of the gods, and thus come to share in their life, a divine 'music' which transcends audible and theoretical music. The theoretical music which the philosopher might possess is then not just a paradigm for lower (audible) music, but is also an image of divine music.

We might note how the theme of the unification of a multiplicity through rational order pervades these hierarchies of virtue and of music. The theme is already formulated by Nicomachus in his definition of concordant intervals in audible music:

> [T13] A system (*systēma*) is an assemblage of two or more intervals. Now while no note in these intervals is consonant with its successor, but always dissonant, some systems (*systēmata*) are consonant and others dissonant. They are consonant when the notes which sound them are different in magnitude, but when struck or sounded simultaneously, mingle with one

> another in such a way that the sound they produce is united (*enoeidē*) and becomes as it were one sound. They are dissonant when the sound from the two of them is heard as divided and unblended.[49]

Consonant intervals (i.e. the proportions constituted by the intervals of the octave, the fifth and the fourth), represent degrees of unification of a multiplicity, of which the octave is the highest degree. These structures of unification obtain in audible music, but also, on a higher level, in harmonics. They serve to organize the diverse strivings in the soul so as to give soul a unified life. The same intensification of unity occurs on the higher levels of virtue, where the different virtues become more and more one. The unification of multiplicity through order increases even further as we transcend the human level and reach a divine life where unification culminates in an activity in which a unifying order is no longer needed, no 'symphony' of the multiple required, where divine activity is one, one 'tone', a truly sublime monotony!

[49] Nicomachus, *Ench.*, ch. 12, transl. Barker 1989, slightly modified.

CHAPTER 11

Harmonics as Theological Paradigm in Proclus

Stephen Gersh

11.1 Proclus' Theological Methods

11.1.1 Four Methods

In the first book of his *Platonic Theology*, Proclus says that there are four modes of theological exposition: the entheastic, the dialectical, the symbolic, and the iconic,[1] which he explains as follows: In the first and entheastic mode – which is used in Plato's *Phaedrus* and in the *Chaldaean Oracles* – the immediate signifieds of the theological discourse are the intellectual gods and the detached gods. However, in the second and dialectical mode – practised by Plato alone in his *Sophist* and *Parmenides* – the immediate signifieds are the One, Being, and the processions from these. The signifying structure is obviously more complicated in the next two modes because Proclus explains that the immediate signifieds are now themselves also signifiers of mediated signifieds. Thus, in the third or symbolic mode – which is used in Plato's *Gorgias*, *Symposium*, and *Protagoras* and in the Orphic poems – the immediate signifieds of the theological discourse are the combats, adulteries, and castrations of the gods, and the mediated signifieds are the three demiurges, union through love, and divine distributions to mortal lives. Finally, in the fourth and iconic mode – which is used in Plato's *Timaeus* and *Statesman* and in the Pythagorean texts – the immediate signifieds are political man, the figures of the four elements, the divisions of psychic substance, and political regimes, and the mediated signifieds are the encosmic gods.[2]

In describing the four methods of theological exposition, Proclus emphasizes the superiority of the first two modes: the entheastic and the

[1] *Th. Pl.* 1.4.17.9–23.11. On this topic see Gersh 2000.
[2] In his *Commentary on the Parmenides*, Proclus states the same theory albeit with less emphasis on the signifying structure, this account providing us with the further information that the entheastic mode has among its immediate signifieds the gods called 'Zonai' and 'Azonai', that the dialectical mode was used by the Eleatics and has among its immediate signifieds whole and parts and same and other, that the symbolic mode has among its immediate signifieds Ouranos, Cronos, and Zeus; and that the

dialectical, over the second two: the symbolic and the iconic, by noting that these methods avoid reference to corporeal and psychic things,[3] and the employment of indirect,[4] ambiguous,[5] and dramaturgical signifiers.[6] In other words, the entheastic and the dialectical methods are to be preferred because their signifieds are exclusively *immediate* and more elevated metaphysically than the immediate *and* mediated signifieds of the symbolic and iconic methods. We might add that Proclus' relative evaluation of the different theological modes is consistent with the primacy of textual authority that he generally accords to the *Chaldaean Oracles* – the quintessential entheastic text – and to Plato's *Parmenides* – the quintessential dialectical text. Moreover, the *Chaldaean Oracles* is the fundamental textbook for the theurgic practices that have been the indispensable complement of philosophy in the Athenian school of Platonism, while the *Parmenides* as interpreted by Proclus' teacher Syrianus has provided the structural basis for the same school's interpretation of the divine hierarchies as a whole.

However, leaving aside Proclus' statements about the theory of theological exposition and turning instead to his practice as an exegete, we discover that in his employment of the four modes there is as much convolution as there is demarcation. First, the dialectical mode frequently overlaps with the entheastic mode: for example, where he argues that the *Parmenides* is the most 'epoptic' dialogue,[7] and that it contains mystical conceptions, the hymnodic genealogy of gods, the kindling of the entire and complete light of theological science, and initiation into mysteries.[8] The references to light and mysteries suggest the entheastic milieu of the *Chaldaean Oracles*. Second, the dialectical mode can overlap with the iconic mode. Thus, Plato's doctrine is said to agree with the mystagogy of Orpheus as transmitted to Aglaophamus and to Pythagoras,[9] and the Platonic theologian is said to require prior training in physics, since physics relates to theology as image to paradigm.[10] Perhaps most importantly, the arrangement of Parmenides' hypotheses in the dialogue named after him – which are themselves *dialectical* – is constantly described as having an *iconic*

iconic mode was used by Philolaus and has among its immediate signifieds arithmetical and geometrical terms (*in Prm.* 1.645.7–647.18).

[3] *Th. Pl.* 1.3.12.11–13.5. [4] *Ibid.* 1.2.9.21–24. [5] *Ibid.* 1.17.81.9–10. [6] *Ibid.* 1.5.26.20–21.

[7] *Ibid.* 1.10.44.6.

[8] *Ibid.* 1.7.31.12–32.12. Cf. *in Prm.* 7.1191.25–26 where the first hypothesis of the dialogue is characterized as a theological hymn. On the overlapping of the dialectical and the entheastic see also *in R.* 2.7.26 ff. and 2.9.27 ff. on Homer as dialectician. A residual element of demarcation between the two modes would be that the entheastic has no need of argument.

[9] *Th. Pl.* 1.5.25.24–26.4. [10] *Ibid.* 1.2.10.25–11.4.

relation to the structure of reality,[11] in that division and resolution imitate procession and reversion,[12] in that the first hypothesis relates to the fourth as paradigm to image with the third hypothesis being a mediator,[13] and in that the middle terms of syllogisms imitate the middle ranks of the divine orders.[14] Here, it is the references to the Pythagorean tradition and to the structure of paradigm and image that point explicitly to the iconic mode. Third, the dialectical mode frequently overlaps with the symbolic mode: for example, where Proclus argues that the One of Parmenides' third hypothesis is no longer transcendent because it is 'swallowed' by being,[15] and that the relation between the fifth and first hypotheses is one of dissimilar similitude.[16] The reference to swallowing suggests the symbolic milieu of the Orphic poems, the notion of dissimilar similitude being elsewhere utilized by Proclus to define 'symbol' as such.[17]

11.1.2 Harmonics as Iconic

The present chapter will consist of a brief exploration of Proclus' handling of iconic theology and especially of the harmonic component within that theology. Although there does not seem to be any passage in which the great Platonic commentator actually introduces the term 'harmonic theology', there is little doubt that he implicitly exploits this conception at considerable length. Given that Plato's *Timaeus* and *Statesman* and the Pythagorean writings have been described as the main texts in which iconic theology is practised, and that the immediate signifieds of this theology have been said to include the figures of the four elements and the divisions of psychic substance, the iconic theology is obviously based primarily on mathematics. Moreover, harmonics is an essential component of the mathematical curriculum for any writer who follows the Nicomachean tradition according to which it is necessary to study four arts in order to ascend to wisdom: arithmetic, the art of absolute multitude; music, the art of relative

11 *Ibid.* 1.7.32.10–12, cf. 1.10.46.2–5. 12 *Ibid.* 1.9.40.5–8. 13 *Ibid.* 1.12.57.8–58.7.

14 *Ibid.* 1.11.53.23–54.11. On the overlapping of the dialectical and the iconic see also *in Tim.* 1.223.31 ff., 235.32–238.5; 240.17 ff.; and 275.3 ff. Diehl where similar hypotheses are applied to the world in its generatedness.

15 *Th. Pl.* 1.12.57.26–58.7. Cf. *in Prm.* 5.1035.4–5. The residual element of demarcation between the two modes would be that the iconic needs the projection of *logoi* into the imagination.

16 *Th. Pl.* 1.12.57.18–20. On the overlapping of the dialectical and the symbolic see also *in R.* essay 6 as a whole.

17 Especially, in his exegesis of Homer. See *in R.* 1.83.26–84.12, etc.

multitude; geometry, the art of stable magnitude; and astronomy, the art of mobile magnitude.[18] The reference noted above to the divisions of psychic substance as the immediate signified of iconic theology points directly to a harmonic subspecies of this theology. The same can be said of Proclus' interpretation of the hypotheses of the *Parmenides* as a structure of extremes and mediation.

There are perhaps two texts that best illustrate Proclus' application of 'harmonic theology': the *Commentary on the Timaeus* and the *Elements of Theology*. Given that the Proclean iconic theology generally overlaps – in the manner described earlier – with the other modes of theological exposition and especially with the dialectical mode, we will with respect to both of these texts combine a more detailed discussion of what they have to say about the harmonic component of iconic theology with some briefer remarks on their doctrinal stance with respect to the corresponding component of dialectical theology.[19]

11.2 The *Timaeus* Commentary

Although the *Timaeus* is seen by Proclus as a text whose unifying 'aim' (*skopos*) concerns physics – at one point he attacks Porphyry for treating the introductory material as ethical and the main body of the text as physical –[20] he also insists on its theological dimension in certain passages. Near the beginning of the commentary, Plato's words 'one, two, three' are said to represent an 'intimation' (*endeixis*) of the divine orders' triadicity.[21] Moreover, Plato's discovery of the efficient, paradigmatic, and final causes unknown to earlier thinkers allowed him to talk about the demiurgic intellect, the intelligible cause, and the Good respectively in the *Timaeus*. This in its turn enabled him to study the intelligible, the intellectual, and the intramundane gods and to render the whole world a 'god endowed with intellect and soul' (*theos ennous empsychos*).[22] The final comment shows that Proclus reconciles the unitary aim of the dialogue with simultaneous physical and theological expositions through the structure of iconicity.[23]

[18] See Nicomachus, *Intr. arithm.* 1.4.20–5.12 and 1.5.13–6.16.

[19] In the present chapter and for obvious reasons, it will not be possible to explain in detail the underlying principles of Proclean theology. For an introduction to some of these questions, see Gersh 2014.

[20] *in Ti.* 1.19.24–29. Cf. 1.77.28–78.1.

[21] *Ibid.* 1.17.9–15.

[22] *Ibid.* 1.4.4–5.

[23] According to *Th. Pl.* 1.2.10.25–11.4 the relation between the physical and the theological would be that in which the former is propaedeutic to the latter.

II.2.1 Harmonics

One of the most concentrated discussions of harmonic theology in the *Commentary on the Timaeus* can be found in the section dealing with the harmony of the soul's substance.[24] After some introductory material this section takes the form of two interpretations of the lemma at *Ti.* 35b4-6: 'He took away a first portion from the whole of it, and after that a second portion twice the first, and again a third which was one and a half times the second and three times the first.'[25] The first interpretation itself is divided into a first subsection comprising a 'mathematical contemplation' (*mathēmatikē theōria*)[26] and a second comprising an 'interpretation of the realities' (*pragmateiōdēs exēgēsis*).[27] It is in this second section that the theological aspects come into relief, and these theological aspects may perhaps be contextualized under two main headings: (1) the soul's substance as *logos* – a term which must be translated into English in various contexts as 'reason', or 'reason-principle', or 'ratio'; and (2) the soul's substance as mean or container of means.

(1) A fundamental premiss of Proclus' interpretation is that the substance of soul is *logos*. This point is set out clearly in a passage where he connects psychology simultaneously with politics and theology in arguing that the soul's substance can be understood as containing three means.[28] These means are held to be the images of the three daughters of Themis, the geometrical mean being the image of *Eunomia*, the harmonic mean that of *Dikē*, and the arithmetical mean that of *Eirēnē*, the cubic proportion that contains the powers of all three being consecrated to Themis herself. Timaeus has called these means 'bonds' (*desmoi*). Because these means are unifying and connective, they can be understood as penetrating through the entire substance of soul, making it a single whole from a multiplicity of parts, and possessing a power of binding a variety of forms. In fact, just as a single ratio (*logos*) pervades the three terms in the case of geometry, so does a single reason-principle (*logos*) penetrate through all first, second, and third things in the sphere of psychology.[29]

But what kind of division of the soul's substance is implicit in its interpretation as *logos*? Proclus provides us with both a negative and a positive answer to this important question. The negative answer is that the

24 For a summary of this section, see *Excursus I* of the present chapter. 25 *in Ti.* 2.174.11–14.
26 *Ibid.* 2.174.15–193.6. 27 *Ibid.* 2.193.7–211.30.
28 The political significance of the means is explained on the basis of Plato, *Laws* 6.757b-e.
29 *in Ti.* 2.198.14–200.21.

division of the soul is neither in the manner of 'bodily division' (*diairesis sōmatikē*), nor according to geometrical 'extensions' (*diastēmata*), nor according to 'quantitative' (*kata to poson*) number, nor in the manner of 'seminal reason-principles' (*logoi spermatikoi*), nor in the manner of 'theorems within science' (*tēs epistēmēs theōrēmata*), nor according to the 'othernesses of essential beings' (*tōn ousiōn heterotētes*).[30] The affirmative answer is that, because the soul is causally dependent on the Demiurge, who fashioned it according to 'perfect measures' (*teleia metra*) and 'intelligible paradigms' (*noēta paradeigmata*), the division of the soul is in an 'incorporeal, intellectual, and undefiled' (*aylos, noeros, achrantos*) manner. The Demiurge perfects the substance of the soul by generating the multiplicity within it and collecting it into order through a 'harmony' (*harmonia*) and holding its divisions together.[31]

The nature of the soul's division specified in these passages obviously implies a particular conception of the soul's substantial *logos*, and Proclus explains clearly what this is in a passage where the last stage of the division is described. Here, when Timaeus says that all the epimoric ratios (4:3) are filled in by the interval of the *epogdoos* and the lemma (256:243),[32] he is interpreted as showing that the terminations of all the 'ratios' (*logoi*) have included more and more partial realities until the point where soul has pre-embraced the causes of the last and most partial things in the universe. According to the will of the Demiurge, the soul has established in itself the principles of these things' 'order' (*taxis*) and 'harmony' (*harmonia*). It therefore contains the principles of 'harmonious procession' (*enarmonios proodos*) and of reversion, and of the division into 'first' (*prōta*), 'middle' (*mesa*), and 'last' (*eschata*). This structure is a single 'intellective reason-principle' (*logos noeros*) composed of all the 'ratios' (*logoi*).[33]

(2) Closely connected with the notion that the soul is a substantial *logos* is the notion that the soul is a 'mean' (*meson*) and a container of means.[34] Both ideas are illustrated in a passage where Proclus explains that the

[30] *Ibid.* 2.193.13–194.4. Proclus also provides a brief justification for each of these points.

[31] *Ibid.* 2.194.4–17. A little later Proclus notes that, in order to understand the soul's structure, it is necessary to ascend in contemplation from the 'apparent' (*phainomenē*) harmony – produced by sounds entering the ears – to the 'substantial and incorporeal' (*ousiōdēs kai aylos*) harmony. See *ibid.* 2.195.11–15.

[32] The amount left over when two tones (9:8) are subtracted from the fourth (4:3).

[33] *Ibid.* 2.207.1–21. The passage provides an excellent illustration of the ambiguity of the term *logos* which appears in two senses in the single final sentence.

[34] Proclus makes the connection between these two ideas very clear when he says at *ibid.* 2.200.9–11 that the Demiurge assigned three 'means' (*mesotētes*) to the soul 'insofar as' (*hōs*) they bind the 'mediate' (*mesē*) order of the wholes, the mediate order being of course the psychic.

Demiurge has two powers – the one producing sameness and the one producing otherness – with which he 'divides' (*diairei*) and 'binds together' (*syndei*) the soul. With respect to the exercise of these powers there are four causes: (1) the final cause: the purposiveness whereby the soul could be 'the mediator of the wholes' (*mesē tōn holōn*) by having two ranks before it – gods or henads and essential beings or unifieds – and two ranks after it – things divided or immanent forms and things totally divided or bodies;[35] (2) efficient causes: the sameness and the otherness just mentioned above; (3) paradigmatic causes: the 'sections' (*tomai*) and the 'bonds' (*desmoi*) of the Father, or Demiurge,[36] by which he first cuts things and then binds them ineffably;[37] and (4) formal causes: the 'numbers' (*arithmoi*) that are the formal causes of the divisions,[38] and the 'means' (*mesotētes*) that are the formal causes of the 'bonds' (*syndesmoi*) and of the 'ratios' (*logoi*) that complete them.[39] From this passage, we can therefore conclude that the soul *is a mean* according to final causality and *contains means* according to formal causality.

The passage, however, points to some apparent ambiguities regarding the status of the bonds and the relation between the bonds and the means. In the description of the paradigmatic causes' relation to the production of soul, bonds appear on the level of the Demiurge himself. This would place them on a metaphysical level prior to the soul-*logos* and presumably to the soul's own bonds. It would also establish these bonds as prior to the means in the metaphysical sense and therefore as causes of the latter. On the other hand, in the account of the formal causes' relation to the production of soul, the bonds appear on the level of immanent forms. This would place the bonds on a metaphysical level subsequent to the soul-*logos* and the soul's own bonds. It would also situate these bonds in metaphysical posteriority to the means and therefore as effects of the latter. The solution to all these questions is undoubtedly that Proclus understands there to be at least three levels of bond or perhaps more truly – holding fast to the

[35] Proclus does not actually specify immanent forms and bodies here, although his intention seems reasonably clear.

[36] The context shows that the 'father' here is the Demiurge, understood symbolically as Jupiter.

[37] Proclus notes that the theologians refer to these enigmatically in speaking of the castration of Kronos and the bonds with which the maker of the universe surrounds himself, and that Socrates refers to these matters in the *Cratylus*. This note is a good illustration of the interweaving of 'iconic' and 'symbolic' theology.

[38] The 'portions' (*moirai*) are said to be according to these numerical formal causes.

[39] *Ibid.* 2.208.20–209.15. Proclus concludes by noting that there is in this context no reference to the 'accessory causes' (*synaitia*) performing the role of matter, since these will not be relevant to the structuring of incorporeal soul.

underlying principles of Proclean metaphysics – a three-level emanation of *desmos*.

The placing of the bonds on a metaphysical level prior to the soul-*logos* and to the soul's own bonds can be paralleled in an earlier explanation in the same commentary where Proclus describes the three bonds, it being important to note here that the commentator in referring to the bonds' relation to the *multiplicity* of souls is clearly assuming the priority of the bonds to the psychic level *as such*.[40] He states that: (1) The geometrical bond connects the totality of *substance* present in souls. Just as the geometrical mean assigns the same ratios to all its terms, so does the geometrical bond reveal the presence of unified substance in all things. (2) The harmonic bond maintains all the *sameness* distributed among the souls and predominates among *universal* things. Just as the harmonic mean assigns the largest ratios to the largest numbers and the smallest ratios to the smallest numbers, so does the harmonic bond reveal that the things greater in substance have more power vested in sameness. (3) The arithmetical bond binds all the *otherness* of procession in soul, and predominates among particular things. Just as the arithmetical mean assigns the smallest ratios to the largest numbers and the largest ratios to the smallest numbers, so does the arithmetical bond reveal that the things lesser in substance have more power vested in otherness.[41] In addition to the metaphysical priority of bonds over means, this passage reveals two further important points: first, that the bonds are analogous to means presumably as the intellectual is analogous to the mathematical;[42] and second, that the three bonds represent the psychogonic instantiation of the intellectual genera of substance, sameness, and otherness.

In the present connection, it is important to emphasize that when Proclus discusses the soul's substance on the one hand as *logos* and on the other as mean or container of means, he is not *only* dealing with psychology. When discussing the soul's substance as *logos*, Proclus noted that the division of the soul is in an 'incorporeal, intellectual, and undefiled' manner and that the structure of soul is a single 'intellective reason-principle' composed of all the 'ratios', while in discussing the soul's substance as mean or container of means, he argued that it had as its paradigmatic causes the 'sections' and the 'bonds' of the Demiurge by which he first cuts things and then binds them ineffably (the paradigmatic

40 The following summary is based on *ibid.* 2.199.6–19 and 199.32–200.9.

41 At *ibid.* 2.200.9–21 there is a briefer summary of the same points. See also *ibid.* 2.209.31–210.5.

42 Intellectual because Demiurgic.

causes being intelligible causes), that the bonds are analogous to means as the intellectual is analogous to the mathematical, and that the three bonds represent the psychogonic instantiation of substance, sameness, and otherness – these being intelligible genera.[43] In other words Proclus, by constantly assimilating soul to the higher spheres of intellectuality and intelligibility, is studying both psychology and theology and assuming an iconic relation between the former and the latter.

II.2.2 Dialectics

Now, in addition to the harmonic aspect of iconic theology *per se* that we have been studying, there is also a harmonic aspect of iconic theology overlapping with dialectical theology that needs to be considered. Given that this is potentially a larger area of study, we will confine ourselves to citing briefly some of the more notable examples, using the features identified as salient to dialectical theology in the discussion of the four modes of theological exposition cited earlier.[44]

According to the first book of Proclus' *Platonic Theology* and the parallel passage of the *Commentary on the Parmenides*, the objects studied in dialectical theology include Being, procession, and the correlative terms sameness-otherness and whole-parts. The discussion of the harmony of the soul's substance in the *Commentary on the Timaeus* contains numerous passages in which components of the psychogonic division are referred to the remaining, procession, and reversion that constitute the mechanism of causality from the level of the gods or henads downwards according to Proclean metaphysics. From the discussion of the 'portions' (*moirai*) of the soul – the numbers 1, 2, 4, 8, 3, 9, 27 – we learn that the soul according to its first portion (#1) remains in the things prior to it,[45] according to its second (#2) and third portions (#3) proceeds and reverts respectively in relation to intellect, according to its fourth (#4) and fifth portions (#9) proceeds and reverts on itself, and according to its sixth (#8) and seventh portions (#27) makes subsequent things proceed and revert respectively.[46] Apart from the passages concerning the four causes and the soul and the relation between

43 The psychogonic instantiation of intelligible genera becomes even more clear when one turns from Proclus' description of the means to his description of the ratios. For some illustrations of these complex arguments, see *Excursus II* of the present chapter.

44 See above pp. 242–3.

45 For 'remaining' see *ibid.* 2.205.32–206.1.

46 *Ibid.* 2.206.13–29. Proclus gives three explanations of the portions in connection with the remaining, procession, and reversion of soul at *ibid.* 2.203.29–205.31, 2.205.31–206.13, and 2.206.13–29, providing various amounts of detail. He says that the last passage – which we have summarized – is most in agreement with the 'realities' (*pragmata*). Cf. also *ibid.* 2.209.16–32.

bonds and means considered earlier,[47] referral of the components of the psychogonic division to the intelligible paradigms of sameness and otherness occurs in a passage where Proclus considers the simultaneously monadic and dyadic aspects of the soul proceeding from beginning to end. Here, the Demiurge is said to have 'guided upwards' (*anagein*) the soul's *hyparxis* towards being, sameness, and otherness, and then to have contemplated the number emerging from the first portion and divided it in a twofold manner into the double and triple series.[48] Finally, referral of the components of the psychogonic division to the intelligible paradigms of whole and parts occurs in a passage where Proclus explains that the Demiurge fashioned the soul as a whole 'before the parts' (*pro tōn merōn*) in that he allowed it to remain undiminished in the derivation of its parts, as a whole 'of parts' (*ek tōn merōn*) in that he exhausts the soul as a mixture in its division into parts but reconstituted it as harmony as these parts are fitted together, and as a whole 'in each of the parts' (*en hekastōi tōn merōn*) in that he divided it into circles and placed all of the *logoi* into each one.[49]

11.3 Elements of Theology

Now if the argument of this essay – that Proclus has a prominent albeit secondary agenda of 'harmonic theology' in the *Commentary on the Timaeus* – is valid, then we ought to find some evidence confirming this fact in his primarily theological writings. In the study of the commentary, it emerged that Proclus' discussions of the substance of the soul as *logos* and of the substance of the soul as mean and as container of means were important indices of the theological tendency in his treatment of the soul's harmony. Therefore, the most appropriate questions for us to pose now should probably include the following: Do the notions of *logos* and mean play a role in the theological writings of Proclus and, if so, what roles precisely do they play? We will take the *Elements of Theology* as being the most likely place to find answers to these questions.[50]

[47] See above pp. 247–9. On the connection between the means and the triad of substance, sameness, and otherness, see also *ibid.* 2.210.1–2.

[48] *Ibid.* 2.196.19–23.

[49] *Ibid.* 2.195.25–196.8. Proclus next adds an important clarification: namely, that each of the three genera mentioned earlier – being, sameness, and otherness – exists in the part 'just as' (*kathaper*) it does in the whole. Therefore, every part is 'somehow' (*pōs*) the whole in having a similarly triadic structure.

[50] It will not be necessary here to dwell on the obvious fact that the objects of theological exposition earmarked in the *Platonic Theology* – the One, being, procession, sameness-otherness, and whole-parts – are prominent throughout the *Elements of Theology*. For the One, see *El. Th.* props. 1–6

11.3.1 Logoi

The term *logos* appears only occasionally in the *Elements of Theology*. However, the relative infrequency of the term itself should not lead us to conclude that the notions underlying the term are less important in that text. On the contrary, the entire work consists of propositions and proofs which exemplify one of the main senses of *logos* as a combination of thinking and the relation between the one and the many in syllogistic argument.[51] Moreover, a sense of *logos* that is of more direct relevance to harmonic theology: that of 'proportional relation' – this expression being perhaps the best in English to capture the simultaneous connotations of 'reason-principle', 'relation', and 'ratio' – is particularly common in this treatise. Here, the proportional relation is between the whole and the part or else between the one and the many or more properly within both these correlative pairs simultaneously, being thereby fundamental to Proclus' conception of the numerous orders and series of hypostases as set out in the work's propositions and proofs.[52]

The most important points regarding this sense of *logos* may perhaps be summarized briefly as follows: (1) *Logoi govern simple relations between parts and wholes.* Proclus argues that in each order or causal chain among the higher realities there exists a single monad prior to the manifold which determines for the members of the order their 'unique proportional relation to one another and to the whole' (*hena logon … pros te allēla kai pros to holon*).[53] (2) *Logoi are multiple relations. They govern sets of relations between one part and another.* One proposition states that every particular soul with respect to the divine soul under which it is ranked 'has the same proportional relation' (*touton echei ton logon*) as does its vehicle to the vehicle of the divine soul.[54] (3) *Logoi are multiple relations. They govern sets of relations not only between one part and another but between parts and the whole.* Within the proof of another proposition, stating that the first members of a

Dodds; for being, *ibid.*, props. 66, 73, 86–89; for procession, *ibid.*, props. 33–35; for sameness-otherness, *ibid.*, props. 30 and 35; for whole-part, *ibid.*, props. 65–67.

51 For *logos* as argument, see Proclus, *El. Th.* props. 59, proof 58.2; 62, proof 58.32; 145, proof 128.16; for *logos* as demonstration: prop. 111.98.31–32. Proclus also restates his general view that *logos* is an aspect of cognition. As such it is a real thing and relates to real things in prop. 123, proof 108.29–31. All 'knowledge through a reason-principle' (*dia logou gnōsis*), inasmuch as it grasps intelligible notions and subsists in acts of intellections, is knowledge 'of real existents' (*tōn ontōn*). Its power of apprehending truth is 'among real things' (*en tois ousin*).

52 For the general structuring function of *logos*, see *ibid.*, prop. 18, proof 20.14–16.

53 *Ibid.*, prop. 21, proof 24.15–18.

54 *Ibid.*, prop. 205.180.4–6. Cf. prop. 164, proof 142.19–22; 185, proof 162.6–9; 203, proof 178.5–7. In these cases, *logos* = *analogy*.

monadic series are conjoined by community of nature with the members of the series placed above it, whereas the last members of the series have no contact with the latter, Proclus observes: 'Such terms are not identical in their proportional relation but in the relation whereby they are derived from and referred back to a single term' (*oude gar heis ho logos, all'hōs aph'henos kai pros hen*).[55] (4) *Logoi are more universal and less universal, and they determine the status of things 'according to participation'.* Another proposition states that all those characters 'having the proportional relation of a substratum in participants' (*en tois metechousin hypokeimenōn echonta logon*) proceed from more perfect and more universal causes.[56] (5) *Logoi are more universal and less universal, and they determine the status of things 'according to causality'.* Within another proof, we read that fathers differ as 'more universal or less universal' (*olikōteroi ... merikōteroi*) – as do the divine orders themselves – according to the 'proportional relation of their causality' (*kata ton tēs aitias logon*).[57] (6) *A logos determines the status of a monadic term as 'monadic'.* Within the proof of a proposition stating that there are series of terms beginning with a monad and proceeding to a coordinate multiplicity, Proclus introduces the words: 'For the monad, having the proportional relation of an originative principle ... ' (*hē men gar monas, archēs echousa logon*).[58] (7) *A logos determines the status of an unparticipated term as 'unparticipated'.* Within the proof of a proposition stating that the first term in each series must be unique, Proclus includes the words: 'For the unparticipated, having the proportional relation of a monad ... ' (*to men gar amethekton, monados echon logon ...*).[59]

II.3.2 Means

As in the case of the *Commentary on the Timaeus*, the notion of *logos* – understood especially with emphasis on its harmonic connotations – is closely connected with the notion of mean, and in the *Elements of Theology*, the notion of mediation supplies one of the major building blocks of the complex structure of henads-gods, intellects, and souls that represents the Proclean order of reality. According to one of Proclus' propositions, every causal principle establishes things similar to itself before it establishes things dissimilar to itself.[60] The proof shows that the effect cannot be

[55] *Ibid.*, prop. 110, proof 98.12–14.
[56] *Ibid.*, prop. 72.68.17–18. Further examples of the application of the term *logos* in the next four cases can be found at prop. 195, proof 170.10–13 and prop. 194, proof 168.31–170.3.
[57] *Ibid.*, prop. 151, proof 132.34–134.1. [58] *Ibid.*, prop. 21, proof 24.4.
[59] *Ibid.*, prop. 23, proof 26.25. [60] *Ibid.*, prop. 28.32.10–11.

the same as the cause and that, if it is other than the cause, it cannot be completely other than it, or partly other than it and partly the same as it in equal degrees, or partly other than it and partly the same as it but other to a greater degree. The result is that the effect must be partly other than the cause and partly the same as it but the same to a greater degree: in other words, every causal principle produces relatively dissimilar effects through the mediation of relatively similar ones.[61] Having established in a further proposition and proof that the reversion of effects to causes is as much dependent on this rule of similarity as is procession,[62] Proclus concludes in a later proof that an effect which proceeds 'immediately' (*amesōs*) from any cause immediately reverts towards it, whereas an effect that requires 'mediation' (*mesotēs*) in its procession also requires mediation in its reversion.[63] Here, the immediate effect corresponds to the similar effect mentioned in the earlier proposition, and the mediated effect to the dissimilar effect.

It is because Proclus is applying the general rule of causation stated above that we find so many metaphysical principles arranged in triadic configurations where either the first and third terms are the extremes and the second is the mean or the first and second are the extremes and the third is the mean, the difference between these two arrangements seemingly resulting from whether the triad is viewed as more static or as more dynamic. Thus, he describes the henads-gods in various propositions by saying that 'all the orders of gods are bound together by means' (*pasai tōn theōn hai taxeis mesotēti syndedentai*),[64] that every divine order is united to itself in a threefold manner 'from its highest extreme, from its mean, and from its last term' (*apo te tēs akrotētos tēs en autēi kai apo tēs mesotētos kai apo tou telous*),[65] and that the powers of the gods beginning from above and 'proceeding through the suitable means' (*dia tōn oikeiōn proiousai mesotētōn*) reach down to the last things.[66] Given that the henads-gods are classified – in accordance with Syrianus' interpretation of the *Parmenides* – according to the other things that participate in them, we find Proclus applying the same structure of extremes and means to all the levels of intelligible, intelligible-and-intellectual, intellectual, psychic, and physical realities. The justification for positing means in this manner is perhaps rendered most explicit in another passage where Proclus proves that there must be a mean between that which is participated in a separable manner – the soul – and that

[61] *Ibid.*, prop. 28, proof 32.12–34.2. [62] *Ibid.*, prop. 32, proof 36.3–10.

[63] *Ibid.*, prop. 38, proof 40.20–25. Proclus adds that the effect will revert first to the 'mean term' (*to meson*) and second to 'the term superior to the mean' (*to tou mesou kreitton*).

[64] *Ibid.*, prop. 132.116.28. [65] *Ibid.*, prop. 148.130.4–5. [66] *Ibid.*, prop. 140.124.1–3.

which participates – the body, this mean being an irradiation of the soul;[67] and again where he argues that there must be a mean between that which exists eternally – the things above and on the level of soul – and that which comes to be in parts of time – the sublunary elements, the mean here being that which is or comes to be for the whole of time: namely, the world or the heaven.[68]

Excursus I

Analysis of 'in Ti.' 2.193.7–211.30 Diehl

For purposes of better conceptualization, it may be useful to summarize briefly the complete argument of the primary text concerning 'harmonic theology' that was considered above in a piecemeal manner.[69]

1 In the first section, Proclus makes some preliminary remarks regarding the harmonic structure of the soul's substance. He will follow this with sections devoted to the means, ratios, and portions of the soul (**2**), the complete harmony of the soul (**3**), and the causes of the soul's harmonic structure (**4**). The discussion concludes with a summary (**5**).

   1.1 How the analysis to be pursued in this part of his commentary is to be contrasted with that conducted in the previous part.

   1.2 The type of division to be made is contrasted with six other types of division ranked in ascending ontological order.

   1.3 The type of division of the soul is determined by the fact that it was made by the Demiurge in contemplating the Paradigm. We must attempt to understand this type of division by contemplating the Demiurge. In section **4**, Proclus will associate the discussion of section **1.3** with the final causality of the soul's harmonic structure.

   1.4 The soul's substance considered in terms of three kinds of wholeness. That the ensuing discussion is concerned with the soul's substance rather than its power or activity (knowledge) is reiterated in section **5.2**.

   1.5 The monadic and dyadic structure of soul. Through its monadic and dyadic elements, the soul participates in limit and infinity and

[67] *Ibid.*, prop. 81, proof 76.12–21.

[68] *Ibid.*, prop. 55, proof 52.17–29. Of course, there are actually *two* means here.

[69] See pp. 246ff.

manifests Apollonian and Dionysian characteristics. Because of these divine characteristics, the structure of the soul is sevenfold.

2 Detailed analysis of the different levels of the soul's division. Section **2.1** deals with the three means, section **2.2** with seven types of ratio, and section **2.3** with the seven portions. Proclus appears to be moving in a descending order of generality and power.

2.1 The three means and the corresponding 'bonds'. The three bonds are related to soul and souls in themselves. The geometrical bond relates to the harmonic and arithmetical bonds as monad to dyad. The geometrical bond is associated with substance, the harmonic bond with sameness, and the arithmetical bond with otherness. According to section **4**, this discussion concerns part of the soul's formal causality.

2.2 The seven types of ratio in the soul. Proclus provides two distinct analyses in sections **2.21** and **2.23** respectively, inserting a reference to the soul as a sevenfold structure in section **2.22**. He follows the arrangement of the portions in the lambda figure moving across the figure from left to right (1, 2, 3, 4, 9, 8, 27).

2.21 The seven types of ratio in the soul with respect to forms and series.

2.22 The sevenfold structure of soul. The origin of this structure has been described in section **1.5**.

2.23 A further interpretation: the seven types of ratio in the soul with respect to the relation of substance, sameness, and otherness to the lower reason-principles.

2.3 The seven portions in the soul. Proclus provides three distinct analyses in sections **2.31**, **2.32**, and **2.33** which correspond to increasingly elevated viewpoints. In the first and last sections he follows the arrangement of the portions in the lambda figure moving from left to right (1, 2, 3, 4, 9, 8, 27), but in the middle section he follows the arrangement moving from top to bottom on the left and then from top to bottom on the right (1, 2, 4, 8 + 1, 3, 9, 27). In all three sections, he relates the portions to remaining, procession, and reversion, and concludes in section **2.34** by stressing the circular motion of the entire structure.

2.31 First analysis of the soul's portions. The soul's portions are divided into a higher group (1, 2) correlated with intellectual principles above soul and with incorporeal aspects of principles below soul, a middle item (3) correlated with the soul itself and with an incorporeal aspect of principles below soul, and a lower group (4, 9, 8, 27) correlated with the dynamic unfolding of the incorporeal aspects of principles below soul. The description of the third portion supplements section **2.2** by describing the association between the epimoric ratio and reversion.

2.32 Second analysis of the soul's portions. The portions are correlated with aspects of the soul's activity with respect to itself, to the most proximate principles above and below, and to more distant principles above and below.

2.33 Third analysis of the soul's portions. The portions are correlated with the soul's relation to intellect, to itself, and to the subsequent.

2.34 The circular motion of the entire structure.

2.4 The dependence of the ratios upon the means, the hierarchical order of the ratios, and the single reason-principle underlying the system.

3 The total harmony of the soul consisting of four octaves, a fifth, and a whole tone.

3.1 Applications of the total harmony. Correlation of the four octaves with the soul, of the fifth with the world, and of the tone with the relation between soul and world. Introduction of further numbers. The monadic character of intellect, the tetradic character of soul, and the decadic character of world.

3.21 Further applications of the total harmony. The world's numerical structure in itself.

3.22 The world's numerical structure in relation to the Paradigm and the Five Figures.

4 The soul's substance considered with respect to four types of cause: the final, the efficient, the paradigmatic, and the formal. The argument returns to the more general discussion at the end of **1.5**.

5 Summary and conclusion. Because the soul is mediate between the undivided and the divided substance, the first three portions (1, 2, 3) imitate the higher motions of remaining, procession, and reversion, while the subsequent portions (4, 9, 8, 27) pre-contain the incorporeal and corporeal characters of lower things.

5.12 The means. Their relation to substance, sameness, and otherness.

5.13 The ratios. Dependence of the ratios upon the means. Relation between the ratios and aspects of the world. Hierarchy among the ratios. Character of divisions in the higher world.

5.2 The foregoing discussion is restricted to the substance of soul.

Excursus II

Harmonic Theology and Ratios in the 'Commentary on the Timaeus'

Proclus' metaphysical interpretation of the *logoi* as ratios follows the pattern of his interpretation of the means as analysed above and, although he does not usually make the distinction between metaphysical and mathematical modalities among ratios that he did earlier among the means, it seems clear that we must assume something along similar lines.[70] At the beginning of his main discussion of ratio-theory,[71] he states that the soul is a 'plenitude of ratios' (*logōn plērōma*) and that the latter are seven in number: namely, the equal (e.g. 3:3, 10:10), the multiple (e.g. 2:1, 3:1, 4:1), the submultiple (e.g. 1:2, 1:3, 1:4), the epimoric (e.g. 3:2, 4:3, 5:4), the epimeric (e.g. 5:3, 7:4), the subepimoric (e.g. 2:3, 3:4, 4:5), and the subepimeric (e.g. 3:5, 4:7).[72]

Next, Proclus turns to the explanation of the relations between the *logoi* and the corporeal (divisible) world. Here, it is argued that the soul exercises causality with respect to the world by means of these principles, in the first instance exploiting their characteristic of being both indivisible and divisible. Through the indivisibility implicit in them the ratios effect the indivisibility that constitutes the limits of all corporeal things; through their divisibility 'in one way' (*monachē*) – with respect to the larger term in a ratio (e.g. as in multiples such as 2:1) – they produce the line; through their divisibility 'in two ways' (*dichē*) – with respect to both the larger and the smaller term (e.g. as in epimorics such as 3:2) – they produce the plane; and through their divisibility 'in three ways' (*trichē*) – with respect to both the larger and the smaller terms and the difference between them (e.g. as in epimerics such as 5:3) – they produce the solid. Moreover, the following general considerations result from the fact that the simpler numbers are 'greater in causality' (*archikōteroi*) than the more composite ones. Through the *equal*,[73] the soul imparts to everything a common measure and an appearance bearing the 'image' (*eikōn*) of sameness. Through the *submultiple* and *multiple*, it presides

[70] The problem is that there is no handy terminological distinction – as between 'bonds' and 'means' – that he can fall back on. The term *logos* in all its polysemy must therefore be retained in both cases. However, at *ibid.* 2.210.18–20 (and perhaps elsewhere) he seems to refer to the metaphysical analogue of the mathematical ratio by speaking of 'bonds' (δεσμοί).

[71] *Ibid.* 2.210.20–28.

[72] Not the multiples of the latter, which apply only to the bodily sphere. For possible identification of these ratios see the note by Baltzly 2009, *ad loc.*

[73] In his references to 'equal', 'multiple', and so forth in this passage, Proclus is obviously talking about a *general character* implicit in types of ratio.

over the 'series' (*seira*), revealing the 'whole form' (*holon eidos*) of each of the intra-mundane beings 'in all the things patterned after it' (*en tois pasin eidopoioumenois*):[74] for example, the solar form in divine, daemonic, and human souls, irrational animals, plants, and minerals – here, the multiple reveals the unity of the series, and the submultiple the variegation in the progression of the form. Finally, the soul arranges 'more particular genera' (*merikōtera genē*) within 'the more universal series' (*hai seirai hai holikōterai*) as follows: According to the *subepimoric* and *epimoric*, it arranges all the genera that are participated as a whole but only according to one of their constituent species: for example, a horse participates in the genus animal (= a whole) together with the one species horse (= one part of whole). According to the *subepimeric* and *epimeric*, it arranges all the genera that are participated as a whole but also according to a multiplicity of their constituent species: for example, a mule participates in the genus animal (= a whole) together with the two species horse (= one part of whole) and donkey (= another part of whole).[75]

A few paragraphs later, Proclus gives a further explanation of the seven types of ratio in the soul, this time stressing not only the relation between the psychic *logoi* and the corporeal (divisible) world below – as in the previous passage – but also their relation to the intelligible (indivisible) world above.[76] The latter is specified in terms of the genera of being, sameness, and otherness. In addition, the psychic *logoi* here connect the intelligible and corporeal worlds not only through the assumed relation between paradigm and image – as in the previous passage – but through the Proclean principle that everything is in everything else but in each in a manner appropriate to it.[77] Thus, the *equal* imparts to all the psychic reason-principles a communion whereby 'all things share in all things' (*pantes pantōn koinōnein*).[78] This presumably occurs in the case of the relation between unity and the reason-principles.[79] The *multiple* and *submultiple* provide an 'indication' (*endeixis*)[80] of the manner in which the more unified measure the more multiplied, and the more undivided the more

[74] Using Diehl's reasonable conjecture. [75] Proclus, *in Ti.* 2.200.20–202.19.

[76] However, Proclus has already told us in the previous passage that the multiple ratio imparts an image of the intelligible genus of sameness to corporeal things.

[77] For this principle, see Proclus, *El. Th.* prop. 103.92.13–14.

[78] Given that Proclus is here exploring relations between the intelligible and the corporeal worlds, there is clearly a shift in meaning from the purely mathematical sense of *logos* (ratio to a combined metaphysical and mathematical sense [ratio = reason-principle]).

[79] There is a lacuna in the text here, which can, however, be filled by analogy with two passages further along.

[80] The term *endeixis* is a technical term employed by Proclus to describe the revelation of higher (intelligible, theological) truths through lower phenomena.

divided, in both cases with 'the wholes permeating the wholes' (*holoi di'holōn phoitōntes*). This occurs in the case of the relation between being and the reason-principles.[81] The *epimorics* and *subepimorics* are indicative of a mode of sharing in which 'wholes do not share in wholes' (*ouch holoi holois … koinōnousin*), although things are connected 'according to their primary component' (*kath' hen ti*). This occurs in the case of the relation between sameness and the reason-principles. The *epimerics* and *subepimerics* are indicative of a mode of sharing which is 'something divided and multiplied' (*meristē tis … kai peplēthysmenē*) because of the lowering of rank. This occurs in the case of the relation between otherness and the reason-principles.[82]

A little later, Proclus again considers the relation between the psychic *logoi* and the corporeal (divisible) worlds. Here, he examines the dependence of the ratios upon the means[83] – it is because of the arithmetical and harmonic means that the hemiolic (3:2), epitritic (4:3), and *epogdoos* (9:8) appear – and argues that in their causality with respect to subsequent realities the ratios are associated with more particular divisions than are the means. Thus, the hemiolics 'bear the image' (*eikona pherein*) of divisible sharing among the higher partial things, the epitritics the image of divisible sharing among middle-ranking partial things, and the *epogdoos* the image of divisible sharing among the lowest partial things. He adds that Timaeus' statement that all the epitritic ratios (4:3) are filled in by the interval of the *epogdoos* and the lemma (256:243)[84] indicates that the 'terminations' (*apoperatōseis*) of all the ratios – the completion of their causal activity in relation to corporeal things – have included more and more partial realities until the point where soul has pre-embraced the causes of the last and most partial things in the universe.[85] A few paragraphs later Proclus gives some illustrations of how the ratios govern these 'second and third processions of reason-principles' (*deuterai kai tritai tōn logōn proodoi*).[86] The hemiolics bind the harmony of the reason-principles by means of the five centres (i.e. the five regular solids), the epitritics manifest their power through the four elements present everywhere,[87] and the *epogdooi* bring into harmony the division of nine and eight (i.e. the number of the

[81] The connection between being, sameness, and otherness and the three levels of ratios is stated in summary form at the end of the present passage.

[82] Proclus, *in Ti.* 2.203.4–29.

[83] Proclus is now focusing on the mathematical sense of *logos* (ratio) rather than the metaphysical sense.

[84] The amount left over when two tones (9:8) are subtracted from the fourth (4:3).

[85] *Ibid.* 2.207.1–18.

[86] Proclus is again working with both the mathematical and metaphysical sense of *logos*. Here, mathematical *logoi* govern the unfolding of physical *logoi*, presumably the 'seminal' (*spermatikoi*) *logoi* described elsewhere.

[87] Cf. Plato, *Resp.* 8.546b-c.

Muses and Sirens respectively).[88] Having noted that the hemiolics and epitritics are more universal than the *epogdooi*, since they produce a more perfect 'concord' (*symphōnia*) of the world with smaller numbers, and that among the 'incorporeal reason-principles' (*asōmatoi logoi*) the more universal are continuous with the more particular, Proclus now introduces the lowest stage in the procession of the ratios. Thus, if the *epogdooi* are the causes of the most partial concord, 'the ratio that follows them' (*to met'autous*) – presumably the one underlying the semitone – is rightly relegated to the lowest rank of the universe although it is not 'unharmonious' (*asymphōnos*) with the totality, since it draws partial emanations from each of the elements down to the subterranean places.[89]

[88] Hence, the ancients' references to eight Sirens and nine Muses.
[89] Proclus, *in Ti.* 2.210.6–211.10.

CHAPTER 12

Calcidius on Cosmic Harmony

Christina Hoenig

12.1 Introduction

In Plato's *Republic* Socrates describes in flowery terms the influence of beautiful products of art that, like a breeze (*ayra*) flowing to the eyes or ears of the city's future leaders, guides them towards 'likeness, friendship and concord (*symphōnia*) with beautiful reason' (*tōi kalōi logōi*, *Resp.* 401d1-2). That the young men's *symphōnia* with reason is more than a hopeful metaphor becomes clear as Socrates, subsequently, ascribes to musical rhythm and harmony a specific educational role: 'more than anything else rhythm and harmony (*rhythmos kai harmonia*) find their way to the inmost soul and take the strongest hold upon it, bringing with them and imparting grace, if one is rightly trained, and otherwise the contrary'.[1] Further on in Socrates' discussion, at *Resp.* 522c-531d, harmonics is listed as one of the disciplines featuring in the curriculum for the intended leaders of the state, following arithmetic, geometry, stereometry and astronomy. Socrates observes the kinship between astronomy and harmonics: 'as eyes are made for astronomy, so ears are made for harmonious movements. These are sister sciences, as the Pythagoreans say, and we admit' (530d6-9). He subsequently stresses that it is the intended objective for students to recognize the mutual kinship not only between astronomy and harmonics, but between all the disciplines which, if exercised properly, are conducive to thought that is removed from the world of change. For this purpose, nevertheless, scientific training can merely play a preparatory role: 'if the mode of inquiry (*methodos*) into all these studies we mentioned brings us to understand their mutual communion and kinship, and to infer how they are related, then it is useful for our intentions to busy ourselves with them, and our toil is not in vain' (531c9-d4). In the same breath, Socrates concedes

[1] *Resp.* 3.401d5-e1. Cf. 400d-402c, *Leg.* 3.689d-e.

that all these efforts are merely the 'prelude' (πάντα ταῦτα προοίμιά ἐστιν, 531d8) for the students' actual goal, the mastery of dialectic.

Elsewhere, in Plato's *Timaeus*, the dialogue's namesake draws a more explicit connection between the effects of music and the condition of the human soul. The benefits of music are taken out of the exclusive context of the *Republic*'s educational program for the future leaders of the state and are shown to be accessible to a less context-specific group of recipients. 'Those who make intelligent use of the Muses' can benefit from harmonious sound that restores their souls to their former concord (*symphōnia*).

> ... that part of music which is serviceable with respect to the hearing of sound is given for the sake of harmony; and harmony, whose motions are akin (*syggeneis*) to the revolutions of the soul within us, has been given by the Muses to him who makes intelligent use of them (*tōi meta nou proschrōmenōi*),[2] not for the sake of irrational pleasure (which is now thought to be its utility), but as an ally against the inward discord that has come into the revolution of the soul, to bring it into order and concord with itself.[3]

The fourth-century Latin translator and commentator Calcidius recasts the significance of musical education by associating the training received by the *Republic*'s leaders with the knowledge acquired by individuals whom he portrays as experts in the Platonic doctrine that he sets out in his commentary on Plato's *Timaeus*.[4] Harmonic theory is part of an educational program Calcidius describes as *studia humanitatis*, a 'liberal education'.[5] This phrase appears, initially, in his translation of *Ti.* 20a, where it replaces the somewhat vague phrase 'the things of which we are talking' which, in the Greek text, refers to the general expertise in politics and philosophy Socrates ascribes to his interlocutor Critias. In the concluding chapter of his commentary, in turn, Calcidius discusses his Latin translation of *Ti.* 53c, in which his protagonist had announced to the others that the structure of the visible cosmos is to be unfolded 'with a mode of demonstration (*genere demonstrationis*) that, although new and unfamiliar, is not

[2] Cf. the description at *Ti.* 80b6 of such individuals as ἔμφρονες, as opposed to the ἄφρονες who merely derive pleasure from music.

[3] *Ti.* 47c7-d7. Transl. Cornford with minor modifications. Cf. *Ti.* 80b5-8; *Epinomis* 991b.

[4] In his translation of *Ti.* 26d Calcidius deviates from the Greek by drawing specific attention to the fact that a part of the education of the *Republic*'s future leaders was 'musical gentleness' (*musica mansuetudo*), an apparent addition to the original text.

[5] Cf. further, Calc. *in Ti.* 128.366.3, where early humans are described as lacking the *studia humanitatis*, and 168.402.1, where Calcidius uses the phrase *liberalis educatio* to delineate the path towards wisdom (*sapientia*). All citations of Calcidius are according to Bakhouche 2011. All translations of Calcidius are according to Magee 2016, unless indicated otherwise.

unknown to you, who have traveled all the paths of a liberal erudition (*eruditionis ingenuae*), and which will become clear with gentle reminding'.[6] In the Greek original, Timaeus merely notes that his listeners 'have some acquaintance with the technical method (*hodos*) which I must necessarily employ in my exposition',[7] referring, it appears, specifically to the geometrical method that serves to exhibit the composition of the shapes assigned to the four primary bodies by the demiurge. Calcidius' commentary on the passage explains that the *ingenua eruditio* possessed by the dialogue's interlocutors included 'specialized doctrines (*praecipuis doctrinis*) which he (i.e. Plato) called the liberal disciplines (*ingenuas disciplinas*) because in those days people were steeped from childhood in geometry, music (*musica*), arithmetic and astronomy, the first steps, as it were, of higher doctrine (*altioris doctrinae*).'[8] Interestingly, Calcidius in his translation and commentary appears intent on emphasizing that the interlocutors will not be troubled by an unfamiliar 'mode of demonstration', given their broad exposure to the *eruditio ingenua,* which comprises the various disciplines listed. This point is not explicitly made by the Greek speaker, but is rather more in line with Socrates' discussion in Book Seven of the *Republic*, where he makes clear that the scientific disciplines under discussion require an abstract *mode of inquiry* (*methodos, Resp.* 531d1, 523a), a requirement that accounts for their affinity. While Calcidius' emphasis on doctrinal content alongside method, such as it is visible in his translation of *Ti.* 53c, is certainly in line with his general dogmatic approach, it may serve to align his (Latin) protagonist's perspective with that of Socrates in the *Republic.*[9] Overall, in Calcidius' interpretation, this passage of the *Timaeus* appears rather more 'Platonic' than it does in its original context, as was presumably the desired outcome.

The expertise in the four disciplines geometry, music, arithmetic and astronomy Calcidius ascribes to the dialogue's interlocutors is, notably, also what qualifies him as a commentator. It is his professed aim to elucidate by way of his commentary those passages of Plato's work that remain obscure to the non-expert in these disciplines. In chapter 2 of the

6 355.582.20–22. Transl. Magee with slight modification.

7 *Ti.* 53c1-2: μετέχετε τῶν κατὰ παίδευσιν ὁδῶν δι' ὧν ἐνδείκνυσθαι τὰ λεγόμενα ἀνάγκη.

8 355.582.31–34. Arithmetic and geometry guide Calcidius' discussion in chapters 8 to 39, followed by harmonics in chapters 40 to 55, and finally astronomy in chapters 61 until 118. Cf. Reydams-Schils 2007, 314–19; Hicks 2017, 81.

9 Calcidius stresses the connection between the two dialogues at the outset of his commentary, where he presents the *Timaeus* as the sequel to the *Republic*: 'On the previous day, Socrates had given a disputation on the state, in ten complete books . . .' (5.206.19–20), likely in reference to Socrates' remarks at *Ti.* 17c-19a.

work, he announces that a thorough understanding of the obscure Platonic doctrine requires the 'technical assistance (*artificialibus remediis*) of all the sciences, arithmetic, astronomy, geometry and music',[10] the four sciences that, grouped together as the 'quadrivium' and alongside the 'trivium' (grammar, logic and rhetoric), would in the later medieval academic setting constitute the seven liberal arts. In demonstrating his expertise in these disciplines throughout his commentary, Calcidius inserts himself, on a narratorial level, among the Timaean interlocutors. Moreover, he associates the expertise conveyed by his commentary with the philosophical insights acquired by those who will, eventually, be able to emerge from the *Republic*'s cave. The likemindedness Calcidius perceives between the recipients of 'liberal studies', such as they appear in his commentary, and the rulers in Plato's *Republic* is emphasized towards the end of the commentary where, after pointing to the case of the captives who are 'buried away in the perpetual darkness of an opaque, densely shadowed cave', he explains:

> Those, however, who despite the difficulty free themselves from their profound ignorance, emerge out of the darkness into the light and aspire to the clarity of knowledge and truth, and they do not resent the fact that men who excel in a liberal education (*studiis humanitatis*) divide and distinguish between sensible and intelligible nature. . . .[11]

By passing on his knowledge of liberal studies in his commentary Calcidius allows his readers, likewise, to follow an educational program that prepares them to 'emerge from the cave'. Calcidius finds room in his erudite circle also for his patron Osius. The latter is credited with 'all forms of liberal education' (*omnia studia humanitatis*)[12] in the prefatory letter preceding Calcidius' translation of the dialogue. As noted by John Magee,[13] Calcidius' use of this phrase to describe both the character Critias at *Ti.* 20a (as addressed by Socrates in his translation of the dialogue) and Calcidius' own patron implicitly puts Osius on a par with Critias while aligning Calcidius, the narrator of the Latin translation, with the Greek narrator Socrates.

The significance of mathematics in Calcidius' philosophical project has been showcased by Anna Somfai, who draws attention to the manner in which geometrical proportion shapes Calcidius' exegesis on demons, and the distribution of the demonic class and other living creatures in the

[10] Calc. *in Ti.* 2.204.18–20. Cf. Theon, *Exp.* 1.1–10. [11] Calc. *in Ti.* 349.576.7–10.
[12] Calc. *Ep. Os.* 132.9. [13] Magee 2016, 716.

universe.[14] In what follows, I shall draw attention to the fact that it is the discipline of harmonics, in particular, which provides an important frame of reference for Calcidius throughout his translation and commentary. Emphasis is placed on harmonic theory with the help of recurring references to harmonious patterns in various contexts of his exegesis: alongside its unsurprisingly prominent role in the construction of the world soul, to which I shall turn first, we perceive echoes of musical harmony also in Calcidius' discussion of the world soul's role in the material realm. Harmonious relations are then shown to feature in the structural make-up of the sensible universe and of the human soul. Most significantly, the continuing emphasis on musical harmony forms a natural segue to Calcidius' interpretation of Plato's creation account, in which he rephrases Timaeus' language of createdness in the terms of musical consonance.

12.2 Geometry, Arithmetic, Harmonics and Astronomy: The Creation of Cosmic Soul and Body

12.2.1 Plato's Timaeus

Before we turn to Calcidius, let me briefly point to those passages in Plato's dialogue that are relevant for our understanding of the harmonious nature of the Timaean universe. Our path begins with geometry. Geometrical structure features in the construction of the world body out of the four primary bodies fire, air, water and earth, described at *Ti.* 31b-32c. The cosmic body's three-dimensional solidity and its structural unity and cohesion are owing to its specific elemental make-up. The demiurge combined the four primary bodies in accordance with the continuous geometrical proportion a:b :: b:c :: c:d, where b and c correspond to the elements of air and water, respectively, and are placed between the two extremes a, corresponding to fire, and d, corresponding to earth:

> . . . the world was to be solid in form, and solids are always conjoined, not by one mean (*mesotēs*), but by two. Accordingly, the god set water and air between fire and earth, and made them, so far as was possible, proportional to one another, so that as fire is to air, so is air to water, and as air is to water, so is water to earth, and thus he bound together the frame of a world visible and tangible . . . [the body of the universe came] into concord by means of proportion (*di'analogias*), and from these it acquired amity (*philian*), so that

[14] Somfai 2003, esp. 130–1, discusses Calcidius' application of the continuous geometrical proportion to the cosmic habitats that feature in his demonology.

> coming into unity with itself it became indissoluble by any other save him who bound it together.[15]

Previously at *Ti.* 31c2-4 Timaeus had announced that 'of all bonds the best is that which makes itself and the terms it connects a unity (*hen*) in the fullest sense; and it is of the nature of a proportion (*analogia*) to effect this most perfectly.'[16] The continuous geometrical proportion plays a role also in Timaeus' description of the composition of the cosmic soul. From *Ti.* 35a onward, the mixture of the psychic ingredients Being, Sameness and Difference, having been formed into a type of 'band', are marked off by the demiurge as individual portions of differing quantities. The diagram chosen by many commentators, both ancient and modern, to illustrate this division and the proportional relation of the different portions towards one another comes in the shape of the Greek letter lambda.[17] One leg exhibits the portions that correspond to the powers of two: 1, 2, 4, 8, representing the geometrical surface; the other leg exhibits portions in accordance with the powers of three, representing the three-dimensional body. Both series present a continuous geometrical proportion of the type we encountered earlier in the context of the composition of the world body. The powers of two may thus be expressed by the continuous geometric proportion 1:2 :: 2:4 :: 4:8, and the powers of three by 1:3 :: 3:9 :: 9:27.

Between the individual integers that feature in each series, the demiurge adds further numerical ratios that correspond both to the arithmetic and the harmonic means of the integers aligned on either side. These further insertions result in a numerical series in which the intervals between the original powers of two and three correspond to the ratio of 3:2, the arithmetic mean, and the ratio of 4:3, the harmonic mean. It is these ratios that showcase the harmonious nature of the series. The ratio of 3:2 corresponds to the musical 'fifth' concordance, the ratio of 4:3 to the 'fourth'.[18] This results in the following series of intervals: 1, 4:3, 3:2, 2, 8:3, 3, 4, 9:2, 16:3, 6, 8, 9, 27:2, 18, 27. Finally, the intervals of 4:3 are filled, in addition, with the ratio 9:8, corresponding to the musical tone, and with the remaining portion (*morion*, 36b1) of the ratio 256:243, intended to

[15] *Ti.* 32b1-c4. Transl. Cornford, with minor modifications.

[16] δεσμῶν δὲ κάλλιστος ὃς ἂν αὑτὸν καὶ τὰ συνδούμενα ὅτι μάλιστα ἓν ποιῇ, τοῦτο δὲ πέφυκεν ἀναλογία κάλλιστα ἀποτελεῖν.

[17] Plut. *De an. procr.* 29.1027D, attributes the diagram to Crantor. Cf. Bakhouche 2011, 81, with further references; cf. n. 30 below.

[18] The move from 1 to the power 2, from the perspective of harmonics, corresponds to the octave 2:1; the move from one to 3 to the octave + fifth (2:1 + 3:2).

correspond to the musical semitone. The band of psychic material is thus divided in accordance with arithmetic, harmonic and geometrical relations.

Timaeus suggests, moreover, that the proportions according to which the band of the psychic mixture is portioned off correspond to the relative distances between the spherical courses traveled by the heavenly bodies. Having split the psychic material into two strips and having crossed these in the form of the letter 'chi' and bent the arrangement into a spherical shape, the creator god 'divided the inner revolution six times into seven unequal circles, in accordance with the double and the triple intervals, there being three of each' (*Ti.* 36d2-4: τὴν δ' ἐντὸς [φορὰν] σχίσας ἑξαχῇ ἑπτὰ κύκλους ἀνίσους κατὰ τὴν τοῦ διπλασίου καὶ τριπλασίου διάστασιν ἑκάστην, οὐσῶν ἑκατέρων τριῶν). Once he had fashioned the heavenly bodies, 'the god placed them into the spherical courses performed by the revolution of the Different [i.e. the inner revolution], setting seven planets into seven spherical courses' (*Ti.* 38c7-d1: ὁ θεὸς ἔθηκεν [τὰ ἄστρα] εἰς τὰς περιφορὰς ἃς ἡ θατέρου περίοδος ᾔειν, ἑπτὰ οὔσας ὄντα ἑπτά). The relevance of, and the mutual kinship between, the four disciplines geometry, arithmetic, harmonics and astronomy is amply demonstrated by Timaeus' descriptions.

12.2.2 Calcidius' Translation

Calcidius' translation largely follows the sense of the Greek text in the above passages, and a few notes on his translation will suffice as our entry point to his discussion. In the earlier context of *Ti.* 32c, while focusing on the construction of the world body according to the continuous geometrical proportion, Calcidius loosely translates that the cosmos (*machinam*) was 'bound together by a friendly proportion in the equilibrium of its parts' (*amica partium aequilibritatis ratione sociatam*).[19] Turning to the composition of the world soul, Calcidius translates that the demiurge divided the psychic mixture 'proportionately', *competenter*, where the Greek states that it was divided 'into as many parts as was fitting' (*Ti.* 35b2: μοίρας ὅσας προσῆκεν). Setting out the detailed arithmetic and harmonic ratios at *Ti.* 36a6, Calcidius transliterates and glosses the Greek terms *epitritē* [*diastasis*] (i.e. 4:3, the musical 'fourth') as 'those [terms] on

[19] *amica ratione* captures both the Greek δι' ἀναλογίας as well as the Empedoclean notion of φιλία, 'friendship', between the elements, while *partium aequilibritas* captures the participle ὁμολογῆσαν 'in agreement with itself', as well as εἰς ταὐτὸν αὑτῷ συνελθόν, 'coming into unity with itself'.

which a third part supervenes', and *epogdoos* (i.e. 9:8, a whole musical 'tone') as 'those [terms] on which an eighth part supervenes', while rendering the straightforward *sescuplum* for *hēmiolia*, the musical 'fifth' (i.e. 3:2).[20] Describing, in turn, the joining together of the two lengthwise-cut portions of psychic mixture into the shape of the letter *chi*,[21] Calcidius, dutiful interpreter that he is, accounts for the surprising fact that Timaeus calls the spherical motion of the outer psychic ring 'the motion of the nature of the Same' (*tēs tautou physeōs*, 36c5) even though it had been composed from mixed types of Same as well as of Difference and Being. Calcidius translates 'he called the motion of the outer circle the motion of the Same', adding 'since it was cognate with the nature of the Same' (*quod erat eiusdem naturae consanguineus*), an explanation that is not found in the Greek.

12.2.3 Calcidius' Commentary

It has long been acknowledged that Calcidius' commentary betrays close parallels, in particular in chapters 37–91 of the commentary, with the second-century Platonist Theon of Smyrna's *Exposition of Mathematical Subjects Useful for the Study of Plato*.[22] Opinions remain divided on the question of whether Theon was Calcidius' direct source, or whether the parallels between these two authors are to be accounted for by their mutually independent use of a common source, a no longer extant work, perhaps a commentary on Plato's *Timaeus* by the Peripatetic Adrastus, whose influence is openly acknowledged by Theon on multiple occasions. A recent evaluation of the parallels between Theon and Calcidius by F. Petrucci suggests a greater degree of independence between them than had previously been assumed, which in turn suggests that both authors appropriated Adrastean material while pursuing rather different programmatic lines and emphasis. Theon, in the early chapters of his work, indicates that the learning he is about to disseminate in his exegesis of the *Timaeus* will accomplish the philosophical pursuit of obtaining happiness.[23] The scope

20 Although he remains reasonably close to the sense of the Greek, Calcidius confuses the ratio of the remaining part short of the 'fourth', translating 243:256 for 256:243, as noted by Magee *comm. ad loc.*

21 Calcidius writes 'in the form of the Greek letter *chi*', *in speciem chi Graecae litterae*. Like his other references to the aforementioned Greek technical terms, this is a somewhat superfluous explanation, given that the translation appears to be put back into the mouth of Timaeus' Greek *persona*. Cf. Magee *comm. ad loc.*

22 For example, Waszink, Jensen 1962 and Waszink 1964; Bakhouche 2011, 36–7.

23 *Exp.* 1.1–10. Petrucci 2012a, 514–21, esp. 517–18 discusses the parallels between Theon and Calcidius *vis-à-vis* Adrastus in the technical passages of this part of the dialogue. See also Petrucci 2012b, where

of his discussion remains, for the most part, reasonably close to the confines of his chosen disciplines and is largely conducted with technical precision. Calcidius appears to handle his source material in the technical parts of his commentary somewhat more freely and follows a broader educational program,[24] as determined by the Timaean creation account – in fact, he moves beyond the thematic scope of the dialogue itself, as is visible in his extensive discussions on topics as varied as fate, demons, and matter.

Calcidius' discussion concerning the construction of the cosmic body and soul – as we will find in due course – draws particular attention to the close relationship between mathematics and music. Initially, however, chapter 15 sets out the mathematical principles that are applied for the construction of the cosmic body from the four elements fire, air, water and earth. Following a lengthy mathematical proof, Calcidius concludes: 'The two extremes among the solid bodies are bound by two means (*duabus medietatibus*), as the certain and incontestable authority of arithmetic confirms in support of Plato.'[25] In chapter 16, in turn, he points to the affinity of the arithmetic with the geometrical mean: 'This same discrete or double mean (*distantiva seu duplex medietas*) between two solid bodies is analogously (*pro competenti modo*) shown to conjoin discrete bodies also by geometrical ratios (*geometricis etiam rationibus*).'[26] At this point, Calcidius feels the need to assist his reader by explaining the technical terms he has just introduced, 'ratio' and 'proportion'. *Competens*, 'proportion', is his chosen rendering for *analogia*, which he transliterates. A *ratio*, by contrast, 'is a reciprocal relation, a kind of convergence of two terms, such that proportion consists of comparison between a number of ratios … a continuous proportion emerges with a minimum of three terms, as the first is to the second, so the second is to the third.'[27] With his readers thus

the author draws similar conclusions on Calcidius' and Theon's use of Adrastean material from a more exhaustive comparison between the two authors.

[24] Bakhouche 2011, vol. 2, 658, implies that Calcidius may have been challenged in the field of musical theory. Earlier work by Bakhouche, which comes to a similar conclusion concerning Calcidius' expertise in the field, investigates the author's discussion of music from a technical perspective and explores parallels in the discussions of Boethius and other Latin authors. Cf. Bakhouche 1997, 217–18.

[25] In response to Waszink 1964, 7–8, who attributes chapters 9–29 of Calcidius' commentary to Adrastus, see Petrucci 2012a, 520–1, who points to differences between Theon and Calcidius in their respective discussions of the geometrical proportion. Waszink had further argued that Calcidius depends upon Adrastus in chapters 1–25, 32–50, 44–6, and 58–118.

[26] 16.220.18–20.

[27] 16.220.26–28: *ratio vero est duorum finium iuxta semet ipsos habitus et quasi quaedam conventio. itaque competens ex complurium rationum comparatione subsistit, et continuum quidem competens in tribus, ut parum, finibus invenitur: sicut primus iuxta secundum, sic secundus iuxta tertium* . . . . Cf. Theon, *Exp.* 82.6-11.

up to speed, Calcidius is able to explain that the demiurge 'uses the ratio or remedy of a continuous proportion (*ratione ac remedio continui competentis*), since it is by its nature a unifier capable of conjoining discrete terms (*coniugabilis est et adunatrix distantium limitum*) and is akin to the ratio which the god used in the fabrication of the sensible world, since he inserted the means of air and water between the extreme limits of world, fire and earth'.[28] He concludes: 'the science of arithmetic explains the extent to which between these two solid bodies two other solids will by their intercalation produce a continuous bond according to the ratio of a continuous proportion (*continuationem iuxta rationem continui competentis*) ... And in this way is preserved as well the geometric *analogia* according to the ratio of a continuous proportion: as fire is to air so air is to water, and finally, water to earth. Conversely: as earth is to water so water is to air and air to fire.'[29]

For the ensuing construction of the world soul, Calcidius expands his discussion to include musical theory. Initially, he ascribes the use of the familiar lambda-shaped diagram to the demiurge himself. Noting that '[the demiurge] placed [the number 2] under 1 on the left of the diagram ...' (*postea duplicem eius sumpsit quam sumpserat, hoc est duo, quae subter unum posita sunt in laeva parte formulae*: 33.242.4–5), Calcidius elaborates on the purpose of the diagram, which 'reflects as in a mirror an image of the powers (*virium*) of the soul. For the partitioning offers an ordered theoretical perspective (*consideratio ordinatioque*) on its powers and activities (*virium, actuum eius officiorumque*) as though on its parts, and points to the congruence of all its tasks and functions (*munerum*) as asserted by three disciplines, in particular, geometry, arithmetic and harmonic theory, for which geometry serves as a foundation and the others as a superstructure (*ceterae vero superstructionis*).'[30] The 'parts' of soul (i.e. the individual

28 17.222.7–10.

29 22.228.19–34. Calcidius addresses the fact that, *prima facie*, the contrasting physical qualities possessed by the individual material elements would render their conjoining difficult. In a somewhat questionable line of argument, he contends that 'they nevertheless have a certain likeness deriving from their very contrariety (for like is compared to like no more than unlike to unlike), and this is their *analogia* i.e. their ratio of continuous proportion ...' (21.228.12–14). For a more detailed discussion of this passage and Calcidius' assignment of these and other qualities to the individual elements, cf. Gersh 1996, 130–4.

30 32.240.4–9. Calcidius may be following Adrastus, cf. Procl. *in Ti.* 3.171.4–8; Theon, *Exp.* 95–96. See Petrucci 2012b: 6–8 and esp. 12; Gersh 1986, 476–8 suggests that Porphyry may have acted as an intermediary between Adrastus and Calcidius. On the foundational role of geometry, cf. Theon, *Exp.* 106.16–19. In chapter 39, Calcidius provides a more metaphysical explanation for the shape of the diagram: 'An explanation should now be offered for the triangular shape ... no shape is more suitable than this one, in which the unity placed at the top is seen to hold the place of the summit or pinnacle, so that through it as a kind of conduit, so to speak, a certain bountiful river, as it were,

quantities portioned off in accordance with specific ratios) represent soul's activities and tasks, all of which occur within the congruent numerical parameters of the three disciplines geometry, arithmetic and harmonics. The role and function of the world soul is to provide a cosmic scaffolding or underlying structure whose cohesion is secured by the reciprocal relations between the numerical ratios that are, as is particularly stressed by Calcidius, congenital to each of the three disciplines.

In chapter 35, after exploring the Pythagorean beliefs concerning the integers featured in the lambda-diagram, Calcidius comments on the close relationship between numerical value and harmonical ratio: 'Harmonic ratio, as well, flows from a sort of fountainhead, as it were (*quasi quodam fonte demanat*), of the same four numbers which make up 10 (1, 2, 3, 4) since from them arise numbers and musical intervals in the ratios of the epitritic, hemiolic, double, triple and quadruple ... now, for purposes of calculation, the epitriton is the same as that which in harmonic terms is called the *diatessaron* [i.e. the musical fourth] while the hemiolic is the same as the *diapente* [the fifth], the double the same as the *diapason* [the octave] and the quadruple the same as the *disdiapason* [double octave].'[31] The Pythagorean origin of harmonic theory is acknowledged in chapter 45, where Calcidius notes that 'Pythagoras was the first to remark that these mutually concordant pitches have a particular affinity with numbers' (*habere aliquam cum numeris germanitatem*).[32] A pun reaffirms the Pythagorean insight at the end of chapter 46: 'musical concordance is found to harmonize (*concinere*) with numerical concord'.[33]

Calcidius' reference to Pythagoras' authority in the context of Timaean harmonic theory implicitly serves to reinforce Plato's own policy of

might flow as if from depths of the perennial fount to provident intelligence and the unity itself be understood to be mind, intelligence or the craftsman god himself.' (*nunc praestanda est ratio formae istius triangularis ... nullam dico esse aptiorem figuram quam est haec in qua singularitas cacumini superimposita summitatem atque arcem obtinere consideratur, ut per eam velut emissaculum quoddam tamquam e sinu fontis perennis providae intellegentiae quasi quidam largus amnis efflueret ipsaque singularitas mens sive intellegentia vel ipse deus opifex intellegatur esse*, 39.248.29–250.1). A similar reference to the number one or monad as representing the highest god is found in Macrobius' *In somn.* 1.6.7–9 and Nicomachus of Gerasa, *ap.* [Iambl.] *Theol. arithm.* 4. Cf. Bakhouche 2011, 657 n. 203, for further references. Bakhouche conjectures that Calcidius' chosen imagery in this passage may be Neopythagorean in character. Van Winden 1965, 105–6 detects a Numenian influence. As pointed out by Magee, *comm. ad loc.*, Calcidius calls matter the 'fountainhead of corporeality' (*fons corporum*) at 29.236.16, a Crantorian idea, according to Plut. *De an procr.* 3.1013C.

31 35.244.9–20. Cf. Theon, *Exp.* 58.2–59.2.

32 45.256.24–29. For the entire chapter, cf. Theon, *Exp.* 56.10–58.9, but see Petrucci 2012a, 515 for differences between Calcidius and Theon.

33 46.258.10–11: *symphonia musicae symphoniae numerorum concinere invenitur*

inquiry, as set out at *Ti.* 29b4-5. There, Timaeus emphasizes that 'accounts are akin (*syggeneis*) [to the subject matters] of which they serve as exegetes' (*hōnper eisin exēgētai*).[34] In chapter 50, Plato's choice of conferring upon Timaeus, a 'follower of Pythagoras (*ex Pythagorae magisterio*)', the role of protagonist is explained by Calcidius as being in line with the use of 'related and familiar proofs' (*domesticis et familiaribus sibi probationibus*) intended to show that 'soul has both a natural correspondence with number and a harmony with musical accords (*animae naturam congruere numeris, concinere etiam modulationibus musicae*).'[35] The appeal to Pythagoras in the context of number and musical theory, while natural enough, is particularly apt given that Calcidius had stressed at the outset of his commentary that the sister disciplines mathematics, harmonics and astronomy are 'cognate' (*consanguineus*, 2.204.20) with the very subject matter at hand, the nature and composition of the cosmos.

Soon thereafter, in chapter 55, Calcidius closes this part of his discussion by reaffirming that 'enough has been said concerning the world soul that consists of the coalescence of two forms of Being, the nature of the Same and Other, and concerning the division of it that has been drawn according to the harmonic, arithmetic and geometrical ratios, and how its nature comports with number and sound' (*quove modo natura eius numeris sonisque conveniat*).[36] However, the relevance of soul's harmonious nature to Calcidius' exegesis does not end here.

12.3 Recurring Harmonious Patterns in Calcidius' Commentary

12.3.1 The World Soul as Median

The significance of musical theory and of its kinship with the other disciplines for Calcidius' exegesis becomes more evident as we discover in other parts of his commentary the imprint of the harmonious patterns first defined in the context of the construction of the cosmic soul. It emerges from Calcidius' discussion that the role of the mathematical and harmonic means as connecting bonds within the structural make-up of the world soul is mirrored by soul's own role within the cosmos, where it serves as an

[34] Calcidius translates 'causal accounts revelatory of why each and every thing is are naturally akin to those same things' (*causae quae cur unaquaeque res sit ostendunt, earundem rerum consanguineae sunt*).

[35] 50.264.25–28.

[36] 55.270.3–6. Similarly also chapter 52, where Calcidius stresses that soul has been divided by the demiurge 'into parts according to certain geometric, arithmetic and musical ratios' (*in partes iuxta quasdam geometricas et arithmeticas et musicas rationes*).

ontological median by connecting the material sphere with the intelligible realm.[37] Given its composition from both divisible and indivisible being, interpreted by Calcidius as soul's participation in the material and intelligible spheres, respectively,[38] the world soul stands in a kindred relation to both metaphysical planes. This relation enables a meaningful interaction with either plane, summed up by Calcidius with the principle 'like knows like', an insight with which he, once more, credits the Pythagoreans.[39]

With reference to his translation of *Ti.* 36a-37a, which lays out the division of the psychic mixture according to the familiar patterns, Calcidius elaborates in chapter 102 also on the metaphysical and epistemological mediation performed by the harmonious world soul that permeates the physical universe:

> With the assertion that the same soul is possessed of harmony he recalls and harkens back to its origin and elements, as it were, from which he constructed it in the initial stages, such that by virtue of its threefold origins . . . it easily distinguishes the similarity and dissimilarity of things . . . for being divisible by numbers, composed of proportions, tightly packed with mathematical means, ordered according to musical ratios, divided six ways by god and then bound by immortal linkages which comport with the diverse and varied movement of the whole world body, soul knows and understands all things according to their proper nature.[40]

[37] Gersh 1996, 128–38, ascribes an 'extensive theory of mediation' (128) to Calcidius.

[38] 53.266.28–268.13: 'And so, since the most ancient beginnings of things are Being or Substance, and since in both its manifestations (indivisible and divisible) this twofold diversity of nature is by far the oldest, it is clear that soul, being a conflation of each type of Being (the natures of the Same and Other) consists of all the original elements and that its nature therefore comports in the highest degree with the nature of numbers; and the latter are clearly more ancient even than geometrical forms themselves, which necessarily are found to depend upon number in some sense . . . we reach the conclusion that soul, being composed of a double Being and twofold nature, in harmony with the potency of numbers, and vivifying the celestial bodies and living beings that possess the faculty of reason and scientific knowledge, has the capacity to know all the things from the combination of whose potencies it itself consists' (*habere omnium rerum conscientiam ex quarum potentiis ipsa constet*).

[39] 51.266.2–12: 'Now, he maintains by a kind of right appropriation that the soul of the sensible world is born yet knows all realities. There is, moreover, the Pythagorean doctrine that "like is comprehended only by like" . . . These, of course, he established as the elements and first beginnings of all reality, from which he held the substance of soul to consist as well; and thus he held that soul possesses full knowledge of all realities, grasping likeness by the likeness within itself.' For similar references to Pythagoras and Empedocles, cf. Alcin. *Didask.* 14.169.29–31; cf. Arist. *de An.* 404b11–18, *Metaph.* 1000b5.

[40] 102.336.11–21: *porro quod eandem modulatam esse asserit, originem eius et quasi quaedam elementa, ex quibus eandem inter initia constituit, recordatur et repetit, ut ex ternis originibus . . . coagmentata similitudinem dissimilitudinemque rerum . . . facile ipsis in rebus recognoscat . . . utpote quae divisa sit numeris, composita analogiis, stipata medietatibus, ordinata rationibus musicis scissaque adeo sexies et rursum devincta immortalibus vinculis convenientibus diverso varioque totius mundani corporis motui omnia sciat et omnia iuxta naturam propriam assequatur.*

The kinship of soul with both the material and the intelligible spheres, and its reciprocal relations with them, rendered possible by mutually shared essential properties, evokes Calcidius' earlier explanation of the manner in which the four elements fire, air, water and earth were conjoined, proportionally, by the demiurge into an everlasting bond.

Its kinship with both spheres, moreover, makes the world soul an effective mediator also in the context of Calcidius' exegesis on fate. Within a triadic divine hierarchy, Calcidius identifies a highest, intelligible god, a subordinate hypostasis referred to as 'providence', 'second power' and 'intellect' (*providentia, secunda eminentia, nous*),[41] and a third hypostasis introduced as 'fate'. Earlier in chapter 143, we learn that fate is to be identified with the world soul in its essential aspect or substantiated form (*in substantia positum*, 143.380.17–18, cf. 149.384.19–20). In chapter 144 the world soul is further said to act, as it were, as the executive arm of divine providence in the material realm. It is identified with the demiurge's 'inevitable decree' (*inevitabile scitum*, 144.380.13) and the laws of fate (*nomous heimarmenous*) that are declared to the created human souls at *Ti.* 41e2-3.[42] Calcidius initially resorts to the geometrical terms 'premise' (*praecessio*) and 'axiom' (*theorema*, transliterated, 150.384.27–386.13)[43] to describe the relationship between the divine Laws, identified with fate, and its issuing authority, divine providence. Divine Law itself, however, is 'promulgated (*promulgata*) by the wise *attunement* (*modulamine*) of intelligence for the governance of all things' (177.408.27–28). Intellect (*nous*), the second hypostasis in Calcidius' metaphysical scheme, takes on the role of the Timaean demiurge. It is responsible for the 'attunement' of the divine Law which, in its substantiated form, is the harmoniously attuned world soul that, in turn, exacts its orderly and regulating influence upon the universe in accordance with the designs of divine providence.

More specifically, soul as fate substantiated in the material realm is further subdivided into three astronomical planes, the 'non-wandering'

41 As pointed out by Den Boeft 1970, 90 and Bakhouche 2011, *comm. ad loc.*, it is Plotinus who first identifies νοῦς with the second hypostasis only. Numenius (fr. 16) distinguishes between a first and a second νοῦς. Ps.-Plutarch at *Fat.* 572F-573A speaks of a πρόνοια that is the νόησις of a first god.

42 It is at *Resp.* 617d, in the context of the eschatological myth of Er, that the three Fates are assigned their respective positions in the universe. As noted, for example, by Bakhouche 2011, *comm. ad loc.*, Calcidius' order in the assignment of the spheres to the three Fates follows that of Plutarch (e.g. *Quaest. conv.* 745B) but differs from that in the *Republic*. Ps.-Plutarch (*Fat.* 568E6-9) and Proclus (*in R.* 2.94.20) offer yet another order of assignment.

43 For the doctrine of fate as ἐξ ὑποθέσεως, see also Calc., chapter 176; Ps.-Plut. *Fat.* 569D-E, 570A-B, Nem. *Nat. hom.* 38. Moreover, fate is described as substantiated by the world soul at Ps.-Plut. *Fat.* 568E, while Nemesius at *De natura hominis* 35, similar to Calcidius, discusses fate in the context of Stoic doctrine; cf. also Ps.-Plut. *Fat.* 574C-F.

plane of the fixed stars, the 'wandering' plane of the planets, and the 'sublunary' plane. The three levels are associated by Calcidius with the three Fates Atropos, Clotho and Lachesis, respectively (144.380.16–24), whereby he once more establishes an exegetical link between the *Timaeus* and the *Republic*. Calcidius had already pointed to its direct impact on the heavenly constellations at an earlier stage, in the context of the discussion of soul's harmonious nature. Without delving, in this earlier context, into the relationship between the individual astronomical planes and the workings of fate, in chapter 56 Calcidius had set out the manner in which soul's own structure, that is, its 'division' (*sectio*), determines that of the heavenly bodies (*caelestia membra*) and their specific orbits, 'with whose motions its own conversion runs concurrent' (56.270.8–10). Given the structural affinity of the manifest heavenly bodies with soul, they revolve in identical, circular orbits. Somewhat later in this discussion, Calcidius turns to examining several heavenly bodies in greater detail since this will be useful for the 'observation of the celestial chorus' (*ad spectaculum caelestis choreae*, 65.280.21–22), supplying a musical image we will encounter again in due course.[44]

While the harmonious patterns Calcidius first identified in the construction of the cosmic soul necessarily recede into the background as his discussion touches on other subjects, they continue to leave noticeable imprints on his exegetical narrative.

12.3.2 Harmonious Habitats

Remaining in the material sphere, soul's harmonious patterns are reflected on a structural level, as demonstrated by the spatial relations of the different habitats into which the universe is divided. In chapter 129 of the commentary Calcidius explains, initially, that the continuous proportion served as a rationale behind the structuring of the material cosmos into five domains of varying magnitudes.

> Plato says that there are in the world five regions or places suitable for living beings and that they exhibit mutual differences in position owing to the difference in the bodies that inhabit those same places ... the difference obtaining between regions is found to be the same as between magnitudes as

[44] A close parallel appears in Theon, *Exp.* 130.20–22, who believes that 'it is useful to know these heavenly bodies for the observation of their courses in the heaven' (οὓς χρήσιμον εἰδέναι πρὸς τὴν τῶν κατὰ τὸν οὐρανὸν ἐπιτελουμένων θεωρίαν) but, unlike Calcidius, does not supply a more explicit reference to the *harmonious* nature of their movement.

> well: the heavenly region is the largest, bringing all things within its embrace, the smallest is that of earth, surrounded by all other bodies, and the rest are intermediate, according to the ratio of a continuous proportion.[45]

These habitats are occupied, in turn, by five different kinds of living creatures that are assigned their respective habitat due to their affinity with its elemental make-up.[46] Calcidius' demonology is thus introduced in the context of the material realm which, in accordance with the familiar proportions, required a mediating link between two extreme material elements, and whose cohesion is due to the shared physical properties of its individual elements. Calcidius reminds us that, as in the case of the harmonious bonds that help connect the psychic tissue, so also in the case of the various living creatures there was a need for a median, sharing in properties of either extreme, to ensure the continuity and unison of the sensible realm.

> Given, then, that the divine and immortal race of living beings is celestial, associated with stars, while the temporary, perishable one subject to passion is associated with earth, it is necessary that there should be between these two some intermediate to connect the extreme limits (*medietatem aliquam conectentem extimos limites*) just as we see in the cases of musical harmony (*harmonia*) and the world itself.[47]

It is worthy of note that Calcidius' demonology, incorporated as it is into the context of the physical universe, stands separate from his discussion on fate and providence in chapters 158–174, in which he had associated the mediatory role with the world soul and made no noticeable room for demons in his providential hierarchy.[48]

12.3.3 Harmony in the Human Soul

Commenting on the nature of the world soul, Calcidius had suggested that it is able, due to its twofold ontological nature, to serve as a guide and ordering principle of the human sphere:

> This is the rational world soul which by virtue of its being endowed with a double nature (*gemina*) contemplates with great veneration the author of

[45] Calc. *in Ti.* 129.366.13–23. [46] Somfai 2003, esp. 130–1. [47] Calc. *in Ti.* 131.368.11–14.

[48] A providential aspect to the demons' function in the cosmos is hinted at 131.368.21–24: 'And such, I suppose, is the nature of demons, having a close connection with divinity by virtue of its immortality, and having a close relation with perishable beings in that it is passible, not immune to passions, *and whose sense of empathy even looks after us* (*cuius affectus nobis quoque consulit*)' (my emphasis). For a discussion of Calcidius' demonology in the broader context of his commentary and of his sources, cf. Hoenig 2018, 201–6.

> the world according to its higher nature while offering guidance to lower things according to its lower nature, complying with the divine commands ... blessed by its likeness to eternal things based on its natural affinity to them, an aid and protectress (*auxiliatrix et patrona*) to things subject to dissolution ... and so human life is tempered (*temperatur*) by the cohabitation of the natural and rational soul.[49]

It is not until later in the commentary that Calcidius further explains how human existence, in particular, is impacted upon by the cosmic soul. Once again, we recognize the pervasive presence of the continuous geometrical proportion that often appears in triadic form. This structure is reflected, we learn, in yet another aspect of cosmic existence: the relationship between the human soul and body. Replicating the triadic structure of the earlier group celestial creatures – demons – terrestrial creatures, Calcidius now establishes a direct comparison of the cosmic body and soul with the human body and soul.

> ... if the world [body] and world soul are ordered so that the summit is assigned to celestial beings and the regions beneath them to divine powers called angels and demons whereas earth is assigned to terrestrial beings, and the celestial beings command whereas angelic powers execute and terrestrial things are ruled, the first of these obtaining the highest place, the second the middle position, and those situated beneath them the bottom, then it follows that in the nature of man as well there is a certain regal element and another thing located in the middle and a third at the bottom, the highest being that which commands, the middle that which acts, and the third that which is ruled and administered. The soul, then, rules, the power of the soul situated in the chest executes, the rest, down to and below the genitals, are ruled and regulated. And we have come upon this same ordering also in books of the *Republic*.[50]

Calcidius here refers to the world body and soul as a joined construct, with the 'summit that is assigned to celestial beings' presumably referring to the positioning of the heavenly bodies within the revolutions of the world soul, as described at *Ti.* 38c-d. The demons, in turn, are placed on a par with the 'power (*vigor*) of soul', capturing the human soul's embodied executive element, which Calcidius locates in the chest. Finally, terrestrial existence must be regulated by the influence of the cosmic soul, as the human body is regulated by its soul from the chest down.[51]

[49] 54.268.14–26.

[50] 232.462.8–233.462.19. Cf. Plato, *Resp.* 434d-35b and 439d-e. Gersh 2011, 137, and 1986, 482–8.

[51] For references on the analogy between cosmos and human being, cf. Bakhouche 2011, 788 n. 479; Gersh 1986, 77–9 and 483.

Earlier in the commentary, however, Calcidius makes use of an alternative scenario to describe the management of earthly affairs by the world soul. In this earlier scenario, the executive action ascribed to the demons in the passage just quoted appears to be somewhat superfluous. Calcidius explains, instead, that each of the heavenly bodies, while traveling along their spherical paths, produces its own specific sound as determined by the harmonic concordances arranged by the demiurge when composing the world soul. Their conjoined movements, in turn, result in a harmonious cosmic symphony, the 'harmony of the spheres', a concept for which, given that it is alien to the *Timaeus*, Calcidius once more points to the *Republic*:

> . . . the stars, according to Pythagoras, in harmonized movement produce musical modes as they rotate in their spinning; this is consistent with [Plato's] claim in the *Republic* that the Sirens, each positioned on its own orbit, set a single mellifluous song into motion as they rotate along with the orbits, and that from the eight different sounds, one harmonious consonance is stirred up.[52]

The harmonious ensemble of the heavenly spheres is subsequently associated by Calcidius with the structural make-up of the human soul. The latter produces its own psychic symphony, with each soul part fulfilling its appointed role and thus, conjointly, producing the virtue of justice.[53] Calcidius continues our preceding passage from chapter 95 as follows:

> The *aplanes* [i.e. fixed heavenly bodies], then, will be the rational part within the soul, and the planets will be analogous to the spirited and appetitive parts and to the other associated movements through whose attunement (*concentu*) the life of the entire world is tempered (*modificata*).[54]

The symphony that is produced by the heavenly bodies and ultimately results from the world soul's intrinsic harmonious structure, as translated into the specific positions and 'songs' of the stars, enables the human soul to expose itself to the modulating influence of its cosmic counterpart. It is this scenario, rather than the soul–body analogy between the universal

[52] 95.328.26–30: *iuxta Pythagoram motu harmonico stellae rotatae musicos in vertigine modos edant, similiter ut in Politia Sirenas singulis insistere circulis dicens, quas rotatas cum circulis unam ciere mellifluam cantilenam atque ex imparibus octo sonis unum concordem concentum excitari*. The context is the division of the various soul parts described in *Ti.* 36d. Theon, *Exp.* 146.1–147.6, with reference to Adrastus; cf. Petrucci 2012b, 19. For variants on the commonplace association of the Sirens with the music of the spheres, cf. Bakhouche 2011, *comm. ad loc.*

[53] Cf. Hicks 2017, 60–1. The occasional elasticity of Calcidius' exegesis, here in the context of the various divisions of the human soul that feature in different contexts of the commentary, has been noted by Gersh 1986, 487–8, and Hicks 2017, 60 n. 91.

[54] 95.328.30–330.2.

macrocosm and human microcosm,[55] that allows Calcidius to create an exegetical link between the *Republic*'s tripartite psychology and *Ti.* 47c-e, the passage touched upon at the outset of the present study.[56] The relation between the rational, spirited and appetitive parts of the human soul that results in a virtuous nature is associated with the specific numerical relations inherent in musical concordance. Calcidius' exegesis of *Ti.* 47c-e thus noticeably expands the dialogue's focus from the harmonious revolutions of soul's rational element (cf. *hē par'hēmin dianoēsis* at *Ti.* 47b8) to the harmonious relations between the individual parts comprising soul in its entirety. If soul's balance is lost, it is remedied not only by studying, with the help of our eyesight, the arrangement and movements of the heavenly bodies but by exposing our ears to the harmonious celestial symphony reproduced in the human realm. In chapter 267 of Calcidius' commentary, a discussion of *Ti.* 47c-d, the passage cited at the outset of the present inquiry, the image of a cosmic soul whose harmonious structural pattern exerts influence in the sublunary sphere comes full circle:

> In earlier sections Plato constructed the soul in accordance with harmonic ratio (*iuxta rationem harmonicam*) and indicated that its natural activity consists of rhythms and modes (*rhythmis modisque*), but that the latter fade owing to soul's association with body, as the state of oblivion inevitably takes hold, and that the souls of many are consequently deprived of modulation (*immodulatas*). The remedy for this defect, he says, is found . . . in the divine music that is never disposed to separation from reason and intelligence. For he holds that this is the music that finally calls souls that stray from the right path back to their original state of harmony (*symphoniam*). And the noblest form of harmony in our character is justice, chief among all the virtues, by way of which the other virtues too execute their task and work, so that reason leads while an inner power resembling irascibility willingly offers itself as its supporter. These things, moreover, cannot occur without modulation; but there would ultimately be no modulation without harmony, while harmony itself follows from music (*ipsa*

[55] Cf. Gersh 1986, 482–3. The soul–body analogy does hint at the *Republic*'s tripartite soul division by distinguishing a ruling, an executive and a ruled element. Calcidius, however, conceives of the intermediate and lowest element as embodied.

[56] Cf. p. 2 above with n. 4. Calcidius' translation runs as follows: '. . . the vocal utility as is captured in connection with music (*ex musica*) has been conferred upon mankind entirely for the sake of harmony (*propter harmoniam*). And harmony, i.e. modulation (*modulatio*), being a regulated tension (*intentio modificata*) and having agitations that are cognate with and, as it were, akin to the circumlations of our soul, is quite beneficial for those who use the gift of the Muses wisely and for the sake of moderation rather than pleasure, for with the help of the Muses it recalls the soul's discordant and unharmonious agitations back into attunement and ordered concord, and rhythm has been given as the remedy for a nature which is for the most part unruly, ignorant of number and limit, and devoid of grace.'

> *symphonia sequitur musicam*). Without any doubt, music provides the adornment of reason to the soul (*musica exornat animam rationabiliter*) by calling it back to its primordial nature and finally rendering it as the craftsman god originally made it. And so the whole of music is found in voice, hearing and sounds. Thus this sense too is useful for the understanding of philosophy as a whole as regards the observation of intelligible reality.[57]

The particular relevance of musical expertise for an understanding of (what Calcidius presents as) Platonic psychology once more validates the scientific discussions that form the foundation to his Timaean exegesis.

12.3.4 Composing the Cosmos

Finally, the harmonious structure of the world soul comes to play a perhaps unexpected role also in Calcidius' overall interpretation of the *Timaeus*. Calcidius reads the creation of the universe described in the dialogue in a non-literal manner,[58] explaining in chapters 23 to 26 of the commentary that the 'origin and beginning of the works of god' is 'incomprehensible', that there was 'no indication of the time from which they began to be' (*dei operum origo et initium incomprehensibile . . . nullum indicium temporis ex quo esse coeperunt*: 23.230.13–15), and that their origin was 'causative, not temporal' (*causativa, non temporaria*: 23.230.25). While chapter 23 does not address, specifically, the creation of the world soul, we may infer that soul counts among the *opera dei* to which this description applies. This is confirmed in chapter 26, where Calcidius deals with the creation of the world soul proper. He explains that Plato decided to 'feign the createdness of eternal things' (*aeternarum rerum genituras comminisci*: 26.232.25–26) to ensure that those who heard that things had an origin 'but had never been born' (*ibid.* l. 27) would not consider those things to be rivaling the 'primacy' (*principatus, ibid.*) of god himself. In the case of divine things, 'origin' is used with a very different meaning than in the case of perishable things (*longe aliter dici originem rerum aeternarum et item caducarum*, 26.232.29).

57 267.496.10–27.

58 Cf. Petrucci 2016c, who points out that in the case of Middle Platonic authors in general, the terminology 'sempiternalistic vs. temporal' rather than the habitual pair 'literal-metaphorical' would more suitably describe their interpretations of the *Timaeus*. Attention should be paid not to entangle 'literal' with 'temporal'. In Calcidius' case, nevertheless, the term 'non-literal' suitably expresses the fact that Calcidius decodes the language of 'createdness' in such a manner as to end up with a cosmos he identifies as uncreated; cf. Hoenig 2014.

Calcidius further explains Plato's decision by pointing to the latter's authorial agenda. Since it was not Plato's primary concern in the *Timaeus* to prove the immortality of the soul, but to exhibit the constitution of the world (*constitutio mundi, hoc est universae rei*: 26.234.12–13), 'it was for present purposes relevant to present the world soul as being born (*nascentem*) and, as it were, brought into the light of day, so that those who heard it might imagine soul as having a form of some sort, precisely as they see in the case of all the things that are born'.

In the course of Calcidius' discussion, the image of the craftsman god is adjusted to that of a musician, an image that naturally falls in line with Calcidius' programmatic emphasis on harmonic theory and its affiliated disciplines while, at the same time, fulfilling the specific exegetical function of dissociating Plato's creation account from a literal interpretation. In chapter 228, Calcidius disparages the deplorable individuals who, given the apparently contradictory portrayal of an uncreated soul in the *Phaedrus*, do not know 'that a composite is that the making of which commences at a fixed point in time, as in the case of a ship or house'. He then appears to summarize alternative types of createdness:

> There is a type of thing which, although non-composite, nevertheless has a structure comparable to that associated with a process of composition (*rationem compositionis*), as with the musical consonance (*musica symphonia*) known as the diatessaron and geometrical theorems (*geometrica theoremata*); so too that which is likewise generated, the coming to be or making of which commences at a fixed point in time (*ex aliquo temporis initio natum factumve sit*), as in the case of a statue; and that which, as in the case of a sphere (*rationem generationis intellegibilis*), has a structure originating in intelligible generation is something else and very different again.[59]

Parallels emerge between Calcidius' list of examples and examples recorded by John Philoponus at *De aeternitate*. The example of a house and a boat is attributed by Philoponus to Porphyry (148.25–149.1) and may ultimately go back to Aristotle's *Protrepticus* fr. 11. Like Aristotle, Porphyry adds a living creature (*zōon*) and a plant (*phyton*) to his list of examples, items that are not found in Calcidius.[60] According to Philoponus, Porphyry had also

[59] 228.458.17–28, cf. Baltes 1976, vol. 1, 137 with n. 213, who points to Procl. *in Ti.* 1.219.7, for a possible parallel in Alcinous. Note, moreover, Calcidius' conclusion in chapter 228: 'when Plato says that soul came into being and was made and put together by the craftsman god, he does not mean that it takes the starting point for its being from a fixed point in time, or that a previously non-existent soul subsequently began to be, but that it has a structure analogous to that associated with coming-to-be and a process of composition. And when he says that it is without a process of generation or composition, he explicitly denies it any origin in a process of composition.'

[60] Porph. *in Ti.* fr. 36.

likened the type of createdness that is portrayed in the *Timaeus* to the composition of syllables from letters and to that of geometrical figures (*diagrammata*: *Aet. mund.* 148.13 = Porph. fr. 37).[61] The former image is reminiscent of chapter 44 in Calcidius' commentary, where the author likens individual notes and the musical consonances (*symphoniae*) of the fourth, fifth, tone and octave to individual syllables and words.[62] Finally, Philoponus at *Aet. mund.* 146.1.14–5 credits the Middle Platonist Taurus with the comparison of the world's createdness to the composition of musical concords, in the context of the latter's list of non-temporal meanings of the term *genēton*: 'Also described as "generated" [by Taurus] are things that are notionally composite, even if they have not [actually] been put together. In this sense the middle note [of the scale] is composed of the highest and lowest; even though it has not [actually] been put together, we detect in it the value that they have relative to each other.'[63]

Philoponus' Greek text in the present passage, *Aet. mund.* 146.14–15, reads *outōs synthetos hē mesē ek nētēs kai hypatēs*, 'in this sense the middle note [of the scale] is composed of the highest and lowest.' An interesting parallel appears in Calcidius' commentary, albeit not in the context of the above-quoted passage from chapter 228. Instead, it appears in chapter 40, introducing Calcidius' discussion 'On Modulation or Harmony' (*de modulatione sive harmonia*), where the author memorably depicts the demiurge as a musician who attunes the various portions of psychic material to harmonious consonances:

> As when musicians in tuning instruments (*ut harmonici modulantes organa*) within the two extremes set by the outer strings, the lowest being the *hypate* and the highest the *nete*, insert other intermediate ones of varying tone and pitch, ones higher than the lowest but lower than the highest, and by way of the attunement work their way up to the tone associated with the final pitch, like the plucking by fingers or plectrum up and down the scale, so god is represented as attuning the world soul (*animam mundi modulans*), filling each of the six intervals of the multiples of the double and triple by two means, such that of the two means one is greater than the smaller term by

[61] Cf. Baltes 1976, vol. 1, 58, with notes 147 and 148; Hoenig 2014, 87 with n. 20.

[62] 44.254.23–256.4.

[63] Translated by Share, with minor modification. Cf. the discussion of this passage by Petrucci 2018a, 53–5, who further clarifies that 'the *mese*, being intermediate and fixed, determines the reciprocal relationships of opposite notes, with which it identifies steadily defined intervals. So, the *mese* is composed, or generated, by the *nete* and *hypate* since it occupies a certain intrinsically defined position between the *nete* and the *hypate*' (55), translating 'in this sense the *mese* too is composed of the *nete* and the *hypate*: for even if the *mese* has not been composed, the intrinsic function of the one with respect to the other can be observed in it' for the same passage in Philoponus (*ibid.* 231–3).

a third of it but smaller than the greater term by the same proportion, a third, of it.[64]

While we find parallels to Calcidius' non-literal interpretation of the term 'generated' in other authors, it is worthy of note that the image of musical consonance that helps convey the uncreated nature of the world soul and body, among the most controversial aspects of Plato's *Timaeus* faced by a commentator, naturally aligns with the earlier parts of Calcidius' commentary, where he provides a rather technical treatment of harmonic theory in a strikingly idiosyncratic arrangement of an exegetical narrative that stresses, from the outset, the significance of harmonic theory for an overall appraisal of his Timaean doctrine.

12.4 Conclusion

Calcidius' association, early on in his translation and commentary, of the technical disciplines that feature in Timaeus' discussion – geometry, arithmetic, harmony and astronomy – with the education of future leaders in Plato's *Republic* sets this dialogue in close relation with the *Timaeus*, with the effect not only of stressing the continuity between Plato's own philosophical program but of exhibiting Calcidius' breadth as a Platonic commentator. At the same time, by providing an exhaustive commentary which, itself, builds upon these disciplines, Calcidius implicitly associates the learning he disseminates in his work with the philosophical knowledge acquired by the future leaders of Kallipolis.

The early chapters in his commentary, which deal with the composition of the cosmic soul according to harmonic ratios, draw particular attention to the kinship of harmonic theory with the mathematical and astronomical disciplines, an effort that is bolstered by the authority of Pythagorean teaching aligned with the Timaean doctrine Calcidius expounds. In the ensuing parts of the commentary, the effects of Calcidius' early emphasis on the role of harmonics allow us to perceive echoes, both firm and faint, of harmonious patterns even in seemingly unexpected contexts.

The 'musical' nature of the cosmic soul qualifies it as a mediating instance between the intelligible and the material spheres. It impacts upon the structure of the physical cosmos by determining the spherical courses of the heavenly bodies. The harmonious arrangement of these bodies, at the same time, is portrayed as the physical manifestation of an

64 40.250.15–23.

elaborate system of divine providence and fate. Harmonious relations, moreover, play a role in the structure of the material realm, in which demons are likened to a harmonic mean, drawing together the habitats on either extreme of their physical environment. In the context of human psychology, the cosmic consonance produced by the heavenly bodies acts as a healing influence on human souls which suffer from internal discord. Finally, the noticeable emphasis Calcidius places on musical theory from the start lays the exegetical groundwork for a non-literal reading of the *Timaeus* in which he recasts the notion of createdness in the language of harmonious consonance. The Timaean creator god, it appears, puts down his tools and picks up the lyre.[65]

[65] I would like to express my sincere gratitude to the editors of this volume for their illuminating insights and comments on this chapter.

CHAPTER 13

Harmonia *in Philoponus'* Commentary on Nicomachus' Introduction to Arithmetic

Giovanna R. Giardina

13.1 Mathematical Sciences and Harmonics

At the beginning of his *Commentary* on Nicomachus, John Philoponus, who follows the latter's text as a guiding thread, addresses the epistemological question raised by Platonic ontological dualism, namely how it is possible for sensible, material, temporal and changeable entities to know intelligible, immaterial, timeless and immutable entities. As is evident, this question is used to introduce the idea of the mathematical sciences as an intermediary between the sensible and the intelligible, which constitutes the very *raison d'être* of Nicomachus' *Introduction to Arithmetic* and therefore of Philoponus' *Commentary*.[1]

On the other hand, it is quite clear that this discussion on the mathematical sciences is a distinctly philosophical one, insofar as it sets out from the problem of assigning a specific meaning to the term 'philosophy', which for Nicomachus as much as Philoponus is synonymous with 'wisdom', understood as the highest science of all, namely 'dialectic' in the strictly Platonic sense of the term.[2] Philosophy means 'love of wisdom',[3] Nicomachus states, drawing upon a definition that may be traced back to the ancients, starting from Pythagoras. The latter, as Nicomachus emphasises, contributed to disseminating the specific meanings of the terms 'wisdom' and 'science', so as to avoid that these terms might be indiscriminately applied to just any art.[4] Philoponus believes that Nicomachus opens his book about mathematics on this note because he is a Platonist

[1] Critical edition: Hoche 1866; English translation, D'Ooge 1926; French translation, Bertier 1978; see Giardina 1999.

[2] In Philop. *in Nicom.* 1.30 wisdom, conceived as the truest and loftiest kind of philosophy, coincides with Platonic dialectic, as already maintained by Plot. *Enn.* 1.3.3.5–10.

[3] Cf. [Pl.] *Def.* 414b7; Alcin. *Didask.* 1.1.152.2.

[4] On this testimony, which credits Pythagoras with the definition of philosophy and the narrowing down of the meaning of the terms 'philosophy' and 'science', see Diog. Laert. 1.12, Cic. *Tusc.* 5.3.8, and Ammon. *in Porph. Isag.* 9.7–9.

philosopher and hence intends to teach his readers what the ultimate purpose of wisdom is and what path leads to it. Philoponus clarifies that the ultimate aim of wisdom lies in the knowledge of intelligible entities and divine matters (Philop. *in Nicom.* 1.1.9–14). Indeed, the goal of human life is to live well, but given that we are rational animals, we cannot live well without knowing the good (Philop. *in Nicom.* 1.15).[5] The path leading to the supreme science, which is to say to the knowledge of intelligibles and of the good, is provided by the mathematical sciences, as Plato and Plotinus have also taught.[6]

After having established the relation between the mathematical sciences and philosophy, Philoponus immediately embarks on his discussion of the former by showing that they are sciences that study a class of entities which represent intermediaries within the framework of Platonic dualism. It is useful to grasp Philoponus' description of the ontological structure of reality, developed once again on the basis of the 'Platonist' Nicomachus, because it allows us to understand the role played by harmonics within this differentiated picture of reality and of being. Philoponus first of all identifies physical entities, which are mixed with non-being both because they are material and because physical reality is characterised by time and motion, which causes natural entities to constantly undergo change. Celestial bodies too, which unlike the bodies in the sublunary world are more stable, insofar as their substance does not change, nonetheless change place, since they travel from east to west, or vice versa. All these natural entities are images of other entities that serve as their archetypes, namely the intelligibles, which according to Plato's teaching are 'entities in the proper sense, i.e. entities that truly exist, which are always the same, eternal, and immutable'.[7] As already noted, this ontological dualism raises the question of the knowability of intelligible entities. Philoponus illustrates just how evident this question is by referring to Aristotle, who in the *Metaphysics* explains that the intelligibles are entities which are difficult to know even though by nature they are pure and bright. The commentator also invokes Plato, who in the *Phaedo* stresses the difficulty of knowing the

[5] Cf. Ammon. *in Porph. Isag.* 2.22–23 and 3.1–2, who describes philosophy as the knowledge of entities *qua* entities and as the knowledge of divine and human matters.

[6] Plot. *Enn.* 1.3.3.5–10 states that the mathematical sciences are propaedeutic to dialectic because they make those who are following the philosophical path familiar with the notion of incorporeal entities. Philop. *in Nicom.* 1.21 mentions that the Pythagorean Androcydes and Archytas of Tarentum upheld arguments similar to Plotinus'.

[7] Philop. *in Nicom.* 1.3.1–2: Ὄντα καλοῦμεν κυρίως τὰ ὄντως ὄντα, τὰ ἀεὶ καὶ ὡσαύτως ἔχοντα, τὰ ἀΐδια, τὰ ἀμετάβλητα. The Greek text of Philoponus' *Commentary on Nicomachus* and the English translation are based on Giardina 1999.

intelligibles both because the body represents an obstacle in this respect and because the faculty of the imagination (*phantasia*) produces images that do not allow us to contemplate the intelligibles in a direct way, without any falsification. In the *Timaeus* Plato draws a distinction between intelligibles and sensibles, describing the former as entities that are ever-existent and have no beginning, and the latter as entities that are generated and are never-existent (Philop. *in Nicom.* 1.3.41–72).[8]

The epistemological problem emerging from this ontological distinction, namely the impossibility of acquiring direct knowledge of intelligible entities that are entirely separate from bodies through corporeal entities,[9] can only be solved through the ontological and epistemological intermediation of mathematical entities. The latter are in bodies and in this respect are inseparable from matter; yet they can be thought of apart from bodies and in this sense are separate from matter (Philop. *in Nicom.* 1.1.61–73). Therefore, mathematical entities share with natural entities the fact that they are not separate from matter, but share with intelligible entities the fact that they are separate from matter. Philoponus is here referring to different aspects of numbers: for when he speaks of mathematical entities that are in bodies, he is referring to physical numbers, which – as in Iamblichus – correspond to the Aristotelian forms that are immanent in matter, or *enyla eidē*;[10] but when he speaks of mathematical entities that are separate from matter, he is referring to dianoetic or psychic numbers. For Philoponus, and for Neoplatonists more generally, the numerical, or more broadly mathematical, nature of the physical world – which is to say the numbers that constitute the structure of the cosmos – is related to the dianoetic or psychic numbers, which are thus called because they occur in our soul (Philop. *in Nicom.* 1.42), that is, to the numbers which constitute the structure of thought, and ultimately to intelligible numeric reality (i.e. the numbers present in the demiurgic intellect). In other words, according to the interpretation provided by Philoponus, and more generally by Neoplatonists after Iamblichus, we have: (1) the Platonic forms, which are principles of measurement and determination (so much so that

[8] Cf. Arist. *Metaph.* α1.993a30-31 and b7-11; Pl. *Phd.* 66b5 ff. (paraphrased in the same way by Ascl. *in Nicom.* 1.3.45–53); Pl. *Ti.* 27d6-28a5 (also quoted by Ascl. *in Nicom.* 1.3.68–71).

[9] Philop. *in Nicom.* 1.1.57–59 writes: ἀδύνατον ἦν ἀμέσως ἐξ αὐτῶν ἐπὶ τὰ νοητὰ καὶ κεχωρισμένα παντελῶς σωμάτων ἐλθεῖν.

[10] On Philoponus' distinction of different ontological degrees in relation to mathematical entities, see Giardina 2000. As regards Iamblichus' ontological distinction of different mathematical entities, I refer to O'Meara 1989, 79 ff.

Pythagoras and Plato called the forms numbers),[11] and which therefore constitute the models for noetic numbers; (2) noetic numbers, which are the rational principles of forms, *logoi*, present in the demiurgic intellect (i.e. those intelligible numbers and images of forms that the demiurge has used to generate the cosmos). Therefore, as Philoponus tells us, arithmetic is the foremost mathematical science, because it dwells (*politeuetai*) with the demiurge (Philop. *in Nicom.* 1.34.1–7), meaning that on the level of the demiurgic intellect the Platonic forms constitute an arithmetical system, insofar as the demiurge conceives the forms as numbers; (3) physical numbers, which are immanent in matter; (4) mathematical entities or dianoetic numbers, which are intermediate between the noetic numbers thought by the demiurge and physical numbers, which have the same nature as intelligibles insofar as they are separable from matter, and the same nature as sensibles insofar as they are not separable from matter. Thanks to their intermediate position, mathematical entities can serve as ladders allowing the philosopher to attain knowledge of the Platonic forms, which is to say to ascend to the level of dialectic.[12]

As we can see, Platonic ontological dualism is interpreted in terms of a distinction between different classes of entities which nonetheless are not unrelated, since the different kinds of numbers – noetic, dianoetic and physical – constitute increasingly weaker ontological degrees in the unfolding of the Platonic forms. But what is most interesting for the sake of the present enquiry is that the creation of the cosmos on the part of the demiurge occurs by virtue of the fact that the latter establishes relations between the numbers he has in the form of *logoi* of intelligible forms. These *logoi* are like the technical reasons (*hōs logon technikon*, to quote Nicomachus, *Intr. arithm.* 12.10) of demiurgic creation. The technical model in question is clearly illustrated by Philoponus, *in Nicom.* 1.34.7–12:

> Hence too poets say that Athena builds, Hephaestus works metals, Apollo provides music, the art of archery and medicine, and another god takes care of something else, not because they provide the handicrafts (for this is only a fanciful tale) but because the rational principles, which is to say the models of these arts, reside with them; likewise, the physician possesses the rational principles of the sick even though he is not sick himself.

[11] Philop. *in Nicom.* 1.34.2–6: 'Plato and the Pythagoreans call the forms numbers because just as number is capable of measuring and even of determining that of which it is number, so all forms are capable of determining, measuring and ordering matter which is indeterminate and disorderly'; see also Philop. *in Nicom.* 1.42.

[12] Cf. Philop. *in Nicom.* 1.30, based on Nicom. *Intr. arithm.* 7.21–8.7.

In this passage, Athena, Hephaestus, Apollo and the other gods are presented as mythical personifications of divine wisdom, which coincides with the wisdom of the demiurge and which, already in ancient mythical lore, is considered a technical form of knowledge, as the gods are said to possess the rational principles of the sciences.

For Neoplatonic philosophers, and in particular for Philoponus, this numerical arrangement of the various degrees of being represents a description of what Plato has taught in the *Timaeus*, a dialogue which is central to both Nicomachus' and Philoponus' expositions. In *Timaeus* 69a-b, the demiurge produces the cosmos by lending it order and measure, which is to say proportion and symmetry. His cosmogonic activity consists in the establishment of numerical relations that allow all things to be proportioned and symmetrical both in relation to one another and in themselves. In creating man, the created gods receive from the demiurge the immortal principle of the soul, which is to say the rational soul of man, which belongs to the same genus as the cosmic soul; around it they craft the head, just as the demiurge has crafted the body of the world. Hence, already in the *Timaeus* the world soul and human thought are presented as the outcome of the same kind of harmonious composition.

Now, as has just been noted, the action of the demiurge consists in the establishment of numerical relations of a certain kind, whereby the cosmos is the outcome of a harmonious composition. In commenting on Nicomachus' work, which affirms the priority of arithmetic over astronomy, in *in Nicom.* 1.41, Philoponus speaks of astronomical harmony: in his view, the movements of the stars are linked by musical relations; therefore, the Pythagoreans were right to observe that the movement of each star produces a melodious harmony, even though we are incapable of perceiving it. But how was the demiurge able to harmoniously create the cosmos through numbers? To answer this question, we must first ask: what does harmony consist in exactly? In his commentary on Nicomachus, Philoponus often quotes the definition of harmony given by the Pythagoreans, according to whom 'harmony is the union of very confused things and of people with conflicting opinions'.[13] What this means – Philoponus explains in 1.42 – is

[13] Philolaus, B61 DK. In Philoponus' commentary this Pythagorean definition first occurs at 1.25 as a way to explain the expression ἁρμονίας σύστασιν ἅπασαν used in [Pl.] *Epin.* 991e2, a dialogue which both Nicomachus and Philoponus considered to be authentic and regarded as Book 13 of the *Laws*. On the Neoplatonic interpretation of the whole mathematical passage from the *Epinomis*, see Giardina 2012, 341–78. With regard to this Pythagorean definition of harmony, see Philop. *in De an.* 358.14–15.

that harmony is a composition of opposites.[14] This definition must further be refined, because no composition can be obtained from entities that are mere opposites – such as white and heat or white and sweetness. Likewise, from two or more entities that are homogeneous yet not different as well – such as for instance two watercourses – we cannot obtain any composition, but only an addition. In order for there to be a composition and harmony, the entities that are being composed must be marked by both equality and inequality (i.e. they must be both homogeneous and opposite); and this is precisely the nature of number, which is the accordance of even and odd. Even and odd constitute the first species of number and are in turn subdivided into other species: even is distinguished into even-times even, even-times odd and odd-times even,[15] while odd is distinguished into prime and incomposite, secondary and composite and, finally, secondary and composite in itself but relatively prime and incomposite.

Again in 1.42, Philoponus observes that Nicomachus' *Introduction to Arithmetic* teaches precisely the theory of numbers, which is to say first of all the theory of absolute quantity (i.e. the theory of even and odd and of the species just mentioned), and then the theory of relative quantity. But what is most significant for our enquiry, which focuses on harmony, is the fact that Philoponus' whole investigation into absolute quantity and relative quantity – like that of Nicomachus before him – revolves around the relation between equality and inequality, between sameness and difference, between odd and even, the composition of which, as we have seen, is harmony.

13.2 How Harmony Is the Composition of Equality and Inequality

Equality and inequality, sameness and difference, are first of all the distinguishing features of number in itself, since each number, as we have seen, is the harmony of odd and even. Therefore, Philoponus' four definitions of even and odd, three of which are reportedly Pythagorean, allow us to identify odd and even numbers through the notions of equality and inequality, or sameness and difference. For example, the third definition, which corresponds to the second Pythagorean definition, states that an even number is one that can be divided both into equal parts and unequal

[14] Cf. Philop. *in De an.* 146.1.

[15] For the definition of even-times even number, ἀρτιάκις ἄρτιος, see Theon, *Exp.* 25.7, and Eucl. *Elem.* 7 def. 8; for the definition of the even-times odd, ἀρτιοπέριττος, see Theon, *Exp.* 25.19 ff. and Eucl. *Elem.* 7 def. 9 and, finally, for the odd-times even, περισσάρτιος, see Theon, *Exp.* 26.5, and Eucl. *Elem.* 7 def. 10.

parts, whereas an odd number can only be divided into unequal parts (Philop. *in Nicom.* 1.58). The fourth definition, which corresponds to the third Pythagorean definition and focuses on the relation between even and odd numbers, defines an odd number as that which differs from an even number by having one unit more or less, and an even number as that which differs from an odd number by having one unit more or less. On the other hand, numbers derive equality and inequality, sameness and difference, from their very origins (i.e. from 1), which is the origin of all numbers, both even and odd, and from 2, which is the origin only of even numbers. The number 1 is the origin and constitutive element of all numbers, Philoponus tells us in *in Nicom.* 1.62–63: it is their origin because, while each number is half the sum of all numbers that come before it and after it, 1 has no number before it, which clearly reveals its original nature; it is their constitutive element because all numbers, both even and odd, are made up of units. Now, 1 is the principle of sameness for numbers: for when it is multiplied by itself, it remains the same, as does any number that is multiplied by 1. The number 2 is not the origin of numbers as 1 is, since it derives from the latter, yet it is akin to 1 as an origin. As we have seen, 2, which is only the origin of even numbers, presents certain features which distinguish it from all other numbers: for example, it can only be divided into two equal parts, and not into two unequal parts as well. It is the principle of difference for numbers: for when it is multiplied by itself or by another number, it produces a different number; but if it is divided, it becomes two units, immediately displaying sameness. Nicomachus (*Intr. arithm.* 109.3–5) credits Pythagoras and the Pythagoreans with the identification of sameness with 1 and alterity with 2. In line with this interpretation, Philoponus argues that, since Plato is a Pythagorean, 'he called the external circle of the universe, which is one and indivisible and has only one specific movement, <the circle> of sameness, and the inner one, which is divided into several circles and movements, <the circle> of difference' (*in Nicom.* 2.55.20–23). It is evident, then, not only that all numbers are marked by both sameness and difference, which derive from the very nature of their origins, but that the sameness and difference which characterise the arithmetical system of numbers find their physical counterpart in the cosmic structure of the Platonic *Timaeus*.

Later on in *in Nicom.* 2.60, Philoponus returns to the question of 1 and 2 when commenting on *Intr. arithm.* 112.13–21. Here, to clarify the relation between physics and mathematics, Nicomachus states that according to both physicians and mathematicians sameness and differences are the principles of the universe, with sameness corresponding to 1 and difference to 2. Philoponus confirms that 1 is synonymous with sameness, since it is indivisible; hence, sameness is also attributed to all odd numbers, of which 1 is the absolute origin, and to all square numbers, which are generated from odd numbers.[16] On the contrary, difference coincides with 2, which is divisible; hence, difference is also attributed to all even numbers, of which 2 is the origin, and to all heteromecic and promecic numbers, which are generated from even numbers.[17] Odd numbers and square numbers, therefore, have the nature of what is limited, since 1 serves as their limit, whereas even, heteromecic and promecic numbers have the nature of what is unlimited, so much so that when these numbers are configured geometrically, the difference between their sides increases indefinitely. Number, then, is a composition of limited and unlimited; and since the universe was fashioned in the likeness of number and is therefore made up of opposites, it necessarily requires harmony. Given, then, that number is intrinsically a harmony, since it is the accordance of even and odd, sameness and difference, limited and unlimited, Philoponus always tends to consider number in itself chiefly as the arithmetical model of the world and to emphasise the role of harmony when discussing relative number. Besides, the cosmic structure produced by the demiurge is the outcome of complex numerical relations, which the demiurge establishes by virtue of the fact that he possesses noetic numbers (i.e. that he conceives of the Platonic forms arithmetically).

From *in Nicom.* 1.123 onwards, Philoponus discusses relative number by commenting on Nicomachus, *Intr. arithm.* 44.10–13, a passage that makes it perfectly clear that equality and inequality are the distinctive features of the very nature of number. Nicomachus writes:

> Of relative quantity, then, the highest generic divisions are two, equality and inequality; for everything viewed in comparison with another thing is either equal or unequal, and there is no third thing besides these.[18]

[16] Indeed, we get square numbers by adding odd numbers. The first square, 4, is obtained by adding the first odd number, 3, to 1; the second square, 9, is obtained by adding the second odd number, 5, to the first square, and so on. On this theory, see Philop. *in Nicom.* 2.34. Sameness is reflected by squares because they have equal sides (1.33). Moreover, if we take a sequence of multiples, doubles, triples, quadruples and so on, square numbers will always occur in odd positions, which confirms that oddness is the absolute cause of sameness: see Philop. *in Nicom.* 2.68.

[17] Heteromecics are rectangles whose sides differ by only one unit (e.g. 6 [= 3 × 2]), whereas promecics are rectangles whose sides differ by more than one unit (e.g. 15 [= 3 × 5]). For this reason, difference is to be found more in promecics than in heteromecics. The first heteromecic is 2 (= 1 × 2), whose sides differ by one unit; the second heteromecic is obtained by adding to the first even number the second one: 2 + 4 = 6 (see Philop. *in Nicom.* 2.55–56).

[18] Transl. by M. L. D'Ooge in D'Ooge 1926.

Philoponus observes that equality cannot be subdivided, since there is no difference between equals, whereas we find different numerical species of inequality, which can exist according to the greater or the less. Hence, in the case of relative number, according to the greater we will have the multiple, the epimoric, the epimeric, the multiple epimoric and the multiple epimeric. Philoponus provides an extensive and detailed discussion of these species of number considered not in itself but in relation to something else; but what is most interesting for our purposes is the philosophical meaning and theoretical aim of this exposition. While each number considered in itself, as an arithmetical entity, already coincides with a harmony of even and odd, the role of harmony becomes even more evident when we consider numerical relations. The knowledge of the ten numerical relations just mentioned leads towards knowledge of the universe, since the mathematical sciences can explain the physical structure of the universe. In *in Nicom.* 1.178–179, Philoponus sets out to explain Nicomachus' 'marvellous rule'[19] that shows how all species of inequality originate from and may be resolved into equality. He therefore draws a connection between the relation between equality and inequality we find in number, the relation between form and matter in the universe and the relation between the rational part of the soul and the irrational one. By providing order and measure, equality, form and the rational soul respectively determine inequality, matter and the irrational soul.[20] Shortly afterwards, Philoponus once again clarifies what the goal of this theory is, which – on the basis of a discussion of absolute number and relative number – seeks to prove that number is the harmonious composition of equality and inequality, of sameness and difference. In *in Nicom.* 2.12, Philoponus comments on Nicomachus, *Intr. arithm.* 75.14–17, which states:

[19] Philop. *in Nicom.* 1.179.4–5, θαυμαστοῦ προστάγματος. Cf. Ascl. *in Nicom.* 1.152.6. This rule consists in taking three equal numbers, for example three units, and in drawing from them another three numbers, such that the first number is equal to the first, the second to the first plus the second, and the third to the first plus two times the second plus the third. Thus, by way of addition, we will obtain all numerical relations through a succession which is consequential by nature, starting from equality.

[20] With regard to the soul, for instance, Philop. *in Nicom.* 1.178.12–21 states: 'In truth, the rational faculty of the soul is similar to equality, whereas the appetitive faculty and the spirited one are similar to the two species of inequality. Indeed, it seems as though the appetitive faculty resembles inequality according to the less, because it lessens the tension of the soul and weakens the rational activities that derive from it, whereas the spirited faculty resembles inequality according to the greater, because the soul is more active and provides a stimulus for irrational acts. Instead, equality is the rational faculty which regulates each of those two faculties, orders them, leads them towards equalisation and brings them into accordance and in tune with reason, smoothing out the harsh and fierce character of the former, and censuring the weak and relaxed aspect of the latter'.

> There follows upon this speculation a most elegant principle, extremely useful in its application to the Platonic psychogony and the problem of all harmonic intervals.[21]

Referring to *Timaeus* 35a-36d, Philoponus here explains:

> By symbolically teaching about the birth of the soul, he [*scil.* Plato] states that the god, taking the essence that is always self-identical and that which is divided among bodies, and mixing them as in a cauldron, and then reducing this mixture to a straight line, creates a single line which he divides according to harmonic ratios – hemiolics, epitritics and epogdoics – and after having cut them in half lengthwise and folded back in the shape of a χ, creates two circles; then, after having cut six times the internal one, he creates seven circles and moves to the right the external circle and to the left the internal one, and calls the external one <the circle> of 'sameness' and the internal one that of 'difference'.[22]

From this summary (*syntomōs*: Philop. *in Nicom.* 2.12.12) description of the operation performed by the Platonic demiurge, it may clearly be inferred that according to Plato the demiurge has created the world soul by establishing, on the basis of sameness and difference, numerical relations that give rise to harmonic ratios. At this stage, Philoponus is concerned with the fact that it is not easy to understand how the demiurge was able to proceed in his creation of the world soul, since – without a reliable method – it is difficult to find the hemiolics, epitritics, and other ratios by which Plato fills the intervals between the multiple parts of the mixture he has posited. It is necessary, therefore, for those who wish to understand philosophy and in particular the complex psychogony of the *Timaeus*, to learn how to successively and methodically take as many hemiolic, epitritic, and other ratios as required. In *in Nicom.* 2.12.13–15, Philoponus writes:

> [. . .] what will be stated henceforth will also help understand harmonic theorems and discover the musical ratios established by Plato in his psychogony (ὡς τὰ νῦν ἐντεῦθεν λεχθησόμενα συμβάλλεται ἡμῖν εἰς ἁρμονικὰ θεωρήματα καὶ εἰς τὴν εὕρεσιν τῶν ἐν ψυχογονίᾳ παρὰ Πλάτωνι κελευομένων μουσικῶν λόγων λαμβάνεσθαι).

From this point onwards, then, Philoponus presents a complete analytical theory about the theorems by which it is possible to find the various numerical species, and about the various types of number and their

[21] Transl. by M. L. D'Ooge in D'Ooge 1926.

[22] This passage on the generation of the world soul according to the *Timaeus* occurs, in a less simplified form, also in Philop. *in De an.* 115.22–122.26 and *De aeternitate mundi contra Proclum* 195.13–200.3. Both passages have been studied by Segonds 1992.

geometrical configurations. This paves the way for an explanation of the harmonious ratios by which the demiurgic activity of the *Timaeus* unfolds. It is not by chance, then, that Philoponus' mathematical theory reaches its culmination with the discussion of proportions, which require an in-depth knowledge of numerical relations and of the geometrical configurations of numbers. In his discussion on proportions, Philoponus sets out from the relations that can be established between square numbers and heteromecic numbers.

As the theory of proportions represents a necessary tool to fully understand the cosmogony of the *Timaeus* and, through it, the harmonious structure of the universe, it is worth devoting a separate section to this theory.

13.3 The Theory of Proportions and the Harmony of the Universe

The theory of numerical relations and of the geometrical configuration of numbers is the focus of Book 2 of Philoponus' *Commentary* on Nicomachus, down to Chapter 59. In *in Nicom.* 2.60, the commentator introduces the theory of proportions by resuming the discussion from the beginning, which is to say from the question of sameness and difference as principles. In *in Nicom.* 2.60.3–13, Philoponus writes:

> Just as by nature there are two principles of the world, sameness and difference, so there are also two principles of numbers: 1 is the cause of sameness and 2 of difference; and these things are confirmed by the opinion of the ancients, of Plato and Philolaus, and by reality itself. He [*scil.* Nicomachus] presents the things <stated> by the ancients word by word, whereas those <which may be inferred> from reality are evident. Indeed, there is sameness in the universe, for the universe is one and issues forth from the one as its creator;[23] but there is also diversity and the division of the one into multiplicity, since it is impossible for multiplicity to exist without any difference or diversity – in brief, the unity of all is <composed> of opposites. Such too is the genus of numbers, since they have two principles, 1 and 2, yet in neither case – as I have often showed – what we have is number, but only the principles of numbers.

The passage just quoted clearly sums up what has been stated so far with regard to the fact that 1 and 2 are merely sameness and difference expressed as numerical principles; that they are the principles by which the Platonic demiurge has created the universe, which consequently is both one and

[23] This passage may reflect the influence of Pl. *Ti.* 31a-b, which emphasises the unity of the heavens.

many; and, finally, that insofar as the universe derives from opposites – from sameness and difference, limited and unlimited, 1 and 2, even and odd – it requires harmony. In *in Nicom.* 2.60.45, Philoponus explicitly writes that 'the universe is composed of opposites and therefore requires harmony' (τὸ πᾶν γὰρ ἐξ ἐναντίων συνέστηκε, διὸ καὶ ἁρμονίας ἐδεήθη). The theory of proportions meets precisely this need to explain how the composition of the universe is harmonious, according to Plato's teaching. The fact that there is a harmony between sameness and difference becomes clear from the comparison that may be drawn between squares – which, as we have seen, are those numbers which originate from odd numbers and are characterised by sameness – and the first species of inequality, namely heteromecics. Following Nicomachus, Philoponus illustrates different ways of comparing sequences of numbers of this sort, all of which reveal how there is 'accordance, friendship and collaboration' (συμπνοίας τε καὶ φιλίας καὶ συναντιλήψεως: Philop. *in Nicom.* 2.60.50–51) between square numbers and heteromecics, which produces all numerical relations in sequence. The same occurs when we take three – rather than two – terms in a relation, because if we place the heteromecic between the squares (the first heteromecic between the first two squares and so on), we will find – as in the case of the previous two-term relations – first the double and then all the species of epimorics, and will discover that the relation between the last term and the middle term is always the same as that between the medium term and the first. If, on the contrary, we place the square between two heteromecics (the first square between the first two heteromecics and so on), we will find that the relation between the terms is not the same, but that the excess is the same: for the middle term exceeds the former by as much as it is exceeded by the last term. All this leads us to the theory of proportions proper, the usefulness of which lies in the fact that 'unless we know it, we cannot even understand what Plato states about psychogony in the *Timaeus*' (Philop. *in Nicom.* 2.70.8–9).

I will not delve into the technical details of Philoponus' exposition of the theory of proportions, because I am only interested in showing for what philosophical reasons it is important to know this theory according to the commentator, who here expresses a view shared by all Platonists from the Imperial Age onwards. I will only note that (1) if a relation must have at least two terms, a proportion must have at least two relations, whereby at least three terms are necessary in order for there to be a proportion;[24] (2) Philoponus, like Nicomachus, is familiar with ten types of proportion; (3)

[24] Cf. Eucl. *Elem.* 5 def. 8.

Philoponus explicitly credits Pythagoras, the Pythagoreans, Plato and Aristotle with knowledge of the first three types of proportion, namely arithmetic, geometry and harmonics (Philop. *in Nicom.* 2.120.4).[25] The arithmetical proportion is characterised by a quantitative relation, since one extreme exceeds the middle term by as much as the latter exceeds the other extreme (i.e. $a - b = b - c$),[26] and its priority over other kinds of proportion is due to the fact that it manifests itself in the simple natural flow of numbers from 1 to infinity. The geometrical proportion is characterised by a qualitative relation, as it consists in the ratio between the extremes and the middle term (i.e. $a{:}b = b{:}c$).[27] The harmonic proportion differs from both, as it establishes the equality of the relation of the extremes to one another with that of the difference between the larger terms to the difference between the smaller terms (i.e. $a{:}c = [a - b]{:}[b - c]$).[28] Moreover, in the harmonic proportion it is possible to determine the middle term, because this is equal to the quotient obtained from the double product of the extremes and their sum.[29] This proportion is called harmonic because it stands at the basis of the relations between the strings of musical instruments, the relations that give rise to specific sounds. Nicomachus, *Intr. arithm.* 134.1–5, had already taught that all that is relative (*to de pros ti*) pertains to harmonic theory, and that therefore the musical relations of harmonic chords have to do with the harmonic proportion. Philoponus explains that ancient music was familiar with three harmonic systems – the tetrachord, the pentachord and the octachord – which are based on multiples and epimorics, within which the harmonic proportion falls. In the tetrachord the two external strings, that is the *nētē* and the *hypatē*, stand in an epitritic ratio to one another because the *nētē* stands to the *hypatē* as 4 stands to 3;[30] in the pentachord, the *nētē* and the *hypatē* stand in a hemiolic ratio to one another, as 6 stands to 4. The combination of these two systems gives us the octave or octachord, which is expressed by the numbers 3, 4, 6, where the ratio between the extremes is 1:2, while 4 is the epitritic of 3 and 6 is the hemiolic of 4. 'Harmony' derives from the combination of the fifth and the octave, because the ratio between the extremes is 1:3. Finally, the double octave is obtained by turning the previous proportion into a four-term proportion through the addition of 12 to the aforementioned numbers. In such a way,

[25] Cf. Iambl. *in Nicom.* 100–101. [26] Cf. Philop. *in Nicom.* 2.76–84.

[27] Cf. Philop. *in Nicom.* 2.85–92. [28] Cf. Philop. *in Nicom.* 2.93–109.

[29] For example, in the case of the harmonic mean 6, 4, 3, we find that $4 = 2 \times (6 \times 3)/(6 + 3)$. See Nicom. *Intr. arithm.* 139.21–140.13 and Philop. *in Nicom.* 2.119.

[30] *Nētē* and *hypatē* are outermost strings in any musical system in Antiquity. These terms also describe the sounds produced by these strings, which are respectively the highest pitch and the lowest one.

the ratio between the extremes will be 1:4, as 12 is four times 3; and we will have two doubles, 6 as the double of 3 and 12 as the double of 6. The double octave is the last possible chord, since there is no higher harmonic sound: any attempt to go beyond the double octave would create such tension as to snap one's vocal chords or the strings on an instrument (Philop. *in Nicom.* 2.104). Philoponus notes that music is the concrete and perceivable aspect of harmony, because the numerical relations in harmony correspond to the degrees of tension between the strings in music (Philop. *in Nicom.* 2.103.41–43).[31]

Following Nicomachus' text and invoking the authority of Philolaus, in *in Nicom.* 2.105.3–11 Philoponus explains that all the harmonic ratios may be found in the cube:

> <The cube> has 12 sides, because as there are 6 planes, each of which has 4 sides, one might conclude that there are 24 sides; but given that each <side> serves two planes, the existing sides are only 12. It thus has 8 solid angles and 6 planes.[32] Take, then, 12, 8 and 6; the mean term of 12 and 6 is 8, for 12 is the hemiolic of 8 and 8 is the epitritic of 6, and we get that 12 is the double of 6. Such were the harmonic means: the epitritic of the tetrachord, the hemiolic of the pentachord, the double of the octachord composed of both.

As in the cube we find all the relations within which the harmonic proportion falls, the cube is rightly regarded and referred to as geometrical harmony. According to Philoponus, who refers to points already made by Nicomachus, the cube was already considered and described in such terms by the ancients, who followed Philolaus' opinion.[33] However, it is not the result of the relations that constitute harmonic proportions because, on the contrary, it precedes harmony: the cube expresses a relation of equality, as it is the same in all three dimensions – width, depth and length (Philop. *in Nicom.* 2.105.1–2) – while the harmonic proportion reveals relations of

[31] Philop. *in An. post.* 180.5 ff., explains that Pythagorean musical theory distinguishes tones according to their numerical relation and not on the basis of perception, whereas music in the popular sense is only based on the concrete perception of sounds. This does not mean that music should be completely dismissed, since in *in An. post.* 215.1–5 Philoponus states that by lifting our eyes to the heavens and seeing the order it reflects, we come to think of the one who has ordered the cosmos and therefore ascend from the thought of corporeal things to that of incorporeal ones; likewise, from sensible harmony we may ascend to the universal formulas of harmony. For this reason, Plato states that the demiurge has given us ears and eyes through which to attain philosophy (*Ti.* 47a-c). The fact that the soul does not acquire knowledge of things from sensibles – Philoponus further notes – has adequately been proven in the commentary on the *Phaedo* (a possible reference to Damascius' commentary on the *Phaedo*: see Mckirahan 2012, 138 n. 504).

[32] For a definition of solid angle, see Eucl. *Elem.* 11 def. 11.

[33] Philolaus, A24 DK. Cf. Philop. *in Nicom.* 2.105; 108; 133; along with Nicom. *Intr. arithm.* 135.10–12.

inequality, which – as we have seen – follows, derives from and ultimately may be resolved into equality (Philop. *in Nicom.* 2.108).[34]

The theory of the cube opens the culminating argument of Nicomachus' *Introduction to Arithmetic* and of Philoponus' commentary, namely the discussion on solid ratios and on the 'perfect mean',[35] which sums up the first three ratios. Whereas plane means only require one middle term because they are two-dimensional, solid means require two middle terms because they are three-dimensional, as taught by Plato. In *Timaeus* 32a-b[36] the latter states that if the body of the universe were a plane surface, one mean would be enough to keep it together, but since the universe is solid, a single mean cannot preserve its harmony (i.e. it cannot establish a relation with the two solids), it is necessary for there to be two proportional mean terms. The perfect mean is a proportion whose terms preserve harmonic relations, arithmetical relations and geometrical ratios. One example of a numeric formula expressing the perfect mean – the harmony combining the first three proportions – is 6, 8, 9, 12. According to the geometric proportion, 12:8 = 9:6 and 8:6 = 12:9; according to the arithmetical mean, 12 exceeds 9 by as much as 9 exceeds 6; and, finally, according to the harmonic mean, 8 exceeds 6 by 2, which is to say by 1/3 of 6, and 12 exceeds 8 by 4, which is to say by 1/3 of 12. The sequence 6, 8, 9, 12, expresses an exemplary three-dimensionality of the terms it comprises, and within it the proportional means measure the intervals of the harmonic scale of the world soul.[37]

13.4 Conclusions

At this stage, it is worth briefly getting back to Philoponus' argument and recapitulating what role harmony plays in the Neopythagorean and Neoplatonic mathematical theory so eloquently illustrated by John Philoponus' *Commentary on Nicomachus*.

We have established that, from a Platonic perspective, mathematical entities have an intermediate ontological status between the sensible and the intelligible, and that the mathematical sciences play a fundamental epistemological role, as they are the only sciences capable of leading to the knowledge of the intelligibles and hence the only ones capable of leading philosophers to a happy life – a life which cannot be achieved without

[34] On the cube, which is to say the regular hexahedron, see Pl. *Ti.* 55c.

[35] Cf. Pl. *Ti.* 36a; Sext. Emp. *Pyr.* 3.155, *Math.* 4.6 and 7.98; Procl. *in Ti.* 2.29.24–37.14.

[36] See Heath 1921, vol. I, 89.

[37] Procl. *in Ti.* 3.175.21 ff. presents a complex system to determine other harmonic intervals, which develop numerical sequences starting from the basic one: 6, 8, 9, 12.

knowledge of the good. In the light of all this, harmonics acquires an essential role among the mathematical sciences. Harmonics is that mathematical science which accounts for the accordance between even and odd in numbers (i.e. the accordance that each number has with itself, as well as the accordance it has with other numbers) within two, three or four-term relations. This accordance, which is the focus of harmonics as a science, is nothing but the mathematical expression of the accordance existing in the universe between equality and inequality, sameness and difference, limited and unlimited: the aspects of cosmic reality, which – as Plato has taught – is the creation of the demiurge, who has fashioned the cosmos precisely by harmonising these discordant aspects, deriving from his contemplation of the ideas. By virtue of this contemplation, the demiurge possesses those technical reasons which have allowed him to operate like a craftsman. The demiurge, then, has fashioned the world mathematically, insofar as he has used *logoi* which are the arithmetical expression of ideal paradigms. If this is the case, and if the creation of the cosmos coincides with the establishment of harmonious numerical relations, then the philosopher can follow the reverse course: through knowledge of the mathematical sciences, he can ascend to the contemplation of the ideas. It is no coincidence, therefore, that throughout Book 1 of his *Commentary on Nicomachus* Philoponus – also drawing upon the *Republic*[38] – stresses that the usefulness of the mathematical sciences lies in the fact that they lead to the contemplation of the ideas. As has been repeatedly noted, only by knowing these sciences is it possible to understand the psychogony of the *Timaeus*; and once we have grasped the structure of the universe, which is a structure marked by order, proportion and symmetry (i.e. an harmonious structure), we can reach its model, which is to say the ideas and the idea of the good.

Such is the overall framework within which harmonics operates. Without it, as Philoponus repeatedly warns us, it is impossible to understand the technical aspects of the psychogony of the *Timaeus* and, therefore, to grasp the structure of the natural world, which consists in the harmonious composition of sameness and difference as universal principles, as Plato himself has taught us in *Timaeus* 35a ff.[39] Since everything in the cosmos stems from demiurgic creation, all parts of the cosmos are arranged according to the same harmonic laws. Therefore, not only the universe in general and the cosmic soul in particular have an harmonious mathematical structure, but our own soul – which shares the same genus as the cosmic soul – results from the

[38] See Philop. *in Nicom.* 1.32 and the reference to Pl. *Resp.* 7.527d-e.

[39] See Philop. *in Nicom.* 1.178, 2.70, 2.133.

harmonising of rationality and irrationality, whereby the rational part of the soul gives order and measure to the irrational part. Likewise, the laws stem from the order and measure which lawgivers bestow on the city, imitating the intelligible order they have come to know.[40] As the whole of reality has the intelligible forms as its model, which according to Philoponus are the principles of measurement and determination, every aspect of reality – be it physical, psychological, ethical or political – reflects the harmony deriving from this paradigmatic measure.

In his *Commentary*, Philoponus constantly emphasises this philosophical function of harmony, but the treatment of it he provides is a technical one, since the philosopher must have a firm technical knowledge of mathematical harmony, if he is to understand the harmony of the cosmos and of its various parts. Harmony, then, is first of all the accordance of even and odd, which is to say the accordance existing in number considered in itself; we encounter it even more when we take numerical relations into consideration: harmony concerns the relations between pairs of numbers, the relations between three numbers, which is to say plane proportions, and finally the relations between four numbers, which is to say solid proportions, according to a theoretical crescendo. The mathematical teaching imparted by Nicomachus and commented upon by Philoponus reaches its climax with the perfect mean, which is also the perfect harmony, which is to say the numerical series 6, 8, 9, 12, which harmonises the first three proportions – the arithmetic, geometric and harmonic – and shows all the chords that produce harmony and may be translated into specific musical strings.

Through mathematical theory, which explains how on the one hand arithmetic is the primary science, insofar as it constitutes the numerical system employed by the Platonic demiurge, and on the other how everything springs from the harmonisation of arithmetical entities, Philoponus provides all the resources required for the Platonic philosopher to understand the dialogue which, more than any other, had posed some exegetical difficulties in the Platonic tradition: the *Timaeus*. But what is most significant is the fact that through arithmetic and harmonics the commentator is able to explain how each sphere of existence constitutes one mode of manifestation of the one and only reality. Hence, the Platonic philosophical system emerges as a strongly unitary one: from the Platonic forms to sensible entities, from the world soul to the laws of the city, not to mention the human soul and the crucial need for those who have embarked on the philosophical path – in agreement with Plato's teaching – to attain the good.

40 See Philop. *in Nicom.* 1.15.

Bibliography

Abert, H. 1899. *Die Lehre vom Ethos in der griechischen Musik*. Leipzig, Breitkopf & Härtel.

Asmis, E. 1991. 'Epicurean poetics', *Proceedings of the Boston Area Colloquium in Ancient Philosophy* 7: 63–105.

Aubry, G. 2007. *Dieu sans la puissance.* Dunamis *et* energeia *chez Aristote et Plotin.* Paris, Vrin.

Babut, D. 1969. *Plutarque.* De la vertu éthique. *Introduction, texte, traduction et commentaire.* Paris, Les Belles Lettres.

Bakhouche, B. (ed.) 1997. 'Musique et philosophie: le *De Institutione Musica* de Boèce dans la tradition encyclopédique latine', *Bulletin de l'Association Guillame Budé* 3: 210–32.

2011. *Calcidius.* Commentaire au Timée de Platon. Paris, Vrin.

Baltes, M. 1976. *Die Weltentstehung des platonischen* Timaios *nach den antiken Interpreten I.* Leiden-Boston, Brill.

Baltes, M., and D'Ancona Costa, C. 2005. 'Plotino, L'immortalità dell'anima IV. 7 (2) 8[4]', in R. Chiaradonna (ed.), *Studi sull'anima in Plotino.* Naples, Bibliopolis, 19–58.

Baltzly, D. 2009. *Proclus,* Commentary on Plato's Timaeus, *vol. IV, bk. 3, pt. 2.* Cambridge University Press.

Barbera, A. 1991. *The Euclidean division of the canon. Greek and Latin sources.* Lincoln and London, University of Nebraska Press.

Barker, A. 1978. 'Music and perception: a study in Aristoxenus', *Journal of Hellenic Studies* 98: 9–16.

1984. *Greek Musical Writings. Volume I: The musician and his art.* Cambridge University Press.

1989. *Greek Musical Writings. Volume II: Harmonic and acoustic theory.* Cambridge University Press.

2000a. *Scientific method in Ptolemy's* Harmonics. Cambridge University Press.

2000b. 'Timaeus on music and the liver', in M. R. Wright (ed.), *Reason and necessity. Essays on Plato's* Timaeus. London-Swansea, Duckworth and The Classical Press of Wales, 85–99.

2001. 'Diogenes of Babylon and Hellenistic musical theory', in C. Auvray-Assayas and D. Delattre (eds.), *Cicéron et Philodème: la polémique en philosophie.* Paris, Éditions Rue d'Ulm, 353–70.

2007. *The science of harmonics in Classical Greece*. Cambridge University Press.

2009. 'Shifting conceptions of "schools" of harmonic theory, 400 BC–200 AD', in Martinelli (ed.), 165–90.

2014. *Ancient Greek writers on their musical past. Studies in Greek musical historiography*. Pisa-Rome, Fabrizio Serra Editore.

2015. *Porphyry's* Commentary on Ptolemy's Harmonics. *A Greek text and annotated translation*. Cambridge University Press.

2016. 'Plutarch, *Quaestiones convivales*, 704c4-705b6: the host and the musician', in L. Bravi, L. Lomiento, A. Meriani, and G. Pace (eds.), *Tra* lyra *e* aulos. *Tradizioni musicali e generi poetici*. Pisa-Rome, Fabrizio Serra Editore, 15–28.

2018. 'Disreputable music: a performance, a defence, and their intertextual and intermedial resonances (Plutarch *Quaest. conv.* 704c4-705b6)', in T. Phillips and A. D'Angour (eds.), *Music, text, and culture in ancient Greece*. Oxford University Press, 233–55.

Barnes, J. 1988. 'Scepticism and the arts', *Apeiron* 21/2: 53–77.

Behr, J. (ed.) 2017. *Origen.* On first principles, 2 vols. Oxford University Press.

Bélis, A. 1986. *Aristoxène de Tarente et Aristote*. Le traité d'harmonique. Paris, Klincksieck.

Bénatouïl, Th. 2003. 'Logos et *scala naturae* dans le stoïcisme de Zénon et Cléanthe', *Elenchos* 23: 297–331.

Benveniste, É. 1966. 'La notion de "rythme" dans son expression linguistique', in Id. *Problèmes de linguistique générale* I. Paris, Gallimard, 327–35.

Bermond, C. 2001. *La danza negli scritti di Filone, Clemente Alessandrino e Origene: storia e simbologia*. Frankfurt am Main, Domus Editoria Europaea.

Bertier, J. 1978. *Nicomaque de Gérase*. Introduction arithmétique. Paris, Vrin.

Besnier, B. 2003. 'La conception stoïcienne de la matière', *Revue de Métaphysique et de Morale* 37: 51–64.

Betegh, G. 2010. 'What makes a myth εἰκώς? Remarks inspired by Myles Burnyeat's εἰκὼς μῦθος', in R. D. Mohr and B. M. Sattler (eds.), *One book, the whole universe. Plato's* Timaeus *today*. Las Vegas-Zurich-Athens, Parmenides Publishing, 213–23.

Bett, R. 2006. 'La double "schizophrénie" d'*Adversus mathematicos* I–VI, et son origine historique', in J. Delattre (ed.), 17–34.

2013. 'A Sceptic looks at art (but not very closely): Sextus Empiricus on music', *International Journal for the Study of Skepticism* 3: 155–81.

2018. *Sextus Empiricus*, Against those in the disciplines. *Translated with introduction and notes*. Oxford University Press.

Blank, D. L. 1998. *Sextus Empiricus*, Against the grammarians (Adversus mathematicos I). *Translated with an introduction and commentary*. Oxford, Clarendon Press.

2009. '*Philosophia* and *technē*: Epicureans on the arts', in J. Warren (ed.), *The Cambridge companion to Epicureanism*. Cambridge University Press, 216–33.

Blomqvist, J. 1974. 'Die Skeptika des Sextus Empiricus', *Grazer Beiträge* 2: 7–14.

Bobzien, S. 2015. 'Time: *M* 10.169-247', in K. Algra and K. Ierodiakonou (eds.), *Sextus Empiricus and ancient physics*. Cambridge University Press, 275–323.
Bonazzi, M. 2003. *Academici e Platonici. Il dibattito antico sullo scetticismo di Platone*. Milan, LED.
2004. 'Un lettore antico della *Repubblica*: Numenio di Apamea', *Méthexis* 17: 71–84.
2007. 'Eudorus' psychology and Stoic ethics', in M. Bonazzi and Ch. Helmig (eds.), *Platonic Stoicism, Stoic Platonism. The dialogue between Platonism and Stoicism in Antiquity*, Leuven University Press, 109–32.
2013. 'Pythagoreanising Aristotle: Eudorus and the systematisation of Platonism', in Schofield (ed.), 160–86.
2015. *À la recherche des idées. Platonisme et philosophie hellénistique d'Antiochus à Plotin*. Paris, Vrin.
Bowie, E. L. 2004. 'Poetry and music in the life of Plutarch's statesman', in L. de Blois, J. Bons, T. Kessels, and D. M. Schenkeveld (eds.), *The statesman in Plutarch's works. Vol. I*. Leiden-Boston, Brill, 115–23.
Boyancé, P. 1946. 'Les muses et l'harmonie des sphères', in *Mélanges dédies à la mémoire de Félix Grat I*. Paris, Mme Pecqueur-Grat, 3–16.
Boys-Stones, G. R. 2001. *Post-Hellenistic philosophy. A study of its development from the Stoics to Origen*, Oxford University Press.
2018. *Platonist philosophy 80 BC to AD 250. An introduction and collection of sources in translation*. Cambridge University Press.
Brague, R. 1999. *La sagesse du monde. Histoire de l'expérience humaine de l'univers*. Paris, Fayard.
Brancacci, A. 1984. 'Aristosseno e lo statuto epistemologico della scienza armonica', in G. Giannantoni and M. Vegetti (eds.), *La scienza ellenistica. Atti delle tre giornate di studio tenutesi a Pavia dal 14 al 16 aprile 1982*. Naples, Bibliopolis, 151–86.
Brigham, F. 1962. 'The concept of new song in Clement of Alexandria's *Exhortation to the Greeks*', *Classical Folia* 16/1: 9–13.
Brisson, L. (ed.) 2005. *Porphyre,* Sentences, 2 vols. Paris, Vrin.
Brochard, V. 2002. *Les Sceptiques grecs*. Paris, Le Livre de Poche (or. ed. Paris, Imprimerie Nationale, 1887).
Bruns, I. (ed.) 1887–92. *Alexandri Aphrodisiensis praeter commentaria scripta minora*, 2 vols. Berlin, Reimer.
Brunschwig, J. 1994a. 'The conjunctive model', in Id. *Papers in Hellenistic philosophy*. Cambridge University Press, 72–91.
1994b. 'Sextus Empiricus on the KRITHPION: the sceptic as conceptual legatee', in Id. *Papers in Hellenistic philosophy*. Cambridge University Press, 230–43.
Burkert, W. 1972. *Lore and science in ancient Pythagoreanism*. Cambridge (MA), Harvard University Press.
Burnyeat, M. F. 2005. 'Εἰκὼς μῦθος', *Rhizai* 2: 143–65.
Bury, R. G. (ed.) 1949. *Sextus Empiricus,* Against professors. Translated by R. G. Bury. Cambridge (MA), Harvard University Press.

Busch, O. 1998. *Logos Syntheseos. Die euklidische* Sectio Canonis, *Aristoxenos, und die Rolle der Mathematik in der antiken Musiktheorie.* Berlin, Staatliches Institut für Musikforschung Preussischer Kulturbesitz.

Butterworth, G. W. 1916. 'Clement of Alexandria's *Protrepticus* and the *Phaedrus* of Plato', *Classical Quarterly* 10/4: 198–205.

1919. *Clement of Alexandria.* The Exhortation to the Greeks. The rich man's salvation. *And the fragment of an address entitled to the newly baptized.* London, Heinemann.

Calabi, F. 2007. *God's acting, man's acting. Tradition and philosophy in Philo of Alexandria*, Leiden-Boston, Brill.

Calabi, F., Munnich, O., Reydams-Schils, G., and Vimercati E. (eds.) 2015. *Pouvoir et puissances chez Philon d'Alexandrie.* Turnhout, Brepols.

Castagnoli, L. 2017. 'Aporia and enquiry in ancient Pyrrhonism', in G. Karamanolis and V. Politis (eds.), *The aporetic tradition in ancient philosophy.* Cambridge University Press, 205–27.

Castelli, L. M. 2018. *Aristotle.* Metaphysics. *Book Iota.* Oxford, Clarendon Press.

Caston, V. 1997. 'Epiphenomenalisms, ancient and modern', *The Philosophical Review* 106/3: 309–63.

2012. *Alexander of Aphrodisias,* On the Soul. *Part I: Soul as form of the body, parts of the soul, nourishment, and perception.* London, Bloomsbury.

Celkyte, A. 2017. 'Epicurus and aesthetic disinterestedness', *Mare Nostrum* 7: 56–75.

Centrone, B. 2000. 'Cosa significa essere pitagorico in età imperiale. Per una riconsiderazione della categoria storiografica del neopitagorismo', in A. Brancacci (ed.), *La filosofia in età imperiale. Le scuole e le tradizioni filosofiche.* Naples, Bibliopolis, 137–68.

2015. 'Medioplatonismo e neopitagorismo: un confronto difficile', *Rivista di storia della filosofia* 70/2: 399–423.

Chadwick, H. 1953. *Origen.* Contra Celsum. *Translated with an introduction and notes.* Cambridge University Press.

Chase, M. 2010. 'Porphyry on the cognitive process', *Ancient Philosophy* 30: 383–405.

Cherniss, H. (ed.) 1976. *Plutarch.* Moralia. *Volume XIII, part I.* Cambridge (MA), Harvard University Press.

Chiaradonna, R. 2007. 'Porphyry's views on the immanent incorporeals', in G. Karamanolis and A. Sheppard (eds.), *Studies on Porphyry* (supplement to the *Bulletin of the Institute of Classical Studies*, vol. 98). London, Institute of Classical Studies, 34–49.

2013. 'Platonist approaches to Aristotle: from Antiochus of Ascalon to Eudorus of Alexandria (and beyond)', in Schofield (ed.), 28–52.

2014. 'Plotinus' metaphorical reading of the *Timaeus*: soul, mathematics, providence', in P. d'Hoine and G. van Riel (eds.), *Fate, providence and moral responsibility in ancient, medieval and early modern thought. Studies in honour of Carlos Steel.* Leuven University Press, 187–210.

2015. 'Plotinus' account of demiurgic causation and its philosophical background', in A. Marmodoro and B. Prince (eds.), *Causation and creation in late Antiquity*. Cambridge University Press, 31–50.

2019. 'Plotinus on memory, recollection and discursive thought', in L. Castagnoli and P. Ceccarelli (eds.), *Greek memories. Theories and practices*. Cambridge University Press, 310–24.

(unpublished), 'The early Peripatetic commentators on Aristotle's *Categories* and the previous philosophical tradition', in A. Joosse and A. Ulacco (eds.), *Dealing with disagreement. The construction of traditions in later ancient philosophy*.

Chrétien J.-L. 1990. *La Voix Nue. Phénoménologie de la promesse*. Paris, Éditions de Minuit.

1997. *Corps à corps. À l'écoute de l'œuvre d'art*. Paris, Éditions de Minuit.

2001. 'Plotin en mouvement', *Archives de Philosophie* 64/2: 243–58.

Clark, P. 2016. *Plotinus: Myth, metaphor and philosophical practice*. University of Chicago Press.

Cooper, J. M. (ed.) 1997. *Plato. Complete works*. Indianapolis, Hackett.

2012. *Pursuits of wisdom. Six ways of life in ancient philosophy from Socrates to Plotinus*. Princeton University Press.

Cornford, F. M. 1937. *Plato's cosmology. The* Timaeus *of Plato translated with a running commentary*. London, Routledge & Kegan Paul.

Cortassa, G. 1981. 'Sesto Empirico e gli ἐγκύκλια μαθήματα: un'introduzione a Sext. Emp. *Adv. Math.* I–VI', in G. Giannantoni (ed.), *Lo scetticismo antico*, 2 vols. Naples, Bibliopolis, 713–24.

Corti, L. 2015. 'Scepticism, number and appearances. The ἀριθμητική τέκνη and Sextus' targets in *M* I–VI', *Philosophie Antique* 15: 121–45.

Cosgrove, C. H. 2006. 'Clement of Alexandria and early Christian music', *Journal of Early Christian Studies* 14/3: 255–82.

Costache, D. 2014. 'Worldview and melodic imagery in Clement the Alexandrian, Saint Athanasius, and their antecedents in Saints Ignatius and Irenaeus', *Phronema* 29/1: 21–60.

Creese, D. 2010. *The monochord in ancient Greek harmonic science*. Cambridge University Press.

Crippa, S. 2009. 'Voce e musica *au cœur* del sapere oracolare in Plutarco', in D. Castaldo, D. Restani, and C. Tassi (eds.), *Il sapere musicale e i suoi contesti da Teofrasto a Claudio Tolemeo*. Ravenna, Longo Editore, 87–94.

da Rocha Júnior, A. R. 2008. 'Plutarch and the music', in A. G. Nikolaidis (ed.), *The unity of Plutarch's work.* Moralia *themes in the* Lives, *features of the* Lives *in the* Moralia. Berlin-New York, De Gruyter, 651–6.

Darras-Worms, A.-L. (ed.) 2007. *Plotin,* Traité 1 (I, 6). *Introduction, traduction, commentaires et notes*. Paris, Éditions du Cerf.

Davidson Greaves, D. (ed.) 1986. *Sextus Empiricus,* Against the Musicians (Adversus musicos). *A new critical text and translation*. Lincoln-London, University of Nebraska Press.

Decleva Caizzi, F. 1992. 'Sesto e gli scettici', *Elenchos* 13: 277–327.

de Haas, F. 2020. 'The utility of musical theory and performance for the good life. A comparison between the ancient philosophical discussion and Cornelius Agrippa's *De incertitudine et vanitate scientiarum et artium*', in G. Gerbino and J. Prins (eds.), *Hearing the Voice, Hearing the Soul: Music, Mind, and Body in Renaissance Thought.* Turnhout, Brepols.

de Jésus, C. A. Martins 2009. 'Dancing with Plutarch. Dance and dance theory in Plutarch's *Table Talks*', in J. Ribeiro Ferreira, D. Leão, M. Tröster, and P. Barata Dias (eds.), Symposion *and* Philanthropia *in Plutarch.* Coimbra, Classica Digitalia/Centro de Estudos Clássicos e Humanísticos da Universidade de Coimbra, 403–14.

Delattre, D. 2001. 'Vers une reconstruction de l'esthétique musicale de Philodème (à partir du livre IV des *Commentaires sur la musique*)', in C. Auvray-Assayas and D. Delattre (eds.), *Cicéron et Philodème: la polémique en philosophie.* Paris, Éditions Rue d'Ulm, 371–84.

2006. 'Présence de l'épicurisme dans le *Contre les grammairiens* et le *Contre les musiciens* de Sextus Empiricus', in J. Delattre (ed.), 47–65.

(ed.) 2007. *Philodème de Gadara,* Sur la musique, *Livre IV. 2 vols.* Paris, Les Belles Lettres.

Delattre, J. (ed.) 2006. *Sur le* Contre les professeurs *de Sextus Empiricus.* Lille, Presses de l'Université de Charles-de Gaulle-Lille 3.

Delling, G. 1984. 'The one who sees God in Philo', in F. E. Grenspahn, E. Hilgert, and B. L. Mack (eds.), *Nourished with peace. Studies in Hellenistic Judaism in memory of Samuel Sandmel.* Chico (CA), Scholars Press, 27–41.

De Marco, V. 1956. 'L'introduzione al Πρὸς Μαθηματικούς di Sesto Empirico', *Rendiconti della Accademia di archeologia, lettere e belle arti di Napoli* 31: 117–60.

Demulder, B. 2017a. 'Dining with the demiurge. Cosmic imagery and cosmological ethics in Plutarch's *Quaestiones Convivales* 1.2', in S. Amendola, G. Pace, and P. Volpe Cacciatore (eds.), *Immagini letterarie e iconografia nelle opere di Plutarco.* Madrid, Ediciones Clásicas, 35–44.

2017b. 'Is dualism a Greek word? Plutarch's dualism as a cultural and historical phenomenon', in A. Georgiadou and K. Oikonomopoulou (eds.), *Space, time and language in Plutarch.* Berlin-New York, De Gruyter, 205–14.

Den Boeft, J. 1970. *Calcidius on fate. His doctrine and sources.* Leiden-Boston, Brill.

1977. *Calcidius on demons.* Leiden-Boston, Brill.

Denniston, J. D. 1954. *The Greek particles.* 2nd ed. Oxford, Clarendon Press.

Desbordes, F. 1990. 'Le scepticisme et les "arts libéraux": une étude de Sextus Empiricus, *Adversus Mathematicos* I–VI', in A.-J. Voelke (ed.), *Le scepticisme antique. Perspectives historiques et systématiques.* Lausanne, Cahiers de la Revue de théologie et de philosophie, n. 15, 167–79.

Dillon, J. 1977. *The Middle Platonists. A study of Platonism 80 B.C. to A.D. 220.* London, Duckworth.

1993. *Alcinous,* The handbook of Platonism. *Translated with an introduction and commentary.* Oxford, Clarendon Press.

1996. *The Middle Platonists. 80 B.C. to A.D. 220. Revised edition with a new afterword.* Ithaca (NY), Cornell University Press.

2014a. 'The Muses in the Platonic Academy', in K. W. Christian, C. E. L. Guest, and C. Wedepohl (eds.), *The Muses and their afterlife in post-classical Europe.* London, Warburg Institute, 1–11.

2014b. 'Pythagoreanism in the Academic tradition: the Early Academy to Numenius', in Huffman 2014a, 250–73.

D'Ippolito, G. 2011. 'Il *De musica* nel *corpus* plutarcheo: una paternità recuperabile', *Quaderni Urbinati di Cultura Classica* 99: 207–25.

Donini, P. 1982. *Le scuole, l'anima, l'impero: la filosofia antica da Antioco a Plotino.* Turin, Rosenberg & Sellier.

1988. 'La connaissance de Dieu et la hiérarchie divine chez Albinos', in R. Van den Broek, T. Baarda, and J. Mansfeld (eds.), *Knowledge of God in the Graeco-Roman world.* Leiden-Boston, Brill, 118–31.

2002. 'Apuleio: ineffabilità o inconoscibilità del principio?', in F. Calabi (ed.), *Arrhetos theos. L'ineffabilità del primo principio nel medioplatonismo.* Pisa, ETS, 93–102.

2011. *Plutarco,* Il volto della luna. *Introduzione, testo critico, traduzione e commento.* Naples, D'Auria.

2017. *Plutarco,* Il demone di Socrate. *Introduzione, traduzione e commento.* Rome, Carocci.

D'Ooge, M. L. 1926. *Nicomachus of Gerasa,* Introduction to Arithmetic. Translated into English by M. L. D'Ooge, with studies in Greek arithmetic by M. L. Robbins and F. E. Karpinski. Ann Arbor, University of Michigan Press.

Dooley, W. E. 1989. *Alexander of Aphrodisias,* On Aristotle Metaphysics 1. Translated by W. E. Dooley. London, Bloomsbury.

Dörrie, H., and Baltes, M. 1998. *Der Platonismus in der Antike, IV 2: Einige grundlegende Axiome / Platonische Physik (im antiken Verständnis) II. Bausteine 125–150.* Stuttgart-Bad Cannstatt, Frommann-Holzboog.

Durán Mañas, M. 2005. 'La *paideia* y la música en Plutarco', in M. Jufresa, F. Mestre, P. Gómez, and P. Gilabert (eds.), *Plutarc a la seva època. Paideia i societat.* Barcelona, Imagraf Impresores, 69–76.

Emilsson E. K. 1988. *Plotinus on sense-perception. A philosophical study.* Cambridge University Press.

2017. *Plotinus.* London-New York, Routledge.

Falcon, A. (ed.) 2016. *The Brill's companion to the reception of Aristotle in Antiquity.* Leiden-Boston, Brill.

Feke, J. 2018. *Ptolemy's philosophy: mathematics as a way of life.* Princeton University Press.

Fera, M. C. 2011. 'Plutarco nel *De musica*', *Quaderni Urbinati di Cultura Classica* 99: 191–206.

Ferrari, F. 1995. *Dio, idee e materia. La struttura del cosmo in Plutarco di Cheronea.* Naples, D'Auria.

1996. 'La generazione precosmica e la struttura della materia in Plutarco', *Museum Helveticum* 53: 44–55.

2000. 'Plutarch: Platonismus und Tradition', in M. Erler and A. Graeser (eds.), *Philosophen des Altertums. Vom Hellenismus bis zur Spätantike. Eine Einführung*. Darmstadt, Primus Verlag, 109–27.

2001. 'Struttura e funzione dell'esegesi testuale nel medioplatonismo: il caso del *Timeo*', *Athenaeum* 89: 525–74.

2004. 'Platone in Plutarco', in I. Gallo (ed.), *La biblioteca di Plutarco*. Naples, D'Auria, 225–35.

2012. 'L'esegesi medioplatonica del *Timeo*: metodi, finaltà, risultati', in F. Celia and A. Ulacco (eds.), *Il* Timeo. *Esegesi greche, arabe, latine*. Pisa University Press, 81–131.

2014. 'Materia, movimento, anima e tempo prima della nascita dell'universo: Plutarco e Attico sulla cosmologia del *Timeo*', in E. Coda and C. Martini Bonadeo (eds.), *Études de logique et de cosmologie offertes à Henri Hugonnard-Roche*. Paris, Vrin, 255–76.

2015. 'Lucio Calveno Tauro e l'interpretazione didascalica della cosmogenesi del *Timeo*', in L. Cardullo and D. Iozzia (eds.), *Bellezza e virtù. Studi in onore di Maria Barbanti*. Acireale, Bonanno, 307–19.

Ferrari, F., and Baldi, L. 2002. *Plutarco,* La generazione dell'anima nel Timeo. Naples, D'Auria.

Festugière, A. J. (ed.) 1970. *Proclus,* Commentaire sur la République, 3 vols. Paris, Vrin.

Finamore, J. F. 2006. 'Apuleius on the Platonic gods', in H. Tarrant and D. Baltzly (eds.), *Reading Plato in Antiquity*. London, Bloomsbury, 33–48.

Foley, E. 1996. *Foundations of Christian music. The music of pre-constantinian Christianity*. Collegeville (MN), The Liturgical Press.

Fortuna, S. 1987. 'Sesto Empirico: ἐγκύκλια μαθήματα e arte utili alla vita', *Studi Classici e Orientali* 36: 123–37.

Fowler, D. 1984. 'Sceptics and Epicureans: a discussion of M. Gigante 1981', *Oxford Studies in Ancient Philosophy* 2: 237–67.

Fowler, R. 2018. 'Variations of receptions of Plato during the Second Sophistic', in Tarrant, Layne, Baltzly, and Renaud (eds.), 223–49.

2014. *Plato in the Third Sophistic*. Berlin-New York, De Gruyter.

Frick, P. 1999. *The concept of divine providence in Philo of Alexandria*. Tübingen, Mohr Siebeck.

Froidefond, C. 1987. 'Plutarque et le platonisme', *Aufstieg und Niedergang der römischen Welt* 2.36.1: 184–233.

García López, J. 1999. 'Banquete, vino y teoría musical en Plutarco: *Quaestiones convivales* (*Moralia* 612C-748D)', in J. G. Montes Cala, M. Sánchez Ortiz de Landaluce, and R. J. Gallé Cejudo (eds.), *Plutarco, Dioniso y el vino*. Madrid, Ediciones Clásicas, 243–53.

2000. 'Terminología musical y géneros poéticos en *Moralia* de Plutarco', in I. Gallo and C. Moreschini (eds.), *I generi letterari in Plutarco*. Naples, D'Auria, 287–98.

2002. 'La μουσικὴ τέχνη en Plu. *Quaestiones Convivales* (*Mor.* 612C-748D)', in L. Torraca (ed.), *Scritti in onore di Italo Gallo*. Naples, Edizioni Scientifiche Italiane, 303–14.

2003. 'Oἱ ὀργανικοί y τὰ ὄργανα musicales en las *Vidas* (griegas) de Plutarco', in J. M. Nieto Ibáñez (ed.), *Lógos Hellenikós. Homenaje al Profesor Gaspar Morocho Gayo, Vol. I*. Universidad de León, 251–8.

2005. 'Teoría musical y régimen político en las *Vidas* (griegas) de Plutarco', in M. Jufresa, F. Mestre, P. Gómez, and P. Gilabert (eds.), *Plutarc a la seva època. Paideia i societat*. Barcelona, Imagraf Impresores, 577–85.

Gelineau, J. 1962. *Chant et musique dans le culte chrétien. Principes, lois et applications*. Paris, Fleurus.

Gérold, T. 1931. *Les Pères de l'Église et la musique*. Paris, Alcan.

Gersh, S. 1986. *Middle Platonism and Neoplatonism. The Latin tradition*. University of Notre Dame.

Gersh, S. 1992. 'Porphyry's commentary on the Harmonics of Ptolemy and Neoplatonist musical theory', in S. Gersh and C. Kennengiesser (eds.), *Platonism in Late Antiquity*. University of Notre Dame, 141–55 (reprinted in S. Gersh, *Reading Plato, Tracing Plato*, Variorum, Ashgate 2005, Item III).

1996. *Concord in discourse. Harmonics and semiotics in late classical and early Medieval Platonism*. Berlin-New York, De Gruyter.

2000. 'Proclus' theological methods. The programme of *Theol. Plat.* I. 4', in A. Ph. Segonds and C. Steel (eds.), *Proclus et la théologie Platonicienne. Actes du Colloque International de Louvain, 13–16 mai 1998, en l'honneur de H. D. Saffrey et L. G. Westerink*. Leuven University Press, 15–27 (reprinted in Id., *Reading Plato, tracing Plato. From ancient commentary to medieval reception*. Aldershot, Ashgate 2005, Item VI).

2014. 'Proclus as theologian', in Id. (ed.), *Interpreting Proclus. From Antiquity to the Renaissance*. Cambridge University Press, 80–107.

2017. 'The Metaphysics of power, *logos*, and harmony in Porphyry', in J. F. Finamore and S. Klitenic Wear (eds.), *Defining Platonism. Essays in honor of the 75th birthday of John M. Dillon*. Steubenville (OH), Franciscan University Press, 198–217.

Gerson, L. P. (ed.) 2010. *The Cambridge history of philosophy in late Antiquity*. Cambridge University Press.

2013. *From Plato to Platonism*. Ithaca (NY), Cornell University Press.

Giardina, G. R. 1999. *Giovanni Filopono matematico tra neopitagorismo e neoplatonismo*. Commentario alla Introduzione Aritmetica di Nicomaco di Gerasa. *Introduzione, testo, traduzione e note*. Catania, CUECM.

2000. 'Il concetto di numero nell'*In Nicomachum* di Giovanni Filopono', in G. Bechtle and D. J. O'Meara (eds.), *La philosophie des mathématiques de l'Antiquité tardive*. Éditions Universitaires Fribourg Suisse, 149–71.

2012. 'L'*Epinomide* negli scritti matematici neopitagorici e neoplatonici', in F. Alesse and F. Ferrari (eds.), *Epinomide. Studi sull'opera e la sua ricezione*. Naples, Bibliopolis, 341–78.

Gibson, S. 2005. *Aristoxenus of Tarentum and the birth of musicology*. New York-London, Routledge.

Gigante, M. 1981. *Scetticismo e epicureismo. Per l'avviamento di un discorso storiografico*. Naples, Bibliopolis.

Gioè, A. 2002. *Filosofi medioplatonici del II secolo d.C.* Naples, Bibliopolis.

Glucker, J. 1978. *Antiochus and the late Academy*. Göttingen, Vandenhoeck & Ruprecht.

Görgemanns, H., and Hirsch-Luipold, R. 2010. 'Plutarch', in S. L. Sorgner and M. Schramm (eds.), *Musik in der antiken Philosophie. Eine Einführung*. Würzburg, Königshausen & Neumann, 249–55.

Gottschalk, H. B. 1971. 'Soul as *harmonia*', *Phronesis* 16: 179–98.

Gourinat, J.-B. 2016. *Plotin,* Traité 20, *Qu'est-ce que la dialectique?* Paris, Vrin.

Granger, H. 1985. 'The *scala naturae* and the continuity of kinds', *Phronesis* 30/2: 181–200.

Greenbaum, D. 2016. *The daimon in Hellenistic astrology. Origins and influence*. Leiden-Boston, Brill.

2018. 'Porphyry of Tyre on the daimon, birth and the stars', in L. Brisson, S. O'Neill, and A. Timotin (eds.), *Neoplatonic demons and angels. Studies in Platonism, Neoplatonism, and the Platonic tradition, volume 20*. Leiden-Boston, Brill, 102–39.

Griffin, M. J. 2015. *Aristotle's* Categories *in the early Roman empire*. Oxford University Press.

2016. 'Why philosophy begins with the categories. Perspectives from the 1st-century Greek commentators', *Documenti e studi sulla tradizione filosofica medievale* 27: 19–42.

Gros, P. 2006. 'Les fondements philosophiques de l'harmonie architecturale selon Vitruve (*De architectura* III–IV)', in Id., *Vitruve et la tradition des traités d'architecture. Fabrica et ratiocinatio*. Rome, École française de Rome, 271–80.

Guitton, J. 1933. *Le temps et l'éternité chez Plotin et saint Augustin*. Paris, Boivin.

Hadot, I. 2005. *Arts libéraux et philosophie dans la pensée antique*, 2nd ed., Paris, Vrin.

2007. 'Versuch einer doktrinalen Neueinordnung der Schule der Sextier', *Rheinisches Museum für Philologie* 150: 179–210.

Hadot, P. 1997. *Plotin ou la simplicité du regard*. Paris, Gallimard.

Hagel, S. 2009. *Ancient Greek music. A new technical history*. Cambridge University Press.

Halliwell, F. S. 2012. '*Amousia:* living without the Muses', in I. Sluiter and R. M. Rosen (eds.), *Aesthetic value in classical Antiquity*. Leiden-Boston, Brill, 15–45.

Halton, T. 1983. 'Clement's lyre: a broken string, a new song', *The Second Century: a Journal of Early Christian Studies* 3–4: 177–99.

Hankinson, R. J. 1995. *The Sceptics*. New York-London, Routledge.

Hardie, Ph. 1995. 'The speech of Pythagoras in Ovid *Metamorphoses* 15: Empedoclean epos', *Classical Quarterly* 45/1: 204–14.

Harl, M. 1983. *Origène*. Philocalie, 1–20. Sur les Écritures. *Introduction, texte, traduction et notes*. Paris, Éditions du Cerf.
Hayduck, M. (ed.) 1891. *Alexandri Aphrodisiensis in Aristotelis Metaphysica commentaria*. Berlin, Reimer.
Heath, Th. 1921. *A history of Greek mathematics*. Oxford, Clarendon Press.
Helmer, J. 1937. *Zu Plutarchs* De animae procreatione in Timaeo. *Ein Beitrag zum Verständnis des Platon-Deuters Plutarch*. Würzburg, Richard Mayr.
Hershbell, J. P. 1987. 'Plutarch's *De animae procreatione in Timaeo*: an analysis of structure and content', *Aufstieg und Niedergang der römischen Welt* 2.36.1: 234–47.
Hicks, A. J. 2017. *Composing the world. Harmony in the Medieval Platonic cosmos*. Oxford University Press.
Hirsch-Luipold, R. 2002. *Plutarchs Denken in Bildern. Studien zur literarischen, philosophischen und religiösen Funktion des Bildhaften*. Tübingen, Mohr Siebeck.
Hoche, R. (ed.) 1866. *Nicomachi Geraseni Pythagorei*, Introductionis arithmeticae libri II. Leipzig, Teubner.
Hoenig, Ch. 2014. 'Calcidius and the creation of the universe', *Rhizomata* 2/1: 80–110.
2018. *Plato's* Timaeus *in the Latin tradition*. Cambridge University Press.
Holzhausen, J. 1993. 'Zur Inspirationslehre Plutarchs in *De Pythiae Oraculis*', *Philologus* 137/1: 72–91.
Horky, P. S. 2013. *Plato and Pythagoreanism*. Oxford University Press.
Huffman, C. A. 1993. *Philolaus of Croton. Pythagorean and Presocratic*. Cambridge University Press.
(ed.) 2014a. *A history of Pythagoreanism*. Cambridge University Press.
2014b. 'The Peripatetics on the Pythagoreans', in Huffman 2014a, 274–95.
Irwin, E. 1982. 'The songs of Orpheus and the new song of Christ', in J. Warden (ed.), *Orpheus. The metamorphoses of a myth*. University of Toronto Press, 51–62.
Janáček, K. 1972. *Sextus Empiricus' sceptical methods*. Prague, Universita Karlova.
2008a. 'Τά δέκα τῶν Σκεπτικῶν', in Id. *Studien zu Sextus Empiricus, Diogenes Laertius und zur pyrrhonischen Skepsis*, ed. by J. Janda and F. Karfik. Berlin-New York, De Gruyter, 146–8 (originally in J. Irmscher, B. Doer, U. Peters, and R. Müller (eds.), *Miscellanea critica* I, Leipzig, 1964, 119–21).
2008b. '*M* I–VI als Schlüssel zu Sextos Empeirikos' Schriften', in Id. *Studien zu Sextus Empiricus, Diogenes Laertius und zur pyrrhonischen Skepsis*, ed. by J. Janda and F. Karfik. Berlin-New York, De Gruyter, 349–57 (originally in *Listy filologické* 117, 1994: 171–8).
Jankélévitch V. 1961. *La musique et l'ineffable*. Paris, Éditions du Seuil.
1998. *Plotin*, Ennéades, I, 3 *Sur la dialectique*. Paris, Éditions du Cerf.
Jones, C. P. 1967. 'The teacher of Plutarch', *Harvard Studies in Classical Philology* 71: 205–13.
Jourdan, F. 2008. 'Le "*Logos*" et l'empereur, nouveaux Orphée. Postérité d'une image entrée dans la littérature avec Clément d'Alexandrie', *Vigiliae Christianae* 62/4: 319–33.

2010. *Orphée et les Chrétiens. La réception du mythe d'Orphée dans la littérature chrétienne grecque des cinq premiers siècles. Tome I : Orphée, du repoussoir au préfigurateur du Christ*. Paris, Les Belles Lettres.

Jufresa, M. 2001. 'El placer de la música supera el del amor', in A. Pérez Jiménez and F. Casadesús Bordoy (eds.), *Estudios sobre Plutarco. Misticismo y religiones mistéricas en la obra de Plutarco*. Madrid, *Ediciones Clásicas*, 539–44.

Jürß, F. 2001. *Sextus Empiricus*, Gegen die Wissenschaftler *1–6. Aus dem Griechischen übersetzt, eingeleitet und kommentiert*. Würzburg, Königshausen & Neumann.

Kalbfleisch, C. (ed.) 1907. *Simplicii* in Aristotelis Categorias commentarium. Berlin, Reimer.

Karamanolis, G. 2006. *Plato and Aristotle in agreement? Platonists on Aristotle from Antiochus to Porphyry*. Oxford, Clarendon Press.

2013. *The philosophy of early Christianity*. London-New York, Routledge.

Kechagia, E. 2011. 'Philosophy in Plutarch's *Table Talk*. In jest or in earnest?', in Klotz and Oikonomopoulou (eds.), 77–104.

Klotz, F. 2011. 'Imagining the past. Plutarch's play with time', in Klotz and Oikonomopoulou (eds.), 161–78.

Klotz, F., and Oikonomopoulou, K. (eds.) 2011. *The philosopher's banquet. Plutarch's* Table Talk *in the intellectual culture of the Roman empire*. Oxford University Press.

König, J. 2007. 'Fragmentation and coherence in Plutarch's *Sympotic Questions*', in J. König and T. Whitmarsh (eds.), *Ordering Knowledge in the Roman Empire*. Cambridge University Press, 43–68.

2011. 'Self-promotion and self-effacement in Plutarch's *Table Talk*', in Klotz and Oikonomopoulou (eds.), 179–203.

Kraeling, C. H., and Mowry, L. 1957. 'Music in the Bible', in E. Wellesz (ed.), *The new Oxford history of music. Vol. 1: Ancient and Oriental music*, Oxford University Press, 283–312.

Kramarz, A. 2016. *The power and value of music. Its effect and ethos in classical authors and contemporary music theory*. New York, Peter Lang.

Kuisma, O. 1996. *Proclus' defence of Homer*. Helsinki, Societas Humanarum Fennica.

Lamberton, R. 1986. *Homer the theologian. Neoplatonist allegorical reading and the growth of the epic tradition*. Berkeley-Los Angeles, University of California Press.

La Sala, R. 2010. 'Sextus Empiricus', in S. L. Sorgner and M. Schramm (eds.), *Musik in der antiken Philosophie. Eine Einführung*. Würzburg, Königshausen & Neumann, 257–73.

Laurent, J. 1992. *Les fondements de la nature selon Plotin*. Paris, Vrin.

2011. *L'éclair dans la nuit. Plotin et la puissance du beau*. Paris, Éditions de la Transparence.

Lautner, P. 2015. 'Mental images in Porphyry's *Commentary on Ptolemy's Harmonics*', *Apeiron* 48/2: 220–51.

Lavaud, L. 2006. 'La *diánoia* médiatrice entre le sensible et l'intelligible', *Études Platoniciennes* 3: 29–55.

Levarie, S. 1991. 'Philo on music', *Journal of Musicology* 9: 124–30.

Lévy, C. 2007. 'La question de la dyade chez Philon d'Alexandrie', in M. Bonazzi, C. Lévy, and C. Steel (eds.), *A Platonic Pythagoras. Platonism and Pythagoreanism in the imperial age*. Turnhout, Brepols, 11–28.

2009. 'Le scepticisme et les arts, de Pyrrhon à Enésidème', in F. Le Blay (ed.), *Transmettre les savoirs dans les mondes hellénistique et romain*. Presses Universitaires de Rennes, 93–106.

2011. 'L'aristotélisme, parent pauvre de la pensée philonienne?', in T. Bénatouïl, E. Maffi, and F. Trabattoni (eds.), *Plato, Aristotle, or both? Dialogues between Platonism and Aristotelianism in Antiquity*. Hildesheim, Georg Olms Verlag, 17–33.

Lewis, E. 1988. 'Diogenes Laertius and the Stoic theory of mixture', *Bulletin of the Institute of Classical Studies* 35: 84–90.

Lilla, S. 1971. *Clement of Alexandria. A study in Christian Platonism and Gnosticism*. Oxford University Press.

Lippman, E. A. 1964. *Musical thought in ancient Greece*. New York-London, Columbia University Press.

Loenen, J. H. 1956. 'Albinus' metaphysics: an attempt at rehabilition. I: The inner consistency and the original character of Albinus' interpretation of Plato', *Mnemosyne* 9/4: 296–319.

Long, A. A. 1991. 'The harmonics of Stoic virtue', in H. Blumenthal and H. Robinson (eds.), *Aristotle and the later tradition (Oxford Studies in Ancient Philosophy*, Supplementary Volume). Oxford, Clarendon Press, 97–116.

1996. *Stoic studies*. Cambridge University Press.

Longo, A. (ed.) 2009. *Plotin,* Traité 2 (IV, 7). Paris, Éditions du Cerf.

Lugaresi, L. 2003. 'Metafore dello spettacolo in Origene', in L. Perrone (ed.), *Origeniana Octava. Origen and the Alexandrian tradition. Papers of the 8th international Origen congress, Pisa 27–31 August 2001*. Leuven University Press, 657–78.

2008. *Il teatro di Dio. Il problema degli spettacoli nel cristianesimo antico* (II–IV secolo). Brescia, Morcelliana.

2011. 'Canto del *Logos*, dramma soteriologico e conoscenza di fede in Clemente Alessandrino', in R. Radice and A. Valvo (eds.), *Dal Logos dei Greci e dei Romani al Logos di Dio*. Milan, Vita e Pensiero, 243–76.

Luna, C. 2001. *Trois études sur la tradition des commentaires anciens à la* Métaphysique *d'Aristote*. Leiden-Boston, Brill.

Lyon, E. L. 2016. 'Ethical aspects of listening in Plato's *Timaeus*. Pleasure and delight in 80b5-8', *Greek and Roman Musical Studies* 4: 253–72.

Magee, J. (ed.) 2016. *Calcidius.* On Plato's Timaeus. Cambridge (MA), Harvard University Press.

Mansfeld, J. 1971. 'Three Notes on Albinus', *Theta-Pi. A Journal for Greek and Early Christian Philosophy* 1: 61–80 = In: J. Mansfeld (1989). *Studies in Later Greek Philosophy and Gnosticism*. London-New York, Routledge, chapt. 6.

1992. *Heresiography in context. Hippolytus'* Elenchos *as a source for Greek philosophy*. Leiden-Boston, Brill.

Marchand, S. 2011. 'Sextus Empiricus' style of writing', in D. E. Machuca (ed.), *New essays on ancient Pyrrhonism*. Leiden-Boston, Brill, 113–41.

Martinelli, M. C. (ed.) 2009. *La Musa dimenticata. Aspetti dell'esperienza musicale greca in età ellenistica*. Pisa, Edizioni della Normale.

McClary, S. 1995. 'Music, the Pythagoreans, and the body', in S. L. Foster (ed.), *Choreographing History*. Bloomington-Indianapolis, Indiana University Press, 82–104.

McKinnon, J. (ed.) 1987. *Music in early Christian literature*. Cambridge University Press.

McKirahan, R. 2012. *Philoponus*, On Aristotle Posterior Analytics *1.9–18*. London, Bloomsbury.

McLynn, N. 2004. 'What was the *Philocalia* of Origen?', *Meddelanden från Collegium Patristicum Lundense* 19: 32–43.

Meeusen, M. 2016. *Plutarch's science of natural problems. A study with commentary on* Quaestiones Naturales. Leuven University Press.

Michalewski, A. 2014. *La puissance de l'intelligible. La théorie plotinienne des Formes au miroir de l'héritage médioplatonicien*. Leuven University Press.

2021. 'Writing in the soul. On some aspects of recollection in Plotinus', in V. Decaix and C. Thomsen Thörnqvist (eds.), *Memory and recollection in the Aristotelian tradition*. Turnhout, Brepols.

Moraux, P. 1973. *Der Aristotelismus bei den Griechen: von Andronikos bis Alexander von Aphrodisias*, vol. 1. Berlin-New York, De Gruyter.

Morel P.-M. 2002. 'La sensation, messagère de l'âme. Plotin V, 3 [49], 3', in M. Dixsaut (ed.), La *connaissance de soi. Études sur le* Traité 49 *de Plotin*. Paris, Vrin, 209–27.

Moreschini, C. 2015. *Apuleius and the metamorphoses of Platonism*. Turnhout, Brepols.

Moro Tornese, S. 2010. *Philosophy of music in the Neoplatonic tradition. Theories of music and harmony in Proclus'* Commentaries on Plato's Timaeus *and* Republic, unpublished doctoral thesis, University of London.

2015. 'Music as therapy: the analogy between music and medicine in Neoplatonism', *Dionysius* 33: 118–31.

Morrow, G. 1992. *Proclus*. A Commentary on the First Book of Euclid's Elements. *Translated with introduction and notes*. Princeton University Press.

Mosconi, G. 2009. '"Governare in armonia": struttura e significato ideologico di un campo metaforico in Plutarco', in D. Castaldo, D. Restani, and C. Tassi (eds.), *Il sapere musicale e i suoi contesti da Teofrasto a Claudio Tolemeo*. Ravenna, Longo Editore, 105–28.

Moutsopoulos, E. 1959. *La musique dans l'œuvre de Platon*. Paris, Presses Universitaires de France.

2004. *La philosophie de la musique dans le système de Proclus*. Athens, Académie d'Athènes.

Murray, P. 2002. 'Plato's Muses. The goddesses that endure', in E. Spentzou and D. Fowler (eds.), *Cultivating the Muse. Struggles for power and inspiration in classical literature*. Oxford University Press, 29–46.

Murray, P., and Wilson, P. (eds.) 2004. *Music and the Muses. The culture of 'Mousikē' in the classical Athenian city*. Oxford University Press.

Nesselrath, H.-G. 2010. *Plutarch*. On the daimonion of Socrates. *Human liberation, divine guidance and philosophy*. Tübingen, Mohr-Siebeck.

Nikolaidis, A. G. 1991. 'Plutarch's contradictions', *Classica et Mediaevalia* 42: 153–86.

Noble, Ch. I. (forthcoming). 'Human nature and normativity in Plotinus', in P. Adamson and C. Rapp (eds.), *State and nature: essays in ancient political philosophy*. Berlin-New York, de Gruyter.

O'Meara, D. J. 1989. *Pythagoras revived. Mathematics and philosophy in late Antiquity*. Oxford, Clarendon Press.

2003. *Platonopolis. Platonic political philosophy in late Antiquity*. Oxford, Clarendon Press.

2005. 'The music of philosophy in late Antiquity', in R. W. Sharples (ed.), *Philosophy and the sciences in Antiquity*. Aldershot, Ashgate, 131–47.

2007. 'Hearing the harmony of the spheres in late Antiquity', in M. Bonazzi, C. Lévy, and C. Steel (eds.), *A Platonic Pythagoras. Platonism and Pythagoreanism in the imperial age*. Turnhout, Brepols, 147–61.

2013. 'Moral virtue in late antique Platonism. Some elements of a background to ethics in early Arabic philosophy', *Mélanges de l'Université Saint-Joseph* (Beirut) 65: 47–61.

Opsomer, J. 1994. 'L'âme du monde et l'âme de l'homme chez Plutarque', in M. García Valdés (ed.), *Estudios sobre Plutarco: ideas religiosas*. Madrid, Ediciones Clásicas, 33–49.

1996. 'Ζητήματα: structure et argumentation dans les *Quaestiones Platonicae*', in J. A. Fernández Delgado and F. Pordomingo Pardo (eds.), *Estudios sobre Plutarco: aspectos formales*. Madrid, Ediciones Clásicas, 71–83.

1998. *In search of the truth. Academic tendencies in Middle Platonism*. Brussels, KAWLSK.

2004. 'Plutarch's *De animae procreatione in Timaeo*: manipulation or search for consistency?', in P. Adamson, H. Baltussen, and M. W. F. Stone (eds.), *Philosophy, science and exegesis in Greek, Latin and Arabic commentaries* (supplement to the *Bulletin of the Institute of Classical Studies* 83). London, Institute of Classical Studies, 137–62.

2005a. 'Plutarch's Platonism revisited', in M. Bonazzi and V. Celluprica (eds.), *L'eredità platonica. Studi sul platonismo da Arcesilao a Proclo*. Naples, Bibliopolis, 163–200.

2005b. 'Demiurges in early Imperial Platonism', in R. Hirsch-Luipold (ed.), *Gott und die Götter bei Plutarch*. Berlin-New York, De Gruyter, 51–99.

2005c. 'A craftsman and his handmaiden. Demiurgy according to Plotinus', in Th. Leinkauf and C. Steel (eds.), *Platons* Timaios *als Grundtext der Kosmologie in Spätantike, Mittelalter und Renaissance. Plato's* Timaeus *and the foundations of cosmology in Late Antiquity, the Middle Ages and Renaissance.* Leuven University Press, 67–102.

2009. 'M. Annius Ammonius, a philosophical profile', in M. Bonazzi and J. Opsomer (eds.), *The origins of the Platonic system. Platonisms of the early empire and their philosophical contexts.* Leuven, Peeters Publishers, 123–86.

2010. 'Arguments non-linéaires et pensée en cercles. Forme et argumentation dans les *Questions Platoniciennes* de Plutarque', in X. Brouillette and A. Giavatto (eds.), *Les dialogues platoniciens chez Plutarque. Stratégies et méthodes exégétiques.* Leuven University Press, 93–116.

2012. 'Plutarch on the division of the soul', in R. Barney, T. Brennan, and C. Brittain (eds.), *Plato and the divided self.* Cambridge University Press, 311–30.

Opsomer, J., Roskam, G., and Titchener, F. B. (eds.) 2016. *A versatile gentleman. Consistency in Plutarch's Writing.* Leuven University Press.

Osborn, E. F. 1957. *The philosophy of Clement of Alexandria.* Cambridge University Press.

Osborne, C. 2010. 'Clement of Alexandria', in Gerson (ed.), 270–82.

Pellegrin, P. 2002. 'Introduction', in P. Pellegrin (ed.), Sextus Empiricus, *Contre les professeurs.* Paris, Éditions du Seuil, 9–47.

2006. 'De l'unité du scepticisme sextien', in J. Delattre (ed.), 35–45.

2010. 'Sextus Empiricus', in Bett, R. (ed.), *The Cambridge companion to ancient Scepticism.* Cambridge University Press, 120–41.

Pelosi, F. 2009. 'Suoni simultanei: prassi esecutiva, *ēthos* e psicologia nei *Problemata* pseudoaristotelici', in Martinelli (ed.), 205–24.

2010. *Plato on music, soul and body.* Cambridge University Press.

2014. 'Dall'unisono alla dissonanza: definizioni di rapporti tra suoni nella teoria musicale greca', *Annali della Scuola Normale Superiore di Pisa (Classe di Lettere e Filosofia)*, serie 5, 6/2: 681–702.

2015. 'Incantare con suoni e parole: l'*epōidē* nei dialoghi platonici', in F. Malhomme and M. Semi (eds.), *Parole e suoni. Contributo a una storia musicale della razionalità antica e moderna.* Milan, Mimesis, 33–46.

2016. 'Music for life: embryology, cookery and *harmonia* in the Hippocratic *On Regimen*', *Greek and Roman Musical Studies* 4/2: 191–208.

2018. 'Eight singing Sirens. Heavenly harmonies in Plato and the Neoplatonists', in J. Prins and M. Vanhaelen (eds.), *Sing aloud harmonious spheres. Renaissance conceptions of cosmic harmony.* New York-London, Routledge, 15–30.

(forthcoming). *Megiste mousike. Filosofia e musica nelle fonti della Grecia antica, vol. 1: dai Presocratici ad Aristosseno.* Berlin-New York, De Gruyter.

Pelosi, F., and Petrucci, F. M. (forthcoming). *Megiste mousike. Filosofia e musica nelle fonti della Grecia antica, vol. 2: dalle filosofie ellenistiche agli autori cristiani.* Berlin-New York, De Gruyter.

Pernigotti, C. 2009. 'Circolazione della cultura letteraria e forme di spettacolarità nel simposio Plutarcheo', in D. Castaldo, D. Restani, and C. Tassi (eds.), *Il sapere musicale e i suoi contesti da Teofrasto a Claudio Tolemeo*. Ravenna, Longo Editore, 95–103.

Petit, A. 1998. 'Philon *et le pythagorisme*: un usage problématique', in C. Lévy (ed.), *Philon d'Alexandrie et le langage de la philosophie*. Turnhout, Brepols, 471–82.

Petrucci, F. M. 2011. 'Una traccia della dialettica scolastica del primo Peripato: le sezioni musicali dei *Problemata physica* (XI e XIX)', in B. Centrone (ed.), *Studi sui* Problemata Physica *Aristotelici*. Naples, Bibliopolis, 175–238.

2012a. *Teone di Smirne,* Expositio rerum mathematicarum ad legendum Platonem utilium. Sankt Augustin, Academia Verlag.

2012b. 'Il *Commento al Timeo* di Adrasto di Afrodisia', *Documenti e Studi sulla Tradizione Filosofica Medievale* 23: 1–32.

2014. 'Le témoignage du deuxième livre du *Commentaire au Timée* de Proclus sur la forme des arguments médio-platoniciens au sujet de la genèse du monde', *Revue des Études Grecques* 127/2: 331–75.

2016a. 'Argumentative strategies in the "Platonic Section" of Plutarch's *De Iside et Osiride* (chapters 45–64)', *Mnemosyne* 69/2: 226–48.

2016b. 'Plutarch's theory of cosmological powers in the *De Iside et Osiride*', *Apeiron* 49/3: 329–67.

2016c. 'Argumentative strategies for interpreting Plato's cosmogony: Taurus and the issue of literalism in Antiquity', *Phronesis* 61/1: 43–59.

2018a. *Taurus of Beirut. The other side of Middle Platonism*. New York-London, Routledge.

2018b. 'Theon of Smyrna and "Plato's system of mathematics": re-thinking Platonic mathematics in Middle Platonism', in Tarrant, Layne, Baltzly, and Renaud (eds.), 143–55.

2019a. 'Making Sense of the Soul's Numbers', *Apeiron* 52: 65–92.

2019b. 'A homeopathic remedy for the human soul. The ethical import of the experience of music in Plutarch and other Middle Platonists', *Ancient Philosophy* 39: 427–50.

Polito, R. 2014. *Aenesidemus of Cnossus: Testimonia*. Cambridge University Press.

Primavesi, O. 2014. 'Aristotle on the "so-called Pythagoreans": from lore to principles', in Huffman 2014a, 227–49.

Provenza, A. 2012. 'Aristoxenus and music therapy: fr. 26 Wehrli within the tradition on music and catharsis', in C. A. Huffman (ed.), *Aristoxenus of Tarentum. Discussion*. New Brunswick-London, Transaction Publishers, 91–128.

Radice, R. 2000. *Oikeiosis. Ricerche sul fondamento del pensiero stoico e sulla sua genesi*. Milan, Vita e Pensiero.

Raffa, M. 2002. La scienza armonica *di Claudio Tolemeo*. Messina, Edizioni Dr. Antonino Sfameni.

2016a. *Claudio Tolemeo*, Armonica *con il* Commentario *di Porfirio*. Milan, Bompiani.

(ed.) 2016b. *Porphyrius,* Commentarius in Claudii Ptolemaei Harmonica. Berlin-New York, De Gruyter.
2017. 'Artificio retorico o sapere musicale? L'accordatura del cosmo in Clemente alessandrino, *Protrettico,* 1, 5, 1–2', *Rivista di Cultura Classica e Medioevale* 59/1: 47–57.
2018. *Theophrastus of Eresus. Commentary, Vol. 9.1. Sources on Music (Texts 714-726 C).* Leiden-Boston, Brill.
Ramelli, I. 2011. 'The philosophical stance of allegory in Stoicism and its reception in Platonism, Pagan and Christian: Origen in dialogue with the Stoics and Plato', *International Journal of the Classical Tradition* 18/3: 335–71.
2018. 'Origen to Evagrius', in Tarrant, Layne, Baltzly, and Renaud (eds.), 271–91.
Rashed, M. 2007. *Essentialisme. Alexandre d'Aphrodise entre logique, physique et cosmologie.* Berlin-New York, De Gruyter.
2013. 'Boethus' Aristotelian ontology', in Schofield (ed.), 53–77.
Ravaisson, F. 1933. *Testament philosophique et fragments.* Paris, Boivin.
Reinhardt, T. 2007. 'Andronicus of Rhodes and Boethus of Sidon on Aristotle's *Categories*', in R. Sorabji and R. W. Sharples (eds.), *Greek and Roman Philosophy 100 BC–200 AD, 2 vols.* (supplement to the *Bulletin of the Institute of Classical Studies* 94). London, Institute of Classical Studies, 513–29.
Reiss, J. 1934. 'Sextus Empiricus przeciw muzykom (Sextus Empiricus contre les musiciens)', *Bulletin International de l'Académie Polonaise des Sciences et des Lettres. Classe de Philologie, Classe d'Histoire et de Philosophie* 7–10: 181–3.
Reydams-Schils, G. J. 1999. *Demiurge and providence. Stoic and Platonist readings of Plato's* Timaeus. Turnhout, Brepols.
(ed.) 2002. *Plato's* Timaeus *as cultural icon.* University of Notre Dame Press.
2007. 'Meta-discourse: Plato's *Timaeus* according to Calcidius', *Phronesis* 52/3: 301–27.
2017. 'Maximus of Tyre on God and providence', in R. Seaford, J. Wilkins, and M. Wright (eds.), *Selfhood and the soul. Essays on ancient thought and literature in honour of Christopher Gill.* Oxford University Press, 125–38.
Riethmüller, A. 1975. 'Die Hinfälligkeit musiktheoretischer Prinzipien nach Sextus Empiricus, *Adversus Musicos*', *Archiv für Musikwissenschaft* 32: 184–95.
Rispoli, G. M. 1992. 'Sesto Empirico e Filodemo contro i musici', in A. H. S. El-Mosalawy (ed.), *Proceedings of the XIXth International Congress of Papyrology, Cairo 2–9* September *1989.* Cairo, Ain Shams University Center of Papyrological Studies, 213–48.
Ritoók, Zs. 2004. *Griechische Musikästhetik. Quellen zur Geschichte der antiken griechischen Musikästhetik.* Frankfurt a.M., Peter Lang.
Rocconi, E. 2009. 'Il suono musicale tra età ellenistica ed età imperiale', in Martinelli (ed.), 191–204.
2012. 'Aristoxenus and musical *Ēthos*', in C. A. Huffman (ed.), *Aristoxenus of Tarentum. Discussion.* New Brunswick-London, Transaction Publishers, 65–90.

Roessli, J.-M. 2002. 'Convergence et divergence dans l'interprétation du mythe d'Orphée. De Clément d'Alexandrie à Eusèbe de Césarée', *Revue de l'histoire des religions* 219/4: 503–13.
2008. 'Imágenes de Orfeo en el arte judío y cristiano', in A. Bernabé and F. Casadesús (eds.), *Orfeo y la tradición órfica: un reencuentro*, vol. 1. Madrid, Akal, 179–226.
2014. 'Assimilation chrétienne d'éléments païens. Construction apologétique ou réalité culturelle?', *Laval théologique et philosophique* 70/3: 507–16.
Romano, F. 1979. *Porfirio di Tiro: filosofia e cultura nel III secolo d.C.* Università di Catania.
Romeyer-Dherbey, G. 1985. *Les sophistes.* Paris, Presses Universitaires de France.
Roskam, G. 2011. 'Two *Quaestiones Socraticae* in Plutarch', in J. M. Candau Morón, F. J. González Ponce, and A. L. Chávez Reino (eds.), *Plutarco transmisor. Actas del X Simposio Internacional de la Sociedad Española de Plutarquistas, Sevilla, 12–14 de noviembre de 2009.* Universidad de Sevilla, 419–31.
2013. 'A ζήτημα on eros and poetry in Plutarch (*Quaest. conv.* 1,5)', in G. Santana Henríquez (ed.), *Plutarco y las artes.* Madrid, Ediciones Clásicas, 95–108.
2014. 'Plutarch's yearning after divinity. The introduction to *On Isis and Osiris*', *Classical Journal* 110/2: 213–39.
2017. 'On the multi-coloured robes of philosophy. Plutarch's approach in *On Isis and Osiris*', in M. Erler and M. A. Stadler (eds.), *Platonismus und spätägyptische Religion. Plutarch und die Ägyptenrezeption in der römischen Kaiserzeit.* Berlin-New York, De Gruyter, 199–218.
Rowe, C. J. 1993. *Plato,* Phaedo. Cambridge University Press.
Rowell, L. 1987. 'Review of Davidson Greaves, *Against the musicians (Adversus musicos)* of Sextus Empiricus 1986', *Journal of Music Theory* 31/2: 359–61.
Ruelle, Ch. É. 1898. 'Sextus Empiricus contre les musiciens', *Revue des Études Grecques* 11/42: 138–58.
Runia, D. T. 1993. 'Was Philo a Middle Platonist? A difficult question revisited', *Studia Philonica Annual* 5: 112–140.
2001. *Philo of Alexandria. On the creation of the cosmos according to Moses.* Leiden-Boston, Brill.
Runia, D. T. and Share, M. 2008. *Proclus,* Commentary on Plato's Timaeus, *vol. II, Book 2: Proclus on the Causes of the Cosmos and Its Creation.* Cambridge University Press.
Russo, A. (ed.) 1972. Sesto Empirico, *Contro i Matematici,* libri I–VI. Bari, Laterza.
Salles, R. 2017. 'Soul as harmony in *Phaedo* 85e-86d and Stoic pneumatic theory', in V. Harte and R. Woolf (eds.), *Rereading ancient philosophy. Old chestnuts and sacred cows.* Cambridge University Press, 221–39.
Sassi, M. M. (2015). 'Parmenides and Empedocles on *krasis* and knowledge', *Apeiron* 45: 1–19.
Scade, P. 2017. 'Music and the soul in Stoicism', in R. Seaford, J. Wilkins, and M. Wright (eds.), *Selfhood and the soul. Essays on ancient thought and literature in honour of Christopher Gill.* Oxford University Press, 197–218.

Schlapbach, K. 2011. 'Dance and discourse in Plutarch's *Table Talks* 9.15', in T. Schmidt and P. Fleury (eds.), *Perceptions of the second sophistic and its times. Regards sur la Seconde Sophistique et son époque*. University of Toronto Press, 149–68.

2018. *The anatomy of dance discourse. Literary and philosophical approaches to dance in the later Graeco-Roman world.* Oxford University Press.

Schofield, M. 2007. 'Aenesidemus: Pyrrhonist and "Heraclitean"', in A. M. Ioppolo and D. N. Sedley (eds.), *Pyrrhonists, Patricians, Platonizers. Hellenistic Philosophy in the period 155–86 BC.* Naples, Bibliopolis, 271–338.

2010. 'Music all pow'rful', in M. L. McPherran (ed.), *Plato's* Republic. *A critical guide*. Cambridge University Press, 229–48.

(ed.) 2013. *Aristotle, Plato and Pythagoreanism in the first century BC. New directions for philosophy.* Cambridge University Press.

Sedley, D. N. 1976. 'Epicurus and his professional rivals', in J. Bollack and A. Laks (eds.), *Études sur l'Epicurisme antique*, Publications de l'Université de Lille, Cahiers de Philologie 1, 121–59.

1985. 'Three notes on Theophrastus' treatment of tastes and smells', in W. W. Fortenbaugh, together with P. M. Huby and A. A. Long (eds.), *Theophrastus of Eresus. On his life and work.* New Brunswick-Oxford, Transaction Books, 205–7.

Segonds, A. Ph. 1992. 'À propos d'une page du *De aeternitate mundi* de Jean Philopon', in M. O. Goulet-Cazé, G. Madec, and D. O'Brien (eds.), *ΣΟΦΙΗΣ ΜΑΙΗΤΟΡΕΣ, Chercheurs de sagesse, Hommage à Jean Pépin*. Paris, Institut d' Etude Augustiniennes, 461–79.

Share, M. 2005. '*John Philoponus,* Against Proclus's on the eternity of the world 1–5'. Ithaca (NY), Cornell University Press.

Sharples, R. W. 1985. 'Theophrastus on tastes and smells', in W. W. Fortenbaugh, together with P. M. Huby and A. A. Long (eds.), *Theophrastus of Eresus. On his life and work.* New Brunswick-Oxford, Transaction Books, 183–204.

2003. 'Threefold providence: the history and background of a doctrine', in R. W. Sharples and A. Sheppard (eds.), *Ancient approaches to Plato's* Timaeus (supplement to the *Bulletin of the Institute of Classical Studies* 78). London, Institute of Classical Studies, 107–27.

(ed.) 2005. *Philosophy and the sciences in Antiquity*. Aldershot, Ashgate.

2010. *Peripatetic philosophy 200 BC to AD 200. An introduction and collection of sources in translation.* Cambridge University Press.

Sheppard, A. 2005. 'Music therapy in Neoplatonism', in R. W. Sharples (ed.), 148–55.

2017. 'Neoplatonists and pantomime dancers', in R. L. Cardullo and F. Coniglione (eds.), *Reason and no-reason from ancient philosophy to neurosciences. Old parameters, new perspectives.* Sankt Augustin, Academia Verlag, 65–78.

Shorey, P. 1916. 'Notes on Sextus Empiricus *ΠΡΟΣ ΜΟΥΣΙΚΟΥΣ* 21', *Classical Philology* 11/1: 99.

Simonetti, E. G. 2017. *A perfect medium? Oracular divination in the thought of Plutarch*. Leuven University Press.

Skeris, R. A. 1976. *ΧΡΩΜΑ ΘΕΟΥ. On the origins and theological interpretation of the musical imagery used by the ecclesiastical writers of the first three centuries, with special reference to the image of Orpheus*. Altötting, Alfred Coppenrath.

Slaveva-Griffin, S. 2009. *Plotinus on number*. Oxford University Press.

Slings, S. R. 1999. *Plato,* Clitophon. Cambridge University Press.

Smith, A. 2010. 'Porphyry and his school', in Gerson (ed.), 325–57.

1974. *Porphyry's place in the Neoplatonic tradition. A study in post-Plotinian Neoplatonism*. The Hague, Martinus Nijhoff.

Smith, W. S. 1962. *Musical aspects of the New Testament*. Amsterdam, Uitgeverij W. Ten Have N.V.

Smits, J. P. H. M. 1970. *Plutarchus en de Griekse muziek*. Bilthoven, Creyghton.

Somfai, A. 2003. 'The nature of daemons. A theological application of the concept of geometrical proportion in Calcidius' *Commentary to Plato's Timaeus* (40d-41a)', in R. W. Sharples and A. Sheppard (eds.), *Ancient approaches to Plato's* Timaeus (supplement to the *Bulletin of the Institute of Classical Studies* 78). London, Institute of Classical Studies, 129–42.

Spinelli, E. 2008. 'Sesto Empirico contro i musici: contesto e senso di una polemica antica', in C. Tatasciore (ed.), *Filosofia e musica*. Milan, Mondadori, 41–56.

2010. 'Pyrrhonism and the specialized sciences', in R. Bett (ed.), *The Cambridge companion to ancient Scepticism*. Cambridge University Press, 249–64.

2014. 'Sesto, Pitagora, la musica', in R. L. Cardullo and D. Iozzia (eds.), ΚΑΛΛΟΣ ΚΑΙ ΑΡΕΤΗ – *Bellezza e virtú: Studi in onore di Maria Barbanti*. Acireale-Rome, Bonanno Editore, 335–47.

2016. '"Are flute-players better than philosophers?" Sextus Empiricus on music, against Pythagoras', in A.-B. Renger and A. Stavru (eds.), *Pythagorean knowledge from the Ancient to the Modern World: askesis, religion, science*. Wiesbaden, Harrassowitz Verlag, 305–18.

Staehle, K. 1931. *Die Zahlenmystik bei Philon von Alexandreia*. Leipzig, Teubner.

Stapert, C. R. 2007. *A new song for an old world. Musical thought in the early Church*. Grand Rapids (MI)-Cambridge (UK), W. B. Eerdmans.

Sterling, G. E. 1993. 'Platonizing Moses: Philo and Middle Platonism', *Studia Philonica Annual* 5: 96–111.

Stover, J. A. (ed.) 2016. *A new work by Apuleius: The lost third book of the* 'De Platone'. *Edited and translated with an introduction and commentary*. Oxford University Press.

Tarrant, H. 1993. *Thrasyllan Platonism*. Ithaca (NY), Cornell University Press.

2004. 'Must commentators know their sources? Proclus' *In Timaeum* and Numenius', in P. Adamson, H. Baltussen, and M. W. F. Stone (eds.), *Philosophy, science and exegesis in Greek, Latin and Arabic commentaries* (supplement to the *Bulletin of the Institute of Classical Studies* 83/1–2). London, Institute of Classical Studies, 175–90.

2017a. *Proclus:* Commentary on Plato's Timaeus, *vol. VI, Book 5: Proclus on the Gods of Generation and the Creation of Humans.* Cambridge University Press.

2017b. 'Plotinus, Origenes, and Ammonius on the King', in G. H. van Kooten and A. K. Petersen (eds.), *Religio-philosophical discourses in the Mediterranean world. From Plato, through Jesus, to late Antiquity.* Leiden-Boston, Brill, 323–37.

Tarrant, H., and Johnson, M. 2018. 'Porphyry and "Neopythagorean" exegesis in *Cave of the Nymphs* and elsewhere', *Méthexis* 30: 154–74.

Tarrant, H., Layne, D. A., Baltzly, D., and Renaud, F. (eds.) 2018. *Brill's companion to the reception of Plato in Antiquity.* Leiden-Boston, Brill.

Tassi, C. 2009. 'Esperienze sonore in Plutarco', in D. Castaldo, D. Restani, and C. Tassi (eds.), *Il sapere musicale e i suoi contesti da Teofrasto a Claudio Tolemeo.* Ravenna, Longo Editore, 129–44.

Teodorsson, S.-T. 1996. *A commentary on Plutarch's* Table Talks. *Vol. III.* Gothenburg, Acta Universitatis Gothoburgensis.

Towey, A. 2000. *Alexander of Aphrodisias,* On Aristotle's On Sense Perception. Ithaca (NY), Cornell University Press.

Tsouna-McKirahan, V. 1996. 'Conservatism and Pyrrhonian Skepticism', *Syllecta Classica* 6: 69–86.

Ulacco, A. 2016. 'The appropriation of Aristotle in the ps-Pythagorean treatises', in Falcon (ed.), 202–17.

Van den Berg, R. 2001. *Proclus'* Hymns. *Essays, translation, commentary.* Leiden-Boston, Brill.

Van den Hoek, A. 1996. 'Techniques of quotation in Clement of Alexandria. A view of ancient literary working methods', *Vigiliae Christianae* 50/3: 223–43.

2005. 'Apologetic and protreptic discourse in Clement of Alexandria', in A. Wlosok and F. Paschoud (eds.), *L'apologétique chrétienne gréco-latine à l'époque prénicénienne* (Entretiens sur l'Antiquité Classique 51), Vandœuvres-Genève, Fondation Hardt, 69–102.

Van der Stockt, L. 1992. 'Plutarch on τέχνη', in I. Gallo (ed.), *Plutarco e le scienze.* Genoa, Sagep Editrice, 287–95.

2009. '"The tunes of death". Music as a way to the divine in Plutarch's *De superstitione, Quaestiones Convivales* IX 14, and *Non posse suaviter vivi secundum Epicurum*', in E. Karamalengou and E. Makrygianni (eds.), *Ἀντιφίλησις: Studies on Classical, Byzantine and Modern Greek literature and culture in honour of Professor John-Theophanes A. Papademetriou.* Stuttgart, Franz Steiner Verlag, 401–13.

Van Winden, J. C. M. 1959. *Calcidius on matter: his doctrine and sources. A chapter in the history of Platonism.* Leiden-Boston, Brill.

1978. 'Quotations from Philo in Clement of Alexandria's *Protrepticus*', *Vigiliae Christianae* 32/3: 208–13.

Veres, M. 2020. 'Keep calm and carry on: Sextus Empiricus on the origins of Pyrrhonism', in J. K. Larsen and P. Steinkrüger (eds.), *Ancient Modes of*

Philosophical Inquiry (special issue of *History of Philosophy and Logical Analysis* 23/1).
Vernière, Y. 1977. *Symboles et mythes dans la pensée de Plutarque. Essai d'interprétation philosophique et religieuse des* Moralia. Paris, Les Belles Lettres.
Viltanioti, I.-F. 2015. *L'harmonie des Sirènes du pythagorisme ancien à Platon.* Berlin-Boston, De Gruyter.
Wakker, G. 1997. 'Emphasis and affirmation. Some aspects of μήν in tragedy', in A. Rijksbaron (ed.), *New approaches to Greek particles.* Amsterdam, J. C. Gieben, 209–31.
Wallies, M. (ed.) 1891. *Alexandri Aphrodisiensis* In Aristotelis Topicorum libros octo commentaria. Berlin, Reimer.
Warren, J. 2002. *Epicurus and Democritean ethics. An archaeology of* ataraxia. Cambridge University Press.
2003. 'Sextus Empiricus and the tripartition of time', *Phronesis* 48/4: 313–43.
Waszink, J. H. 1957. 'Der Platonismus und die altchristliche Gedankenwelt', in *Recherches sur la tradition platonicienne* (Entretiens sur l'Antiquité Classique 3), Vandœuvres-Genève, Fondation Hardt, 137–79.
1964. *Studien zum 'Timaioskommentar' des Calcidius. Die erste Hälfte des Kommentars.* Leiden-Boston, Brill/Warburg Institute.
Waszink, J. H., and Jensen, P. J. (eds.) 1962. *Plato,* Timaeus a Calcidio translatus commentarioque instructus. Leiden-Boston, Brill/Warburg Institute.
Webb, R. 2008a. *Demons and dancers. Performance in late Antiquity*, Cambridge (MA), Harvard University Press.
2008b. 'Inside the mask: pantomime from the performers' perspective', in E. Hall and R. Wyles (eds.), *New directions in ancient pantomime.* Oxford University Press, 43–60.
Weil, H., and Reinach, T. 1900. *Plutarque*, De la musique. Paris, Leroux.
Wendland, P. (ed.) 1901. *Alexandri Aphrodisiensis* in librum de sensu commentarium. Berlin, Reimer.
Wersinger, A. G. 2007. 'La philosophie entre logique et musique. Sextus Empiricus et la *diaphônia* (Discussion de quelques arguments de Jonathan Barnes)', *Revue de Métaphysique et de Morale* 56/4: 499–519.
West, M. L. 1992. *Ancient Greek Music.* Clarendon Press, Oxford.
Whitaker, G. H. 1929. *The Works of Philo of Alexandria*, v. 1. London, William Heinemann.
Wilberding, J. 2008. 'Automatic action in Plotinus', *Oxford Studies in Ancient Philosophy* 34: 373–407.
Wilkinson, L. P. 1938. 'Philodemus on ethos in music', *Classical Quarterly* 32/3–4: 174–81.
Wolff, F. 2015. *Pourquoi la musique?* Paris, Fayard.
Woodruff, P. 1988. 'Aporetic Pyrrhonism', *Oxford Studies in Ancient Philosophy* 6: 139–68.
Woodward, L. 2010. 'Diogenes of Babylon reading Plato on music', in V. Harte, M. M. McCabe, R. W. Sharples, and A. Sheppard (eds.), *Aristotle and the*

Stoics reading Plato (supplement to the *Bulletin of the Institute of Classical Studies* 107). London, Institute of Classical Studies, 233–53.

Zhmud, L. 2012a. *Pythagoras and the early Pythagoreans*. Oxford University Press.

2012b. 'Aristoxenus and the Pythagoreans', in C. A. Huffman (ed.), *Aristoxenus of Tarentum. Discussion*. New Brunswick-London, Transaction Publishers, 223–49.

Index Locorum[1]

[1]We indicate editions and Latin titles only in the case ambiguities may occur.

General Index

Lightning Source UK Ltd.
Milton Keynes UK
UKHW021226050722
405333UK00018B/301

9 781108 940955